THE
CITY PARENT
HANDBOOK

THE
CITY PARENT
HANDBOOK

The **Complete Guide**
to the Ups and Downs
and Ins and Outs of
Raising Young Kids in the City

KATHY BISHOP
JULIA WHITEHEAD

RODALE

© 2004 by Kathy Bishop and Julia Whitehead

Printed in the United States of America
Rodale Inc. makes every effort to use acid-free ∞, recycled paper ♻.

The "Music for Aardvarks and Other Mammals" lyrics on page 220 are by David Weinstone.

Book design by UDG DesignWorks

Library of Congress Cataloging-in-Publication Data

Bishop, Kathy.
    The city parent handbook : the complete guide to the ups and downs and ins and outs of raising young kids in the city / Kathy Bishop and Julia Whitehead.
        p.   cm.
    Includes bibliographical references and index.
    ISBN 1–57954–887–3 paperback
    1. Child rearing—United States—Handbooks, manuals, etc. 2. Parenting—United States—Handbooks, manuals, etc. 3. City children—United States. 4. City and town life—United States. I. Whitehead, Julia. II. Title.
    HQ769.B6124   2004
    649'.1'0973—dc22

                                                                                        2004007767

Distributed to the trade by Holtzbrinck Publishers

2   4   6   8   10   9   7   5   3   1   paperback

For Alice. You are so obviously the inspiration for this book. Thank you for choosing me as a mom and for brightening my life every day. For Jim, my husband and partner in everything, who is sharing this amazing and whacky ride. And for my own city parents—you're just the best. Finally, Jeff, this is for you. But you already knew that. And I *know* how proud you would be. I miss you terribly.

—Kathy Bishop

To my husband and children, first, foremost, and always: Peter, for his unconditional support of anything I do, and Pearson, Katherine, and Malcolm, for giving me so many stories to write about and for promising not to sue me for putting them in a book. And to my parents and sisters because they deserve to have a book dedicated to them too.

—Julia Whitehead

CONTENTS

Chapter 12: The Agony and the Ecstasy: A Private School Primer 303

Chapter 13: You *Can* Win: A Public School Primer 330

A NOTE OF THANKS

■ ■

We are deeply indebted to the many individuals who contributed to making this book possible. At the top of this list is our agent, Brian DeFiore. A city dad himself, Brian immediately "got" the concept of a city parenting book and provided us with invaluable guidance and support throughout the process of putting this baby to bed. Kudos, also, to our editor Lou Cinquino, who recognized why a city parenting book made sense even though his own parenting is done in more bucolic surroundings and who jumped through quite a few hoops to make this book as strong as he knew it could be.

To the many experts who shared their insights on the issues addressed in this book, we could not have done it without you. Thanks especially to: Wendy Mogel, Monsignor Tom Hartman, Dr. Bruce Lanphear, Dr. Wendy Haft, Dr. Michael Shannon, Dr. Ruth Etzel, Dr. Gerald Loughlin, Dr. Pat Allen, Dr. Steven Blaustein, Dr. Louis Cooper, Naomi Siegel, William L. Bainbridge, Robin Aronow, Roxana Reid, Kari Kling, Jane Hammerslough, Rita Finkel, Shantras Lakes, Judith Shupe, Bash Dibra, Roni Hewitt, Lydia Spinelli, Jo Ann Lynch, Pamela Awad, Bonnie Berryman, and MaryLou Stettaford.

And to all those parents across the country who shared their personal experiences with us, we are sincerely appreciative of your help, most notably Lenore Michaels, Leslie Bennetts, Laura Broadwell, Susan Bower, Nancy Eder, Leigh Anne O'Connor, Sylvie Anapol, Andrea Picard, Pat Wexler, Susan Webb, and Jane Ray. Our miracle-worker award goes to Richard Berenson, who managed to take an authors' picture that we were both happy with. A special thanks goes to Kathy's assistants Elizabeth Cobb and Marisa Lowenstein, whose fresh ideas and research were always appreciated, and to Jennifer Moore for her contribution as well. We also are indebted to the women who help care for our children: Rita Almeida Pfeiffer, Alreka Morgan, and Carmen Stephens.

Finally, thank you to those very special friends and family members whom we relied on to get us through this process with a minimum of therapy and medicinal aid, most especially Mary Berner, Liz Whitehead, Lynn Edens, Adrienne Koch, and Craig Albert. We owe you one.

INTRODUCTION

Why did we write this book? The short answer—because no one else had. Amazing, given the millions of parents raising their young'uns in cities across the country, but true nonetheless. Sure, there were great city-family retail guides that did a fine job identifying the places to go for kids' shoes, birthday parties, and mommy-and-me classes, and even more tourist-oriented ones that were terrific compilations of museums, landmarks, and other must-see stops for sightseeing families. But when it came to actual *parenting*, there was simply nothing out there that addressed the issues and intricacies of urban child-rearing.

It's not like city parents don't have questions; we've asked a few ourselves. Is it true, as so many suburban friends insist, that raising our kids in the city will turn them into neurotic, jaded, and hardened human beings? Or that, deprived of accessible backyards and independent outdoor lives, our kids are doomed to grow into fitness-phobes and nature sissies? And, where can one turn to find out how to deal with a caregiver who's illegal or non-English speaking or both? Then there's the guilty little secret of so many city parents who are really staying in the city because *they* love the excitement, the restaurants, the culture. What could they read to find out if that great urban lifestyle and kids really mix?

Hey, city parents are people too. They deserve to have their questions answered. Out of sheer ignorance, we decided to take on the challenge. Of course, we didn't know then what we know now—that city parenting is infinitely more complicated than just worrying about the stuff that's in your face (ohmigod, what to do if my child doesn't get *in*; can we keep our apartment from looking and feeling like an overcrowded rat cage). Just as important are all the questions you don't think to ask, myriad issues of health and safety, of psychology, and of space planning that don't necessarily announce themselves upfront or even at all. Those are the questions that'll really come back and bite you. Knowing about these more subtle matters—the importance of developing "connections" for city kids, how the city influences a developing young psyche, the right way to take advantage of urban medical resources, and the ease with which you can build culture into your life—can be of enormous benefit to your city family.

So while we designed this book to be a ready reference suitable for quick dips when the next city issue smacks you in the face, we also hope readers will consider giving each section its due. At the end of the day, the process of writing this book has made the both of us better city parents. In gratitude to whatever insane spirit impelled us to take on this project, we hope you will find it does the same for you.

PART ONE

FAMILY
LIFE

CHAPTER 1

APARTMENT LIVING

■ ■

F ar too many city families end up leaving town for the 'burbs because the idea of raising their kids in the same locale where they sowed their wild oats is just too much of a mental leap for them to handle. Or maybe they give it a try and then flee in disgust after too many 10-block schleps to get baby to the nearest swing or a few too many visits from Mr. Bonaduce next door who's complaining yet again about Briana's colicky crying. But we're here to say that finding the perfect neighborhood, the perfect family-friendly building, and, yes, the perfect neighbors is eminently doable. Follow our lead, and you'll not only have all that, but your family will be a little more perfect too.

TROLLING FOR HOUSING—THE INS AND OUTS OF FINDING URBAN FAMILY HOUSING

Before you deal with all the quirks of living in urban housing, you first need to know how to *find* a place that will work for your family. It won't be hard but, as they say, the devil is in the details. Failing to consider some of the finer points today can mean getting caught short 3 months or 3 years down the road when the impact of your inattention hits home. In broad strokes, you'll need to:

1. Research the neighborhood, before, not after, the fact. (And that does mean thinking about school options, even if Raven is still in diapers.)
2. Pick a family-friendly building, or at least understand the consequences of not doing so.
3. Inspect the apartment really, really thoroughly, with your current and future family in mind.

Location, Location, Location— Sleuthing the Neighborhood

In your prior incarnation as a happy-go-lucky single or couple, worrying about the area you lived in might have seemed wholly unimportant. As long as there was a bar nearby with a hopping scene, you were set. But you're in a family way now, and distance and accessibility have just become A VERY BIG DEAL.

When you have a child at the hip, you're well advised to factor in family-friendly characteristics when evaluating areas. Keep in mind the facility with which you can move around your city. New Yorkers, for instance, who live in a relatively compact city, take their kids uptown, downtown, and crosstown without batting an eye; but in LA, where many minutes of freeway driving separate one neighborhood from another, you need to look more carefully at what you have in the few blocks around your home. Perhaps you'll choose to live with some family inconveniences—say, poor access to public transportation or less-than-generous secondary services like dry cleaners, supermarkets, and drugstores. But at least if you're forewarned, you can start working on a realistic plan to access what your neighborhood doesn't provide—especially, especially, especially with regard to schools. The angst that city parents go through in getting and keeping their kids in school can be greatly mitigated by preliminarily investigating the public and private school options in a potential new neighborhood. (For suggestions on how to do this, see chapter 11, "Getting Off to a Great Start.")

The following list of subjects is meant to guide you in your search for the perfect 'hood. No doubt you'll have your own issues you'll want addressed (say you're a runner and can't live without access to a good outdoor path, or a yogi who wants classes nearby).

Education. It may not feel so urgent when little Janie's primary educational focus is grabbing the beak on Big Bird, but if you plan on staying in your dwelling for the long haul, you absolutely must think about the school options now. And not just the preschool and elementary years, but also middle school and even later. Key words to consider are: quality, location, availability, choice, and cost. What do you have to do to get in? What are the test scores of your local public elementary school? How about programs for younger kids: Are there accessible toddler (and pretoddler, if you're so inclined) options —art, music, physical activity, language? Check the Ys, churches, and franchises such as Gymboree. What about day care, if that's something you need and want—is it in the neighborhood or en route to work?

Getting around. Are you going to be sitting in the car for two hours a day just to secure a parking spot? Or is there adequate (and affordable) parking? How about access to public transportation? Remember, just because you have (and need) a car doesn't mean your babysitter will. Keep in mind the places you want to go to: If you commute east and the public transportation in your area is only north and south, you'll need to figure out what transfers will add to your day. Ditto for getting the kids to school and back as well as to any of their other activities.

Daily errands. Never underestimate the value of proximity to milk, bread, and diapers. Also, if food is really important to you, think about how close you are to greengrocers, butchers, fish markets, and bakeries. And don't forget the less-glamorous essential services—dry cleaner, drugstore/pharmacy (24-hour and regular hours), shoe repair, deli (for quick pickups), and fast food for delivery (pizza, ethnic).

Entertainment. Reading: Is a public library branch nearby (and is it good or bad)? What about bookstores? Playgrounds: One is essential; a variety is a nice benefit. Consider state of repair, whether it has a sprinkler (highly desirable in summer months), and age orientation (toddlers only or will it be good for them when they're older too?). Park/nature spots: Is there a place to ride bikes, picnic, in-line skate, run? Do nearby parks have special public events like plays and concerts? Family restaurants: What's available for eat-in/eat-out with kids? Museums: Check out all your options big and small, weekend hours, extended hours, kids' programs.

Crime. Ask your real estate agent or local police precinct for crime stats. Then stop cops on the street and ask them about the neighborhood. They're often willing to give you specifics about which blocks to avoid.

THE CITY PARENT RULES
How to Get the Neighborhood Inside Skinny

Rule #1: Ask around. Word-of-mouth is a great launching pad as long as you keep in mind, always, that it is completely subjective.

Rule #2: Visit the neighborhood at different times. Maybe this seems obvious, but you can really get a feel for how the area ticks if you see it in action at various hours of the day, weekend and workweek. The critical times for great family-watching include right before school (7:30–8:30 A.M. in the North and East; 7:00–8:00 A.M. in the South, Midwest, and West Coast), when school's out (noon, 3–5 P.M., depending on age), and afternoons at local parks and playgrounds. These time periods are particularly enlightening. You can really see who your neighbors are (and who's taking care of their kids) as well as get a sense of the tempo and tenor of the neighborhood. How many families are out strolling about on a Saturday or Sunday afternoon? What's the mix and rapport between them and childless folks—is it comfortable or does one group seem out of place? Where are families going—which restaurants, stores—and how are they received?

Rule #3: Trot over to the neighborhood park/playground. Unless your apartment is palatial—and even if it is—your younger youngsters will be spending lots of their waking hours there. Ideally, the local tot hotspot will have options for various ages—infant and toddler areas (look for swings with baby seats and sandboxes) as well as plenty of climbing equipment and slides for the older kids (remember to check the state of repair; if it's not good, you can try and find out from the locals or whoever's in charge at the city's parks department if it's slated for renovation). And here, voyeurism goes a long way. Estimate the ratio of moms to nannies during the week. That might yield important information, depending on whether you or a caregiver will be taking your child to the park. What do the parents act like? Are there tons of them? Are they interacting with one another? Are there nanny klatches? All of these behaviors are clues to the type of parents and families living in the 'hood. And don't forget weekends—are the families still there, or did they all decamp for their country houses?

Rule #4: Google it. Many cities' Web sites— Dallas (dallascityhall.com), New York (nyc.gov), and Boston (cityofboston.gov) among them—have specific tools to help you research neighborhoods, providing a remarkably efficient way of figuring out school districts, crimes, park areas, and more for any area that catches your fancy.

The Family-Friendly Building

Maybe you've scored a single-family residence, in which case much of this section won't pertain to you. But if you find yourself looking at any kind of multifamily arrangement, pay attention. Finding that kid-friendly apartment building provides a lot more benefits than you might think. Does it really make a difference? Let's put it this way: Does a kid-friendly babysitter, teacher, or pediatrician make a difference?

Granted, we recognize that finances, time constraints, and the real estate market can puncture the airy dreams of housing seekers. But if you are lucky enough to have a choice, you should seriously consider the reasons why a family building will serve you well.

First of all, misery loves company. Unlike the suburbs, where people with similar backgrounds and income levels generally gravitate to the same neighborhoods, in a city, next-door neighbors can easily be mentally, socially, and economically worlds apart. But as much as you tell yourself that this exciting urban mix is one of the best things about living in the city, it doesn't seem as attractive when the childless-by-choice couple in apartment 6B, with their Biedermeier furniture, Klimt paintings, and fin de siècle objets d'art, asks you to remove little Homer's finger painting from your front door because it disturbs the aesthetic of your shared hallway. It's possible that, after a hard day at work, they may find Homer's in-your-face elevator banter to be, well, just a tad intrusive, particularly if he chooses to bring his "outside" voice in. And, as cute as all your friends tell you little Tonya is, don't assume that those golden-agers—finally enjoying their hard-earned moments of peace after 30 years of feeding, clothing, schlepping, and paying up the wazoo for their own children—will appreciate having to start all over again dealing with yours.

Here's a City Parent axiom: If you're the only family living in a building, you are going to stand out in ways you really can't control and your family antics will be scrutinized and clucked over endlessly. Trust us, it will happen. Kids are definitely louder, messier, and more unruly than adults. At some point, all city kids WILL irritate the neighbors.

All things being equal, or nearly so, why not choose a place where you feel comfortable and fit in right from the start? In buildings where there is a decent percentage of families, yours will just be another glorious brick in its dynamic social architecture. No need to blend in with the woodwork: The solidarity that comes from living among other families goes a long way to counteract the natural (and understandable) bias that people have when living with little ones who are not theirs.

The second reason why a family building will serve you well is related to the first: There's safety (and joy) in numbers. There's a lot to be said for friendships, or at least acquaintanceships, developed out of propinquity. In case of emergency, neighbors with children can be excellent sources of spur-of-the-moment child care. Most of them will be sympathetic to the midnight knock of a desperate parent cradling one child who's on the way to the emergency room and proffering another who's in need of a temporary home—after all, the time may come when they can use a helping hand, in return.

On the social plane, having families with children in your building is just plain fun—for you and for the kids. Children get instant playmates and another play space when they're stir-crazy from inclement weather. Moreover, pals in the building provide a valuable life experience for city kids. To the 6-and-under set, being able to run across the hall or up and down a few flights of stairs to their friend's "house" may be the closest they'll come to experiencing the freedom enjoyed by their suburban counterparts. In fact, a Sacramento study showed kids preferred apartment living over other types and concluded that kids "may view apartment complexes as having a greater sense of community than in the empty streets of many suburban neighborhoods." And more often than not, the parents end up enjoying socializing with *their* building "friends" over a glass of wine at the end of the day (remember, nobody has to drive home) while the kids are running amok.

There are other advantages to living in a kid-friendly residence. Many buildings organize kiddie events like Halloween and Easter egg hunts, which make city holidays a much safer and more entertaining proposition. Plus, if you're the chatty type or if the building has a bulletin board, you can swap local parenting advice (the scoop on schools, restaurants, nannies who work in the neighborhood, extracurricular activities, and the like). The skyscraper's the limit.

Happily, knowing how to seek out and secure family-friendly apartment digs

Build a Better Building

Just because your building doesn't have any organized children's events doesn't mean it can't. Take a little initiative. It's really easy to leave a note under your fellow parents' doors or posted in the elevator. If there's a relatively high degree of interest, go as a group to the managing agent or landlord with your suggestions or plan. Chances are they'll be accommodating, particularly if you take on the organizing.

is as much science as art. The "City Parent Tipsheet" on page 10 identifies the apartment variables most important to a family and should come in handy when checking out whether a building will be right for yours. By the way, we assume that if you are a buyer you have also done the necessary due diligence on price, building financial condition, percentage of owners versus renters, etc. If this sounds like some dead language to you, do yourself a favor and get a book on buying an apartment, go online, and do the basic research that you would for any major investment.

Home Sweet Home—Evaluating the Apartment

So, you're totally into the neighborhood, the building seems fabulous—now you're down to checking out the actual apartment. We trust you know yourself well enough to have already made the basic tradeoffs—space, light, neighborhood quality, building quality, and cost—but when you're securing space for a family, particularly if the "family" is only a gleam in your eye at this point, there are a couple of special subtle and not so subtle unit considerations that should be high up in your decision-making process.

Space. First, there is never enough of it in the city for families. Whatever you estimated as the minimum amount of closet space (for clothes, equipment, cleaning supplies) will be insufficient, so think ahead when the broker cavalierly says you can buy armoires to supplement the broom closet that passes as the apartment's one and only enclosed storage space. Second, don't ignore room count if you have more than one child. We'd swap one large one for two tiny kids rooms any day because at some point, they *all* want their own space (though there's good reason to have them share bedrooms until they do). At least make sure that you have a decent way of dividing a room to accommodate a growing population—unless you're completely certain of your family size.

Apartment condition. Look at the physical characteristics of the apartment with an eagle eye. Problems get magnified because your kids will be spending so much time in the apartment. Lack of light is more oppressive, water drips more annoying, and lead paint more dangerous than you'd otherwise think.

If you are renting, you also want to be sure that you are not blamed for physical damage that was there before your kids became residents. If you don't have a before-the-fact record, you won't have a leg to stand on when you're trying to get that security deposit back. So protect yourself. Sometime before the apartment is legally yours, take a formal, written damage inventory, accompanied by videotape if possible. It's only an hour out of your day, and it may save you a lot of money and aggravation later. Just be sure to send this assessment to the landlord after you move in so you are on record as to the way things were before your little tykes went to town.

Some specific defects to watch out for:

- Pesticide smell. The chemicals are not good for your kids, and if you can smell it, somebody may have felt there was a big enough problem to really douse the place.
- Broken window seals/evidence of water stains/humid "feel"/swelling plaster/ separation of baseboards from floor. Any or all of these might indicate that the apartment, or the building, has a mold problem.
- Recent repainting/renovation. In an older building, any kind of fix-up work can create potentially harmful lead paint problems if proper procedures weren't followed; at least ask.

Physical relationship to other units. Most apartment buildings tend to be developed in a line plan—that is, apartments above and below are the same configuration, so bedrooms, kitchens, and living rooms all stack up. That's a good thing. It means that your kid's room is probably not over the adult master bedroom downstairs—but check it out anyway, because there are plenty of

CITY SAVVY

The Best Time to Check Out a Potential Apartment . . .

. . . is when the neighbors are home! Ideally, go during the dinner hour if you can swing it (even later would be better, but you'll have to dance a little to come up with a plausible reason for that intrusion) so that you can assess the noise transfer between your unit and the ones above and below.

City Parent Tipsheet: Evaluating Your Building

WHAT TO LOOK FOR:	WHY	HOW TO FIND OUT
Cleanliness, security, safety of public areas	Says a lot about how building is operated and maintained—and what kind of problems might be in your future as a resident and how tight a leash you should be prepared to keep your kids on inter-building.	*Observe, observe, observe:* *Exterior:* Is the building entrance well lit? Are external doors solid/working dead bolt, or is there a glass panel? Does building have audio, video security? *Back halls, entry foyers, exterior walls:* Look for lights out, peeling paint, general dirt level, wires hanging out of windows—the more signs of decrepitude, the more likely the building is under-maintained, maybe in financial difficulty. Also check for emergency lighting for fires, sprinkler systems—it'll help you see how up-to-date the building is from a safety point of view. Do the halls have fire extinguishers, smoke detectors, fire alarms? *Front/back door policy:* How easy is it for non-building residents to get in the building—is there more than one entrance? If there's a doorman, does it look like he's checking with a resident before letting someone go up? Also, ask the super and/or doormen if there have been any incidents. If you're buying the apartment, request to see the super's repair log—it'll give you a great indication of what's going on in the building (at least physically).
Doorman	It's safer than the alternative: Cuts down on unwanted intruders, helps you manage getting kids, etc. into the building in one piece.	Ask the managing agent; make sure you get the exact hours (and days) of coverage if it's important to you that the door is manned 24/7.
Resident super	Boy, can this make a difference with those middle-of-the-night stopped-up toilets, etc.	Ask the managing agent; if the super's not in residence, find out what hours he's at the building, where he's located when he's not there, how he stays in touch.
Occupant demographics	Remember: Safety in numbers—it'll shape building attitudes toward children, playmate possibilities, emergency child care backup.	Use your eyes—how many window guards are there? Ask to see a bike room and check for kids' equipment. See if doors, halls have kids' artwork. And feel free to ask; you're entitled to know ahead of time.
Storage (lockers/bike rooms)	Any extra space you can get is a godsend.	Ask agent or super if there is a communal storage room; if lockers are available, ask about cost, waiting list; ask to view facilities.
Laundry facilities	So critical with kids. In apartment, is heavenly; in building, is really, really important.	Ask agent or super; if facilities are shared, ask to see them (see how well kept they are and the location) and ask about peak times and waits. Optimum is one washer and dryer for every 8 to 10 units in the building, if it's primarily a family building; if there are a lot of singles, fewer would be okay. Check to make sure laundry facilities are locked at off-peak hours.
Play spaces (basement, outdoor, roof)	Great on rainy days, but our sampling shows that the outdoor play spaces get the most use.	You probably won't even need to ask; any building with child-oriented amenities usually has a fat family demographic, so you are the target market.
Apartment configuration/number	Bigger units means more families; also more possibilities for move-up or combinations, should your family grow larger.	Ask the building agent or manager; no one should give you a problem on this info.

exceptions and the goal is to minimize situations where your boisterous brood is tap-dancing above individuals who relish peace and quiet, and vice versa.

Getting What You Want

Of course, now that you've found what you think will be a happy nest for little chicklets, you do have to make sure you are approved by the powers that be. If you've gotten this far, that shouldn't be a problem. Don't let the brokers terrorize you. Typically, approval interviews—whether condo, co-op, or landlord—occur without children (although occasionally, a co-op board will want to interview you in your home) so the little darlings really shouldn't impede your acceptance. If the building has had problems with rambunctious kids (the teenagers who used to live in Julia's apartment apparently had a habit of throwing things out the window to the sidewalks four stories below), you may get some tentative questions about your intent on obeying house rules ("you will get those floors covered, won't you?"). In the preponderance of cases, as long as you're normal people with normal habits you should be fine—assuming you are financially capable of taking on whatever ownership or tenant obligations you're trying to assume.

LOVE THY NEIGHBOR

There's no question that teaching children neighborly ways takes on new dimensions in the city, where we're all living on top of one another. In so many apartment buildings, we know what they're cooking, when they're not getting along, when they go to the bathroom—geez, even when they're having sex. "Mommy, what are they doing upstairs?" They, in return, know who's winning at cops and robbers, which aspiring pianist should take up a new hobby, and who is in desperate need of Ritalin. Getting along in such close quarters is no easy feat, but as all city dwellers know, it's the only game in town.

Regardless of how hard it may be to achieve, peaceful coexistence is essential. Don't forget, the way you deal with neighbors (and the way they deal with you) is one

CITYWISE WARNING

Co-ops Are Not for Everyone

Co-ops can be great: They offer the security of a controlled environment and residents who have, in some measure, been screened for admittance. They also provide something that some families have trouble with: rules. If you and yours are freewheeling individualists who chafe at restraints on your legal, but maybe slightly antisocial, behavior, you might be happier with a rental or less-restrictive condo—which, generally speaking, have much less power to evict "troublesome" tenants. Same thing goes if the family budget is feeling a little tight and there's a teeny possibility you might get behind on a housing payment or two.

A Word about Discrimination

Technically, discriminating against families is illegal (except for multifamily buildings of four or fewer units and private non-brokered sales, though why they're allowed to discriminate is beyond us). But the cold reality is that some places just do not want families. Renters with kids can have a terrible time finding a place in Boston, as an example, where the lead paint laws are so onerous that landlords regularly dis families because they just don't want to deal with the red tape and expense of de-leading. If you think your family was discriminated against, you do have rights and the ability to fight if you're willing to take on that battle.

The Department of Housing and Urban Development (HUD) handles violations of federal fair housing laws, including discrimination against families. If you think you have a problem, call HUD (800-669-9777), try the Web site at www.hud.gov, or contact your local HUD office.

of those areas that has a far greater impact on your children than you think at the time. How you meet, greet, treat, even talk sweet to the neighbors is the first step in teaching your children how to be good citizens, how to respect others, and how to get along. How and what you do in your building while your children are still impressionable can set them up for life.

Building relations can be a pretty big deal. They can also be a little difficult to gauge because in addition to all those face-to-face interactions, there are so many more that don't even involve face time—like the competition for the use of shared hallway space or the reverberation of Lulu's piano practice into the book club meeting next door.

The Commonsense Approach

Sometimes employing some good, old-fashioned common sense is in order. When you're living in close quarters, it pays to be polite and respectful. After all, why make enemies of people you and your children have to see every day? And really, wouldn't you rather that Mrs. Abernathy from 8C greet little Lawrence with a smile rather than a blank-eyed stare when they meet at the elevator? Normal civilities go a long way in big, bustling, sometimes impersonal cities, and your kids will reap the benefits if you establish a pattern of politeness at home. So good mornings, thank yous, and have a nice days should be the rule for all your family members when they pass neighbors in the hall, see the super fixing some burnt-out light, or share elevator space with the guys from upstairs.

Actually, we'll go even further. We think everyone with kids should be proactively nice (very underrated word: nice) because little guys have a way of stepping over the line sometimes. That's not anyone in your family? Well, how about:

- When your toddler's been screaming in your room three nights running from night terrors
- When your scribbling 2-year-old lets loose on your neighbor's door
- When your kids and their crew track mud all over the shared foyer
- When your inquisitive little genius pushes the emergency stop button in the elevator during the morning commute out

More "interactions" than you realized? We thought so. So be generous with the gestures—drop off a home-baked cake, just because. Slip a little note under your neighbor's door with a warning about your child's upcoming birthday party and an advance apology for the excess noise and strollers stuffing the shared foyer; that might be just the ticket for preventing neighborly irritation. And a bottle of wine or a bouquet of flowers when the neighborly interaction is a little more intrusive (that muddied hallway, those loud tear-filled nights) might save you a month of glares from next door. Don't leave it to your neighbor to complain—it's undoubtedly as unpleasant for them to do as it is for you to hear. So take our advice and build goodwill before an incident

Common Areas—Yours to Use, Not Abuse

Let us introduce the "urban mud room"—the elevator foyer, hallway, or back staircase. These shared "public" spaces can be incredibly useful, assuming they're yours to use. Lots of buildings, sadly for families, have prohibitions against putting *anything* out there. If that's the case, sorry, you need to abide.

But if you are allowed to take a piece of that space, be happy—those few extra square feet can be invaluable, but just keep in mind that you are sharing. Our strong recommendation: Take your lead from what's already there (or on other floors). If everybody seems to use the area around their door for umbrella stands or outdoor footwear, feel free to make that space yours—doormat, boot basket, stroller park, take your pick.

occurs, and be liberal with the peace offerings after the fact of whatever family fracas inevitably occurs.

Noise—The Fear Factor

Okay, you're happily ensconced in your dream apartment; the neighborhood is every bit as great as you thought it would be; Junior, cross fingers, is sleeping through the night in his new bedroom; the commute to work's a breeze; and, wow, your apartment gets even more sunlight than you expected. So in the midst of all this domestic bliss, how come, darn it, you're waking up in the middle of the night in a cold, shaking sweat? Fear of the boogeyman? No, it's worse.

"Can they really make us move, honey?" is a question that's been asked in apartments across every city in the nation. Shh! hear that . . . someone's asking it now . . . and now . . . and now. Of all the issues that come up in apartments or communal living spaces, those pertaining to noise are by far the most likely to turn solid citizens into homicidal maniacs. And if this has escaped your notice before, once kids have entered the picture, we can pretty much guarantee that you will be involved in a noise complaint—and probably not on the giving end. No, you'll most likely be joining the legions of parents who've been absolutely petrified by threats of eviction, haunted by terms such as "violation of covenant of quiet enjoyment," terrified that the cops are going to show up at the door any minute—and all because your kids are acting their age.

But here's the real deal. While most cities regulate noise, they're really not interested in normal people sounds. Typically, noise ordinances were created to handle commercial and industrial noises; they were simply never intended to handle noise within a residential building. Such regulations have lots of words about defined noise nuisances (amplifiers, construction), pro-

> ### CITYWISE WARNING
>
> ### Cover the Floors or Else!
>
> Just because you have nothing to fear from city noise ordinances doesn't mean that you can ignore the rules of your building. Fail to cover your floors the way your lease, co-op, condo, or homeowners association requires and you may buy yourselves a heap of trouble. Most such directives require apartment dwellers to cover 75 to 80 percent of their floors (usually excluding kitchens and bathrooms, and possibly halls or foyers) with rugs or carpet—specifically to hold down the amount of noise seeping between apartments. Fail to obey the regulations and your landlord or board can absolutely invoke the specified penalty, which, depending on your housing circumstances, can be as dramatic as forcing you to leave.

hibit sustained noise that exceeds a certain decibel level, and differ according to the time of day, the zoning, even the type of noise. But we defy you to find anything in any city noise ordinances that could remotely be used to regulate 4-year-olds jumping off a bed. (Warning: If you're one of those urban families pioneering life in that commercial zone, you may find that the allowable "outdoor" noise is a lot greater than you were used to in your earlier residences.)

That's not to say people haven't used these laws successfully to shut down noisemakers who are disturbing their home lives—but the perpetrators are generally loud bars or music joints and emphatically not the 2-year-olds next door. (A well-timed call to the cops, however, may get a little response—watch those teenagers; their parties will at least get a complaint logged in if 2B calls the police.) Bottom line: There is simply no legal basis for forcing people out of their homes just because they have typical, noisy kids—and it doesn't matter whether you're a renter or co-op owner or condo buyer; it's not going to happen to you.

When Your Little Monster's the Monster

All of you with bouncy toddlers are probably relaxing right about now. After all, we just told you that the legal system recognizes that kids are kids and that noise is a by-product of raising them. But just because the law makes it difficult to oust you and your minis, don't assume you're off the hook: A landlord or building board has ways to apply pressure on noisemakers. And then there's the victim of your family's raucous activities.

Never underestimate the lengths an aggrieved neighbor will go to on his or her own. Apparently, there are myriad ways to "get" you and yours. Consider the following Internet posting from a man who moved with his family to an apartment after having lived in a home for most of his adult life. (Please keep in mind that we've read tons of similar postings, maybe none quite as psychotic as the following, but often just as "emotional.")

> *To all those people out there [who] insist on making others' lives hell . . . I have one thing to say to you . . . I will have my revenge, you will never see me coming, you will wonder why all those bad things are happening to you. You will stay awake at night looking out your window, worried if your car will get keyed . . . beware you ungrateful tenants above me, I have been trained by some of the finest in the art of "covert."*

Other "revenge" incidents we've heard of include trash (cigarette butts, discarded chicken bones, and the like) thrown onto another's balcony; tires slashed in the middle of the night; and, in old buildings, purposely flushing toilets when a neighbor is taking a shower to scald him. And then there's that favorite American pastime, the lawsuit. Just because your neighbor has no real legal case against you doesn't mean he won't exercise his God-given right to engage in expensive, pointless litigation. You, of course, will have to spend your own money to defend yourself until such point as the court tells you all to go away.

And sometimes that could take years. Consider the Rubins and the Schilds. These two California neighbors, both fathers and lawyers, engaged in bitter litigation for years over the noise caused by a basketball-playing teen. And although this is a story of house neighbors, it provides almost more of a moral for apartment dwellers, who deal daily with almost exactly the type and scale of problems that these two families had.

It all began in 1987 when the Schilds put a basketball hoop in their backyard, and the Schild son played with it, usually after school by himself, sometimes with his father when he came home from work. The Rubins, who had an infant at the time, complained about the noise, which they said interrupted naps and was generally unpleasant. Their complaint prompted the Schilds to try to dampen the noise by solidifying and padding the backboard pole. Nice gesture, huh? That apparently helped some, but a year later, when Schild told his son he could play for a few more minutes after Rubin had complained again, Rubin grabbed a hose and soaked everything in sight, including the Schild father and son.

Schild sued Rubin for assault; Rubin counter-sued for nuisance and emotional distress, and later for harassment, and they were off to the races. Several temporary restraining orders, enjoinments, and court rulings later, the Schilds ultimately prevailed, with the California Court of Appeals ruling that noise from recreational basketball is not harassment, nor in this particular case played in a way that would cause a *reasonable* person to become emotionally distressed.

When Your Neighbor's the Monster

The legal regime works both ways on noise, so unless your neighbor's running a rock band out of his apartment, you're not likely to get much relief out of court. (If he is, check out www.nolo.com for some pointers on legal action and then consult a lawyer.) Of course, you can appeal to the landlord or building authorities for help, but if that's not sufficient, you may have to take defensive action.

Our ploys to fight their noise:

Vents: If the issue is those, ahem, intimate conversations of your neighbors reverberating from the vents, then by all means close them off. If that doesn't work for you, try installing a fan in the vent.

Not only does it help circulate the air, it also camouflages ambient sound.

White noise machines: The salvation of many a parent, they're great for tuning out loud neighbors—hey, even your own children—and for drowning out honking cars and rowdy passersby as well.

Ear plugs: *Hello*, like they cost $2 at the drugstore. Worth a try, no? If you want to go further (and are willing to spring for the extra cost), get special plugs from an audiologist or ear doctor.

Windows: If street noise is the problem, then installing interior windows, basically a second layer of glass, really works. (It's also really expensive.)

Now we don't know what happened with the Schilds and the Rubins after that. It's fairly difficult to believe that their neighborly relations ever approached normalcy after what they had been through.

We know it's hard to imagine that you and your adorable charges could ever inspire so much hate, loathing, and litigation, but you must remember that in apartments and condominium complexes you do share walls (floors/ceiling) with your neighbors, thus increasing the likelihood of their being disturbed by unwanted sound. This can come in many forms—people walking, cabinets closing, items dropping, people screaming, babies crying, even pipes vibrating from flushing toilets. And, unfortunately, the building boom in the postwar decades contributed a lot of structures that were put up in a hurry, often with flimsy materials. Newer, cheaper buildings might have no insulation between floors or walls. Floors might be made of inexpensive plywood that creaks under the slightest bit of pressure.

Even if some of these noise offenses sound quite benign to you, it might be like a fingernail on a chalkboard to someone else. One family we knew endured months of telephone calls and screaming visits from their downstairs neighbor complaining of the ungodly noise he felt their two young girls were making. The building's board of directors assured them they wouldn't be tossed out, but in desperation suggested the family and their noise-sensitive neighbor go to mediation. They did—and their problems dissolved because it turned out that this particular complainant just wanted to know that somebody cared about his feelings.

But how close it came to a far less happy ending. And as millions of city parents can attest, the tensions and aggravations that noise standoffs breed will take years off your life expectancy. So when you're the noisy neighbor, why not do your part to curtail the family's noise? And understand that, while it's natural for you to get your dander up when someone's haranguing you just because your kids are acting their age, your future may be a lot less tempestuous if you, too, show your neighbors that you are sensitive to their positions and are doing what you can to respect their rights.

THE CITY PARENT RULES
Best Moves to Reduce Noise and Friction

Rule #1: Cover those floors according to your lease's (or house rules') floor coverage requirements; you're being very, very unneighborly (and can get in a lot of trouble to boot) if you don't.

Rule #2: Install padded carpeting, even double-padded, in buildings with particularly poor soundproofing. It sounds expensive but doesn't have to be, especially for hallways where children often like to run. (Many stores and carpeting companies sell remnants, which are cheaper and usually large enough for such spaces.) Plus, it provides good insulation—a help in reducing electric bills. Foam padding (the type used in gyms) is popular with little acrobats, but it tends to deteriorate over time. If you're hoping for more extended life from your padding, pick something fibrous, like fiberglass, nylon, Orlon, or Teflon.

Rule #3: Use window coverings and wall coverings. Fabrics absorb sound, and the more you use, the less noisy your home will be. Hang tapestries or rugs with fiberglass padding, or Peg-Board a wall.

Rule #4: Keep 'em where your neighbors ain't. If the guys downstairs say your boys are disrupting their weekend soirees, keep the little ruffians from running in the living and dining rooms on weekend nights. If your master bedroom is above your neighbors, don't let the kids jump on your bed at 7 A.M. on Sunday morning.

If your neighbor's office shares a wall with a kid's bedroom, maybe that's not the place to put a backboard.

Rule #5: Teach your kids the rules of coexistence (and why). They're never too young to start hearing that while, yes, they are the center of *your* universe, there *are* other people living in the building, so maybe riding their monster wheels indoors is just not the right thing to do.

Finally, if friction looks like it's going to persist, you may want to protect yourself by documenting any of the changes you have made in response to a neighbor's complaint. It could come in handy if an action is taken against you. Remember, just because your neighbor has no real legal case against you, that won't prevent him from taking you to court if he's got the litigation bug.

CHAPTER 2

KEEPING SANE IN SMALL PLACES

■ ■

Comical, confusing, claustrophobic—the life of a family crammed into a space that's smaller than most suburban garages is certainly never dull. But hey, you have to play the hand the apartment god dealt you. From our perspective, making an apartment work for a family requires thought and effort on three main battlefronts: managing space, keeping clean, and controlling the clutter. Fortunately, with enough planning and an endless supply of creativity, you will be able to master apartment life *en famille*—and even have time, money, and energy to spare for decorating your child's bedroom.

SPACE MANAGEMENT

There's no way around the cold, hard, ultimately inescapable fact that no matter where you're raising your family in the city, you're doing so in space that's at least 50 percent less than you'd like. There are benefits, of course—greater family inter- action, less space for kids to make a mess in, more of a need to get them to pick up after themselves (by the way, that is a good thing!), fewer rooms to furnish and care for. But if you can't get beyond that sense of choking claustrophobia to look at the upside of "closeness," take heart: There are many tricks of the trade to make the best of what you've got—from how you use the space you have and how to choose furniture and wall coverings, to how to find clever ways to free up space. Using a few of them can do wonders to contain the damage of your cloistered brood and create storage for those not "of the moment" items.

Smart Room Planning: The Art of Multitasking

While houses in the suburbs are busy supersizing, city apartments are definitely not. Quite to the contrary, premium-priced dwelling space means every square foot needs to work overtime these days, particularly for families who simply have more functions to fit in. Urban singles and couples complain about cramming sleeping, eating, and entertaining into their tiny city co-op—well, puhleeze, when you add kids, you take on a plethora of new space requirements. Think play spaces, art projects, and homework nooks.

The answer is clearly multitasking—dining rooms doubling as family rooms, living rooms with office niches (attractively camouflaged, of course), kitchens prepped for finger painting and homemaking. The combinations and possibilities are only limited by your needs. Helping you out are the interior design and home furnishing worlds that have come to the rescue with an ever-expanding variety of multitasking items. With the flick of a switch or a couple of simple folds and tucks, furniture pieces now move freely from function to function. A dining room table for just dining? How positively small-minded. Today's souped-up numbers are adjustable in length, depth, width, even height and become an ergonomically acceptable writing space, a big or small dining table, and low coffee table all in one. Of course, you can always hire an architect specializing in small spaces, should you be so inclined. But even if you can't afford that space-age model apartment or the services of the designer du jour, there are plenty of opportunities to maximize the use of your space to meet your family's many needs.

THE CITY PARENT RULES
How to Work a Room

Rule #1: Make every room house at least three activities. Why three? No great logic here, but it seems to be better than two and easier than four. Look, if you want to raise a family in a small footprint, you just cannot afford to let any square footage lie idle. The living room that you so carefully preserve for company? We're not suggesting you use the sofa for Play-Doh molding, but it would be perfect for nightly read-aloud time and the coffee table might be great for puzzle fests. Or maybe you can put that desk in the corner for family finances, freeing up that kitchen alcove for kiddie crafts.

CITY SAVVY

Space Saver

Put a baby jumper in the kitchen doorway—you can cook up a storm while baby safely bounces to his heart's delight.

Heave the High Chair

High chairs—you just don't need them. If you have a stable (no glass tops) table, infants and toddlers will do just as well with the much cheaper little seats that clip-on. Just make sure you install the seat properly and over a bench or chair. That way, if there's an equipment failure, little Anna won't go into a 3-foot free fall.

Rule #2: Double duty every room by focusing on activities that are time independent. Dining and office work, for example, can cohabit quite nicely with the dining table, serving as a desk outside of mealtimes, with all the office paraphernalia (staplers, files, pens, pencils, even laptops) stored in a sideboard after quitting time. Ditto the kitchen table for meals and crafts or homework. So think about what your family does and when; you'd be surprised how much more flexibility doubling up gives you in planning your space.

Durable Design

Of course, all the planning in the world won't shield your apartment from the daily roughhousing of an active family (and whose isn't?) that's forced into a shoebox. If you don't want to feel like you're entering Tobacco Road every time you walk into your apartment, you have to think durable (aka kid-resistant) décor. A small investment now will undoubtedly save you money in the long run—or at the very least, minimize the number of times you have to schlep out to buy a new couch, put on a new coat of paint, or even wax the floors. So you might as well let the constraints of city living unleash your inner interior designer. Just bone up on the basics before you trot out the paintbrush.

Up the walls. Particularly when kids are little and prone to careening around corners, apartment walls seem to take more damage than any other part of the structure. But without inhibiting the wholesome physical activity of your tots, there are some easy things you can do to prevent your walls from looking like the inside of a tenement. Sponge painting (actually any paint technique, like marbleizing or ragging, that creates "texture" through nonuniform applications of paint and/or subtle combinations of several colors) works wonders to camouflage the myriad fingerprints, greasy scuff marks, and that occasional unwanted abstract "painting." It's not only one of the more chic and finished routes to take, but repair is easy as well; if "somebody" chips a piece of paint, you just dab on a bit of reasonably close color—no need to match exactly.

Another wall sparer is washable wallpaper. Vinylized wall coverings—ideal for hallways, kids' bedrooms, bathrooms, and other high-traffic areas—are a far cry from the overly plastic-looking psychedelic designs of yesteryear. Better coatings yield an enormous variety of styles, colors, and designs (sold, natch, with coordinating everythings), and today's options are mommy nirvana—attractive, nearly identical to nonspongeable ones, and instantly reincarnated with a damp sponge (add soap for the tough jobs). Plus, you can find them everywhere, from big do-it-yourself stores like Home Depot or Lowe's to your local purveyor of wallpaper.

If all this is just too "Martha" for you and a quick, simple paint job is as far as you're willing to go, well, then choose a high-gloss finish for bathrooms and kitchens and semi-gloss or eggshell finishes for other rooms. They'll be much easier to clean than more matte versions.

Dancin' on the furniture. Every city parent's dilemma: Spend half of each day corralling under sixes out of the living room OR give in wearily to their need to jump (preferably off something). The fabric you choose to cover the sofa, chairs, upholstered beds, etc., can make all the difference between the furniture making it to the child's fourth birthday or falling victim to assault by sneakers . . .

Naturally, slipcovers make the most sense for families, and we have no doubt that it was an inventive mother who came up with this concept. Either go for a casual, unconstructed "shabby chic" look or have them made-to-fit in any style from modern to contemporary—even Victorian, if you must. Just make sure you either prewash the material or buy shrinkage-tested bolts before having anything made-to-order.

Whether we're talking about slipcovers or upholstering, the more expensive the material does *not* mean the more durable it is. (Fabric prices are generally based on availability or on how difficult they are to make, which means you'll be mortgaging the condo for fabrics that are going to wear out in a New York minute.) Do your family and creditors a favor and go instead for cottons and cotton/polyester

"P" Is for Painted Cabinetry

Kitchens and kids' rooms with painted cabinets can take a beating in an apartment. Don't despair—you don't have to repaint the whole installation. Just get a small can of paint that closely matches the current shade (remember, it's aged since it was first applied) and paint the offending area. It may not be an exact match, but you'd be surprised at how easily the eye deceives you into believing that there's no difference.

blends. Heck, they're the fabrics of our lives and they're highly durable; just make sure that any cotton you choose is treated with a fabric protector, because soil is not its friend. Denim (as we all know since we've kept, and still wear, our high school jeans, right?) is nearly indestructible and now comes in almost every color for furnishings. Heavy linen is another excellent choice, and it launders well. Better yet are some of the new synthetics like Sunbrella and Bartsuede, which are attractive and easy to clean.

With all fabrics, a good rule of thumb is to look for tight weaves (hold the fabric up to the light—if you can see through it, do you really think it's going to stand up to your family's punishing ways?), smooth surfaces, and resistance to abrasion (give a little rub to test; any snagging or color rub-off and it's not for you).

Another fashion blast from the past is making it big in the furniture world: Ultrasuede. Yes, it's baaaaaaaack! When Kathy was 8 months pregnant, she went out to buy a larger, more comfy bed in preparation for wee-hour feedings and the inevitable kiddie "sleepovers." She chose one with an upholstered frame and headboard and picked out a vibrant red cotton fabric—primary, of course, so baby could focus on it and so dark stains wouldn't show, or so she thought. Now a sale's a sale, but the saleslady absolutely forbid her this choice: "You're a new mom, you're going with Ultrasuede," she said knowingly. "Any spill—baby bottles, juice, 'accidents,' coffee, pen, you name it, it'll just wash out. Trust me, you'll thank me later."

Well, whoever you are, it is later, and THANK YOU! The tragedies Kathy's brood avoided in one week alone: milk and cookies (from her husband, not her daughter, Alice), newspaper print, and children's vitamins. (Anybody else's tots insist on taking the vitamins out for a look mid-consumption?) And if that's not good enough, the material's resistant to odors and pet hair.

You probably know all the old saws about picking fabrics—like multicolored patterns and tweeds conceal dirt better than solid colors, and if you have to go with a solid, pick something dirt colored like gray or brown. Of course, if you're wor-

---

Shout It Out

The absolute best fast stain remover in the world—good for crayons on couches, chocolate on chintz, and juice on jute—are Shout Wipes. We know they're supposed to be used for pretreating wash, but they've bailed us out of numerous upholstery near-disasters. We buy 'em by the case. And we're not fancy in our technique: We just wipe (or blot, if the fabric police show up) and dry.

Decorate with Loose Cushions, Pillows, and Throws

They're cheap, come in every imaginable color, fabric, and design, and they're made for families with small children. Strategically placed, they can cover all of little Kyle's unwanted additions to your furnishing, like the laundry marker sketch on the back of that living room chair your mother-in-law gave you.

ried about dust or pet hair, stay away from dark-colored materials. All this aside, both of us have had pretty light-colored furniture successfully for years. Our secrets: We don't use them in rooms where kids hang out enormous amounts of time, and we do scan for stains more often than we sync our palms. *And we never, never, never allow shoes on the furniture.*

Stretching Your Storage

Efficient room planning will open up space you never realized you had, but trust us, it'll never be enough for all the stuff your family will amass. We challenge anyone who says that they really comprehended, beforehand, just how much stuff accumulates when kids enter the picture. In fact, the single most underestimated component of any family apartment, we believe, is storage.

Taking the time to analyze the storage you've got and perhaps spending a little money to make up for what's missing is your best course of action. We want to pass on a general "theory" of storage as defined by people in the biz. It sounds a bit pedantic, but we found it to be extremely helpful when rethinking our own homes, and hopefully it will encourage you to organize your space more effectively as well.

Open/semi-open storage. Think of this as basically anything within eyesight, like bookcases, shelves, coat trees, hooks, tabletops, bins, baskets, and boxes. Because it's so visible, open storage is best for items that are carefully edited or have some aesthetic quality (collectibles, stacked games, books). Semi-open (baskets and boxes) give you a lot more flexibility because of closed sides, so they're great for loose clothes, shoes, and boots, etc. Semi-open containers, like floor baskets, are also particularly good for little kid toys because children can see what's in them; when toys are behind closed doors and not so accessible, they often gather dust because tots forget they're there.

Closed/covered storage. Certain things should just stay behind closed doors and under wraps in closets, armoires, cupboards, chests, drawer units, and under-bed drawers. What we mean here are items that can look cluttered—such as stacks of clothing, older kids' school supplies, younger kids' art supplies (cans of crayons, half-used paints)—or are just not particularly attractive out in the open, like luggage, house files, tools, and supplies.

Accessible storage. The things that you and your family use on a frequent basis should be conveniently located (meaning in the apartment) in storage that is easy and fast to get to, probably relatively low down and near the point of use. This is crucial for toys—unless you want to be tugged on every single time your 2-year-old wants to play with LEGOs, you need to make sure his toys are easy for him to access. The same goes for winter garb. Keeping hats and mittens on a closet shelf is going to extend your morning exit by precious minutes; try a basket by the door.

Remote storage. Finally, this misunderstood, underutilized storage option includes all those places where you can stock stuff you use seasonally or irregularly. We include here all those inaccessible stashes both in the apartment—high shelves,

THE URBAN A-LIST
Best Ideas for Family Storage

1. Baskets/boxes for bulky toys (stuffed animals, dolls, vehicles), temporary storage (filing, mail, magazines), and loose stuff on shelves
2. Hooks on wall outside back door for stroller, kid's bike/trike
3. Foyer container (wicker, decorative wood, or chrome) for kids' shoes/boots
4. Vertical storage (shelves, overhead cabinets) over beds, framing doors, and above toilets ("waste not, want not")
5. Under-sink cabinet door hooks/shelves for rags and soaps
6. Under-bed storage—pullout drawer for linens, games, soft luggage, shoes.

Or for a kid's room: Captain's bed with its mega storage options (built-in drawers and/or shelves underneath). We've even seen versions with pullout steps and desks!

7. Inside hooks on closet /bathroom doors for pj's, towels, belts, etc.
8. Bedside cabinets—not tables
9. Laundry bags or stand-up hampers for toys (train tracks, blocks), out-of-season sports gear
10. Foyer storage benches, good for kids to put on/take off shoes, rest a grocery bag, or store infrequently used items, holiday decorations, photos, and Junior's pre-nursery, nursery, pre-k, and ongoing art projects

back closets, and back door hallways—and outside, such as storage lockers, bike rooms, and even your mother's house. These are where you put the sleds and ice skates (in the summer), the bassinet you're saving for that next (?!) baby, and the pants you swear you'll fit into by next year.

If it's not obvious by now, when it comes to family storage, our mantra (or maybe it's more like a whine) is "MORE!" whether you put it up (shelves, cabinets), block it out (an unused corner turned into a mini-closet), or bring it in (furniture with a drawer, a shelf, or a hidden storage space). In storage, as in life, compromises apply. Example: The most effective use of space may be built-ins, though they can be costly and will limit future flexibility (you're not really going to tear down those hand-hewn bookshelves to reposition your bed, are you?). But in many situations, customized cabinetry does pay off in the long run by maximizing the space you've got. Think about it most particularly for living rooms and dining rooms where wall space is often unused or non-utilitarian (books/photo albums can be stored without detracting from your public area aesthetic). And, yes, all those closet outfitters do have a point about how inefficiently most of us use those storage spaces.

Take advantage of storage opportunities and you can easily end up with several hundred feet of extra space (worth about a million bucks in our neck of the urban jungle). No law we know of says that bookcases have to stop at the classic 5 to 6 feet high; go ahead and take them up as far as they'll go. If you have an oddball-shaped nook, cabinets can be constructed to go far deeper than the traditional 12 to 14 inches and as wide or narrow as you need them. Don't be deterred by price: There are slews of furniture and cabinetry and closet companies for every budget and all hell-bent on saving you space. And many have consultants who will come in for free to give you a plan on what you can do. You may not like everything—or anything—they suggest, but we'd be surprised if you don't get some ideas.

KEEPING CLEAN

It's not that city families are dirtier than their country counterparts, it's just that the germs, the dirt, the wear, the tear are all appallingly concentrated in smaller spaces. That means the less you bring in at the outset, the better. And what you do bring in, you'd better clean up. But fighting filth in apartments, like everything else, requires a plan. And a tub of Mr. Clean—or, for fancier types, the Thymes collection mandarin citrus-scented all-purpose cleaner—ain't gonna do it.

Fighting Dirt Devils

Stroller wheels, shopping carts, grocery cartons (especially if you have food delivered in them from supermarkets), shopping bags, and cockroaches all threaten the gleaming clean of your abode. Better to fold up shopping carts outside and remove the contents of delivery cartons before bringing them in the house. And, whenever possible, try to keep strollers in the hall.

But how to handle the single biggest threat to apartment cleanliness—your family's shoes? So simple: Take them off, take them off, take them all off. In Japan, where they are expert at dealing with crowded spaces, custom requires that you remove your shoes whenever you enter an abode. We speak from experience when we say that American city families will spare their rooms mountains of dirt if they adopt the same practice. If you get your kids and their little playmates to off their footwear when they come in from the playground, park, or whatever dirty place they've been hanging out in, you will enormously lessen the amount of filth in your home.

In our homes, this rule goes for most adults as well as kids. Grown-ups who know us well shed their shoes as soon as they're through our portal. (Full disclo-

Footloose and Fancy Free?

We doubt you will be once you consider what's likely to be lurking on the bottom of Derek's glow-in-the-dark Elmo sneakers. Hmm, some teensy soot droplets and then lots of other exciting stuff like remnants of doggie do, pigeon droppings, human saliva, urine from all breeds, sweat, and, sadly (at least until every city adopts a zero-tolerance policy), even human feces.

As for the germs all that crap—literally—carries, think *E. coli*, *Staph aureus* (a charming organism that can cause anything from boils to respiratory infection), Strep D, and even a flesh-eating bacteria—and that's just the beginning. CBS News sent out microbiologists to test 46 public surfaces in New York City, Lincoln, Nebraska, and San Francisco and found more than half contaminated by bacteria that can cause anything from respiratory

ailments to diarrhea, skin infections, gastroenteritis, vomiting, and kidney disease. And if that's not enough to completely nauseate you, there's one more horror tap dancing on your sole: lead. Urban health officials' latest concern is the outdoor lead that tracks in—residue from formerly lead-painted structures like elevated trains, steel beams, and old fire escapes now adhered to your shoe.

Question is: Do you really want your marathon crawler, whose tongue darts out faster and more furiously than a rattlesnake's to come in face-to-face contact with all those germs?

Sources: Philip Tierno Jr., "The Secret Life of Germs: Observations and Lessons from a Microbe Hunter," *CBS News' Eye on America* (correspondent John Roberts), May 12, 1997; Kirk Johnson, "Looking Outside for Lead Risks, Underfoot and Overhead," *New York Times*, November 2, 2003, p. 31ff.

sure: We do maintain kind of casual lifestyles anyway, so going shoeless doesn't necessarily detract from anyone's personal style.) But we don't make a big deal out of it and look the other way for dinner guests who either haven't been to the Orient recently or perhaps have other reasons for wanting to keep their feet clad. Since most adults haven't been digging in the sandbox or rolling around in the dirt and grass in the park, the damage their shoes can do is well within our capabilities to handle. And we do support vigorous doormat use. Our choice of doormat? Two: One inside and one outside the doorway. And while a cozy, pretty pad to welcome friends and strangers is a nice touch, in cities where dirt gets tracked in at skyscraper proportions, you need to bring out the heavy artillery (those thick coir brush mats have been around forever for a reason, you know).

Minimizing What Goes Around

It's amazing how many of our friends have the same carpet pattern—you know, the one dappled with apple juice and stamped in cookie crumbs (or worse, you can't identify what the stains are). But it really doesn't have to be this way. One more basic rule that will extend the life of your carpet and upholstery immeasurably: Restrict all food and drink to the kitchen (and dining room, should you be fortunate to have the space). As far as everyplace else is concerned, off-limits for all vittles—snacks, juice, candy (never let toddlers wander the house with chocolates or lollipops; little kids just don't have the muscle control to stop that little candy dribble from spilling out on those newly chintzed sofas). And if you can hold the line here, you'll be amazed at how helpful it is at containing any roach or rodent problem, let alone maintaining the color scheme you started out with. We do make exceptions in our homes for sick kids; they're allowed to eat on a tray in our bedroom. It's not quite enough of a privilege to fake being sick for, but it does brighten up the day of an under-the-weather child.

CLUTTER CONTROL

We still can't figure out whether it's a space management issue or some undiagnosed psychological condition that plagues city dwellers, but we do know that clutter is a major family affliction. Of course, you can take the easy way out and let your belongings just accumulate on floors and tumble out of overstuffed closets. Maybe you don't find living among all that stuff to be oppressive. But consider this: There is so much going on outside your front door when you live in a city, so many things you can't control, that it becomes especially imperative to create a soothing, serene home environment for your children. Otherwise, they'll grow up thinking that chaos is the only way of life.

Coming home to an orderly environment is crucial, asserts NYC-based child psychologist Wendy Haft, Ph.D., even for those children who absolutely thrive on the hubbub outside. "On a pragmatic level, you want the house to be neat. You don't want the kids to constantly be asking, 'Where's my homework? My scarf?' etc. But on another level, it's profoundly important for them to come home to an organized place. This shows them a kind of modeling for the organization they'll need to internalize in order to deal with the world. Even a little thing like 'Put the truck in the red case where it goes, and you'll always know where the truck is' illustrates how to plan. Eventually, that trades up into organizing their thoughts so it helps with their study skills and then to putting their motivations into play."

One of the biggest problems with small spaces is that when stuff is out, it's in your face. The apparent current trend—to invite children and all their worldly possessions into every conceivable inch of space of every single room in the apartment—is not necessarily the best one for the spatially challenged set. When the toys overtake, you'll always feel just a bit out of control. And dare we offer a bit of judgment here: What message are you sending your children? That there are no rules, no boundaries? That they can do whatever they want, whenever they please (just think of the bucks it'll cost them later in therapy when they have to establish the boundaries you failed to give them)?

Not that the kids' playthings are the only reprobates. The second biggest offender in the family apartments we've been in is paper—mail that just sits on a table, magazines, newspapers, school notices. Sometimes they're in neat piles, it's true; but when you're living in a small space, those small, neat piles have a way of reproducing overnight like the Tribbles on that *Star Trek* episode.

Rounding Up Items Gone AWOL

Remember the drill sergeant approach: three simple steps, high reps, threat of bodily harm. Keep it simple and strict and eventually even your family will get with the program.

1. Put "in process mail" in a drawer or on a shelf in a preset place (and magazines in a basket) when the initial sorting is done; otherwise, it will always be out on a table.

2. Have a family cleanup before bed every night to control the damage.

3. Give your 4-and-overs an overflow basket for junk that they can throw miscellaneous items into during the week, pending a sorting out when there's more time; Saturday mornings are often good.

Reclaiming Your Apartment

It's time to take back your apartment. How do you do that? Lay down the law and get everyone involved. Set a schedule and a timetable for the cleanup. Then keep in mind the words that will bring order back to your house: edit, discard, stow, and, most of all, stop.

Edit your possessions. Getting a handle on household (not just toy) clutter will go a long way to creating a home that feels clean, calm, and safe. But achieving peace in a city apartment comes with a price—mainly your possessions. You simply can't keep everything in an apartment without your family losing its collective sanity. Not that we're proselytizing on behalf of a monastic lifestyle. It's just that this is a case when less is definitely more.

"While there's an inherent element of hope we instill in objects, living with too much of anything has a significant downside," explains Jane Hammerslough, author of *Dematerializing: Taming the Power of Possessions.* "People end up feeling tense, it's overwhelming when they discover that their possessions haven't magically transformed their lives." Hammerslough, who spent several years analyzing the effects that "stuff" has on our psyches and society, suggests dealing head-on with the emotional component to paring down. "If you want the kids to eventually realize that they don't need 800 lbs. of LEGOs, that 400 pounds will do, then you'll have to recognize that 25 pairs of black shoes are unnecessary as well." For city children, Hammerslough especially recommends turning acquisitions to action. "Approach experience as something you 'own.' So the next time you take the kids to hear music or visit a museum, cherish it, own the city's culture and diversity, point out to the kids that yes, they don't have as much space as *Malcolm in the Middle*'s family, but *this* is what you do have."

So just as when you were designing your space, think about what is really needed, by whom, when, and how often. Go ahead and include what your family truly treasures. (Hint: There is simply no room for junk in a small place, discarded toys, books that everyone's outgrown, or too-small clothes and, sadly, you will have to be selective on which of those adorable finger paintings you keep.) Then . . .

Discard with mercy. Regularly examine the family's possessions with a gimlet eye and dispose of anything that you don't absolutely need or have a use for; and if it's something where the need will be in the distant future, do a cost-benefit analysis. (Well, maybe not; if you really figure out the expense of the space devoted to almost any item, you'd chuck everything.) Think long and hard about what really makes sense to keep for the long haul. And do the world a favor, find a local charity that will regularly accept donations of gently used goods (think religious organizations, shelters, and the like) and make your kids part of the program.

Toys, of course, are serious clutter criminals. And you're going to have to work hard to keep them under control. For children who are too sentimental to give up that robot missing his head or the armless Chatty Cathy, we highly recommend a midnight, child-free raid. But beware smart kids who catch on to this ploy: One child we know very well regularly checks the recyclable bin to make sure that Mom hasn't disposed of some of his "favorite" toys on the QT.

Stow for the season. Once you've gotten rid of all the useless tchotchkes taking up space (and for the breakables that remain, museum putty works wonders at keeping them in place and safe from a toddler's roving hands), we recommend one more scan around the apartment. Look for things that are only used for part of the year. Outdoor play equipment, seasonal clothes, holiday decorations,

Your 5-Step Program to Take On Toys

Follow these few simple directives, and you will be saner, richer, and toy thinner.

Step one: Put your toy collection on a diet. That means trim the "fat" and no "empty calories." No broken toys, no puzzles with pieces missing (kids hate it when they make the effort to do a puzzle and then there's one empty space after all their hard work), no games with only half the relevant pieces. And toss the teddy bear without legs unless he's really "special" to someone.

Step two: Focus and consolidate. If little Trevor likes to build, settle on LEGOs or K'NEX or Lincoln Logs or blocks, but not more than one of the same type of toy. There is nothing more wasteful of space or money than a kid with three inadequate collections of stuff. Of course, you will have to determine what it is that catches Trevor's fancy, and that may require exposing him to a few different makes and models – just keep the doses small. You'll figure out pretty quickly what his real interests are.

Step three: Avoid big toy nightmares. If Melissa really wants a dollhouse, you're not going to deny her, are you? But please, try and get a sense of whether she's actually going to use it before you buy one that takes up half her room. Likewise for Jose's ride-on vehicle collection. Does he really need more than one? You thought we were going to say that he doesn't even need one, didn't you? But the amount of use Julia's children got from the plastic cab that her well-meaning, but not space-deprived, sister bought her firstborn years ago was well worth Julia's initial fainting spell. Every one of her children and their friends has ridden in or on it and turned it over and made it into a house or an ice cream machine or a spaceship. Even though it's big and ugly (unless you like *really* bright yellow and orange), it does roll easily behind a door or into a room where visitors are least likely to go.

As for those playthings that by their nature are big, we suggest their apartment-friendly equivalents. A playhouse? Not for city kids, but try a collapsible tent or tube that sets up, folds up, and stores easily. Or if you don't want to spring for that, a sheet hot/cold weather linens—every family harbors lots of these types of items. Force yourself to store seasonal stuff in your remote storage (remember, the places that are relatively inaccessible, high, or inconvenient; lockers; Cousin Maude's garage) rather than stuff everything into the main family closets. It's a little bit of a pain when you have to make the transition between seasons, but it will really expand your breathing room throughout the year.

Stop before you shop. Most important, think before you buy. For an apartment dweller, picking out little Lian's next birthday present is not just a matter of what he wants or the newest Disney sensation. The city parent who forgets

over the dining room or kitchen table is pretty exciting too. Toy kitchens—set aside some kitchen utensils just for play and make a chair the stove or refrigerator—make for pretend play, and most kids will go along. And if you ever throw a cardboard box out without temporarily turning it over to your tots, shame on you. It's a wonderful temporary toy: It's a car, it's a plane, or it's a dollhouse that can be finger-painted (and you can fold it up and slip it in the closet).

Step four: Practice moderation. Children do not need a ton of toys. They just don't. You will do yourself an enormous favor and teach your children a valuable lesson (which they will take to heart at some point, we promise; it just may be way postadolescence) if you limit the presents at birthdays and holidays to a few well-chosen, special items. Spend time, not money, to think about what your little ones really need or want, or both. As Hammerslough points out, with young children especially, the drive to want more is really about their search for the novel. "Try to understand what they

truly enjoy. Is it the quantity, the time spent with you, or the actual activity?" Rather than focus on more, more, more, Hammerslough offers, "Work with your children to reinvent what they already have. 'Who needs more plastic animals, today, we're going to make a circus with the ones we have.'"

And don't forget to pass on the good word to friends and family—particularly those with an edifice complex. (How can you tell? Simple. They only buy the biggest toys in the world for your little sweetie.) For Madison's next birthday, don't hesitate to tell all those who love your child what she (and you) would really like. You'll all be happier in the end.

Step five: Use the public library. The benefits of using the library are so compelling. It's free. Your kids get variety without overflowing their own shelves. And don't forget tapes. Did you know that most public libraries have perfectly current video collections? Even better, they have the classics. Remember *Make Way for Ducklings*? It's still as good as we remember it.

dimensions has only herself to blame! That aqua center, which seemed so modest in the playroom of your sister's house, looks like the *Titanic* in your apartment living room—which, by the way, is the only place it fits. When space is so tight, fewer things can equal more fun.

SPACE'S FINAL FRONTIER: THE KIDS' BEDROOMS

By default, city parents are unique in the amount of time they expend dealing with the limits imposed by their kids' bedrooms. Fear not. Making it all work just takes a little concentration.

Furnishing: The Essentials

Want to do yourself the biggest favor? Really think about what you're buying before you buy, especially if you're a first-time parent. You will save yourself so much money and space if you focus on what's *really* necessary for your child—and that's a lot less than the man in the baby store might tell you. Believe it or not, you won't be considered Mommy Dearest if little Alexander doesn't have a formal changing table or diaper genie. City parents need to be essentialists, which doesn't mean you can't splurge on occasions; just make those splurges conscious ones. If you lust after that wicker bassinet because it's just like the one in your baby pictures, go for it. But recognize that you're doing it for yourself, not for Alexander, who will be just as happy in a crib from the day he comes home. And by all means, if you have space and money to spare, feel free to spend on extra shelves, kid-sized furniture, comfy chairs—we don't want to take the joy out of this for you. Not at all; we just want to distinguish between wants and needs. So, with no further ado, we present our no-frills City Parent room basics, by space and age.

Infants

Here's a shocker to all you new parents: This is the easy stage. In terms of furnishings, the priorities at this age are sleeping, clothing, feeding, and bathing. The

The Makeshift Bassinet

A lined dresser drawer can be an awfully cozy bassinet. Kathy is still proud of the fact that she slept in one placed on the floor on her first trip to Paris at age 3 weeks.

problem for first-time, space-deprived city parents is that they don't have the experience to know what baby paraphernalia is essential—plus the euphoria of impending parenthood tends to drive this urge to buy, to nest, to tangibly celebrate this new stage in life. Much of the "must-haves" are actually unnecessary. Take the diaper bag—not a big item, but you really don't need a special bag, you know. When Julia had her third child—and all the older siblings' baby trappings had long since been dispersed to friends and family—she could not bear to buy it all, all over again; so no changing table, no baby bouncers, and she passed over the high chair in favor of a hook-on chair. It worked out just fine. So take a deep breath, a step back, and really think about those purchases that will clutter up your personal space. What do *we* think you really need?

- A crib (and at least look at the option of buying one that's convertible into a full bed)
- Space for clothes/diapers, which can be a proper dresser or just a set of shelves in a closet or on a wall.
- Changing pad. Who needs a separate piece of furniture just for diaper duty? Lots of options here: Keep one on or in the dresser, store it under the bed or in a closet—just make sure it's convenient to whatever surface you've decided to lay it on (and if you want to change your little honeydew on the floor, that's fine by us). Diapering paraphernalia should be convenient to your designated diapering spot and is easily storable in a basket on the dresser top or hung on the closet or bedroom door.
- Toys/miscellaneous basket. Space under the crib can be used for storing other necessities like baby tub, linens, and backup diapering supplies.

Toddlers to Kindergarten

Ah, the age of toys, toys, and more toys—and books, if you know what's good for you. Crafts, too, can be big-time at this stage. To save wear and tear and scarring and marring, keep crafts in the kitchen, with a tarp on hand that can be spread out for such occasions. In the bedroom, however, you will need:

- A bed. Consider child-sized only if space is a real constraint; spring for a twin (or even a full) bed, which will take your 2-year-old through college (and maybe beyond).
- Shelves and hanging space (clothes are bigger now and you probably do have some items that are better off hung). You can get what you need from a dresser plus a built-in closet. If that's not available, fabricate a closet space: Use a flexible shower rod plus Velcroed fabric "door panels" glued to the ceiling. Another option is an armoire, which can be an unbeatable combo space for this age.

- Toy baskets/boxes/toy shelves. If your child is into Lincoln Logs or the like, you may want to consider plastic boxes for the tiny ones (they can be stashed just about anywhere: on shelves, under beds, stacked on closet floors or in the spaces between open doors and the wall) —and even for the bigger ones, if the vertically oriented containers they come in don't work with your space. Big baskets are great for everything from vehicles and stuffed animals to dolls and dress-up clothes.
- Book storage (racks or shelves or basket).
- Collapsible tents, for make-believe.

Looking Forward

As your kids get older and they move out of the toy stage, their storage needs will blessedly diminish. And they'll shift—with greater space demands for clothes, computer/electronic paraphernalia, and homework. So as you make all those choices for the sleeping space of your baby, do keep his evolution in mind, especially when it comes to built-ins (designing 3-foot-high built-in shelves may be oh so cute, but a couple years down the road, you'll have the carpenter in to take 'em to the ceiling).

By the way, just because your child may be outgrowing some charming piece of furniture doesn't mean it should be tossed. Some items can be recycled. Take the crib mattress. It can be great for sleepovers for quite a few years—just tuck it under a bed or stand it on its end inside of a closet and you're good to go. Other keepers? That baby chair: an excellent seat for large teddy bears and dolls attending tea parties. The glider: so comfortable and you spent so much money on it—don't be afraid to have the cushions re-covered in a fabric to match the big-girl or big-boy room. Or better yet, ahead of time, purchase one that fits the décor of your living room or den and then move it there when the time comes. The changing table: Traditional designs really don't make sense to keep—not enough storage or the right height, etc. But if you've planned in advance, you can get a table that turns into a desk later on.

Decorating Children's Rooms with Space Management in Mind

With small children, it's so easy to get caught up in age-sized furniture, mini chairs, little beds, tiny tables. Bonnie Berryman and Marylou Stettaford, the design powerhouses behind House to Home Makeovers in Rye, New York, and frequent consultants to city apartment dwellers, say that in small spaces, bigger is better. "Go for large pieces of furniture as storage and then don't be afraid to go as high as you can. Bookcases, armoires, wardrobes, and cabinets, all make for excellent toy storage," they recommend. Keep in mind that the furniture pieces offered in children's collections are typically much shorter than their adult counterparts. Cute, yes, but that means less storage, so you may want to forgo the kiddie stuff and buy grown-up units. You can always decorate them in children's themes or colors.

Even if you're designing for someone who doesn't clear a subway stile yet, there's no reason you can't think vertically when you're configuring the room. Reclaim the space above your child's window or door by adding a shelf or even just a ledge. It makes a great area to display collectibles, your child's favorite artwork, or nice things used infrequently. Empty space under a window? Use it for a window seat. Sometimes a pair of stock, over-the-refrigerator cabinets will fit underneath a window; if so, all you have to do is screw them into the window wall studs and add a plywood top and cushion. You get the gist of all this, don't you? Place cabinets and shelves generously—they will get used.

By the way, when you offer kids a convenient place to store their toys, clothes, and treasures, something miraculous happens. They pick up on their own. A few pegs on the back of the door to their room, placed at their height, and they might just remember to hang up their coat, hat, and backpack.

Let the Door Store!

Oh that sturdy, woefully misunderstood door. You think you're multitasking when you hang a simple mirror on it. Well, baby, it can do so much more. Here are five easy conversions:

1. Install a hook or a rack for pj's, bathrobe, slippers, backpack, or clothes ready for the next day's outing.

2. Turn the door into a veritable art gallery. Buy one of those handy over-the-door easels (basically a roll of paper suspended from a string) and hang it, accompanied by a beach pail (slung over the door handle) filled with crayons, markers, and colored pencils and—voila!—a mini-art studio. Alternative art idea: Attach a large slate chalkboard, or buy chalkboard paint to coat an appropriate area of the door, and hang a 2-inch shelf for chalk underneath.

3. Create a portable changing station, hanging diapers, wipes, creams, and a changing pad off of the door.

4. Hang a canvas shoe rack and use the cubbies for crafts, collections, and just about anything your bubbula can think of.

5. Place Velcro strips in several rows of three (about 5 inches apart), adding the sister strip to stuffed animals. Attach the critters to the door when it's not in use. If you really want to have fun, you can paint a zoo or farm background. (If Zach's collection is so extensive that the door won't do, you can always try this idea on one of the walls.)

Sharing Rooms

So many parents feel guilty about not having space, forcing their poor deprived children to share rooms out of sheer necessity. Maybe that's the wrong way to look at it; maybe you're actually doing your kids a favor by doubling them up.

THE URBAN A-LIST
Tricks of the Trade for a Space-Efficient Kid's Room

1. Use toy chests as night tables: the top for lamp, books, a glass of water; underneath for out-of-season clothing or seasonal toys.

2. Place a wooden toy chest near a window; add some cushions and it's a window seat and reading nook.

3. Loft beds or a high bed frame can double your space, especially if you have one of those high-ceilinged pre-war apartments; you can have the bed on top and a desk/play area down below. The IKEA Web site suggests making a secret hideaway underneath the bed comfy with pillows and blankets.

4. Floor pillows and bean bags make durable, affordable, comfortable chairs for reading or hanging out with friends.

5. Give every child a peg rack for the next day's clothing or pajamas or outerwear. It'll help your child organize himself and get clothes off the floor.

6. Can you say armoire? The Europeans have been using these for several hundred years; surely we can try them in the third millennium.

7. Store sports equipment in a standing hamper (bamboo, cloth, or frame) or industrial-size garbage can (chrome, white plastic). They're perfect for everything from baseball bats to lacrosse and hockey sticks to tennis rackets. If the closet's big enough, they can be stashed in there; if not, get a container that's attractive enough to remain out in the open.

8. Make open play space in a small room by organizing furniture along the walls.

9. Canvas laundry bags for laundry? How passé. Use them instead as alternatives to those ubiquitous plastic storage boxes. They can be shoved into any space you have available and are particularly good for train tracks, blocks, and dress-up clothes.

10. Under-the-bed storage is a must. Slide-out drawers can store toys (they're great for vehicles, dolls, art portfolios, puzzles, and games), linens, and out-of-season clothes or clothes being held for the next-in-line. Or go with the trundle bed—you can use the trundle for toys when Bobby's into those and as an extra bed when he's at the sleepover age.

If we've heard it once, we've heard it a hundred times: "Our kids have separate rooms, but they always end up in one."

Dr. Wendy Haft believes, despite the best of intentions, many families today are making a mistake by insisting on giving children their own bedrooms and separate toys and enforcing the "don't touch this or that of your siblings" rules. "People are going overboard these days. Maybe there's more value in learning to negotiate, sharing, helping out, creating an even stronger intimacy," she says.

Sharing rooms fosters a sense of security among siblings. "Wonderful things go on at night after the parents leave; it becomes a kind of slumber party," says Dr. Haft, who shared a room with her younger sister from birth till she went to college. When they're not fighting over toys, siblings can create meaningful bonds, concurs Jan Faull, a child-development and behavior specialist and author of *Unplugging Power Struggles.* In one column she penned for *FamilyFun,* she went so far as to say that all parents should consider having their kids share a bedroom. "Sometimes it remedies nighttime sleep problems, and it always gives siblings daily reasons to learn to share, to compromise and to negotiate," she writes. One of Kathy's happiest memories of her childhood is the goodnight ritual she shared with her older brother, Jeff. Bunking together in a room in Manhattan's Greenwich Village, every night one would start: "Goodnight." The other would reply, "Thank you for saying 'goodnight.'" Then, "Thank you for saying 'thank you' for saying 'goodnight,'" back to the first, and on and on, until someone fell asleep.

"There are so many issues surrounding night time and separation," reminds Dr. Haft, that sharing a room provides siblings "with an additional opportunity to get to know and empathize with another person." Recently, her older daughter offered up a prized stuffed animal to her younger sister when she was afraid to go to sleep. "Because it came from her sister, it was really special, more potent." Needless to say, the ploy worked. "This is just an example of an opportunity that would not have been presented had they not shared a room."

Not that sharing always keeps them out of *your* room. Julia remembers the night she and her husband were happily settling down, alone at last, when she heard a rumbling down the hall. "Do you hear that? They're coming!" Louder and louder the noise got and then a chanting and a rhythmic thumping. Cautiously, Julia peered out her bedroom door and there were her two older kids, her son behind her daughter, his hands on her shoulders as they conga-ed down the hall, "We can't go to sleep (boom)! We can't go to sleep (boom)." Well, maybe sharing a room didn't get them to sleep any better, but they *were* laughing and, for once, cooperating.

So look at your space constraint as a virtue not a deprivation. That said, sharing a room has various logistical problems that need to be addressed. The first issue at hand is the sleeping arrangements. Trundles work nicely for rooms that are spatially challenged—pretty much any room in a city. And if the trundler doesn't like being low down, you can always get one of those pop-up beds that fold down for storage and scissor-up to regular bed height when in use.

Then there are bunk beds. They don't just work in rooms with high ceilings, you know. The bunk bed/loft bed industry has really come into its own over the past few years, a godsend to those of us with many kids and few bedrooms. The variations are just about endless: You can get smaller bunk beds that barely scrape 5 feet tall; you can get triple bunks that purportedly fit under 8-foot ceilings (although these creeped us out). Friends of ours had their three girls bedding down in a bunk bed/trundle combination, which worked fabulously. Want more ideas? Bunk over daybed; twin bed over full bed; twin loft bunk beds; loft bed over hanging space, and on and on.

Concerning bunks, here's a golden rule that best not be broken: No un-potty trained on top bunks. And, in general, it makes more sense to let the older kids sleep on top. First of all, for safety reasons, experts say, you should be 6 years old to be on top. And, psychologically, having the top bunk presents a way for the older sib to reassert his rightful place in the family hierarchy and get a feeling (illusory maybe) of having more control. If you do go for bunk beds, think logistics when you select bedding. Schlepping up there to change the linens is a serious pain, so many parents recommend sleeping bags until Junior learns how to make his own bed. Another option for kids' beds, which works just as well on any bed, is to rely

Bunk Bed Safety

Most kids survive bunk beds quite happily, but a few precautions never hurt anyone:

1. Put a cordless nightlight on the ladder; it'll make it a bit safer if the top bunker wants to descend in the dark of night.
2. Don't allow the bunk bed to be used as a trampoline—ever. Jumping on or from the bed can collapse it and/or cause injuries from poor landings.
3. Make sure your bunk bed has what should be typical safety features: guardrail on the top bunk (with no more than a 3½-inch gap between the guardrail and side rails); upper mattresses supported by wires or slats that are fastened at both ends and run directly under the mattress; and snug-fitting mattresses with no gaps between the mattress and edge of the frame that a small child could get trapped in.

Sources: American Academy of Pediatrics, Medem Medical Library, "Bunk Bed Dangers," from *Caring for Baby and Young Child: Birth to Age 5*, Bantam, 1999; www.pedscenter.yourmd.com

When Your Kids Share a Room

Doubling kids up can be a bumpy ride if kids are of widely different personalities: messy versus neat, quiet versus rambunctious, etc. If you've got a big dichotomy, see if you can divide the room with a temporary wall. If that fails, recognize you are going to have to be diligent about laying down and enforcing laws to keep the peace.

- Respecting each other's personal space is paramount. That way, the neat child won't get tagged with cleaning up her messy sibling's debris and she'll feel a little more comfortable if her own space is as tidy as she likes it. And, of course, if you've got a toddler or younger as one of the sharers, the burden's going to be on you to make sure little Tabitha isn't constantly destroying her older brother's space.
- Time-outs may be required. If one child needs a lot more quiet, you're going to have to build that into the schedule; give them each ownership of the room at different times—for one to color quietly or for the other to indulge in some loud, action-packed vehicle play.
- Watch the post–lights-out talking. If both kids enjoy it, build it into the nighttime routine but stay alert: That type of stuff can go on into the wee hours if you don't step in.
- Let their personalities shine. There are lots of ways to give each kid a voice in the room without making it look like a circus on steroids: special sheets, pillows, or drawer pulls; a place for each one's art and books; special rugs to mark their areas; bookshelves divided so that each has space for his own collection; or even individual chests for storing special objects.

on comforters over a fitted sheet. Any kid can fluff and straighten a comforter; it's when they have to tuck and smooth that the going gets rough.

Shall we talk about sex? The boy/girl thing really doesn't become an issue until the first of the kids approaches adolescence (although a precocious few draw the line at sharing by first grade). Often, different sex kids will share longer than you ever thought possible, even though they gripe about each other. There's something pretty comforting about having someone sequestered next to you in the deep of the night, even if it's your annoying copycat 3-year-old sister. But when it's time to separate the genders, often your children will let you know.

CHAPTER 3

THE RX FOR CITY HEALTH HAZARDS

■ ■

No question, management of your child's health has a distinctively urban tinge, from the good—the plethora of choices you have when managing your families' health—to the bad—problems like pollution, cockroaches, and lead, which may not even blip your suburban friends' radar. For each, there's a unique city component, history, and strategy. We'll tell you how to deal with them, when to deal with them, and, really importantly, what steps to take so you never find yourself in the position of saying, "If only I'd known."

MEDICAL CHOICES YOU HAVE . . . AND SHOULD MAKE

Love this story: In 1946, a small-town Oklahoma boy developed an infection in his leg that traveled to the bone. His local doc advocated standard-issue treatment: *amputation*. But the boy's father refused to believe that was the only option. He drove his 16-year-old for hours until they reached Oklahoma City and The Children's Hospital, where doctors gave the youth a new wonder drug, penicillin. As the boy lay in his bed at the hospital, convalescing, he listened to the 1946 World Series on the radio. You know what? The wonder drug worked, and Mickey Mantle went on to have a pretty fair baseball career of his own.

Fortunately for baseball fans, Mickey's dad knew that when it comes to finding a top-notch hospital or specialist, hands down, there's no better place for your child than a city. Without a doubt, the depth and breadth of urban pediatric medical services make this one of the strongest components of city family living. Our suburban and rural cousins often have to travel far and wide for the health care that's so readily available to us. City hospitals, especially the many children's hospitals across the country, are among the finest in the world. And it doesn't take more than a nanosecond for urban dwellers to access pediatric specialists in every conceivable field—from cardiology and cancer to plastic surgery, allergies, and learning and physical disabilities. There are even docs specializing in health issues common to foreign adoptees.

Sadly, like time-deprived parents everywhere, many urban moms and dads don't always think through the issues before the fact. But when your child has a serious injury and there's no pediatric anesthesiologist in the hospital you ran to, you'll know why you needed to do a little investigation up front. No messing around here. If there's a time to be ahead of the curve as a parent, it's to get your medical options in line. Of course, we're not suggesting you research and prepare for every possible medical happening, but we do insist (please) that you take advantage of your city's offerings in the biggest-bang-for-the-buck categories: emergency care, plastic surgery, and pediatric dentistry.

In this section, we'll explain why you want focused pediatric providers in each of these areas and how to find suitable ones for your family. We'll also give you tips on how to coordinate the activities of these specialty providers with those of your child's primary care physician. Many situations require a joint effort, and your child will be much better served if her pediatrician, pediatric dentist, and plastic surgeon—and any other specialists you use—all know and respect each other and have admitting privileges at the same hospital.

Pediatric Emergency Departments: Why You Want One

In an emergency situation, you can't always choose where your child gets treated, and in a real crisis, you'll just want to get to the nearest emergency room pronto (actually, emergency facilities have gotten so complicated that medical professionals now prefer the term *emergency department*; since most of us are amateurs here, we'll stick with the traditional moniker). But many times you do have options, and there's a world of difference in what your kid's experience will be like if you don't exercise your right to choose with a modicum of responsibility and research. Cities generally have quite a selection of hospitals, but there are big differences in their pediatric capabilities. Most parents treat them as so many Starbucks branches: settling for the one in the 'hood. Maybe your local ER will be everything you want for little Malek. Then again . . .

Consider this. There are more than 31 million child and adolescent emergency room visits a year—that works out to 41 visits for every 100 kids, which makes the odds pretty great that an emergency room visit is in your future. Yes, yes, sure the kids are growing up too fast and all, but they're hardly miniature versions of us, you know. They have different bodies (how can an adult blood pressure cuff possibly fit the arm of a 3-year-old?), different illnesses, and different medication and anesthesia requirements. In fact, the differences are so profound that over the last 10 years, an entirely new medical subspecialty has emerged: pediatric emergency medicine.

Top teaching hospitals now offer this specialty, which gives doctors an extra three years of training in handling children's medical emergencies. But many hospitals still lack deep pediatric knowledge. Here's a scary stat: Ninety percent of the physicians staffing emergency departments have training in Advanced Cardiac Life Support, but less than two-thirds have completed an equivalent course in pediatric resuscitation. Do you really want to take a chance that your unconscious child is in the hands of the one out of three lacking pediatric expertise?

What Pediatric Medics Know: Kids Are Not Mini-You's

Children's bodies are just so different from those of adults. Here are just a few of the dissimilarities that are relevant in terms of emergency care.

1. Kids' bones and joints are soft; they don't always respond to trauma in the same fashion as adults. Lung injuries from trauma are often suspected in adults with rib fractures, but in young children, an impact can damage the lungs while the soft bones appear to be fine. And pediatric fractures can require totally different treatments than adult ones, particularly if they impact the growth plate—which is not so easy to ascertain if you don't know what you're looking for.

2. Shock, from loss of blood or dehydration, is often very difficult to recognize in kids—and the failure to do so results in a really shocking rate of morbidity and mortality among children. In adults, shock often manifests itself through falling blood pressure; kids, on the other hand, have a deceptive ability to maintain normal blood pressure even though the blood flow to other organs, like the kidneys and gut, has effectively shut down.

3. Intubation to get oxygen to the lungs of kids with respiratory issues can be very tricky. Their airways are tiny and more flexible than adults; their tracheas shorter, their larynxes higher. When someone who lacks pediatric experience tries to intubate a child, the tube is often improperly placed or unknowingly dislodged— cutting off the sometimes critical flow of oxygen.

4. So many signs of illness are different. Pneumonia, for instance, usually presents in adults with a cough, fever, and chest pain. Infants may never actually develop a fever to signify an infection; all that may be evident is some lethargy or crankiness.

Even less-than-life-threatening emergencies can turn into traumatic disasters if they involve a child being shoehorned into a normal emergency room's capabilities and equipment. Take Julia's own nightmare experience. When her then 3-year-old ripped open his big toe, she rushed him to the closest hospital. What should have been a 15-minute exercise to sew a few stitches in the toe turned into a 2-hour horror show when the emergency room turned out to lack anything suitable to restrain a small child (including personnel trained to help with the situation). And without a pediatric anesthesiologist on staff, there was apparently no way to give her completely traumatized child any medication either to dull the pain of the multiple aborted stitching attempts or calm his ultimately hysterical mental condition.

Then there's the nonmedical trauma to consider. Sometimes it seems like city emergency facilities harbor more criminals than an episode of *NYPD Blue*. This is scary enough for adults; do you really want your sensitive kindergartner exposed to that if you can avoid it? As Gerald Loughlin, M.D., Nancy C. Paduano, Professor and Chairman, Department of Pediatrics at Weill Medical College of Cornell University and Pediatrician-in-Chief at New York Weill Cornell Medical Center, says, in an urban emergency room, you can find "a 2-year-old with a fever next to a guy with a gunshot wound right next to a drunk." We'll take door number two please.

Choosing the Best ER

Now that you're convinced a pediatric ER is the way to go, how do you pick one? There are three considerations. First: location. You may find the perfect facility, but it's on the south end of the city and you live farther north. Not very helpful if your child's in distress in the middle of the night. Second: the professional criterion. Matters of staffing, staff training, and equipment and supplies are the main issues that pediatric emergency professionals themselves use to judge facilities. Third: your pediatrician. Having a doctor who has privileges at the emergency room you're visiting may not be a lifesaver, but it sure can feel like one. A doctor who calls ahead to the ER to put them on notice that you're coming in (or even meets you there) can make a huge difference in the quality and length of your stay.

We'll leave locational issues to you, but here's some advice on evaluating the professional criteria and working with your pediatrician.

Examining the ER

Once you've identified hospitals within a reasonable distance of your home (and maybe a second option near your child's school or day care), your next concern will be with the emergency room itself. What you are looking for are facilities that can treat a child as a child and can answer most of the following questions in the affirmative:

Does the hospital have a pediatrics department? Easiest question to ask. If the answer is no, this is the last place you want your child to be in an emergency. Chances are there won't be much in the way of specialized pediatric care in the ER, let alone ongoing care should your child's situation be so serious he needs hospitalization.

Does the hospital have a separate pediatric emergency room? Or at least separate waiting and treatment areas? Children's hospitals have these facilities and, quite often, so do big-city general hospitals, especially if they're teaching hospitals. If the hospital doesn't have a specific pediatric ER, the next best option would be a full-time pediatric staff with pediatric specialists (anesthesiologists, neurologists, etc.). But you'll want to check their hours, since that staff may only be on call during certain times. And your child is yours, 24/7.

Do the ER doctors and nurses have specific training in pediatric emergency medicine? Pediatric specialization is key, not only for the very significant medical benefits such training provides but also the emotional ones. As Dr. Loughlin points out, it makes an enormous difference to be treated by a "person who likes kids, who's comfortable with and able to deal with children." There are many, many wonderful and committed medical professionals who just panic at the prospect of working on children in distress. Nurses and doctors who are trained in pediatric emergency care, by contrast, have made that choice willingly.

The gold standard is an emergency room stocked with docs with either "double boards"—meaning they've received separate certification by both the American Board of Pediatrics and the Board of Emergency Medicine—or certifi-

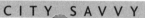

CITY SAVVY

Your Questions for the ER

Call a hospital you are considering and ask to speak with someone who can describe the emergency room's pediatric capabilities—preferably the pediatric nursing director or the ER's general director. Make your calls in the morning, since undoubtedly the individual best able to handle this kind of request is a day-shift worker, plus the ER's less likely to be hopping with activity then. That said, you *are* talking to an *emergency* room, so you never know whether a time is appropriate or not. Check to see how frantic things are before you launch into your interrogation. Remember, you'll attract more flies with honey, so set up your questions without being overly pushy, starting with "Is this a good time to speak?" "I just had a kid" or "I just moved into the neighborhood and am trying to find out about emergency room care, so I was wondering how you handle pediatric emergencies" should do the trick.

The Best-Laid Plans

Maybe you've done the most incredible investigation, you and your doctor are in total agreement, and there's a fantastic pediatric ER just waiting to serve you. But then the emergency happens when your child is visiting friends 2 miles south of your apartment. The ambulance driver may not be able to take you to your desired facility (out of his zone) or he may say there's no time, the child's condition is too critical. If you're in a situation like this, let your research help you with your next move. Explain to the EMS pros about your choices. Maybe there's a pediatric ER nearby that would satisfy them and you. But don't second-guess them on the direness of the emergency: They're trained and you (most of you, anyway) are not.

cation in Pediatrics Emergency Medicine. Your least desirable ER? Those manned solely by regular emergency doctors or worse: moonlighting interns who have even less training in kids and their emergencies. Although these guys can do right by your child in many situations, the fact is their pediatric training is limited to a small percentage of their total medical education (typically just 1 to 3 months out of 3 or 4 years of training), and they will just not be as well versed in the nuances of pediatric care as the specialists are.

In addition to the main ER physicians, there is a cast of supporting characters who can be quite important, depending on your child's emergency needs. In the best of circumstances, pediatric specialists are on-call at all times. Some of the most important are anesthesiologists, trauma surgeons, neurosurgeons, and orthopedic surgeons.

Let's not forget the nurses either. Often the first person you'll see in an ER is the triage nurse, the one responsible for ranking cases by severity of emergency. Because distress symptoms in children can vary so greatly from those of adults, you want a triage nurse to have specific pediatric emergency training. Ideally, the ER nursing staff will also have training in pediatric critical care and pediatric surgery as well.

Does the ER have pediatric equipment? Pediatric medicines? This is a biggie. Your child absolutely will do better with scaled-down equipment. For instance, kids require plastic airway tubes that are less than half the width of those made for adults. Too many hospitals don't have the right intubation gear, and doctors end up having to jury-rig adult tubes. It's one thing if you're bringing in an 11-year-old with a broken arm; but if your toddler is seriously injured, wouldn't you rather be at a facility equipped with child-size breathing tubes, oxygen masks, blood pressure cuffs, and pediatric defibrillators with miniaturized paddles?

Then there are the meds: Does the ER have premeasured doses of emergency drugs organized for children of different weights? This speeds up care, and the last thing you want in an emergency is to find out the doc treating your little one failed Math 101.

Want to know more? The list of recommended equipment and supplies is awe-inspiring. The American Academy of Pediatrics gives a complete rundown at its Web site at www.aap.org.

Does the ER have a child life program? This is one of the smarter, more humane developments in children-focused care. Child life professionals are non-medical members of a child's care team whose primary focus is to reduce the stress a child experiences in the hospital. Not widespread, particularly in these cost-cutting times, they're a godsend when they are part of the emergency room experience. Child life specialists will usually stay with a child from the beginning to the end of his emergency room stay, explaining ER procedures in child-friendly terms, using play or other distractions to take his mind off his pain or worry, and working with the parent or accompanying adult to minimize the child's distress.

Working with Your Pediatrician

Ideally, you and your pediatrician are in perfect sync on the go-to emergency department for your child. Of course, if you're in the stages of picking a pediatrician, you can front-run any potential conflict by taking the advice of Sue Jane Smith, RN, MSN, and the trauma coordinator at Children's Hospital of Michigan: First pick the ER, then find a pediatrician who has admitting privileges at that hospital. "When women are pregnant and they choose an obstetrician, they usually decide where they want to have their baby and then choose a doctor that is on staff. A lot of things go into that decision of choosing the hospital. Those same things need to go into choosing your child's hospital." Many pediatricians have admitting privileges or are on staff at several hospitals, she adds.

Perhaps you've already discussed the whole emergency situation with your pediatrician, but many people have never had that conversation. If you're the laggard, no time to waste. Call or set up an appointment to go over your child's emergency care routine. Ideally you've already followed the instructions above and called the hospitals directly to check out the ER's pediatric capabilities. That doesn't get you out of talking with your doctor: This is a *very* important conversation to have. Dr. Loughlin says that when he's seen "trouble over the years, it's when a parent is uncomfortable talking with his pediatrician." So if you feel you can't have this discussion, you need to do some hard thinking about why.

By the way, if that well-planned-for emergency does arise, call your pediatrician's office before you go to the emergency room, if at all possible. Maybe your doctor can meet you there. At a minimum, he may be able to get you treated faster and more appropriately. Many urban ERs, even pediatric ones, are wildly overcrowded; they even turn away traffic when their waiting rooms are too full. How bad can it get? Just ask the desperate patients in Las Vegas, who have been known to call 911 from the emergency room to get ambulances to bring them back in on a stretcher, in the hopes of getting faster care.

THE URBAN A-LIST
How to Talk the ER Talk

When you're working out your emergency-room plan with your pediatrician:

Don't be confrontational. Putting doc on the defensive never works as well as the situational approach: "What should we do if there's an emergency on a Saturday afternoon at 3 P.M.—where do I go?" If he tells you where, but doesn't elucidate, don't be afraid to ask why he likes that facility. Or, ask why he prefers hospital X more than hospital Y (which you know has a good pediatric ER).

Discuss the choices. It may turn out that hospital X is where he has admitting privileges but does not necessarily have anything to offer a child in a medical emergency. If that's the case, you will need to make some choices. You may, for example, decide that it's fine to go to the hospital your doctor recommends if your kid just has a scrape; but if he's gasping for air or has a serious head wound, advises Dr. Loughlin, you're probably going to want to go to the ER with "all the trappings," regardless of your doctor's admitting capabilities. Or perhaps there's an acceptable compromise. Maybe your doctor has admitting privileges at more than one hospital and maybe his *second* choice will have the pediatric ER you're looking for.

Review other locations. If your child spends regular time in different parts of the city (maybe day care and home are far apart, for example), go through the same drill for any of those places.

Discuss the entire emergency procedure. Ask your doctor for advice on when to take your child to the ER, when to use an ambulance, and when it's okay to get there by your own devices.

Smart Emergency Communications

Now that you've gone to all the trouble of researching your ER options, don't forget to communicate your wishes to any babysitter, nanny, family member, school, or other person or entity in charge of care for your child.

Pediatric Dentists: Today's Tooth Fairies

There are thousands and thousands and thousands of city dentists. But the benefits of a competent, full-coverage pediatric dentist are particularly compelling in the city—where any day you can avoid an emergency room visit is a good day in our book. For starters, there's your child's experience. Julia's children love going to the dentist. We're not kidding. But we're also not surprised. After all, what's not to like about a dentist's office stocked with video games, a playhouse, TV, dentists who crack jokes constantly, cookie dough-flavored toothpaste, plenty of hand-holding, and prizes at the end. All in all, their dental experiences are a far cry from the drill-'em-and-fill-'em nightmares of yesteryear.

Dental practitioners who choose to specialize in children go through traditional dental school but then obtain 2 to 3 years of additional training in the technical aspects of pediatric dental care as well as in child development and patient (and parent) management. So these guys are not only versed in all the particular and unique dental needs of kids, they're also completely and utterly attuned to making the dental visit as painless (emotionally and physically) as possible.

In this business, "you do everything you can to mask the experience," says Louis Cooper, D.D.S., of the Manhattan Pediatric Dental Group. His key tactics are "diversion and distraction." So when Pearson had a recalcitrant tooth pulled, an encounter that he was truly dreading, Dr. Cooper started with a running joke routine—the gags coming so fast that Pearson barely had a chance to think about what was really on the agenda. Next came the special goggles with mirrors to reflect the TV monitor so he could watch *Shrek* while laying back in the chair. A little laughing gas, a little Novocaine—and way faster than Pearson ever expected, the tooth was gone, the visit over, and *Shrek* barely past the opening credits. Will Pearson ever dread dentists the way his father does? Probably not, as long as he keeps going to Dr. Cooper.

But it's not just the fact that your kids won't experience the trauma you did. It's the aggravation you may save them and yourself in avoiding an emergency room visit. Kids have lots of things happen to their mouths that require immediate attention—babies fall off of changing tables or beds, toddlers run into swings, budding athletes take a hockey stick in the jaw or lose teeth in a playground collision. If you follow the inclination of many parents, you'll rush the victim to an emergency room, where the wait may be extensive (3 or more hours is not uncommon in overloaded urban ERs) and where any repair may be done with a surgeon's skill but probably not with pediatric dental particularities top of mind. Here's a far better choice, call your child's dentist (who ideally has round-the-clock coverage) in any mouth-related emergency. Depending on the nature of the emergency, your child's dentist can either meet you at the office, where he's set up to handle many of these kinds of emergencies, or he'll meet you at the emergency room where, chances are, he can greatly expedite your child's care.

Identifying that pediatric dentist who will make your life so much more pleasant needn't be a chore. In addition to the specialized pediatric training, a pediatric dentist should be a member of the American Board of Pediatric Dentistry (the American Academy of Pediatric Dentistry provides a search function for parents on its Web site, www.aapd.org). You want a practitioner who is competent, obviously, and has a personality that you think will work with your child. Office staff is important too. City practices tend to be very busy and crowded, and those

The Lowdown on City Dentist Appointments

Children under 5 should be seen in the morning. Some of this is for the practice's convenience. Dentists figure older kids have more to lose from missing school, so they reserve after-school slots for them. But there are a lot of advantages for the younger children who go early. They tend to be less cranky, so the whole event is likely to progress more smoothly. And they avoid the afternoon crush—Dr. Cooper says there's a "palpable buzz" in his office after 3 P.M., which can greatly add to the tension and stress of a younger child.

First visits should be between 1 and 2 years of age. Many dental problems can be avoided or treated if caught early—notably baby bottle syndrome, where kids who are allowed to fall asleep with a bottle in their mouth develop large numbers of cavities in their baby teeth. In fact, the American Academy of Pediatrics recently recommended children be seen as young as 6 months.

Delays are a fact of life in city pediatric dentists' offices. Emergency situations are often handled there (something you'll be glad of when your child's the accident victim) so there's a sizable degree of randomness in a day's schedule. Plus even though every practice allows a certain amount of time per child, sometimes a 4-year-old takes a little extra coaxing to get into the chair. And, of course, facilities are subject to parent or caregiver error as well. Getting the child to the appointment just "a little bit" late has a predictable snowball effect on the rest of a tightly packed schedule.

on the front line need to be able to deal with questions and tantrums and phones without losing their cool. Your medical professionals can all be good sources for names—including your dentist, doctor, and your child's pediatrician or plastic surgeon.

Plastic Surgery: You're Never Too Young

Who thinks about finding a pediatric plastic surgeon before the fact? We sure didn't. And yet, there are a zillion city scenarios that start off so benignly—say, hopping on the underground or taking Rover to the dog run—that result in the need for a top doc. Here are four common childhood accidents that might require a pediatric plastic surgeon:

1. Hakim bangs his chin on the jungle gym. So many children do this that the temptation is to ignore special treatment, but injuries to the chin can damage facial nerves.
2. The cab door slams on Rosa's finger. These accidents often involve the nail bed, which must be properly reimplanted to prevent permanent loss or disfigurement of the nail.
3. Courtney gets bitten by that sweet little pit bull from the park. Dog bite wounds in children are usually on the face, almost always involving the tearing of soft tissue—with big potential for disfigurement if not properly treated.
4. Joey grabs a hot pot on the stove. Scar tissue, which forms on improperly treated burned hands, can limit future function.

In many of these cases, time will be of the essence. Most of us consider ourselves to be darned lucky just to get any care that's available. And in the highly stressful moment, parents usually won't think about how a scar will heal or disfigure—they just want to make sure their child stops bleeding or infection doesn't creep into a wound, etc. But often there *is* time to call in your own specialist—that is, if you think to do so. When a cut is gushing, for instance, the wound will need to be sutured up quickly; when it isn't, you have up to 6 hours to get it sewn up. In other words, you don't need to rely on that on-call ER plastic surgeon with no pediatric experience. Julia's Malcolm was lucky when he got his foot slammed by a piano bench. Julia thought to call her pediatrician, who immediately called a plastic surgeon to meet them at the emergency room. That action saved Malcolm's toe. With hindsight, Julia knows she was lucky: It never would have occurred to her to have requested a pediatric plastic surgeon. Take her advice and have one on call.

Of course, do your homework ahead of time and find that doctor you like

Smart Emergency Communications, Part 2

Alert your child's day care or nursery, or preschool, etc., that in case of an accident, any facial surgery is to be done by your plastic surgeon. We recommend putting this in writing, alongside the pediatrician, pediatric dentist, and hospital of choice.

and trust. There is an abundance of choices in every city—and for every insurance plan. And here's a great opportunity to feel superior to our country brethren: According to a survey by the American Academy of Pediatrics, only 22 percent of doctors identified as pediatric plastic surgeons practiced in suburban or rural areas; most are found in cities.

Just as with finding the best pediatric dentist for your child, start your search for a plastic surgeon by asking your pediatrician (or your dentist, as they often work hand-in-hand with plastic surgeons) for a referral. Presumably, you trust your existing doctors (if you don't, change).

The best-case scenario is a board certified pediatric plastic surgeon associated or affiliated with the hospital of your choice. Certified physicians will have passed two lengthy and rigorous sets of tests given by the American Board of Plastic Surgery (ABPS). Pediatric plastic surgeons, by definition, devote 50 percent or more of their practice to the care of children and get additional training specifically geared to the needs of children. Plus, they have child-appropriate equipment and materials and usually very pleasant child-friendly décor in their offices. Additionally, physicians who have shown proper credentials to their peers are eligible to become specialty fellows of the American Academy of Pediatrics in the area of plastic surgery.

If you're not satisfied with the credentials of your referral, check with the plastic surgery department of a nearby university or with the county medical society, or obtain information from the Plastic Surgery Section of the American Academy of Pediatrics. And if per chance there is no pediatric plastic surgeon in your area, try and identify a doctor who has done a pediatric fellowship. Finally, if this too doesn't pan out, try to ascertain how much experience the general plastic surgeon has with children (i.e., the number of children he treats in a year, the percent of children in his practice). Once again, the more experience he has with children, the merrier your own child's plastic surgery experience is likely to be.

CITY AFFLICTIONS

As fine as the medical care is that's available to city children, there are still some unhealthy living conditions inherent to city rearing that put our children at risk. Pollution, lead exposure, mold—dang it, we even have to worry about the pigeons and cockroaches. Cheer up—there's plenty you can do to mitigate any potential damage city living may cause to your children.

The Air We Breathe

Nobody ever said city air was great, but now according to the latest research we have to worry about the air inside our homes as well. The combination of outdoor and indoor pollution certainly complicates things, and it means that as a parent you need to be more vigilant than ever. But do we all need to hook up oxygen tanks to the backs of our strollers? Nah, it's not that bad.

Outdoor Air Pollution

Some good news: Thanks to government laws that have worked to reduce major sources of pollution, urban air *is* significantly cleaner than when we all were

Another Reason to Hate Pigeons

A study of kids visiting a Bronx emergency room found that 50 percent of those between the ages of 2 and 5 were infected with the very scary sounding *Cryptococcus neoformans,* as were a whopping 70 percent of those children over 5.[a] Now, *C. neoformans* is a fairly common fungus that is considered harmless in most humans; but in individuals with immune-compromised systems, like HIV/AIDS patients, it causes a relentless infection.[b] That doesn't make us feel too sanguine about having it run rampant in our little ones.

Since *C. neoformans* is typically found in pigeon droppings and all kinds of urban dirt, it seems that we have just found another big reason to avoid massive pigeon gatherings and playing on or about pigeon droppings (and check that sandbox); in fact, you may want to downright discourage pigeon feeding, particularly near playgrounds. And for goodness sakes, if you really needed another reason to wash your kids' hands after they've come in from outside, now you have one.

a. Sarah Ramsay, "C neoformans Common in Urban Children," *Lancet,* May 12, 2001.
b. "Worms Teach Lesson on Mechanism of Fungal Infection," News from Harvard Medical, Dental and Public Health Schools, Nov. 22, 2002.

growing up. Oh, and here's another bright spot (well, sort of): Recent research suggests that city kids may actually be *less* affected by ozone than their suburban cousins. Turns out that all that earthbound ozone generated by our dirty urban industrial activities may be more problematic for kids living *downwind* of pollution-generating cities—a function of wind patterns as well as ozone's unique chemistry that allows it to be broken down in the presence of sunlight and a few noxious chemicals (which cities have in abundance). One study examining the growth of cottonwood trees on the East Coast found that those growing in New York City grew twice as big as those in far more pastoral surroundings elsewhere in New York State. Why? Because the non-city areas had much higher ozone buildups than those in the urban area itself.

But don't break out the champagne just yet. Ground-level ozone can build up in warm weather in any city, and it's nasty when it does. Plus cities have way more than their share of smog, particulates, and all the other toxins that are part of the daily crusty urban fallout. And a gazillion studies of the impact of pollution on children have shown it to be associated with a bunch of unpleasant health problems—including middle ear and respiratory infections, increased colds, headaches, allergies, and episodes of bronchitis.

Furthermore, just because you seem to be relatively unscathed from a bad air day doesn't mean you can assume your child is escaping the harmful impacts of pollution. Their airways are narrower than yours. They need more oxygen relative to their size than you do. They breathe more rapidly and inhale more pollutants per pound of body weight. Their higher metabolic rates can increase the absorption of toxins. Their lungs are still growing, creating millions of air sacs throughout childhood. And yo, they are just closer to the ground, breathing in dust, dirt, and toxic heavy metals that are deposited on city cement and soil. Compounding kids' natural vulnerability is the fact that they often play outside on summer afternoons—when excessive pollution is most likely to occur.

What does all this mean to the city parent? You've got to be sensible about pollution.

THE CITY PARENT RULES
Protecting Your Progeny from Outdoor Pollution

Rule #1: Pay attention to air alerts in your city. Tracking pollution is not difficult. Air pollution levels are monitored and reported publicly in every city, often with the next day's weather forecast.

Rule #2: Adjust your kid's activities. It's surprising how many people let kids play outside with abandon on the worst of bad air days. We know it's a pain to keep active kids indoors when the sun is shining, but we're really not asking that much. Most cities are only subject to a very few days of excessively bad air each year, if that. Remember, not only are children *not* immune to pollution effects, they are, in fact, much more sensitive to them than grown-ups. So adjust their schedules according to the pollution forecast. On days when air quality is expected to be at its worst levels, no running around the playground during suspect times. If the issue is carbon monoxide, the worst time would be morning; if it's ozone, nix outdoor play in the afternoon.

Rule #3: Monitor your child's appearance and physical condition. Unlike adults, a child won't necessarily be conscious of the fact that he's suffering from pollution. If he's coughing or wheezing or simply short of breath, he needs to stop running around—no matter how much fun he's having. Another thing: You may be thrilled that you have a happy, healthy, active kid. You should be. But active kids are particularly susceptible to the effects of ozone and particulate matter because they breathe so much while running around. So if your child is a whirlwind of motion, be particularly sensitive to any display of symptoms when the air quality is questionable.

Rule #4: Consider some enlightening food for thought. Ruth Etzel, M.D., Ph.D., former chair of the American Academy of Pediatrics' Committee on Environmental Health and editor of its handbook *Pediatric Environmental Health*, speaks about tantalizing studies showing potential benefits for asthma sufferers from eating apples or fish and even from vitamins C and E. While such studies are still limited, the issues are "worthy of further study," concurs Dr. Loughlin, who before coming to New York was credited with building Johns Hopkins' highly regarded pediatric respiratory disease program. The way we look at this, you've got one more reason to make sure your children are eating well-balanced diets.

Indoor Air Quality

Here's the 20-million-dollar question: Why would indoor air quality (IAQ to insiders) have suddenly become such a concern? After all, humans have been living inside for thousands of years (and how well ventilated do you think that winter cave was?). Indoor pollution seems to be a result of the way we build and use modern structures, including: (1) the lack of ventilation, particularly in the abundance of new city buildings with their energy-efficient sealed windows; (2) the many pollutants and allergens we bring into our homes as a consequence of modern living, i.e., chemical pollutants like pesticides and cleaning fluids, tobacco smoke, and

Pollution Where You Least Expect It

The concept of indoor air pollution is so new that most people aren't even familiar with some of the worst sources. Dirt and dust, pollen, and animal hair are up there, but so are a host of less obvious but equally unpleasant polluters. Get educated, because like it or not, you probably have some of the worst offenders in your home.

- Carpet. New carpeting can be a problem for anyone with allergies or asthma because they emit volatile organic compounds (VOCs) for several days after they're installed. Before you buy new carpets and rugs, see if they (and any padding and adhesives) are tagged with the green label of the Carpet and Rug Institute, Indoor Air Quality Testing Program—which signifies that the products meet government standards for VOC emissions. And, if you have the discipline and desire, follow the EPA's recommendations: Have all family members out of the house when the new carpet's installed, run every piece of venting equipment you've got— window fans and air conditioners— and open the windows for 48 to 72 hours after the carpet has been laid.

- Furniture. New furniture is a particularly strong source of unhealthy chemical emissions. Formaldehyde is the problem here. Keep your windows open for a while when you first bring in new pieces.
- Dry cleaning. Keep your dry cleaning out of the apartment if it smells like chemicals (let it air outside awhile and consider getting a new cleaner if this persists). And watch your use of moth repellants; many use paradichlorobenzene (as do quite a few air fresheners), which is one of those mysterious substances that wreaks havoc in animals but hasn't been tested yet on humans.
- Gas stoves. Make sure fumes from cooking with gas are thoroughly vented to the outdoors. We're told the flame should be blue-tipped; yellow-tipped flames cause more pollutant emissions (like carbon monoxide). Your gas company should be able to adjust your stove to the proper "hue." And if you're getting a new stove, get one with a pilotless ignition so that you won't always have a pilot light burning.

Beware That First-Floor Business

If your family lives one or two floors above a dry cleaner or gas station, you should strongly consider talking to the local health department about getting your apartment monitored because of the very strong pollutants involved in both establishments. If they're not following the necessary procedures to maintain and clean up their operations, your kids could really get hurt.

biological contaminants like bacteria and pollen; and (3) in the case of city kids, the fact that so many are spending so much of their time in concentrated indoor spaces that any negative aspects of that air are magnified.

But how do you know if you have a problem? Well, just as with outdoor pollution, if your child has asthma, assume that you do, because kids who suffer from this condition are particularly susceptible to minor degradations in air quality. Or maybe your dwelling has some of the characteristics that would suggest less-than-desirable air quality: stale smelling air; lingering odors; eye, nose, or throat irritation (is everybody in your family always coughing?); very high (above 60 percent) or very low (below 30 percent) relative humidity levels; excessive dust (do you feel like you're constantly dusting just to keep it down to a thin coat?); or allergens like pet dander. On second thought, the more we read about indoor air issues and possible connections with asthma and other sicknesses, the more we are convinced that even if you think that you're home free, you're not. We all can, and should, be alert to the issue and take measures to clean up our acts and our air.

The EPA and the American Lung Association—both of which have been studying indoor air quality fairly exhaustively—come out strongly in favor of what is called "source control," eliminating the sources of pollution, as the most important strategy you can adopt for improving your apartment air. Second? Ventilation, which they describe as bringing the outdoor in (though obviously not during a Bad Air Alert day). A very distant third is air cleaning through portable or in-duct devices. Studies are inconclusive, and the variables that have to be considered to determine if one solution will work for your problem are so complex, you need a doctorate just to figure out the right questions to ask, let alone divine the answers. But you can make a difference.

THE CITY PARENT RULES
How to Improve Your Indoor Air

Rule #1: Control indoor pollutants. Minimizing what is brought into a home—especially into those tight apartment spaces—is just about the leading recommendation for addressing air quality of almost every expert we've encountered.

The Air Cleaning Frenzy: HEPA or Hype?

Seems not a day goes by that we don't get another glitzy gizmo catalog touting some HEPA-filtered device as the answer to our indoor air prayers. So do they live up to all the hoopla? There is general accord that vacuum cleaners with HEPA filters are quite effective in sucking up dust from floors. But for HEPA air filters, the verdict is mixed at best. A 2000 Institute of Medicine[a] report says that the common recommendation that allergic and asthmatic individuals should use HEPA "is not supported by either experiments or theoretical predictions." And it's important to note that, HEPA or not, air cleaners are only effective with *airborne* particles. If your issue is pollen and dust mites—big particles that tend to settle—air cleaners are not going to give you much relief. However, they do appear to be effective at removing smaller particles like tobacco smoke, droplet nuclei, and grass and cat allergen particles.

In the face of such unclear direction, what would we do? Disagree, of course! In the absence of obvious family asthma or allergies, Julia is waiting to spend the money till she feels she has some clearer direction. Kathy, who had a huge problem with allergies at her in-laws, went for the big, powerful HEPA model and feels she sleeps much better for the purchase. Our advice to you? First and foremost, do everything you can in terms of source control; then if you still want to get a HEPA air cleaner, shop right:

- Ignore the tabletop models. We couldn't find anybody with any kind of authority who recommends them.
- Don't assume that product ratings have anything to do with your health. Only a few devices are what the FDA calls Class II medical devices, that is actually able to demonstrate a medical benefit. Such products have an Underwriters Laboratory, or UL seal, and a statement indicating the product has received FDA Class II approval.
- Stay away from ozone-generating models (electrostatic precipitators and ionizers produce ozone, so be careful).
- Don't expect a room cleaner to take care of a whole apartment. They are effective for one room only; make sure the windows and doors are shut when they're in use (and, by the way, their effectiveness diminishes significantly if they're not running all the time).
- Don't stick the appliance in a corner. You're trying to circulate the air, remember?
- Make sure you can stand the noise, particularly at night.
- Read the maintenance instructions. A lot of these systems require significant cleaning or filter changing. If you ignore them, you'll not only lose much of the cleaning benefit, you may also be creating a little bacterial colony right in the machine.

a. Committee on the Assessment of Asthma and Indoor Air, "Cleaning the Air: Asthma and Indoor Air Exposure," Division of Health Promotion and Disease Prevention, Institute of Medicine, 2000, p. 384.

Rule #2: Don't smoke. Duh.

Rule #3: Limit your intentional use of pollutants. For example, you can try cleaning with less-toxic substances. Baking soda and vinegar is often recommended by back-to-nature types as a home-cleaning scrub, replacing industrial-strength cleaning solvents.

Rule #4: Ventilate, ventilate, ventilate. To mitigate the effects of indoor pollutants, consider more venting. The more "bad" stuff you can direct outdoors, the better off you will be. This may be harder to pull off if you rent, but if you can afford it, there are numerous models of outside venting exhaust fans you can install in bathrooms, kitchens, and laundry areas that will help rid you of the organic pollution that emanates from the hot water used in those rooms. If that's too big a deal, vent the old-fashioned way—open windows and doors—when you're doing your industrial-strength apartment cleaning and when you're using air freshener, hair spray, or nail polish.

Rule #5: Take good care of the a/c. Whether it's central, through the wall, or in the window, at a minimum follow the recommended maintenance procedures (one of those things no one does, but if you saw an analysis of what's in equipment that hasn't been cleaned, you'd be afraid to take in another breath). After 9/11, Kathy had all her units cleaned; she's still in shock about what came out.

Rule #6: Clean the duct system. If you have a duct system, get it cleaned properly if someone in your family seems to be suffering from the effects of bad air or if you see large dust or mold deposits. (Only a lab can tell you if what looks like mold is really mold; some microbiology firms can do an analysis off a piece of sticky tape with some of your sample on it for about $50.) Just make sure that whoever does the cleaning follows EPA recommendations; otherwise, you may be doing more harm than good. Finally, make sure they clean the entire system, use HEPA vacuum equipment, and protect your furnishings during the work. Better yet, if you really want to know what should be done and when, contact your local EPA office for the fine pamphlet "Should You Have the Air Ducts in Your Home Cleaned?"

Don't hire any firm to clean your ducts that says it's EPA certified—there's no such thing—or that wants you to clean ducts regularly or touts the health benefits (as yet unclear). Call the National Air Duct Cleaners Association and check references for at least three candidates as well as state licenses if they're relevant (as they are in California, Texas, and Florida, among others). If the servicer wants to use chemical sealants or biocides, think about it very carefully; the EPA has very mixed feelings on their application.

Rule #7: Give space heaters some space. Those of you who are in old buildings with less-than-adequate heat may be tempted to use unvented space heaters to notch up the temperature a degree or two. Do so only with appropriate precautions. Old or malfunctioning models can release all sorts of noxious elements into the air while sucking out the oxygen (in fact, in many states, unvented heaters are illegal and/or may vitiate your insurance coverage if used). If you need the heat, get a UL-approved newer model with an automatic sensor that shuts the heater off when the oxygen gets too low. And crack a window, please.

When You Share the Venting System

Many apartment buildings have some form of shared ventilation and venting—from full centrally controlled HVAC systems to simpler shared hot water pipes and ducting. Those joint air supplies can be an important source of pollution, and there's no reason to think that your building is any better at caring for it appropriately than you. You'll need some help with:

1. Duct work and HVAC systems. Since there are as yet no federal standards on what your ducts should look like, it may be a little hard to get the people in charge of a building system to agree on the wisdom of cleaning general duct work in the absence of any apparent problem. HVAC systems present a different issue, however, because of the presence of moisture and filters. The opportunities for mold growth are pretty extensive in a poorly maintained system, as are the possibilities that dust and debris are effectively exhaled by the system when filters get clogged (more on this in our section on mold). How lovely.

Ask your management company what their maintenance routine is, and report any incidents of moisture, dust, or odd smells. More proactive: Ask them to survey the building population frequently for HVAC issues that need to be addressed.

2. Building management of pollutants. There are many areas where good building management can contribute to the "health" of all residents: its policies regarding dust and debris control during apartment renovation, CO_2 monitoring in the basement, general maintenance of public areas, and storage, or the use and care of, cleaning and treatment supplies and pesticides. (One New York co-op, now much maligned by civil libertarians, actually banned smoking anywhere in the building.) With standards and concrete guidance still in the offing, the best we can suggest is that you and some like-minded neighbors meet with building management if you think your families are being exposed to harmful materials.

Rule #8: Scrub that humidifier. If you use cool mist or ultrasonic humidifiers, follow the directions, clean them often, and change the water daily. Pediatricians recommend humidifiers to counter the effect of dry winter heat on kid's sensitive membranes. But these become enormous bacterial breeding grounds if you don't treat them right. Better yet, get one of the latest models with a dishwasher-safe tank.

Rule #9: Clean, clean, clean. If you have a child with asthma or allergies, of course you'll want to talk to your doctors and check local groups for detailed instructions on what you can do to minimize dust mites and the like. But what we all should do, even those of us who tend to breathe freely, is suck/mop/sponge up the dust at least twice a week. But do it right or, again, you'll stir up more problems than you resolve. Damp mop or sponge sills and floors and use a HEPA-filter vacuum to vacuum floors and furniture (and look under those couch cushions).

Asthma: An Urban Epidemic

Experts agree that childhood asthma is now of epidemic proportions and on the rise, particularly in children under 4 where the prevalence of asthma has increased nearly 160 percent between 1980 and 1994. Called by many a disease of the modern age, the dramatic trend is far more apparent in industrialized countries than in developing ones. But why certain children develop asthma and others do not is still largely a mystery.

The rap used to be that asthma, a chronic inflammation of the bronchial airways, was predominantly an inner city problem brought on because young children were exposed to high levels of cockroach dust, industrial pollution, lead, and other toxic elements that are endemic in substandard living conditions. Asthma absolutely still afflicts inner city children in disproportionate numbers, but it's no longer so discriminatory: Recent large-scale studies have concluded that, today, all urban children are at higher risk for asthma, regardless of race or family income. And it's our city air—both outdoors and in—that is aggravating the asthma problem, according to Michael Shannon, M.D., MPH, chair of

CITYWISE WARNING !

Don't Let Asthma Go Undetected

Despite the increased prevalence of asthma, much of it is undiagnosed, so it's essential to pay attention to your child. Be on the lookout for early warning signs: wheezes (or audible whistles upon exhaling); frequent cough, particularly one that's spasmodic; waking at night with coughing or wheezing; shortness of breath without exercising, or excessively so with exercise; little stamina; recurrent bouts of bronchitis or pneumonia. If your child is exhibiting any of these symptoms, get her to a doctor, ideally an allergy/immunology specialist. Proper treatment can do much to prevent midnight emergency room visits.

the American Academy of Pediatrics' Committee on Environmental Health and chief of Emergency Medicine at Children's Hospital Boston. "Indoor air pollutants are more responsible for leading children to develop asthma," Dr. Shannon explains, "while the outdoor environment seems to be more responsible for making asthma and allergy cases worse." Other researchers are concerned about the increased amounts of time kids are spending indoors, wondering whether the hours spent in airtight environments chock-full of trapped indoor pollutants is an issue or whether the villain is simply the lack of exercise. Maybe, some suspect, young lungs don't get the workout they need to develop. Still others wonder if urban stress is triggering young brains to send out hormones and neurotransmitters that negatively impact their immature immune systems.

An Ounce of Prevention . . .

The fact is, asthma is an extremely complicated disease. Some experts believe there are substantial, meaningful differences between varieties of asthma, including exercise-induced, allergic, and bacterial fungal—with possibly multiple causes and multiple manifestations. But as a city parent, you might as well assume your child is at higher risk just by virtue of your habitation (especially if one or more parents is asthmatic as well). We hope that assumption will make you more vigilant about taking protective steps; there's no downside to your doing so.

THE CITY PARENT RULES
Fighting Asthma

Rule #1: Start early. According to Dr. Etzel, prevention of asthma "begins while the baby is still in the womb." She highly recommends breastfeeding for as long as possible. And consider getting a dog. Mounting evidence suggests that kids with early pet exposure may be less likely to get allergies later on.

Rule #2: Mitigate your child's exposure to potential risk factors. This is especially crucial in the first years of his life, which mostly means adhering closely to the measures we've suggested in keeping your city home clean: eliminating as much as possible cockroaches, mice, dust mites, and mold and minimizing indoor air pollutants (remember to air out your dry cleaning and new furnishings). And, of course, don't smoke or let anyone around your child smoke.

Rule #3: Pay attention to your child's life outside the home. If you're shopping for day care or nursery schools, pick one that makes reduction of asthma contributors one of its standard operating procedures. There should be no evidence of cockroaches or mold. The space should be well-ventilated: You shouldn't be able to smell fumes from the arts and crafts areas or cleaning chemicals. And the staff should be trained to spot and deal with asthma symptoms. But you'll only know if you ask.

Rule #4: Get your kids outside for exercise as much as possible. It's good for them, fun for them, and may be a key to protecting their lungs for life. But remember: On hot, sunny days when the prediction is that ozone levels will be high, switch outdoor play to the morning or evening, avoiding heavy exertion during the hours of 3 to 5 P.M., when ozone levels peak.

Exposure to Lead

Maybe it's not true, as pundits were saying a few years back, that lead paint is the new asbestos. Then again, maybe it is. After fading from public consciousness for a few years, questions about lead's impacts have reemerged, stimulating renewed debate about whether we are appropriately protecting our children—especially in cities where the sources of lead are both prolific and pervasive and where new awareness of lead poisoning in middle- and upper-income city kids is setting up alarms in the medical establishment. But with public policy makers sparring with children's advocates and scientists often at odds with one another, it's hard to get a fix on what it all means for you.

What is incontrovertible is the fact that lead and children do not mix. The absorption, either by ingestion or inhalation, of too much lead by young children (particularly those under 6 whose bodies absorb more of it than older kids or adults when exposed) can result in the development of severe physical problems—damaged kidneys and central nervous systems, interference with blood cell formation, even death. Clearly, this is not something to trifle with. Cognitively, it's ugly too. Children with high blood lead levels (BLLs) are at greater risk for developmental delays, permanent learning disabilities, fine motor coordination issues, even a drop in IQ. Furthermore, while a causal relationship has not yet been established, there is mounting evidence that lead exposure may be associated with many of the symptoms associated with ADHD.

What is still very much up for grabs is: (1) how much lead in the blood is "safe," (2) what sources of lead are the ones to worry about, and (3) how crazy parents should get about protecting their children against lead.

How Much Lead Is Too Much?

The government has done an excellent job of reducing lead exposure by banning the use of lead-based paint and lead plumbing supplies and through the phasing out of lead in gasoline. The decrease in the incidence of lead poisoning has been dramatic—88 percent of children under the age of 6 were found to have had elevated blood levels between 1976 and 1980, compared to just 2 percent (an admittedly soft number) in the survey period running from 1999 to 2000.

But most of these stats measure results under guidelines issued by the Centers for Disease Control and Prevention (CDC) in 1991, which classify toxicity as BLLs of 10 micrograms per deciliter or greater. These guidelines are now under strong attack. Studies by researchers such as Bruce Lanphear, M.D., MPH, director of the Cincinnati Children's Environmental Health Center at the Cincinnati Children's Hospital Medical Center and considered by many to be the country's top pediatric lead researcher, have demonstrated that much smaller amounts of lead than those permissible under the current CDC rules could put children at risk for all the cognitive damage excessive lead can wreak. In one 5-year study, in which researchers from Cornell University and the University of Rochester School of Medicine participated, children with BLLs below the 10 micrograms per deciliter threshold showed "intellectual impairment" from the lead exposure, with the amount of impairment *most pronounced* at the *lower* levels. What type of impairment? Maybe 5 IQ points at the lower levels, which is not nothing. We wouldn't be at all surprised if new guidelines are eventually issued that will reduce the previous standard for acceptable blood levels in children by as much as 50 percent. But *eventually* is the operative word here. As Dr. Lanphear warns, "The laws catching up to the science could take a week, a month, or 5 years . . ."

Should you care? Well, in the 1970s, when the bulk of today's parents were toddling around, the average BLL for *all* American kids was *25* micrograms (and look how great we all turned out). But after reading reams of material and talking with many top docs who are so concerned about lead, we believe keeping your kids at very conservative BLLs (below the proposed replacement standard of 5 BLLs) is both warranted and attainable without enormous amounts of effort on your part. Besides, we do all want our children to turn out even better than we did, don't we?

How Does a Child Get Exposed?

Screening blood is not sufficient however. "If it's true that there is no discernible threshold for intellectual impairments, as our studies are showing," suggests Dr. Lanphear, "then our focus must shift away from waiting until a child has been unduly exposed, to primary prevention. First thing I would tell parents: Primary emphasis should be on screening housing and reducing exposures; screening blood should be considered a safety net."

The prevailing wisdom (so far, at least)—is that most cases of lead poisoning are the result of exposure in homes, primarily when children in older buildings eat peeling lead paint chips (which have an especially high concentration) that have fallen on the floor or are chipping off walls or window frames. Exposure also occurs when teething toddlers chew on windowsills, doors, even radiators and/or when kids ingest or inhale lead-tinged dust particles that get on their toys, on food that's been stored uncovered, or on the floors on which they're playing.

Don't ignore your own walls because you think this type of stuff only happens in substandard housing. Lead dust can exist in the most meticulously maintained home and can even be a significant issue in a newly renovated apartment because of the disturbance of old paint. So the antebellum dream house you've been fantasizing about restoring in Atlanta, or that "perfect" 1920s bungalow in Portland? It may turn out to be more of a nightmare for your kids if you don't take precautions. Sheldon Whitehouse, former attorney general of Rhode Island, found this out the hard way. He and his wife renovated their house in a lovely historic district in Providence. All was well until a routine blood test post-renovation resulted in the stunning news that his children had elevated blood lead levels.

According to recent CDC research, remodeling and repainting projects may be the cause of as much as 10 percent of all lead poisoning in American children. In fact, over the last decade, doctors have been reporting a real shift in the demographics of lead-poisoned children. Dr. Lanphear notes that only a decade ago, children from the poorest neighborhoods comprised about 90 percent of the cases treated at Cincinnati Children's Hospital Medical Center. Now, he says, a good 50 percent of exposed children treated at his hospital come from affluent families who have been inadvertently poisoned when their old homes were renovated. So please, do not assume that your child will be immune from lead's deadly effects just because you have nice digs. Nor is it safe to believe that you've protected your child simply because you kept him out of your abode during the renovation itself; lead levels can be persistently high even after the job is completed. (By the way, if you're pregnant, you need to be just as concerned: Lead ingested during pregnancy can have devastating results on the baby's development.)

There are, of course, other sources of lead intake besides paint, but they tend

Is Your House or Apartment Likely to Be a Problem?

Well, since lead-based residential-use paint has been banned partially since 1960 and only entirely since 1978, it could be a danger in any pre-1978 home. The older the home, the more problematic the issue. According to the New York State attorney general's office, 20 percent of all housing built between 1959 and 1974 has some lead paint, 70 percent of housing built between 1940 and 1959 has some lead paint, and 99 percent of the housing built before 1940 has some lead paint.[a] If that paint dates to the 1940s or before, it may have as much as 50 percent more lead than the later-produced lead paint, so it really packs a punch.

a. State of New York Attorney General, Environmental Protection Bureau, "Look Out for Lead! A Guide for Tenants with Preschool-Age Children," revised 1999.

to be more elusive. According to the American Academy of Pediatrics, for kids with low, but still elevated, blood levels (between 10 and 14 BLLs), the source of the lead exposure is often a mystery. One possibility is dirt from sidewalks, parks, playgrounds, and building foundations. Howard Mielke, M.S., Ph.D., has been researching the incidence of lead in urban soil over the two decades since his own daughter's high blood lead levels were traced to the soil in her day care center's outdoor play area. He and other scientists conducting studies in cities as diverse as Baltimore, Minneapolis, and New Orleans, and the results suggest that, in traffic-congested urban areas, "many children face their greatest risk for exposure in the yards around their houses and, to a lesser extent, in the open spaces such as public playgrounds in which they play." While there's considerable debate as to the sources of urban soil lead—from traffic exhaust to building paint residue and fallout from industrial pollution—there's no question that its buildup can be substantial. A Chicago residential neighborhood study documented median soil lead levels more than four times the acceptable EPA standard, causing health professionals at the renowned Children's Memorial Hospital to warn parents that protecting kids from lead in soil should be as important as safeguarding them against paint-based sources.

Finally, there's the issue of lead found in water. Many cities, including Atlanta, New York, Pittsburgh, Philadelphia, and New Orleans, add an anticorrosive called orthophosphate to the water supply and have achieved great success in reducing the lead content of water found in older buildings, but there are no guarantees. Lead can still leach in from old pipes and from brass fittings on faucets or pipes in your building, particularly if you are using hot water. Washington D.C. residents are still reeling from the news that ⅔ of tested homes had water exceeding EPA lead limits (some by as much as 36 times), a result of additives which corroded lead pipes.

Should You Be Concerned?

There seems to be little question that urban kids are more at risk than suburban children because they suffer from the unhappy combination of old housing stock and industrial contamination. Certainly some locales seem to have more problems than others. Cities on record with high incidences of lead poisoning include Providence, Chicago, Rochester, Philadelphia, Detroit, and Boston, though Beantown seems to have cleared up much of the problem with its very stringent lead abatement program. But it's not just the old-time industrial cities with problems; even San Francisco estimated that 8 percent of its children had elevated blood levels.

When do you really have reason to worry, reason to take action?

1. If you live in poorly maintained, inner city housing.
2. If you live in a building built before 1978—especially, if the apartment's been renovated or you're doing the renovation.

3. If your child plays on dirt at your home, day care, school, or playground and that area is located near high traffic roads.
4. If your child has a BLL of 5 or more.

We've tried hard to sift through the conflicting facts and ever-changing landscape with regards to lead impact and law to come up with a reasonable game plan for all city parents.

THE CITY PARENT RULES
Preventing and Dealing with Lead Poisoning

Rule #1: Get your children screened regularly. Not all doctors do this, so you need to take charge if it's not a regular feature of your children's pediatric exams. In some states, it's mandated for the youngest children; federally, it's required for those in the Medicaid program. But compliance isn't always guaranteed. If it were us (and it is), we'd spring for the screening at least for the first couple of years—and after that if the family abode undergoes any renovation. (Oh, and don't relax just because your child tested fine as a 1-year-old. Research in Chicago showed that 21 percent of children tested at age 1 ended up with elevated BLLs during a later screening—an "expected" result given the greater mobility, oral behaviors, and outdoor play typical of 2- and 3-year-olds.) Get the doctor to explain the results, but if it's above 5 micrograms per deciliter (half of the current "safe" level of 10 micrograms), we would strongly recommend finding and removing the source of lead exposure.

Rule #2: Evaluate the presence of high-risk conditions at home or anyplace where your child spends a substantial amount of time. The most effective way to reduce exposures to hazards is to make sure they don't exist or to eliminate them if they do. So, if your home predates 1978 (even if it's been updated in the interim) and has any

Need More Info on Lead Risks?

Start with the EPA's National Lead Information Center at (800) 424-LEAD (www.epa.gov/lead/nlic.htm). The center publishes numerous brochures about protecting your family from lead, which you can order by phone or print off the site. If you think you need someone to check out the lead in your apartment, make sure that person is EPA-*certified*; you can get a list of suitable practitioners from your local health department, HUD office, or the EPA.

Phosphate Power

If you're wet-mopping for lead dust, do it with a solution of automatic dishwasher soap and warm water. The soap contains phosphate, which promotes the dissolution of the lead.

peeling paint or other deteriorating surfaces, leaks, or rubbing doors or windows (or, heaven forbid, your child has elevated lead levels), you need to have your home evaluated for the potential and scope of any lead paint hazard. Do not, do not, do not try and evaluate the situation through home testing. According to the EPA, home test kits are not reliable enough to give accurate readings. You need professional help.

Rule #3: Check the dirt. If your children play in areas where they're exposed to bare soil that is located near high-trafficked roads or older buildings with peeling paint, get the soil tested or keep your children away. Since the EPA does not find home-tests to be reliable, we suggest you hire an EPA-certified professional to evaluate your soil if you have concerns. And if it turns out you do have a problem? Besides making sure that toys and hands that spend time outside are cleaned often, you'll need to cover any bare soil with a thick barrier layer—of mulch, sod, sand, whatever—to raise ground levels. And, certainly, reconsider those plans to plant any vegetables or herbs there. Lead-laden soil is not exactly the best base for food that may hit your family's table.

Rule #4: Clean with a purpose. While there's some controversy about how much good cleaning can do if you have substantial lead dust in your home, in the absence of any conclusive results, we'll go with the suggested practices of just about every government agency we've looked at in this regard. Keep dust to a minimum by wet-mopping regularly—particularly sills, floors, and around the entrance—and clean the mops and sponges thoroughly after use. Avoid cleaning techniques and equipment that abrade or wear down painted surfaces, such as vacuum beater bars, mops with scrubber strips, abrasive cleaners, or steel wool. Clean your kids' toys regularly, especially any teething toys or pacifiers. And look at it this way: Even if the effectiveness of all this elbow grease isn't completely clear as far as lead dust is concerned, at least you'll be helping to mitigate other dust-driven maladies like asthma, allergies, and unpleasant-looking furniture.

Rule #5: Watch your families' diet and hygiene. Just add lead protection to the list of reasons why your family should stay away from fat, which increases lead absorption, and eat nutritious meals—especially ones with lots of calcium and iron, which can help to minimize the body's ability to absorb lead (within limits).

Calcium, however, can also reduce the body's ability to absorb iron, so ask your pediatrician how much calcium your children should be getting each day. On the hygiene front, if the threat of colds is not enough of a reason, then the threat of lead ingestion should hopefully convince you to get all your kids in the habit of washing their hands (and faces) often, especially before meals, naps, and bedtimes. Finally, this should be a given but, whatever you do, don't let your tot chew on windowsills, doors, or painted furniture surfaces.

Rule #6: Don't ignore the dangers of renovation. We only know of one person who even considered lead when she was renovating her apartment—and we know tons of people who have made glorious apartments out of wrecks. We're better informed now. If you're renovating a pre-1978 home, follow approved procedures for conducting the work. Both the EPA and your local health department provide guidelines, but essentially anything that disturbs a lead-painted surface—like drilling, nailing, wall demolition, making holes for pipes or electrical wire or cable, scraping or sanding, etc.—can create a major problem. If you're in a potential lead-paint hazard area, there are steps you must follow that cover everything from sealing off work areas while the work's being done (ideally, keeping kids out of the home while the work's in progress) to covering furniture to cleaning up after it's all over. Just make sure that you and your contractor agree on what needs to be done and follow the rules religiously. And if you really want some peace of mind, think about having a hazard assessment done after you've finished it all and before the kids are back home.

Rule #7: Make everybody take their shoes off before entering the home. This may be just about one of our favorite rules. It's possibly the most helpful way of keeping lead from outside dirt from entering your home—and, oh yeah, it keeps the dirt out too.

Rule #8: Watch out for the H$_2$O. Minimize your child's exposure to other potential sources of lead like water. It's generally only a problem if lead is leaching into cooking or drinking water via old pipes made with lead or lead fittings (such as those that exist in many prewar buildings), and it is a particular issue with hot water. The easiest way to control this is to limit your water use for cooking or drinking to the *cold water tap*. As a safety mechanism, run it for a minute first— well, at least 30 seconds, if you can't be that disciplined. The only problem with this is that "flushing" the pipes isn't always effective in high-rise buildings, which may have large-diameter supply pipes. If you are concerned, get the water tested. In some cities, New York for one, the Department of Environmental Protection will test your building for free. In less-generous cities, you should be able to get it done for about $50 or so (but beware of getting services from any testing group that may have a vested interest in how your results come in).

The 911 for H₂O

Does your water have a problem? Certain commercial filters are effective at filtering out lead from water, but you have to choose carefully. A few years back, some under-sink filters were found to actually *add* lead to the water. Turns out, brass fittings on the filters leached lead into the very water they were supposed to be filtering.

The EPA recommends that you buy a water filter that's been certified for lead by NSF, International, a nonprofit testing and standards organization (NSE filtering efficacy at lead levels of up to 150 parts per billion only). "Pitcher" versions use disposable filters to treat tap water and are a bargain at $25 to $30, plus the cost of filters you replace every couple of months or so. Or you can go for the pricier filter "appliances" that get installed directly on the plumbing system. Finally, if you're really a nervous Nellie and are only going to use bottled water, check with the dentist to see if your child needs fluoride supplements.

Rule #9: Never ignore the problem. If, by any chance, it is determined that lead hazards exist in your home, they must be taken care of. Views on the proper handling of lead paint vary, particularly whether abatement (permanent elimination of hazards) is preferable to interim control (treatments that temporarily reduce the risk of a hazard, like repairing chipped paint surfaces). Procedures are complicated. This is not a do-it-yourself job, and anyone you hire should be EPA-certified. Don't mess around: Get help from your pediatrician, your city health or environmental department, and the EPA if need be.

Mold in Your Abode

Yuck, yuck, yeecchh. That pretty much sums up how we feel about this topic, particularly when we found out that it's not just an issue for tract houses in Florida. In fact, mold appears to be an equal opportunity plague, attacking even the toniest buildings. (According to the *New York Post*, real estate investor Richard Kramer filed a $400 million lawsuit alleging that the mold in his newly built, $10 million Park Avenue condo had disabled his wife and child.) Of course, the upswing in mold issues is not just city-centric. Airtight buildings and the use of less-durable building materials—like wallboard, whose high "failure" rate allows moisture to accumulate—are providing wonderful homes for mold in all sorts of venues. But an extra urban complication is associated with buildingwide HVAC systems or plumbing pipes that can spread a mold problem throughout a building, making mold control a particularly challenging activity from a number of perspectives.

Speaking of perspectives, here are some. Most of the more than 100,000 species of mold are not particularly hazardous, although like any other substance, their presence can exacerbate the suffering of allergy or asthma victims. And just so you clearly understand the issue, mold is everywhere; so we're not talking "zero tolerance," just managing it to a less-than-ill-health-causing level. Don't get hysterical, just cautious. In the face of continued debates about mold impact, we'll follow public health officials who have decided to get out in front of the debates by giving very simple advice: If you see or smell mold in your home, identify and eliminate the moisture that's causing the mold to grow and then attack the mold itself.

Control Moisture, Prevent Mold

Mold cannot grow without water or moisture. There are many mold spores in the air where we live. The problem develops when they land on a wet spot, so managing moisture is the key to mold control. While in many cases, a building owner or manager will be taking the lead in this effort, particularly if there's a central HVAC system, you as the resident are the first line of defense. You need to be vigilant about monitoring your overall humidity level, caring for areas that come into contact with moisture, and reporting problems that require input from or action by building management.

You've Got Mold

If you see a moldy condition, you have no choice. Something has to be done.

Renters should immediately notify the landlord or super or management company, so they can commence appropriate remediation steps. If you own a unit and a central system is involved, you definitely need to bring the building in on the fix (you could be liable, by the way, if some action you take results in mold

Mold ID

How do you know if you have mold?

- You can see it: visible growth in any color from white to yellow to orange to green to brown to black.
- You can smell it: musty, mildewy air.
- You suspect it: You've had water damage, and you have warping wood or cracking plasterboard, or someone in your family is inexplicably ill (their asthma's taken a turn for the worse or they're displaying allergic symptoms like rashes, red eyes, sneezing).

THE URBAN A-LIST
Easy Moldbusters To Try Right Now

Here's what you can do to keep mold from invading your apartment.

Monitor the humidity level. Experts like to see home humidity between 30 and 50 percent. Drier than that and everyone will be complaining about dry eyes and sinuses; more humid and you're providing the perfect breeding ground for all sorts of nasty molds (if you're not sure you've got the right balance, pick up a moisture or humidity meter from your local hardware store—there should be a good selection of models under $50). If mold's your concern, keeping the air dry will obviously be your focus. Air conditioners can help dry out air (especially if they're set on recirculate, although then you don't get the benefit of outside air coming in) as can dehumidifiers and venting. Also, be vigilant in maintaining your moisture-sensitive appliances—which no one ever does, but it can make a big difference to the health of your home.

- Have your air conditioners or a/c system inspected at the beginning of every season by an appropriate professional, and make sure you change the filters, clean coils, and drain pans as directed in your manufacturer's instructions. It will cut down on mold growth and increase their operating efficiency.
- Clean your refrigerator drip pan and make sure the doors seal so that mold doesn't get a chance to grow.

Fix problems fast. If your home springs a leak or a sink or toilet overflows, get the problem fixed immediately and remove any excess water. Make sure that areas affected by the overflow are cleaned and dried quickly and appropriately. If possible, move any furniture or carpeting involved to as dry an area as possible. Fans, dehumidifiers, and window air conditioners can help, as long as you use them within 2 days of the overflow; beyond that, mold's already started to grow and you'll just be spreading it by making it airborne. Gross. Turning off the heat, on the other hand, is a mistake—that actually helps the mold, especially in colder temperatures when moisture condenses on cold surfaces like windows to become a fine breeding ground. If the water has soaked a wall, you're going to need help because you must get inside to see what's up.

Modify your behavior. There are some easy practices you can adopt that will definitely improve your odds in the mold fight:

- Do open a window when you shower or use the dishwasher or dryer.
- Do air out that closet by keeping the door open as often as possible.
- Don't use carpeting in spill-prone locations like the kitchen and bathroom.
- Do keep a clean apartment. Spills, dishes in the sink, dirty clothes left languishing, and rarely cleaned appliances are happy habitats for mold.

getting into the building conduits). If the issue seems to be localized, you can and probably will have to deal with it yourself, although the building management company may have helpful ideas or directions for you to take.

But we don't want to mislead you here. With the parameters of the mold issue still being defined, we know what we will do if either of us suspects our apartments harbor mold. We will get right on the phone (or the computer; our city's Web sites are pretty good) and get the latest, most up-to-date directives from the EPA and our local health department.

Pests and Pesticides

A scourge of urban life, prevalent in the poshest apartments in Dallas, NYC, and San Fran, pests may be the ultimate democrats. So much so, that in apartment buildings across the nation, monthly visits from the exterminator are as common as fliers from the local Chinese restaurant. How do you fight city vermin and bugs? For starters, don't invite them in.

Along with the heightened public consciousness regarding indoor air quality and mold has come a reexamination of the use of pesticides. A team at the Environmental and Occupational Health Sciences Institute at Rutgers University analyzed the movement of chlorpyrifos (an incredibly common insecticide in this country) in a test involving two apartments. Instead of the pesticides dissipating as was expected, the sprays adhered to children's plastic toys and stuffed animals, with the residue lasting for weeks. Even when the toys were removed from the test apartments and not put back until after the spraying, they still collected more of the pesticide than any other objects (probably because of the foam's absorption ability and some electrostatic action of the plastics), with the peak deposits a full *36 hours* after the spraying occurred.

These findings are particularly daunting when you consider the immature systems of children who might be exposed to pesticides and the propensity of many

Pest in the City: A Primer

PEST OF THE DAY	CITY HANGOUTS	HOW TO DISCOURAGE THEIR STAY
Cockroaches	Kitchens, grocery bags (you might want to rethink saving money by saving them to use later); unrefrigerated vegetables; toasters, radios and TVs; electrical and plumbing conduits; floor drains.	Clean up spilled foods and water; eliminate harborage and pathway areas by sealing or screening; repair water leaks; increase ventilation; inspect incoming foods and packaging.
Mice and Rats	Kitchen cabinets; stored food; storage areas; wall voids; inside appliances; closets.	Install physical barriers like metal screen or special sealants; eliminate food and water; remove nesting sites; inspect incoming boxes.
Pantry/Fabric Pests	Flour; potpourri; spices, cereals; rice; beans; dry pet food; stored clothing; woolen rugs.	Inspect foods and packaging prior to storage; store foods in glass/plastic containers; clean up spilled foods; rotate dry goods; store only clean cloths.

Source: National Pest Management Association, Inc., www.pestworld.org.

of them to not only touch their toys but to put them in their mouths. Combined with the "grasshopper" effect by which dried pesticides move around a room, jumping from object to object, it's clear that just signing up automatically on your building's monthly pesticide list is a little cavalier. Not that we expect all of you to give up pesticides completely. Heck, many apartment dwellers would give up part of their paycheck before they considered forgoing their monthly spray. While we're not suggesting you just turn your keys over to the lower rungs of the animal and insect kingdoms, from what we now know, it seems clear that greater emphasis should be placed on pest prevention and preparation for pesticide use.

So by all means, follow the directions given above for the pest of your choice, and really consider using more health-friendly alternatives to poison if the pests start winning the war. What might those options be? It depends on the pest, and there are some strong regional variations. Your building management and/or local pest control companies can give you advice. To give you a feel for the types of actions they'll recommend, we are providing for your reading pleasure a special section on that unwelcome guest in so many apartments across the nation: the cockroach.

The Cockroach: Friend or Foe?

Seems to us that the cockroach may be one organism with very few friends; so we'll assume you're not one of them. And if you have kids, you have no business harboring these folks. Cockroach detritus has been implicated in study after study as a major contributor to urban asthma. We won't bore you with our collection of data on the female and her ootheca or the male's developmental time in lab conditions . . . Okay, just one fact. The prolific female German cockroach (the number one urban household pest in terms of frequency) can produce up to 30,000 new progeny in a year. Kind of makes you look at that lone critter scuttling across your kitchen floor a little differently, doesn't it? And we don't need to tell you that they like warm, humid places. Your kitchen's ideal, but the bathroom will do in a pinch, as will just about anyplace you eat and drink (they'll eat almost anything, by the way, even toothpaste, soap, and glue).

How'd they get in your home anyway? Maybe they were there before you moved in, but you've probably brought in more relatives in garbage bags or cardboard boxes. Three-quarters of the time, the cockroaches in your apartment are just hanging out in a crack near food, so it really is effective to find those cracks and seal them up. Check walls, baseboards, inside cabinets, under kitchen appliances, pipes and plumbing connections, and around toilet bottoms—and don't stint on the sealant. If you've got bigger openings to deal with, try duct tape (just don't cover any vents). You should also make it a little harder for them to find food. Never leave dirty dishes overnight in the sink or dishwasher and, by all means, clean up after meals and kids' spills. If you have a real issue with these guys, you will want to seal up all food in containers or keep as much as possible in the fridge or freezer. Bag your garbage, and if you recycle, rinse out bottles well—otherwise, you're just inviting roaches to your door, and once they're there, do you think they'll knock before coming into your apartment? Of course, it will also help matters if your super keeps a clean building; if he doesn't, join forces with some neighbors to put some pressure where it's due.

Despite your best efforts, if you do see roaches scampering across your floors, there are a few things you can try before resorting to professional help. Baits are often effective (although maybe not as fast-working as sprays) and much easier on your health; they're just kind of disgusting, that's all.

When you opt for professional roachbusters, follow the EPA's recommendation: Make sure the pesticide is sprayed in a fine stream in cracks and crevices, not misted over the floor area. And *STORE KIDS' TOYS FOR A WEEK AFTER THE SPRAYING* (the EPA is silent on how to explain that to your kids, though). That may require a little work on your part; state law doesn't always require landlords to notify tenants prior to pesticide application (although in a condo or co-op, you have control over whether you want the visit). We heartily suggest someone be in the apartment to monitor the spraying at least on a few occasions. And take advantage of your servicer's knowledge; he might be able to help you figure out where the cockroaches are really taking root and where you may be able to apply more efforts to make your home less homey for the roach and his friends.

CHAPTER 4

THE INS AND OUTS OF CITY SAFETY

■ ■

We steadfastly refuse to believe that safety in the city is an oxymoron. In fact, we think our kids are just as safe here as anywhere else—which isn't to say that we don't take precautions. After all, toddling about in the congestion of the city does mean your child will be perambulating in the presence of a few mobile dangers, not to mention those he will encounter should you all live 20 stories up (think elevators, fire emergencies). And, of course, there's the newest city threat: terrorism. We don't want to terrorize you, though. Odds are, your child will never suffer the slightest harm from any of these. We just want to help you make those probabilities skew even more his way.

TODDLERS IN TRANSIT

Half the fun of being a city parent is venturing out into the exciting surroundings with a little one in tow. But it's also half of the anxiety. Nothing—oh, except for getting into school, of course—stresses out the city parent more than keeping Junior safe outside. Cars, buses, crowds—it's not enough that you have to protect your child in the midst of all of this: You also have to teach him how to do it for himself. After all, Emilio will be out there on his own someday.

On the Hoof

Sorry to scare you, but in most cities traffic-related pedestrian death rates are twice as high among young children as they are in rural areas. Granted, a large number of these incidents occur as kids dart into traffic—which tends to be more of a problem among kids over the age of 5 who are less closely supervised than younger ones. But parents of their younger brethren need to be just as concerned about pedestrian safety. Why? Most of us don't have the best pedestrian practices to begin with. (Who out there can honestly say they've never jaywalked or crossed when the

*Take Extra Care at
Stoplight Intersections*

According to a study in Philadelphia, drivers who approach a traffic light gear up to try and make the light, focusing on the signal, not pedestrians. Conversely, drivers who see a stop sign tend to slow down and look for pedestrians or other traffic to see if it's safe to move through the intersection. The moral of this story: Parent and child need to be especially cautious when crossing at intersections with stoplights because that's where the most trouble occurs. Case in point: Of the 8,029 high-risk intersections identified in a 2001 New York City survey, only *9 percent* were stop-sign intersections even though stop-sign intersections represent nearly 75 percent of all intersections in the city.

a. "Large City Transportation Issues," Rudin Center for Transportation Policy and Management at the Robert F. Wagner Graduate School of Public Service, New York University, November 2000, p. 135.
b. City of New York, Office of the Comptroller, "Red Means 'Go,' A Survey of Red Light Violations in New York City and Red Light Camera Usage in Other Major Cities," May 20, 2001, p. 4.

DON'T WALK sign was flashing?) And even the most safety-conscious of us walk around our cities in a way that assumes drivers are careful. Hello! Lastly, once your child starts to motor around on his own, constant reinforcement of safe habits is key. Set a good example.

Clearly, we all need to be a lot more defensive in our walking habits. But it's not just a question of watching out for the other guy. Parents of young kids have to contend with a stroller. And all too often, grown-ups adopt safe practices for themselves but forget that the stroller is an appendage sticking out several feet in front of them. Every year, in every city, there are tragic, tragic accidents involving children in strollers who were hit by traffic (including bikes) because the adult in charge had the stroller off the curb while waiting to cross or started crossing and the stroller got hit by a fast-turning car.

THE CITY PARENT RULES
Navigating Traffic with Young Children

Rule #1: Stand well back from the street when waiting to cross. It's not safe to stand right on the curb. If you talk to your local police, they'll back us up on the frequency with which cars or buses find themselves forced up onto a sidewalk. You need to give yourself some margin of safety against that occurrence. Most safety experts recommend that pedestrians (and strollers) stand 2 feet back from the curb when waiting at an intersection. And we've heard of some cops who, based on what they've seen, think you need to stand at the building line to really be safe.

Rule #2: Keep conscious about the stroller. There are way too many accidents involving vehicles and strollers. Quite often the driver can see you but the stroller might be out of his field of vision. So you have to be extra careful and account for the stroller's extra length in every crossing decision you make. To the extent you

Kid Harness: Horror or Help?

A friend of ours has a harness for her 2-year-old son. She doesn't use it all the time, but whenever she is going to be in a crowded place or is walking with him on the street, she takes it along. "He's really active, and I just don't want to take the chance that he breaks loose," she says. But from the remarks she gets from passersby, you'd think she'd invented child labor. Harness-using adults get catcalls hurled at them all the time, with comments ranging from the not particularly humorous "Let the kid off the leash, lady" to the downright enraged "Keeping a child roped up like that is barbaric!" But, you know what? If that's what you need to do to keep your kid safe, then to heck with those mindless critics.

Most city kids learn early to hold hands when walking or stay within a safe distance of an accompanying adult. But some of you may have young'uns who are a little impetuous. Many kids have a "runaway phase," particularly between the ages of 18 months and 2½ years, and sometimes they're the ones who decide early on that they can't stand a stroller, either. If that sounds like your tot, then by all means, harness her up. A few suggestions, though:

- Don't get a harness that attaches itself to the wrist via Velcro. This type unattaches way too easily.
- Don't get overconfident, particularly near intersections. Just because a child is attached to you doesn't mean he can't get in trouble—especially if the distance between you and him is extended. Keep your child close, and when you get to a crossing, make sure you're holding hands and not relying on the harness to keep him safe.
- Do teach your child how to walk appropriately in the city. Using a harness doesn't mean you can forget that your child should be learning how to walk appropriately unrestrained.

can, reduce the length between you and the end of the stroller; keep it close and be vigilant.

Rule #3: Don't cross unless the light says walk. We all know this and, of course, we all ignore this with abandon. Who has time, after all, to wait for the next light change? But you're really pressing your luck if you've got young children in tow. Their legs are shorter, and they just can't make it as fast as you can. Want to know when grown-ups violate this dictum? Running to make a bus. In fact, at a busy intersection near Julia's apartment, the local police precinct posted notices admonishing pedestrians not to do just that. Apparently, there had been a rash of accidents involving pedestrians who had rushed across the intersection to catch a waiting bus at the stop on the other side. Also, points out Barbara Boisi, safety expert for the Parents League of New York, lights have different ways of working. One busy intersection near Julia's sons' school has a series of lights designed to clear the intersection from turning cars before the walk signal goes on. However, many pedestrians don't realize that and start walking too early, which has led to an unfortunate number of pedestrian incidents.

Rule #4: Use the pedestrian button. Signal crossing times differ among cities, among intersections, and can even change with the time of day. Who knew? In pedestrian-friendly Center City Philly, WALK signals run 7 seconds or more compared to typical city times of only 4 or 5 seconds. (Of course, you also get a few more seconds from the flashing DON'T WALK interval, but that's not a whole lot of time.) If you're not familiar with the dynamics of a particular intersection, you may find that a leisurely stroll with your 2-year-old turns into a terrified run as the WALK signal changes to DON'T WALK before you've taken 10 steps. On that theory, use the pedestrian button. Assuming it's working, it will get you dif-

Stupid Traffic Moves (That We See Over and Over)

- Letting kids run way ahead on the block—only to have to sprint wildly after them as they approach an intersection with no sign of stopping. Not to be sexist, but in our observation it's mostly dads who err here.
- Kids riding a tricycle or big wheels–type vehicle across the street accompanied by an adult whose hands are otherwise occupied (with groceries, pushing a stroller, etc.). Big mistake. Young kids on wheels often have problems making it across the street—they get stuck or tip over. They need an adult's firm hand to make sure they get across in time and in one piece.

- Parents riding bikes in traffic with their kids as a passenger—and no one's wearing a helmet. Of course, in many of these cases, the kid is not even in a legal bike seat, so we don't even know where to start on this one.
- Little kids playing with a ball in front of their building. Ten to one, the ball ends up in the street. And if a ballplayer is young enough, the temptation to run into the street to get the ball may be stronger than any possible thought he might harbor of traffic dangers.
- People standing on a curb holding onto a stroller that's in the street. We just said it, but this one occurs so often and is so stupid that we have to repeat it again.

ferent benefits in different places. At a minimum, it will speed up the time that the light changes to WALK again, but in some spots it actually lengthens crossing times. (In Boston, for example, where streets are typically allotted 7 or 8 seconds for crossings, button-pushing gets you 20.) As an extra added benefit, little kids love to push the button, so they will eagerly look forward to pursuing this exercise every time you need to cross.

Rule #5: Hold hands. As children get beyond 2, a little more willful and a little more independent, there is a great tendency among city parents and caregivers to give them maybe a tad more freedom than is prudent. You may think they know to stop at the curb but, according to the experts, you're taking an awfully big chance. Kids really don't have the maturity to take care of themselves in traffic until they're 9, so how can you expect your 4-year-old to make appropriate decisions? Hold their hands firmly when nearing a crossing and all the way through to the other side. In the same vein, horseplay at a street corner should be strictly forbidden. Young kids will get lost in the moment, and the next thing you know, one of them will be out in the street.

Lost in the Crowd

City kids are undeniably more involved with crowds and crowded situations than those living in the suburbs or the country, so the opportunities to become separated from a supervising adult are far greater. For that simple reason, we believe it is imperative that you take measures, if only for your own peace of mind, to help your wee ones help themselves if they get lost—on an age-appropriate basis, of course.

Make sure your child has some identifying information on him—particularly 4 and unders who generally are not able to do much on their own. At a minimum, put your name and phone number on the name tag in his clothes; some children's outerwear have inside pockets perfect for an ID card. Or get a more formal ID from the cottage industry that's developed around parental fears—anything from a plastic name bracelet (of course, Paulina has to be willing to wear this; good luck on that one) to premade laminated labels for inside the soles of her shoes. Your local police precinct may also provide an ID kit.

City Parent Pop Quiz

Whom do you tell your child to go to if he or she gets lost?

A: Policeman

B: Fireman

C: Mother with child

D: Shopkeeper

If you answered A, as most people do, you're wrong. Policemen would be a great option if you could guarantee they'd be around. Chances are you won't find many men in blue or firemen roaming the spring sales at Saks. What about someone who works at the place where the child is lost? Nope; requires too much discrimination for young kids. (Who is on duty and, more importantly, who is not is not necessarily apparent to a 4 or 5 year old—and certainly not to someone younger.) The answer: Try a woman with a stroller or young child—she's unlikely to turn away a lost little boy or girl. Statistics show quite strongly that lost children have far more to fear from men than women and the *most* to fear from someone who seeks them out rather than a person they select. This isn't going to help you when your toddler wanders off, but a 4-year-old (and sometimes a mature 3-year-old) should be able to handle this level of instruction.

Otherwise, the rule is stay put. The last thing you want to enter into is a game of chase, where you both are roaming around a store or a park looking for each other. And, of course, the corollary to that is to tell your child not to go somewhere even if an adult tells them to. That may frustrate a concerned stranger who's just trying to get them to the proper authorities, but we'd take that risk over a bet that the concerned stranger is really a good guy.

CITYWISE WARNING

No Name Backpacks

In our neck of the woods, it's a really big deal when preschoolers get their first backpacks, and many of our kids' friends have their names printed in big letters on the outside. We resisted because we were once told that individuals up to no good could come on to your child by calling his name (conveniently read off the backpack). That was enough for us. We stick to initials only.

Tots and Public Transportation

Kids in cities often spend a lot of time in mass transit vehicles. In terms of convenience, subways and buses may seem a little problematic: They don't take you door to door, and they're often excruciatingly slow (buses will take you about 40 percent longer in most places than cabs or cars). But they're great from a safety perspective and much cheaper to boot. Taxis and livery cars, on the other hand, have tremendous flexibility; but as far as your kid's safety is concerned, they are less than ideal, particularly if you travel *without* car seats. So, if you haven't factored taxi safety records into your transportation decisions, you may want to do so. It could tip the balance on any number of occasions when time is not a major issue.

Taxi Troubles

We've collected a few facts that should get your attention if you plan on using cabs to ferry around your little ones.

- Just because your cab is not speeding along some highway doesn't mean that you and yours won't be subject to serious injury or even death in the event of a crash. It's the combination of sudden deceleration and body weight that creates a crushing force even at low speeds. In a 30-mph crash, for example, even a little 10-pound baby will propel forward with the force of *hundreds of pounds*—a veritable missile that you surely will not be able to hold safely in your arms.

- Not that you always have a choice, but leased taxis have a far greater rate of accidents than owner-operated cars and other vehicles for hire. It's not necessarily a case of "it's not his car so what does he care if it gets hit," but probably more a factor of the driver's need to make money. One has to drive very aggressively to make enough money in a day to cover the rental payment for the taxi and, hopefully, make a little money over that to take home. How can you tell who leases their cab and who doesn't? If you see an ad board on the top of the cab, it's probably leased or part of a corporate fleet since individual owner-operators don't usually get advertising deals.

Why Is Riding in a Taxi So Dangerous?

For some bizarre reason, once people get into a taxi, everything they've ever been taught about seat belts just goes out the window. In one study examining taxi crashes in New York City, only 17 percent of the riders were identified as having used seat belts.[a] Kind of silly, it seems to us—in fact downright insane because if you do strap on a belt, your risk of injury is cut approximately in half. That said, even seatbelted passengers have a high injury rate. The likely cause? The partition between the driver's and passenger's seats: Hit it during a collision or abrupt stop and you might as well have run into a brick wall.

a. Schaller Consulting, "Taxi and Livery Crashes in New York City, 1990-1999," February 28, 2001.

- Passengers in taxis are *three times* more likely to be injured in an accident than if they are in livery cars or "black cars" (the latter being the industry term for those radio service town cars). In one study, nearly 12 percent of rear-seat passengers who were involved in a taxi crash suffered relatively severe injuries, as opposed to around 3 percent of rear-seat passengers in other vehicles.
- Carrying a child on your lap in a car, a favorite of taxi-riding parents, is referred to in the biz as the "child-crusher" position. We won't give you the gory details; suffice to say, the rather graphic label is entirely apt.

But do we really need to use restraints in taxis? Sometimes, the law actually gives you a choice about restraining your child, but that doesn't mean not doing so is an appropriate parental option (hey, in Honolulu you can *allow* your little lassie to get married at 15; is that a good idea too?). For sure, the physical evidence is overwhelming—there is no effective way to secure a small child in a taxi using adult seat belts. But the hassle of lugging a car seat around usually defeats parents. Even the most diligent of us throw our child into a taxi without a car seat or a booster seat as soon as they're out of the infant stage.

For the most part, the law has let us get away with this because in many venues, taxis have long been exempt from child restraint regulations. Not anymore. Cabs in more and more cities are now required to use the same devices as those demanded in passenger cars because the benefits are indisputable. Hail a taxi with a tot in Boston or Providence, for instance, and the law says your child better be appropriately seated. Think the law will never catch up with you? Think again. In some states, the statute requiring child seats in cabs is considered a "primary enforcement law," which means the cops can stop the cab

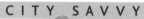

CITY SAVVY

Car Seat Safety

Since we know that you've now decided to protect your baby, make sure you do it right. There's a lot to know about buying and installing a car seat to really get the protection you're after. You can check out the recall list at the excellent www.carseat.org, a site run by a 20-year-old child safety advocacy group. Other good sites for seats and safety instructions include the American Academy of Pediatrics, www.aap.org/family/carseatguide.htm (you can also write the AAP for a copy of the guide) and the National Highway Traffic Safety Administration, www.nhtsa.dot.gov/people/injury/childps.

just because your child is missing a car seat. And, by the way, in some places, you, as the miscreant caregiver, will be the one paying the fine, not the hapless driver.

Still wanna play Russian roulette on this one because taxis *never* get stopped for car seat offenses in *your* city? You might want to consider the fact that your insurance carrier could deny you coverage should your child be in an accident and you failed to uphold your part of the law. Feeling lucky still?

You shouldn't. Whether you simply want to keep your child safe or you're just interested in staying on the right side of the law (hopefully both), you need to invest in keeping your child safely restrained. Of course, you can always go whole hog and carry a regular car seat for lugging in and out of taxis. But there are easier ways.

The Best Safety Restraints for Taxi-ing Kids

For the youngest children, you pretty much have two options:

Frame strollers. Essentially carriage frames onto which you snap your car seat, these are great for parents who have to navigate taxis *and* stairs. Running about $40 (without the car seat), they're made by a number of manufacturers. The Kolcraft Universal car seat carrier is a current city fave: It works well with a decent variety of infant car seats (including the Cosco Designer, which fits little ones up to 35 pounds), plus it's light and can be folded with one hand.

Travel systems. Costing a couple hundred dollars and up, this option is offered by many manufacturers. It provides you with two interchangeable seating options, one for the car (infant only) and one for "strolling," so once the child outgrows the child seat, he can still use the system with the stroller seat. On the negative side, its dual purpose service means the design suffers: They are heavier and less maneuverable than strollers designed specifically for city moving.

For older kids, you can choose from:

Backless boosters. "In a pinch, backless boosters'll do the trick," says Toby McAdams, Child Passenger Safety Technician, mother of two, and the brains behind www.carseatsafety.org, a wonderful compendium of info and comments on car seats. These stripped-down seats weigh only a few pounds, can be bought for as little as $15, and attach to taxis without a high degree of difficulty. (What's more, with a little bungee cord, you can attach these boosters to stroller handles quite nicely.) The other great thing about these seats is their weight range (some work for kids from 30–100 pounds), solving the problem of where to stash your taxi-ing city child when she outgrows her infant seat in an economic, space-efficient way. A couple of points: These are only suitable for taxis and cars with high back seats or head restraints; they must always be used with

Car Seats Are Not Stroller Substitutes

Doctors advise that infants, especially preterm ones, should be limited to no more than an hour at a time in car seats because the upright position can cause breathing problems. That means you might want to reconsider using your universal car seat carrier or a Sit 'n Stroll as your primary stroller, particularly if baby has any kind of breathing issues. Better yet, consult your pediatrician.

a shoulder belt; and you should buy one that uses the vehicle's belt assembly for restraint, not a "shield booster" (the latter forces the child's weight against his abdomen in a crash).

Safeline Kids Sit 'n Stroll stroller. Basically, this is a very low frame stroller with wheels that tuck away to become a car seat. If your child is out of his regular car seat and you're not comfortable with the backless booster for such a little kid, you may want to try this. However, we find them cumbersome and not cheap ($200 or thereabouts for a stroller that you will definitely not use on a day-to-day basis and a car seat that would not be your first choice except for the fact that it fits on this stroller). But, on the plus side, it'll definitely do the job in the cab and on planes.

Safety or travel vest. Essentially a harness attached to a rigid back that you buckle into the taxi's own seat belt assembly—and typically rated for children who weigh between 25 and 40 pounds—these look like the perfect solution. Costing about $30, they're quite portable (weighing only about 4 pounds). There's just one little problem: They're really, really difficult to use. You have to fit the vest to both the child and the vehicle; neither activity is all that easy. So, if you want to try it out (Cosco makes one, and you'll see other private labels), do the adjustments for the child before you hit the road and definitely find a vehicle to try it out on before you hail your first taxi.

Whichever of these options you choose, and we sincerely hope you do choose one of them, don't rush the installation. As Toby McAdams says, "It is okay to spend an extra couple minutes before the taxi pulls away," making sure your child is secured. And don't struggle if you are in any way concerned about your ability to manage the stroller extrication while keeping the child (or children) firmly in hand and out of the traffic stream passing you by. Ask the driver to help you. Some may grumble, but few will refuse. And for gosh sakes, tell him to start the meter running while you're working on getting kids and car seat installed.

Buses and Subways

Easily safer than taxis, buses and subways can become a regular part of any urban child's routine. The obvious rules apply: Children should be kept at a safe distance from train tracks and the street, holding adult hands if they're independently mobile. Seating is much more flexible than in taxis. And seat belts are not available, so you don't have to worry about them—in fact, studies involving school buses have shown that they may do more harm than good. But without any kind of restraint, you do need to keep a hand on your children or they'll go flying at every stop and start. And please resist the temptation to let them face backwards on the seat in either train or bus, something many toddlers love to do because they can see outside. It's a much more precarious position in the event of a sudden speed change.

If subways are your preferred mode of travel, be aware that not every subway has elevator access down to the tracks. This means that you (or some kind stranger) will have to haul stroller, tot, and other baggage up and down stairs—with each added pound increasing the trickiness of your ascents and descents. Even buses are no picnic. So when your child is small, Snuglis and similar slings are much, much easier to manage. Similarly, carrying any paraphernalia in a backpack rather than in bags attached to the stroller will help you make your way without losing your equilibrium.

FIRE DRILL

One of the problems with fires is that people think it will never happen to them. Don't be so sure. In prewar buildings, which house millions of apartment dwellers across the country, archaic electrical wiring is hardly up to the Internet age. Not that it takes some computer mogul attaching commercial capacity servers to the building's 1910 circuitry to cause an apartment fire. Electrical dishwasher shorts are often a cause (they've resulted in two fires in Julia's building in 5 years). Even if the odds of a fire in your own home are small, when you factor in the possibilities of fire in all the other apartments in your building, you're at much more risk of facing a fire emergency in a multifamily situation than if you lived in a single-family home.

And here's the thing. We are so inundated with fire safety communications that we all think we know it all—but come some emergency and all that prep goes right out of our heads. Remember the horrific 1998 apartment fire involving the family of actor Macaulay Culkin? Sparks from a wall-mounted heater ignited a Christmas tree, setting off a breakfast-time inferno. The family had the presence of mind to call 911 and evacuated safely but, in their haste to escape, forgot to shut doors—allowing smoke to filter up and down stairwells, ultimately killing four people who died of smoke inhalation in a stairwell while attempting to escape from upper floors.

The incident reminded the national fire safety community how lethally unaware most civilians are about what to do in a fire. Certainly, in the case of the Culkin fire, the failure to close doors was a significant factor in the four deaths. But don't forget about "staying put"—that old fire safety dictum, which, if followed, would have saved lives in the Culkin fire (whose victims died nearly 10 floors above the fire's origin). Is that still the best advice? What about the World Trade Center attack, where staying where you were was clearly a mistake? Have the rules changed, then? Read on to find out.

City Fire Facts

In case you didn't realize it:

- Kitchen fires are a big cause of fire everywhere, but since urban kitchens tend to be small, they are often cluttered, possibly increasing the unwanted flame potential. Please resist the urge to use a counter by a stove as a storage place. Keep all papers away from burners. That simple oversight has caused innumerable unnecessary fires.

- Candle fires have increased astonishingly over the past few years as aromatherapy and decorative uses of candles have become wildly popular. Across the United States, they have a higher death rate than most other causes of fire, particularly for kids under 6.[a] Even if your apartment is tiny and the rooms merely steps apart, there's no excuse for leaving your child alone in the presence of a lit candle.

- Overloaded circuits are another big city fire starter. We urban dwellers have fewer outlets and jam more stuff into each—courtesy of those multi-plug adapters and multi-outlet strips. Be careful; don't overload.

- You just cannot afford to ignore your smoke alarm batteries. A huge portion of fatalities in fires occur in a home with a nonworking or nonexistent smoke alarm. They really do save lives—if they're working, that is. Unfortunately, we've seen estimates that while 90 percent of American homes have alarms, only two-thirds of them are functional (and we know that people in apartments think their place is so small they'll notice smoke before a fire alarm would go off). For goodness' sake, this is a very easy safety measure. Don't ignore your alarm. Don't disable it. And don't forget to keep it in working order.

a. NFPA Public Affairs Office, "Home Fires Caused by Candles Peak in '98, Double Over Decade," September 17, 2001

The Bottom Line on Urban Fire Safety

We researched advice from fire departments, emergency agencies, and independent commentators all over the continent to come up with the most up-to-date views on urban fire safety. We have three conclusions:

1. The old ways are still best. In the many years we've been "drilled" in offices and schools, the edict has always been to stay where you are unless a fire was actually threatening your safety. First, a comforting fact: Urban fire departments are remarkably fast in getting to the scene of the action. In Houston and NYC, for example, typical response time is a shade over 4 minutes—plenty of time to get you help if you need it. There are compelling reasons behind the principle of staying put: Fire safety experts have long held that people in high-rises just don't understand how dangerous smoke is. Not that there aren't times when you should evacuate (see page 90 for a primer on when), but it seems that the advice given by your local fire department and the presentations the kids get in school are probably right on.

2. Emergency planning needs more than lip service from you, your kids, and your caregiver. In New York City, new laws included a provision to increase fire safety awareness. Building managers were required to prepare and distribute a fire safety plan to all building residents, including posting it in an accessible area as well as on the inside of every apartment door. Did it work? Hardly. Apartment dwellers all over town were up in arms because they felt the posting made their homes look like hotel rooms. And we'd bet a thousand bucks that most folks didn't even read the plans. But remember the Culkins: Do you think you'll have more presence of mind than they did? Don't kid yourself. You need to be serious about this stuff. Have a fire safety plan, read it, and go over it with your loved ones again and again.

3. There are numerous things that can be done on a building-wide basis to facilitate fire safety and, indeed, are applicable in other emergencies as well—terrorist attacks, power outages, you name it. If your building is behind the eight ball, why not get involved? All too often, emergency preparation and prevention actions mandated by local laws are just ignored or, as discussed, are less than adequate. Don't let your building be the next cause célèbre. Especially if you're in a building that is older or without sprinklers, you need to get with the program.

If you take all of this stuff as seriously as we do, you'll take the time to understand what each of these points requires from you.

Fire Alarm: Should You Stay or Should You Go?

Tragic errors are made by people who react the wrong way when a fire alarm goes off. Say it's 2 A.M. and you're awakened by a cacophony of sirens. Do you know what to do?

As we said, the basic principle is to stay where you are unless you're actually being threatened by the fire, because far more people are killed by smoke inhalation than by fire itself. That said, the longer you wait to leave, the more risk there is that smoke and fire will have spread, cutting off your exits. If you're in charge, you will have to make the judgment of whether to stay or go—and if you're not there, you need to make sure your caregiver or your kids understand what you want them to do and when and how.

THE CITY PARENT RULES
When to Go and What to Do

Rule #1: When the fire is in your apartment. Get everyone out. Make sure they know how to crawl if there's smoke: Keep low and cover your mouth with a damp towel or washcloth. Shut (but don't lock) all windows and doors as you leave. Call 911. Don't try to put it out unless you have a way out, and if it is spreading quickly, give up and get out.

Rule #2: When the fire is on your floor or the floor below you. Evacuate immediately *if* you can do it safely without travelling through smoke.

Rule #3: If you think the fire has just been discovered or you just heard the alarm and think you can exit safely. Check the door to the hallway with the *back of your hand*—you don't want to take the chance of burning your palm or fingers on a hot door; that could make a crawling escape all the more difficult. If it's cool, open it slowly to check for smoke. If there's no smoke, proceed to the exit and follow the same process to check the exit stairs.

Rule #4: If you are in a combustible or non-fireproof building (generally one with structural components made of wood). Fires in such buildings can spread rapidly inside the walls, so you are much less likely to be safe inside the building in the event a fire occurs in someone else's unit. You should make your way out unless smoke, heat, or fire prevent your leaving.

Any time you leave, (1) grab your fire emergency kit (see page 93), in case you have to abort your exit somewhere along the way; (2) shut all windows and doors as you leave, including entry doors and fire exit doors; and (3) alert anyone you can on the way out.

When to Stay and What to Do

Rule #1: When the fire does not appear to be near your apartment. Like we said, this is the base case and generally will be the behavior you will adopt should you see those engines pulling up outside your building.

Rule #2: When the fire department instructs you to stay. They know more about fires than you do, so you're just going to have to trust their judgment that you are safest (and less of an impediment) where you are.

Rule #3: When there's smoke in the hall or exit stairs. Do not travel through smoke if you encounter it. Take refuge in your apartment or another one if possible.

Rule #4: If you're staying put and feel you're in any kind of danger:
- While you're waiting, seal doors, vents, and air ducts with duct tape and wet towels. Fill a bath tub; you may need to wet down overheating doors.
- Move to a balcony or the least smoky room and seal the door. Open a window for fresh air if you need it. (Don't break it, though; if smoke starts pouring in, you won't be able to seal it up again.)
- Let the fire department know where you are if you feel threatened: (1) call 911 on your cell phone, (2) communicate through your intercom, and/or (3) hang a sheet or towel outside your window or from your balcony.
- If smoke becomes a factor, stay low, hold that towel or cloth over your mouth and nose, take short breaths through your nose, and get instructions through your intercom or cell phone on what to do.

Biggest Apartment Fire Mistakes

- Ignoring the fire alarm (or worse, not even knowing what it sounds like).
- Using the elevator. It might stop, trapping you between floors, or even take you up to where the fire is.
- Moving through smoke.
- Not closing doors.
- Not replacing fire alarm batteries when they're worn out (or not even having fire alarms).
- Not knowing where the building alarms are or how to operate them.
- Wasting time. Don't dress the kids; don't collect belongings.

Making a Family Plan

We know that fire safety is not exactly front and center in most apartment dwellers' lists of daily concerns. After all, most of you have been listening to fire safety speeches since you were 2; surely you've got this stuff down by now. But when push comes to shove, would you really remember how important closing doors is? Do you ever practice drills at home? Have you ever discussed your plan with your caregiver? Good for you if you say yes; for the rest of us, time to get moving. No excuses. Develop your emergency plan and go over it with your kids.

Then practice the evacuation, the whole evacuation, doing just what you would if there really was a fire, including making family members crawl out of their bedrooms through all the possible apartment exits to the exit stairway(s) (count the doors from your apartment, if necessary). Don't stop short. Go all the way out of the building to the designated meeting place. Don't forget to close doors and windows. In fact, practice at night when the kids are sleeping, and see if they wake up (studies suggest that kids sleep right through smoke alarms). No cheating; you really need to practice for your sake and theirs. And do it again with the caregiver.

Drills Equals Thrills: A Program That the Kids Will Love (and Remember)

The NYC Fire Zone is a fire department-run safety program/reality show conducted in a little room built as a fire scene, complete with smoldering embers. The guys on duty (all real firefighters) take kids through some interactive movies of apartment/house fires, all based on real city incidents. At the end of the show, the kids escape from a "real" fire themselves. The room fills with smoke, and, coached by the firefighters, they extricate themselves in true "stay low and go" fashion by crawling along the wall in the dark and haze. It's a little eerie, even frightening, depending on your state of mind, but it's the most memorable, impactful fire drill we've ever seen.

Indianapolis and Chicago both run variants of the Survive Alive program, which also allows kids to participate in "experiential" training during which they go through simulated fires. Check with your local fire department to see if a similar virtual reality experience is available for your kids.

What Your Building Can Do

Our final point concerns building preparedness. Again this may evoke yawns, but there have been way too many tragedies because of improperly locked stairwells and blocked exit ways. So start with your building manager. Ask him what the building fire emergency plan is. In many cities, the manager is required to prepare a plan and have it approved by the fire department. If one hasn't been done yet, check with the board, tenants' association, or your local fire department to get help on getting a plan done properly. Look to see that the building has basic fire safety elements in place, such as:

- Clearly marked and unlocked exit doors (the doors to the roof in the Twin Towers were locked, preventing possible helicopter rescue for evacuees headed for the roof).
- Cleared corridors and stairways—you'll never notice how clogged your back hall is with bikes or strollers or boxes until you need to negotiate it in an emergency.
- Automatic closers on apartment doors and fire stair doors.
- Functioning, effective emergency lighting (in a high-rise, check for a backup emergency lighting system if the electricity goes out; you may have a lot of flights to go down in the dark, and that's a real chore).
- Posted emergency instructions and an emergency communication system. If there's an intercom system, how will it be used? If not, how about communication by phone?

If your building is missing any of this stuff, round up some neighbors and fix what needs fixing. Better yet, try and mobilize for a building-wide drill. It can't hurt anyone, will help you get to know your neighbors, and may even build a little neighborly solidarity.

ELEVATOR ACTION

If you live in an apartment, the odds are good that you have an elevator. No one knows what the real incidence of elevator accidents is because the industry is notoriously poorly supervised and, at least in the case of New York City (which saw the arrest of most of the official elevator inspection hierarchy in the city's 1996 "Operation Up/Down") sometimes corrupt. But many accidents are preventable, so make sure you and your kids understand elevator basics.

THE CITY PARENT RULES
Elevator Safety

Rule #1: Enter and exit carefully. Many of the reported injuries occur when the elevator floor is not aligned with the floor on which it opens and the passenger trips and falls. And, of course, make sure the elevator is actually there before you enter.

Rule #2: Never force a door open. If you're inside and it doesn't open, try pushing the Door Open button. But don't try prying open the door, whether you're inside or outside of the car. You never know when the elevator will restart, carrying you along half in and half out.

Rule #3: Don't lean on the doors. Kids are always leaning, touching, pushing—not a great idea in elevators. Doors can malfunction and open while the car's in between floors. You don't want to depend on them to keep you out of the shaft.

Rule #4: Don't jump when inside the elevator. A gaggle of people, mostly kids, in Julia's old building were caught in a wandering elevator one Halloween when excited kids, trick-or-treating from floor to floor, jumped so much the elevator went slightly off its track. No one was in danger, but the elevator couldn't read the code that sent it to waiting riders. Instead, it traveled aimlessly up and down the building until it finally rested (softly) in the basement. Trust us, those kids won't ever jump in an elevator again.

Rule #5: If the elevator gets stuck, stay put. Use the alarm button or emergency phone to contact help (in a pinch, a cell phone call to 911 will also work) and wait for it to come. And sit down, just in case the elevator restarts with a jolt. Don't even think about climbing out of a stalled elevator. Lots of injuries occur when people try to jump down to a landing; worse, death can result if you miss the landing and enter the shaft.

Rule #6: Never enter an elevator in a fire or in a power failure. The elevators may stop running or malfunction, trapping you in the car.

SAFETY IN A POST-9/11 WORLD

The horrific events of 9/11 created a new set of safety concerns: evacuation, public outings crowds, transportation. How do parents respond to what is undeniably a new consciousness without making their children nervous wrecks? Take a deep breath. The odds that you or your children will be subject to a terrorist attack are so unknowable, and probably so small, that you simply cannot rationally devote a lot of your physical effort or emotional energy to mitigating such a random threat. So, no, we're not recommending you build a $100,000 steel-girded, lead-lined safe room. But we don't believe in ignoring the possibilities anymore than we ignore planning for any other emergency that rears its ugly head. If nothing else, there are likely to be scares and false alarms on an increased basis—which suggests it would be a very good idea to think through what you would do in the event of some emergency evacuation.

Not that survival planning for the city family is so obvious or easy. On the cusp of the 2003 war in Iraq, the country was thrust into a state of high alert. The airwaves and news pages were flooded with recommendations for stocking your home to carry you through a "lockdown" period of a few days and for carrying your family through a multiday evacuation. Many of the most authoritative recommendations, however, were certainly not written with the city family in mind. If you've ever checked out the evacuation kit recommended by the Federal Emergency Management Agency (FEMA), you'll see what we mean. Now, assuredly those guys know what they're talking about, but the totality of their recommended supplies kit is well beyond the scope of pedestrian portability and presumes (1) that you have a car, and (2) that the car actually has a likelihood of being able to go someplace in an emergency—presumptions that rule out a good many of us city dwellers.

Here's what we suggest. Plan at the same level as you would for a fire emergency. You may never activate that plan, but it will make you feel safer just to have gone through the exercise. That means do what you have to do, within reason, to protect your family in the event of a need to "shelter-in-place," as the Red Cross puts it, or evacuate (and if you need to travel light, see "Evacuation Tips" on page 96 for help with a pared-down evac kit). There are lots of places to find thorough descriptions of how to prepare your home for a lockdown, what food to stock, and how to respond differently to different types of emergencies;

if you're going to go down this road at all, we recommend you print out copies of the Red Cross's instructions at http://www.redcross.org/services/disaster/ 0,1082,0_500_,00.html. Of course, whatever level you decide to take your planning to, make sure every adult in charge of your kids knows what you expect them to do and when—including how to tune into an emergency radio station, how to seal up a safe room (if that's in your plan), how to evacuate, and who should be collecting which kids.

Even More Evacuation Tips

- If you have young kids and are really serious about this evacuation stuff, you might want to keep an umbrella stroller handy, even if your youngest is well past that stage. It can be handy for ferrying goods as well as tired tots.
- If you live within spitting distance of a nuclear power plant, you might want to keep potassium iodide pills on hand. They prevent children's thyroids from soaking up radiation from nuclear meltdowns (although they'll do nothing if you're trying to defend yourself against a dirty bomb—that's a different kind of radiation entirely).
- Hoofing it with the recommended amount of water is next to impossible. Consider buying a hydration backpack specially designed for carrying water.
- Lots of people will tell you to create a kit of important documents that you can gather up at a moment's notice. This will certainly make your life easier if your house incinerates. But, even better advice is to send all those documents to a trusted friend or relative, preferably one who lives far out of town, *before* the emergency. That way, you won't have to sweat the collection in an emergency and you'll have someone else able to deal with important matters if you're temporarily incapacitated. Include copies of important documents (drivers' licenses; will; passports) and a list of important contacts and data including relatives' and physicians' telephone numbers, Social Security numbers, credit card accounts and company contacts, insurance (property and health) policy numbers and contacts, mortgage contacts, bank and brokerage account numbers and contacts, PIN numbers, and an inventory of valuable household goods.

In terms of gearing up for an emergency, we have nothing to add to what the professionals have to say, except to point out a few city nuances to keep in mind as you prepare:

Evacuate with mobility in mind. Even if you're in a driving city, should you ever have the need to evacuate, roads might be clogged. If you're in a walking city, you certainly need to think about how to provision your evacuation when you're leaving on foot. Stuck on what to take? See "The City Parent Getaway Kit" on page 98.

Identify a safe room. This is a little trickier for city families who are dealing with a relatively large number of people in a small apartment. There are simply fewer choices. A closet won't do: too little oxygen and it won't support many people for too long. Try a room facing a courtyard with the least amount of access to the outside.

Take timing into account. Most of the disaster preparation we've seen assumes that you're at home or can get home. Yet the events of 9/11 happened at 9:00 in the morning on a bright sunny day. Parents were at work or doing errands, kids were at school or on the playground. You really need to take some time to figure out where everyone might be at different times of the day and how, or if, you're going to round them up. We highly recommend that you consider the merits of having two meeting places: one in your immediate neighborhood and one a farther distance, in the event that travel to your own home is prohibited. And consider keeping a copy of your contact list and emergency meeting points with your child (we have one in an inside pocket in our children's backpacks). You can't be sure where they'll be or in whose care should disaster strike.

Incorporate your schools' plans into yours. Almost every city school has done a disaster plan. If they haven't communicated it to you, make sure you know what they plan to do in the event of an evacuation or emergency, including if kids are off-site (on a field trip, for example). Make sure the school has current, complete contact numbers for you, including e-mail and out-of-city contacts in case local phone lines go down. That was a real problem in New York City on 9/11 when it turned out many contact numbers were out-of-date. Also, many schools have developed a lockdown plan to be implemented in the event authorities request that everyone shelter-in. If your school has a plan to do so, make sure they have supplies and dosage for any medicine your child needs to take (including potassium iodide if that is on your agenda; many schools have no plans to administer it wholesale because of the variability of its effects on children).

The City Parent Getaway Kit

Whether it's a fire in Boston, power outage in LA, or terrorist alert in D.C., urban families have, sadly, more and more reasons to want to plan for a fast exit. Looking at emergency packing suggestions for all the above, we've come up with the least-common-denominator essentials. Our recommendation: Pack a backpack or two and keep them stashed under your bed so you can pull them out quickly when you need them. It won't get you through a week, but it should get you through a day or two until you can make other accommodations. Remember, if it's a fire, you want to get out quickly with just the important stuff that you can't "live" without.

IF YOU HAVE ONE BACKPACK:

Flashlight and extra batteries

Cell phone with extra emergency power

Portable radio, battery or hand-cranked

Bottled water/long-lasting snacks

Cash, credit card

First aid kit, prescription medicine

Matches

Particle mask for everyone

Multi-tool knife

Map of your city with exits marked

Personal hygiene basics: soap, toilet paper, etc.

Extra eyeglasses

Infant/toddler needs if appropriate (diapers/wipes, formula, bottles)

Pet needs if appropriate

Copy of picture ID (passport, drivers' license) for all adults, birth certificates for children

Water purification tablets like Halazone or Globaline (check camping supply stores)

IF YOU HAVE TWO, ADD:

Sweatshirts, extra underwear for everyone

Ground cloth

Rain ponchos for all

More food (shelf-stable, low-salt items, snack bars, trail mix, snack-size canned foods) and water (but if you're on foot, the recommended gallon/day/person of water may not be realistic)

CHAPTER 5

TAKING CARE OF THE CAREGIVING

C ity parents have it all wrong. They quake in their boots anticipating the
struggle, the effort, the sleepless nights of trying to secure a place in the
right preschool or kindergarten. But the event that *really* should've gotten
all that effort and attention probably happened long before: when they decided on
child care.

Having lived in and around city child care situations for 15 years now, we're
willing to lay major money on the table that most parents underestimate the com-
plexity of finding good child care *and* overestimate the success of the arrangement
they finally make.

Fact is, many parents make their choice, pay their money, and then *assume* all
is well. They *think* they're on top of the situation, but suddenly they realize their
daughter's now on her fourth head teacher at day care—and she's only been there
6 months (no wonder she couldn't seem to get their names down pat). Or their
neighbor tells them she saw their nanny and son shopping on the opposite side of
the city from where they live—when, by the way, they thought Nanny Dearest and
Chumley were at the playground.

Here's the drill. City caregiving is unparalleled in terms of the depth and
breadth of its offerings—daycare, family care, and all sorts of in-home caregivers,
from haute haughty grads of prestigious nanny schools to young women far from
home hoping to take on a new occupation in a language they're just beginning to
understand. But it's also complicated—there are lots of city nuances that have to
be considered when you're choosing and using child care of any kind. And if you
don't know enough about what you're in for, there will be repercussions. You'll
make a bad choice (who knew the nanny fabricated her references?) or a suboptimal one (say, not even looking at daycare, which might have been a better option
for your child). Or you make a good choice and fall apart on the follow-through.
(Little Priscilla got a concussion because Nanny took her to that poorly maintained

playground near your house—yes, you're upset with Nanny, but did you ever tell her not to go there?)

Just to complicate things further, what you have to do to find and manage child care wisely is not only different in the city, it's also different for each type of care situation. Don't cringe; a little more knowledge certainly won't hurt you, and it's just what you need to take advantage of all those fabulous caregiving opportunities your city provides.

THE DAY CARE DANCE

Utter the words "urban day care" to many parents and they'll conjure up visions of cramped, dingy spaces jammed with hyper, dirty-faced kids attended to by irritable, snappish child care workers. It's true that city day care has a horrible reputation, often deservedly so. There are loads of stats and studies attesting to the poor quality of many, many centers. So why would anyone consider day care for their child? The answer is, of course, that not every center is bad; in fact the differences among the good centers and the bad ones are huge. In one extensive study of the turnover in day care staff, a pervasive problem, 25 percent of the centers had *no* turnover while a few had 100 percent.

What would be even more surprising to the many city dwellers who would rather eat nails than consider day care for their little babes are the really substantial benefits a *good* center can provide both parent and child. Take the highly regarded Children's All Day School (CADS) in New York City. Here's what that center—and others like it in cities around the country—deliver.

Thoughtful, consistent, and creative care all day long. At a good center, you won't have to worry about your kids being bored, unchallenged, or understimulated—and you'll never have to wonder whether their formative childhood influence is going to be *SpongeBob SquarePants*. At CADS, for instance, kids run through carefully conceived daily schedules full of art, creative play, puzzles, and math and reading readiness activities—specially designed to meet the needs of the small clients who play in rooms specifically designed for their age group. The center also takes advantage of the ready supply of artists in the city by bringing in outside professionals on a regular basis to teach music (even the infants get a special music teacher three times a week) and movement, in addition to all the clowns, magicians, and puppeteers who also visit.

A major bargain. If you're talking about the care of a single child, quality city day care can be quite a bit less expensive than a good nanny. Popular wisdom, however, suggests that when you have two kids, the nanny is easier on your pocket-

Location, Location, Location

Real estate represents a big portion of city day care costs (labor's the biggest). So when you're checking out centers, keep in mind that, all things being equal, the center close to work in the city's busy commercial district is going to be more expensive than that center near the less-pricey residential area in which you live.

book. Not necessarily. When you look at the nanny side of the ledger, you also need to add in the cost of preschool tuition plus any supplemental classes for younger kids (music, movement, art), which are already included in the day care fee. Now do the math.

Staff dedicated to child care. Relying on a child care center is quite different than depending on a nanny who has other duties to manage, a little light house-keeping, maybe, a few daily errands. At a good day care, staff is completely focused on the care of children; that's the mission 100 percent.

Socialization. A biggie and pretty self-evident at that. The social experience provided by daily mixing with the same group of kids is one of the most important developmental exercises for young kids. And in day care, socialization starts early.

Oversight of child's development. The daily, all-day interaction between experienced day care professionals and children can be the basis of significant insight into how a child is progressing. Not only will staff members let parents in on "who" their kids really are and "what" is exciting them, but they can also identify potential issues early on. Many centers even have educational consultants come in on a regular basis to address staff/parent concerns regarding specific children. The heads-up such close care provides parents allows them to get appropriate help early, when it can really pay off.

Extra help when your child needs it. If intervention is indicated for a child—speech, physical, or occupational therapy, for instance—staff members at a great urban day care center can be an invaluable resource. Whatever the issue, they've doubtless seen it and dealt with it before. They can most likely provide recommendations for good therapists and doctors and very often help you work the system to identify and secure whatever government assistance will pay for your child's therapy. And when you do get that help, another plus is that in an all-day center, the therapists often work with the child on-site—which is not only convenient for the parent, but it allows the center to see whether the intervention is working or not.

Minimal exposure to the city admissions rat race. Here's a huge benefit for overstressed parents. Good day care centers can provide just as strong a preschool experience as any of the "names"—and they do so without subjecting parent and child to the angst of the urban preschool admissions process. That pain-free entry doesn't mean you'll lose on the way out, either. The list of kindergartens offering places to the CADS "graduates" would hold its own with the comparable list from any of the hot name preschools in New York City.

What to Look For

What's the big deal you wonder? I'll just sign up for a licensed, accredited center. Hold your horses. *Every* day care center is required to be licensed by the state, which sets the minimum requirements for things such as staffing, space, and health and safety code requirements, so the mere fact that a center is licensed tells you very little. Even accreditation bestowed by the National Association for the Education of Young Children (NAEYC; the industry group attempting to raise the quality of early childhood care across the country), while not a bad thing to have, is no assurance. The 10 percent of the nation's centers that are so recognized often have just as high levels of staff turnover as nonaccredited ones. As researchers have noted, "NAEYC accreditation is not a guarantee of high quality or of a program's ability to sustain quality over time."

Turning to all those research studies again, they strongly emphasize the correlation or association of quality care and such factors as: (1) high adult-to-child ratios (the NAEYC recommends staffing of one adult for four children under age 2; one adult for six to seven children ages 2 and 3, and one for every 10 children ages 4 and 5; more adults would be even better, but you are rarely going to find that); (2) high percentages of teachers and aides with training in child development; (3) staff wages paid at competitive levels for the area that you're in; and (4) low turnover.

Unfortunately, as important as these questions are, it's not so easy to interrogate a center director on all these elements and get answers that will really tell you yes or no on quality. Here's what we'd do.

THE CITY PARENT RULES
Finding a Great Day Care Center

Rule #1: Start with the basics. Get some rudimentary information materials on how to evaluate different centers; www.childcareaware.org (800-424-2246) is a great source of information and provides a handy checklist to use when examining a facility.

Rule #2: Do your background checks. Call the appropriate state regulatory agency to find out if a center you are considering has any licensing violations. While you're at it, check out the actual licensing requirements for your state at http://nrc.uchsc.edu/STATES/states.htm; they can be quite detailed in terms of health and safety requirements and will greatly assist you in spotting violations during your center visit.

Rule #3: Ask the big questions. Continuity of care, dealing with discipline—these are areas you want to get the director to talk about. And *you* must keep your eye out for some of the qualitative aspects of care such as the interaction between the staff and children. Is there a lot of verbal communication? Are babies being held while they're fed? How is discipline meted out?

Rule #4: Get some staffing stats. We've mentioned turnover as an indicator of daycare quality. So, ask the director what percent of the staff has to be replaced every year (or take a more diplomatic tact and ask what the average tenure is). While you're at it, ask what kind of continuing training or education is provided staff members—centers that invest in the skills of their employees have a distinct advantage over those that don't when it comes to attracting and retaining workers. Also inquire about the staff recruitment policy itself: It's a big, wide city out there, so how and where does the center look for help? What sort of screening do potential hires get? And what educational background is required? If the center uses drivers, ask about them too.

Rule #5: Examine the schedules for particular age groups. Quality day care centers have very strong educational/child development programming—i.e., the schedule for 3-year-olds should be like any good preschool: a combination of academics, play, and socialization. If the teaching part doesn't come through to you loud and clear, then you're probably looking at a babysitting service, not quality day care.

Rule #6: Look for a professional atmosphere. God forbid you should ever call an employee at a good center a babysitter. These people take the job of caring for children very

CITYWISE WARNING !

Don't Rely Solely on the Director

Make a point of asking any staff member you encounter the same questions you're asking the director—particularly, how long they've been at the center. If the accumulated answers seem to indicate a lot more turnover than the director has indicated (every other teacher seems to have just started), it might be time for a little talk.

seriously; for them, child care is a career and a calling, not just a job. They are constantly trained, their skills upgraded, their activities evaluated, just as they would be in any profession. And, by the way, the respect accorded to workers in good centers is a key reason why the good centers have low turnover, so you want to make sure that respect is absolutely in evidence.

THE CITY DIFFERENCE:
Evaluating Day Care

Once you have your core questions down pat, you will need to focus on the city elements of day care.

Dealing with density. In sprawling southwestern cities like Houston, the availability of wide-open spaces allows the construction of centers like the enormous Crème de la Crème facilities, replete with classrooms, computer, music and movement rooms, media centers, outdoor water parks, etc. Very, very cool, but you're unlikely to find that kind of acreage in denser cities like New York or Boston, where space is tough to come by and centers are often only 2000 to 3000 square feet. The good news is crowded spaces don't necessarily prevent the delivery of quality care. It's not the overall area that's important, it's how the kids are cared for in that space, right? But tight quarters can impose limitations on day care operations. So, if you're looking at smaller centers, pay strict attention to:

- Management of outdoor activities. Many city centers don't have outdoor space of their own, and in some the kids don't actually go outdoors at all during care hours, *ever*. You need to make a decision whether that bothers you (it would us). So ask the center, and yourself, some questions. Where do the kids play and when? Is there suitable space with appropriate equipment for all age groups? Are the younger ones separated from the older ones? If the outdoor space belongs to the center, is it interesting enough to keep kids happy over the course of a year or is center outdoor time supplemented with visits to local city playgrounds? If so, which are those (and how safe are they) and how do the children get there? Do you feel comfortable with the safety precautions being taken? If you can, observe a group from the day care at the playground to see how comfortable you are with the supervision.
- Separation of kids and activities indoors. Some day care centers consciously mix kids of different ages, family style. If that's the case, be sure that the

very different developmental needs of disparate ages are dealt with appropriately. If the answers give you the feeling that maybe the mix is one of logistics (just not enough separate places to keep everybody), that's probably not great. And even small spaces should have different areas for creative play, reading, and art. Toddler areas should give plenty of opportunity for movement even if it's through the use of creative, albeit compact, climbing structures.

- How sick kids are handled. It's a fact of day care life that your child will have more colds, viruses, and ear infections than if he'd been cared for in his own home (that's not necessarily such a bad thing in the long run, medical experts are now saying, because day care kids get their immune systems fortified at an early age). But it would still be nice to think there's some attempt at quarantining those who start throwing up during arts and crafts. Find out where children who take ill are placed.

- Proximity of the center to public transportation. Dense cities can have very expensive real estate, meaning the staff often has to travel far to get to work. Centers that are near subway or bus stops are advantaged in recruiting teachers.

Health and safety. If you checked out www.childcareaware.org or a similar resource for evaluating day care operations, you should have a sizable list of basic health and safety criterion to examine. Add these city issues as well:

- If the facility is in an older building, ask if the center has done lead paint tests (and ask to see the results); find out where the children's drinking water comes from. If it's from the tap, ask if it's been tested for lead also. Similarly, if the children's outdoor play could bring them into contact with

ground near the building foundation or walls, ask if that soil has been lead tested as well.

- Ask where the children are taken in the event of a medical emergency, and make sure that location has suitable pediatric ER facilities and staff.
- Ask about pesticide use. It'll be a rare city center that can avoid using them entirely, so ask what types of pesticides are used and where and if the kids' toys are protected from the spraying. (By the way, if you can smell it while you're there, that's a bad sign.)
- Ask about the playground equipment. If it looks like pressed wood to you, ask if it's been tested for arsenic; ditto with any neighborhood playgrounds the kids frequent. Also check out the hand-washing policy; all the kids should be washing their hands when they come in from the outside as a matter of course.
- Security is certainly an issue for any day care, but in the city, where loads of people may be passing by a center on a daily basis, you want to be doubly sure that security cameras are in place, access is well controlled, and that any outdoor space is completely protected from kids getting out and from unwelcome guests getting in.

A special note about driving. If you're in a driving city, you may very well want and find a day care that picks up and drops off at your home. It's a great convenience; just be sure it's a safe one too. Most states have quite specific requirements regarding day care transportation, mostly geared to making sure that kids are restrained properly and kept track of (Memphis's recent rash of day care fatalities, which resulted when children were inadvertently left behind in center vans, led to new state requirements for monitoring kids' movement). However, regulation is one thing; observance, quite another. If you can arrange it, monitor a couple of day care pickups—or be at the center when vans roll in at dropoff time or leave to take the children home— to see that:

- Children are checked in on a written list by the driver or other staff member (each child should be individually checked off upon leaving the van too).
- All kids are securely restrained in infant, child, or booster seats, as appropriate, and that the number of kids and supervisors is in compliance with your state's law.
- Another adult is in the van with the children at all times if the driver has to leave the van.
- At dropoff, a staff member checks all seats in the van after all the children have departed.

You can also ask to see the driver's passenger logs at the center (some states require that an additional person at the center verify the driver's log) as well as any written verification of the driver's fitness, which would have included checks of criminal, driving, and medical records; and verification that the driver has received necessary training for child transportation mandated by your state.

THE URBAN A-LIST
Finding That Great Center AND Securing a Spot

Spaces at the best centers don't come easy. You need a plan.

Compile your short list. Recommendations from friends are always helpful; but in lieu of, or in addition to them, you can check out one of your local child care resource and referral organizations (CCR&Rs). These are nonprofit organizations that will tell you about your state's licensing requirements and provide you referrals to state licensed facilities that will meet basic requirements you give them regarding hours, NAEYC accreditation, cost, etc. Some CCR&Rs will go further and actually do some research for you, sometimes for free, sometimes for a small fee; they'll also often cover family care as well as child care. Keep in mind that the operative word in their name is "referral." They are not recommending places to you; they're just giving you a list of places that meet some objective criteria (licensing and accreditation, hours, location). Any assessment of quality is for you to make yourself. If you need help in finding a CCR&R, you can get names by zipcode at www.naccrra.org, the site of the national association for CCR&Rs.

Think outside the 'hood. Even though the selection of day care centers in any city is going to far exceed what you'd find outside, you are still not going to find a lot of high-quality centers that fit your logistical needs and offer that highly interactive, loving, safe care that you seek. Expand your options by considering centers within close proximity to both your house and workplace—or even en route between the two.

Woo the best ones. After you've visited your short list of centers (the best ones more than once, ideally), validated references, and did some spot checks on their van pickups or park trips, you'll whittle the list down to even fewer centers. Go after those actively. If they use wait lists, get on them (but make sure you know how they work; you may need to reregister your interest every so often). Get to know the directors, particularly of your top picks, and if they don't have a space, let them know that you will take one as soon as it's available—and keep checking in until you're in.

The Day Care Admissions Drill

Read the headlines about the paucity of day care slots and you can understand why parents feel they have to get their babies on a waiting list at conception, as they reportedly do in Oakland. But the numbers never tell the whole story, and, without boring you with all the details of how these things are calculated, we can tell you that in every city there are centers with long waiting lists and others with lots of vacancies. What really matters is getting a space at a good center when you want it.

The biggest logjams tend to be for infants (because, by law, they require more caregivers) and preschool-age kids (because more and more parents want their children to benefit from some sort of prekindergarten program). How centers handle excess demand differs considerably. Some keep extensive waiting lists for all age groups; if a vacancy occurs, they run down the wait list until they get a bite. Others don't bother with wait lists at all, which is good news for the persistent parent. If a space frees up in the middle of the year, they'll be glad to take your child. So don't make generalizations and don't give up on a top quality center if you're temporarily shut out.

Here's the bottom line: Since there's so little uniformity in admissions policies, if you're considering day care at all, do some preliminary research early just to see what the process is—even if you may not be using a center for some time. You don't have to go through the whole investigative drill, but certainly you want to get some idea of vacancy rates, wait lists, and capacity at the centers that may be on your list.

CITYWISE WARNING !

Saving Your Place

Be aware that day care parents are increasingly adopting a buy-and-hold strategy: paying for day care when a slot opens up even though they don't plan on putting their child into the center for some months hence. It may not be the most appealing course of action but, since there aren't loads of options out there, we recommend that if need be and you can swing it, you reserve the space and pay the few months of interim costs.

FAMILY CARE: WILL IT WORK FOR YOUR CHILD?

In family care, your child spends his time in the caregiver's home. The benefit, the theory goes, is that your child is in more of a homelike, less institutional setting. The other kids? Another version of an extended family. And theoretically, since you have the same caregiver, the opportunity for forming that long-term bond so important to kids is enhanced. Also in this kind of arrangement, there may be more flexibility—a slightly later pickup schedule or more slack when a child is sick.

Family care is undeniably popular, accounting for a quarter of the child care in this country. Probably the biggest reason people opt for it is cost: It is one of the cheapest child care options. BUT what you save in dollars, you may pay for in other ways.

A major problem with this kind of care is the lack of oversight. Family child care is notoriously unregulated; few states require licensing and even then, a lot of providers just operate under the radar. What licensing requirements that do exist are not exactly comprehensive, either. Providers will *probably* have had to: undergo a home inspection, prove that they meet some modest safety requirements (the presence of a fire extinguisher, for example) and minimum space requirements, provide some documentation on the health of the caregiver, and maybe even complete a modest child care course. That's it. So when you choose family care, you're relying heavily on your own gut to determine if the caregiver can handle the kids with minimal training, downtime, or backup.

If you are keen on this option, we suggest you pay attention to more than the kindness of the caregiver to decide if it really is suitable care for your child—particularly given the additional constraints imposed by being in a city. Take the space issue. Is there enough room to take care of multiple kids? Kids of different age groups playing in the same room can require a lot more attention from the caregiver (someone's got to keep the 5-year-old's puzzle pieces out of the 2-year-old's mouth). And you want to be really sure that the TV is not being used to pick up the slack. What about outdoor space? If you're in a center city, it's unlikely that a group care home will have its own outdoor space. This means for your child to get the fresh air he needs, the caregiver will have to schlep the whole lot to the nearest playground—in which case, you would do well to satisfy yourself that the caregiver can handle multiple kids outdoors (legally, it can be as many as eight per attendant).

If you're in a more spread-out city, good family care may be a more

Family Care Options

There are two types of arrangements:

"Group" or "large" care operations accommodate up to 12 or maybe 14 kids, depending on the state regs. But the primary caregiver must have at least one assistant.

In "regular" care, one caregiver watches over from six to eight kids, depending on the state and the ages of the kids. (Infants reduce the number of kids any caregiver is allowed to take care of.)

accessible option. Clearly, it is helpful to find a licensed caregiver, particularly one who's in some sort of care network that allows some backup if the caregiver's ill as well as more opportunity for training. We strongly recommend that, as with day care, you consult with your local CCR&R regarding your state's licensing requirements and referrals. This is an instance where you may want to take advantage of any "enhanced services" that the CCR&R provides to help parents narrow down choices. And as we advised with day care, examine any potential family care with an eye to how it performs on health and safety issues.

UH OH, THE AU PAIR

The au pair, that "not quite a nanny, more than a babysitter" phenomenon, allows you to tap into a font of youthful overseas energy for not a lot of money. It may not be for everyone, but if you want to try it, you will find lots of teen spirits knocking on your door. And why not? If you were a 20-year-old Swede with wanderlust, where would you rather do your time—among the manicured lawns of Grosse Pointe or in the happening Windy City? In some lovely, but not exactly shaking, Bay Area suburb, or in a hip San Fran Victorian? Oh please. Hands down, au pairs will take that city assignment every time. So they're there if you want them.

But do you? First (and who knew!), *real* au pairs are a legal phenomenon—regulated by the Department of State, which allows foreign young people who pass criminal screens, reference checks, and personal interviews to emigrate to the United States for one year so they can learn about our wonderful country while taking care of your kiddies. That means you can only get an au pair through one of the officially designated au pair administration agencies; you'll find that very short list on the State Department's Office of Exchange Coordination and Designation Web site at http://exchanges.state.gov/education/jexchanges/private/aupair.htm. You're also subject to the rather strict parameters of the program. The key ones:

- Child care can involve no more than 10 hours per day and 45 hours in total a week.
- Au pairs cannot be placed in a home with an infant unless an adult is present at all times, or in a home with children under 2 unless they have 200 hours of infant child care experience.
- Au pairs aren't housekeepers. They can clean up the children's toys and do their laundry, but that's about it.

- They have to earn 6 hours of academic credit over the course of their years in the States—after all, they're supposed to be learning.
- They have to be paid according to the State Department rules—essentially minimum wage based on a 45-hour week, with a credit to you for room and board.

Minimum wage sounds pretty good if you're in a city where caregivers routinely charge $10 to $20 an hour. You are on the hook for about $500 toward education costs, the J-1 visa fee, and the agency processing and placement fees. But even then, the economics are sweet: The total cost is probably, all in, only around $250 a week, which for 45 hours looks mighty fine to an urban parent.

The downside, of course, is you're dealing with a young (18- to 26-year-old) girl (almost always; males don't usually apply *or* get selected) who may have no background or even real interest in child care. And they will have absolutely no experience with your city (or maybe any city), so there'll be a whole new world to educate them about. Of course, plenty of other people will be happy to introduce them to all the seductions of a city. Oh, the stories, we could tell—of au pairs stumbling in at 4 A.M. (and how great do you think they are the next morning taking care of your bambino?) and giving out the private family phone number to persuasive strangers in bars (a swell way for you to make new friends). Then factor in their own developmental changes: They start with you as country-bred sweet young things with lilting accents and within 6 months have discovered their inner goth. Yup, au pairs can be pretty exciting.

But some people do think they're the only way to go. The price is great; you don't, for the most part have to deal with any tax hassles unless you want to (just make sure the au pair hasn't been in this country before, because then taxes are a totally different story); and your kids get exposure to a different culture and maybe language. And when it works, it works. Our suggestions:

1. Use au pairs when your kids are bigger, not when they're babes—we're thinking, not earlier than 5 even. Since au pairs are neither trained nor, generally, intending to pursue caregiving as a career, they're just not going to be particularly attuned to child development. But they can be terrific for schlepping kids around to playdates and after-school activities and for monitoring homework (although they probably won't help much with it), and they're much less likely to find that type of work too taxing or boring.
2. Read our suggestions for dealing with a nanny (see "Nanny, Nanny" on page 112). Many of the same prescriptions regarding language, culture, and getting on the same page apply.

NANNY, NANNY

It's really impossible to be sure because of the lack of documentation, but according to one study, as many as 40 percent of families with income over $75,000 hire caregivers for their children. You're talking a lot of city parents here. But hiring and managing someone to take care of your child in your city home is a quite unique experience. From a wide open, virtually unregulated labor market to dealing with the lightning fast nanny grapevine to navigating cultural and language differences, to just knowing where your child and caregiver are during the day, a full-time nanny requires a lot more interaction on your part than any other type of city caregiving.

O Nanny, Where Art Thou?

We could fill the rest of this book with stories of nanny wanderings. The nanny who will only go to one park because that's where her friends hang out. Maybe that's good, maybe that's bad, but did ya think to check? Or maybe you discover that little Talitha has every single one of the Spy Kids Happy Meal Toys because, apparently, she's a Micky D's frequent diner. You didn't ask, so you didn't know. Or maybe your caregiver's *not* as mobile as you'd like her to be and you can't understand why she keeps finding reasons not to take your son to that sweet little children's museum. Turns out, she doesn't know the bus routes in this part of town and was embarrassed to ask you.

CITY SAVVY

Communication and Oversight

If you have a caregiver, these two words—communication and oversight—should be your mantra. Given the discretion and autonomy of city caregivers, the range of environments they may encounter with your child, and the fact that your caregiver's cultural background may be very different than your own, you need to:

Talk often and clearly. Discuss regularly what's going on in the caregiving relationship, defining (and redefining) your expectations in light of your child's changing needs and caregiver feedback.

Monitor and evolve. Find ways to closely watch what's going on and recognize that the monitoring, also, will evolve as you grow more comfortable with the most important person in your life outside your family.

My, my, my, the places your nanny can go. Not that they're necessarily bad. It's just that most parents don't spend enormous amounts of gray matter pondering the locations, routes, and modes of transportation that should be on their nanny's good-to-go list. Fact is, city nannies have tremendous autonomy (more than you ever dreamed) and major mobility. Without the benefit of big houses and big yards to play in, they're out and about in cities whose gestalt likely changes from block to block. You're the parent, so you need to figure out where you want your child to go and why and how and when, lest mistakes be made.

The Pool Is Wide, The Pool Is Deep. . . And the Prices Are a Scandal

The supply of nanny candidates in every city is huge and diverse. That should be a good thing; you'll have lots of choices. But there's more than a little bit of weirdness about the whole hiring exercise because a sizable part of the supply is comprised of illegal or semi-legal immigrants (allowed to be here but not to work). Think of the impacts: Parents find a great nanny, but she doesn't have work papers, turning Mom and Dad into tax cheats (not since Prohibition have so many otherwise upstanding citizens operated outside the law). Or you're interviewing seven different people from five different countries, only one of whom is a native English speaker, and none of them has any documentation. It can be kinda hard to get a fix on who these people are (and you will be hiring one of them to help raise your child, no less). All in all, the conditions are not exactly ideal for the type of transactions we're used to in this country—you know, characterized by free-flowing, transparent information, resumes and references, oh, and even wage demands that correlate with experience and expertise. In fact, you can get great people for no money and horrible people for top dollar.

Here's the deal. Hiring a caregiver in the city is caveat emptor, if nothing else. Market rules don't work, and sources of good caregivers are all over the place—with the best sometimes coming from the least likely places. You'll need to pay attention.

Nanny Networks

The social networks of urban caregivers—of which the nanny klatches and nanny grapevine are the most obvious manifestations—can be a big part of your caregiver's life. Those social ties can be great (friends in the 'hood, an extra pair of eyes and hands) or horrible (bad influences and bad-mouthing).

Consider the following. In one study of Los Angeles caregivers, the nannies all sat together at the playground, and when trouble brewed, they often responded as a group. A child would cry and one would comfort the child, another would dust off his clothes. Other research on West Indian caregivers notes that, in the islands, child care is typically shared among many and that women carry this practice with them to the United States. In New York, caregivers were observed to "watch and caution other women's charges as well as their own." Julia has long known that her nanny, Alreka, was friends with quite a few nannies just like herself—fiercely conscientious—and that their relationships enveloped the children under their collective care. Julia remembers the time one of Alreka's friends saw Pearson get picked up from school by a van that she didn't recognize. She was so alarmed that when she couldn't find Alreka to check out the situation, she called Julia at work to make sure that all was okay.

Whether it's the result of cultural tradition or simply a situation of friends looking after friends, strong nanny networks can be a wonderful benefit. Caregivers use it in apartment buildings where one nanny may watch the kids while another goes down to the basement to put in some laundry. In the park, a nanny will watch over her kids and another's while the other caregiver takes a charge to the bathroom. Or nanny friends will arrange to picnic or bus to a museum together. It's great when it works: Your nanny's happier, and your kids are doubly cared for.

Then there's the nanny grapevine. Nannies are human; many of them like to chat. And the talk can be exceedingly helpful to the caregiving equation. Best source of nannies, we find, are recommendations from good nannies. Whenever we have a friend looking, we always ask our nannies who they know who might be available. The nanny grapevine can also be a font of great general child info, supplementing your own. It can be tapped to see who likes what after-school activity (the nanny is often the one to pick up and drop off, so she sees whether the kid really enjoys it), what doctor has a good bedside manner, what new playground little Toddie might enjoy, or what bookstore has the best story hour.

CITYWISE WARNING !

There Are No Secrets

Remember, if your nanny knows a lot about you, a lot of other people will too if she's loose-lipped. Be nasty to your nanny and we guarantee you that not only will her friends hear about it but often their employers will as well (and if you are rude, it serves you right). Even when you didn't do anything wrong, caregiver chatter can be a problem. We heard of one woman who fired her nanny after some pretty questionable behavior. Unfortunately, the fired nanny was part of a very tight clique in her apartment building who, when the new nanny entered the scene, took every opportunity to bad-mouth the employer and make life difficult for the replacement. Fortunately, in this particular case, the replacement hung tough and said she wasn't interested in being part of that group anyway.

But before you get too excited about all the fringe benefits you're going to reap from your nanny's friends, consider the flip side—maybe your nanny hangs out with a bad group. Here's an all too common scene: nanny klatches sitting frozen on benches, gossiping, while the kids gambol all over the playground unsupervised. There was one story that captivated members of an Internet message board for days. A passerby happened across a group of nannies in a park whose charges were stuck in strollers a few feet away from them. One of the strollers, set on an incline, started to roll down the hill with a toddler seated helplessly inside. The passerby watched, expecting one of the caregivers to leap up and stop the runaway stroller but, after a few seconds of no action, she ran after the stroller, caught it, and pushed it back up to the group. A nanny, ostensibly in charge of the now-rescued child, stood up and grabbed the stroller handle with no thank you, no comment, nada. The good Samaritan passerby was so horrified by the whole incident that she went to the message board in an effort to find the toddler's mother to let her know how unsafe her child's care was.

We've seen this same scenario (without the rolling stroller) played out countless times in the playgrounds and parks where we live. Certainly, there's always an element of physical danger when a child's poorly supervised, but there're other impacts as well. We've seen nannies snap at a child who dared to interrupt their group confab, even refuse to help a child who needed help. Then there's the gossip itself; bad enough if it were just centered on some soap opera plot twist, but so much of it can revolve around complaining—about their jobs, their bosses, their charges.

Here's the general rule, and we really believe this: Good nannies hang out with good nannies, and the reverse is true too. That's something to be aware of when you hire someone and something to watch over as they work for you.

The Immigration Impact

Great thing about the city, that diversity. And just to make sure Brittany gets enough of a taste of people from different cultures, different socioeconomic backgrounds, and different religions, you're going to start her off *at birth* with exposure to someone whose life experience is going to be worlds apart from the one she'll likely enjoy. Didn't realize you were doing all that when you hired the nanny, did you?

Consider the fact that your caregiver is helping raise your child, may be in your home every day from morning to night, maybe even spends more time with your kids than you do. Don't you think it would be wise to understand where she's coming from? And if it's a different place than where you're from, don't you think that makes a difference? Of course, you do, but maybe you're brighter than we are because neither of us, nor any of our friends, really sat down and analyzed all the ways those economic, social, psychological, and linguistic differences could impact the employer-employee relationship or the kids.

Cultural Views on Child-Rearing

A little story. Friends of ours worried about their nanny because she didn't sit down on the floor to play with their little boy. Jasmine was perfectly pleasant in other respects, but she just wouldn't get down and dirty. No surprise, it wasn't too long before Jasmine and that family went their separate ways. Could this relationship have been saved? Who's to say, but we do know that in the West Indies, where Jasmine was from, grown women just don't sit on the floor; it's considered totally inappropriate behavior, so rolling around with a child would be even more undignified. Maybe Jasmine would never have changed her ways—or maybe she would have if she had understood how important interactive, from-the-ground-up play between caregiver and child was to the parents.

Want some other examples of child-rearing culture clashes just waiting to happen? Think about:

Discipline. While the trend in this country is to spare the rod, corporal punishment is still considered acceptable in many other countries. That doesn't mean your foreign-born nanny's going to swat your child; probably nothing of the kind. But it may mean she'll need some instruction on how you want discipline to be meted out, if at all. The right way to handle the discipline dilemma is to recognize that your nanny's instinct may be to handle it in some other way than you would; so instead of getting alarmed at the difference, recognize it and then explain how and why you want things handled.

Independence. Say you're big on encouraging your children to take care of themselves, but in your caregiver's country, independence in children is not encouraged. In most of Central America, for example, adults like to baby children, which is why you may find a Guatemalan nanny still bathing an 8-year-old-girl. If long-term coddling is not part of your plan, you've got some discussions in front of you.

Deportment. We all want polite kids, but the definition of good manners varies by culture. In St. Croix, children are not supposed to participate in adult conversations or make eye contact (it's considered challenging)—quite the opposite of the more interactive nature of most American families and the almost constant admonitions to kids to look people in the eye. St. Crucians also look askance at children who call adults by their first names, a not uncommon practice in this country. Your nanny may be the one who's mostly around when your kid is interacting with others—at preschool, in the park, at the deli—so make sure you're on the same page with how those interactions are conducted.

Health and medical. Diet and nutrition views can be one big bone of contention. In countries where food is less than plentiful, kids may be encouraged simply to eat, with little discussion of "eating right." And it may not occur to your caregiver that park hot dogs and pizzeria slices are not at the top of your food pyramid. Hey, they're convenient, inexpensive foods to buy; the kids like them. Who could criticize that? Well, maybe the parents who have no idea that Joe-Joe is dining at Ray's Pizza three times a week (so that's how he knows all the pizza places on the avenue!). Lyuba Konopasek, M.D., assistant professor of pediatrics at Weill Medical College, Cornell University, is on top of the urban obesity epidemic and the need to manage the eating habits of city kids who may not be as active as they could be. She was zealous about giving her two kids nutritious snacks but then found out their caregiver was feeding them candy. "It didn't occur to me," she said. And don't forget cures for the common cold or colic or diarrhea: Other countries have different medical traditions, including hefty doses of folk medicine. Some of this stuff may be great—it could make an herbalist out of you—but some of it is downright toxic for your tot (Caribbean "gripe water," a cherished remedy for colic, can contain alcohol; and the Dominican wonder drug litargario, used for foot fungus, burns, and body odor, is nearly 80 percent lead). And don't guess about your nanny's medical expertise. Maybe she's a stranger to Neosporin or the au courant treatment for a vomiting child. Check it out well before the fact.

Interaction. You might be a strong proponent of the virtues of talking and interacting with your kids, and certainly you would be supported and encouraged in your belief by American educators. But this is, in many ways, a relatively new (and maybe distinctly American) phenomenon. So don't assume your nanny is engaging in a running conversation with your child; that may not be an objective she's ever considered.

The Language Impact

Hiring a caregiver who's not fluent in English has a raft of implications, from the impact on the child's language skills to communications between the caregiver and you to interaction with the rest of your child's world. Have you really thought this through?

Bilingual babies. Let's start with the easy stuff: the linguistic impact. Having a caregiver speak to your child in another language can absolutely help him learn something about another tongue. But what, exactly, that is depends. We've heard friends' big talk about how their Spanish or Chinese nanny is teaching their children another language. "Chester's bilingual," they crow. Well maybe he is, maybe he's not.

If one or both of the parents speak the caregiver's language and speak it to the child as well, the opportunity for true bilingualism is immeasurably enhanced. However, if that language is not one you speak, relying on a caregiver to make your child bilingual is simply not going to work if all other aspects of his life are conducted in English. Consider one study of children 3 and under with Latina nannies. Although the nannies generally spoke in Spanish to the children, the children usually conversed in English or with gestures; the kids had some comprehension (receptive language) but little Spanish expression of their own. Those results are typical of the research in this area. Unless you find ways to reinforce and support the caregiver's language, and keep it going over a protracted period of time (like a lifetime), your child's claim to bilingualism will fall short.

Want to Solidify That Second Language?

Here are some tips:

- Whoever is speaking the non-English language to the child should try not to mix English and the other language in their conversations. Be consistent: It's one language or the other.
- Be prepared for some resistance to the other language as the child enters school. If all his friends speak English, he may be uninterested in speaking another language in front of them.
- Consider other ways to reinforce the second language. Find foreign language cartoons or videos (you *must* watch TV, my child); consider a bilingual school or an after-school language program; make frequent visits to areas of your city where that language is spoken; play music in that language; take trips to countries where that language is important.

The Effect on Communications. Beyond the caregiver's impact on your child's bilingual capabilities, and substantially more important than the quality of her native language skills, is her ability to communicate with you and other English speakers.

If you speak her language, you only have to worry about her external communications like routine doctor's appointments and medical situations. How will she tell the doctor what's wrong with the child or even answer his routine questions? Can she convey the doctor's comments to you? If she's the one who has to handle an emergency, does she know how to tell an ambulance driver which hospital to go to? Then there's your child's social calendar. Can she schedule playdates and are they only with people speaking her language? How about neighborhood field trips—can she read Clarie the signs about the animals at the zoo or the children's museum? And what about all that school stuff? Can she communicate enough with your child's teacher to tell her that he's a little tired today, or can the teacher successfully relay messages that he had a bad day or a good day or scratched someone or was scratched?

If you don't speak your nanny's language, the communication issues snowball. How to handle the constant changes in a child's day-to-day activities; that phone call warning her you're stuck in traffic—how will you get important information like this across? If your child seems sick, will the nanny be able to discuss his symptoms over the phone so you can decide whether he needs to go to the doctor? How do you give her constructive criticism? Gosh, how do you even interview her?

Whether you're dealing with an internal language barrier, an external one, or both, you need to make darn sure that your caregiver is equipped to handle emergencies, to expand your child's social horizons, to give you feedback, and to take yours. And you need to be prepared to take a more active role in the whole caregiving equation than you would if your nanny's English was excellent. That means being conscientious about creating and maintaining a consistent flow of communications between you and the caregiver. That means being meticulous about checking and double-checking her understanding of instructions. And that means, absolutely, rounding up a number of intermediaries—doormen, friends, children, office mates, neighbors—who can help in the translation process if language becomes an impediment.

Finally, you'll want to make sure that even if your caregiver is reticent to use English, that she's enthusiastic about interacting in her own language. That interaction between caregiver and child is hugely important in whatever language it occurs. And even if she can't read English, have her read books to your child in her own language—there are still plenty of benefits for your child (of course, you're still on the hook for reading out loud yourself).

THE CITY PARENT RULES
When Caregivers Are Not Fluent in English

Rule #1: Do a 411 on 911. Check to see that your city's 911 can handle your caregiver's language (and make sure she knows how and when to call and what to say).

Rule #2: Take charge of all things medical. First, arrange with your pediatrician to call you directly, during or after any doctor's visit that your caregiver is taking your child to (better yet, go yourself). And absolutely administer children's medicine yourself, or ask a neighbor to—unless you are certain your caregiver knows what's what, including exact dosage amounts, whether it's given with food, if it's refrigerated, etc.

Rule #3: Be proactive about playdates. Plan on taking a very active role in arranging your child's social life; otherwise, your child's playdates may end up limited to children with a parent or caregiver speaking your nanny's language.

Rule #4: Check in regularly at school. Take the initiative in communicating with the teachers in any classes or preschool your kids attend. If your caregiver's English is poor, you may lose the benefit of those quick exchanges at pickup or dropoff. Plan to call or exchange notes with the teacher on a regular basis.

Rule #5: Make a communications plan. Consider how you're going to interact with the caregiver if you're not fluent in the caregiver's language. How are you going to discourse with her about your child's activities? Maybe the caregiver has children or friends who speak English and who can act as a go-between. Some parents we know call such designated intermediaries with questions on a regular basis or send queries or schedule changes home in writing with the caregiver.

Expertise or Emotion

One of the tough things to reconcile about immigrant caregivers is that many of them are not trained in early childhood education—which, of course, goes against every erudite article we've read about the value of such training for people taking care of children. And, of course, it's totally inconsistent with many of the studies in day care that show quite dramatic correlations between the quality of a day care facility and the education levels of its staff. So why do we hesitate here?

Two reasons. First, if an in-home caregiver is what you want, you will substantially limit your choices if you insist on a lot of training, and you will, most likely, increase the salary you'll have to pay. That's a market fact, and it may not be one you can tolerate financially or otherwise. Second, both of us share a strong belief that when it comes to one-on-one caregiving, emotion trumps training—all else being equal. Of course, we are *extremely* fortunate, immensely *blessed* to have found caregivers who adore our children and who take their child care responsibilities incredibly seriously. And while neither Alreka nor Rita had received formal child care education, they had caregiving experience. At the end of the day, we, and others like us, made the decision that we were entirely capable of handling developmental issues or steps as they arose (toilet training, age-appropriate games, teaching sharing, la la, la, la, la) with the help and support of our caregivers; but we *could not do* without the emotional content those women were willing to bring to their child-caring duties.

Our instincts are not completely without academic support. A seminal study on cognitive development and young children by the Institute of Medicine discusses the importance of "emotionally invested, available" caregiving. It asserts that children who don't have that emotional connection, "even in the presence of adequate physical care and cognitive stimulation develop an array of developmental deficits that may endure over time." We just knew we were right.

Of course, we were also aware that our kids would be in supplemental classes as soon as they could benefit (which for us meant 9 months) and then nursery and preschool, so there were plenty of formally trained individuals in on the act. And, finally, we'd seen a couple of these more highly trained in-home caregivers in action, and they'd left us cold.

If this is the way you go, you will definitely need to take on the responsibility of providing some of that missing child care training. It's great that you're up on the latest child-rearing theory, but if it's so important to you, shouldn't it be to your caregiver as well? So keep those discussions going—not just on the kids, what they're doing, and what their teachers say, but also on any views you're developing on child-rearing. And check out classes and seminars on child development offered by local Ys and parent associations that your caregiver could attend. Often, such seminars provide child care or are at night.

A Little Understanding Goes a Long Way

In any locale, the relationship between caregiver and employer is a difficult one to navigate. On the one hand, it's a commercial transaction; on the other, it's about the most intimate, personal relationship you can have. That's just for starters, though, because in the city, you also throw into the mix the fact that so many of these caregivers are far from home and their families (in one city, as many as 40 percent of domestic worker mothers have left at least one child behind), and they are often new to the culture and language, which imposes an emotional burden on your relationship that's like nothing you've ever experienced.

Don't get us wrong; these caregivers clearly work by choice (although every year, we read new stories of virtually enslaved immigrant caregivers). What they don't choose, however, is to be treated as if they lacked brains because their English is a little broken or a little less than human by employers who really would rather not know any of the personal details of their lives (you know, that would just complicate things). We see this all the time—employers who have no clue about their nanny's family situation, don't know when their birthday is, don't know if they have friends, don't know where they go on weekends. And then there are the children who treat the caregiver with the same utter lack of respect that their parents do. We've seen many ugly incidents with petite little things barking commands, even screaming invectives at their nannies. The problem is so endemic that one high-powered city private school actually confronted parents with what it felt was unacceptably rude behavior on the part of their kids.

So a little humanity, please. We're not asking you to loosen your performance standards or default on your oversight responsibilities. Your kids are too important for that. But we do believe you should treat your caregiver with a normal amount of respect *and* a modicum of compassion for the circumstances of her life. And remember, your children are watching. They will be learning some early, probably lasting lessons from how you interact with the person who takes care of them. What lessons will those be?

Finding and Hiring a City Caregiver

Of course, it's one thing to prepare yourself to be a good boss, but it's quite another to actually identify great candidates, cull the "one" who will make your children *and* you happy, and then set her up for that happily-ever-after arrangement you hope to have. One of the most important decisions you're going to have to make concerns money and it's one you'll have to make early since what you pay will, in large part, determine how you will do your search and what you can expect to find at the end of it.

What's It Going to Cost You?

As we've said, there are a lot of caregiver candidates out there, a lot of places to find them, and an enormous range of salaries. Among our own acquaintances, gross compensation for nannies ranges from $250 to over $1,000 a week—and there are good caregivers and bad caregivers at either end of the scale.

What accounts for the pay differential? A few things. For one, there are certainly to-be-expected regional differences in compensation. In the heyday of Silicon Valley millionaires, San Fran nannies were pulling in $15 to $17 an hour, while their Kansas City counterparts were getting a more modest $7 to $10. Nannies making $400 a week in Boston can supposedly move to Los Angeles for an instant salary bump up to $600 a week.

How you find your nanny may also account for some significant salary differences. Really cheap wages tend to go to word-of-mouth hires, while agency hires typically get top dollar. Travel the agency route in the City of Angels, for instance, and according to one agency owner, you'll pay $500 to $750 a week for a nanny with good English skills, a car, and papers. At the bottom of their totem pole, they can get you someone for $150 to $250 weekly but no papers, no car, and little English.

As a matter of record, the biggest salary swings do center around documentation and training—or lack thereof. In Los Angeles, live-in undocumented caregivers can earn less than $1 an hour for working 14-hour days, 100-hour weeks. (Hey, that can't be legal! Maybe not, but neither are "they," goes the thinking— again an ugly impact of their untenable status here.)

Generally, caregivers who don't have work papers work for less, sometimes for next to nothing. Conversely, the more actual training a "legal" nanny has—college degree, nanny school, early childhood education degree—the higher the price. We saw one agency's primer on compensation differences for its caregiver candidates, all of whom are prescreened for their ability to work legally. For a basic nanny (child care, light housekeeping), expect to pay $15–$25 an hour (for the 8–6 P.M., 50-hour week, that's $750 a week, at the *low* end). Hire a *governess* to teach and nanny, and you'll be shelling out up to $35 an hour. Or you could try and save a little money by hiring a live-in; there the agency says you'd be paying $2,500 a month (at the low end, of course).

One axiom: The range of duties narrows as you go up the price ladder. At the lower rungs, you'll find nannies who care for the kids and cook and clean for the whole family. Go up a little higher and you'll lose the housecleaning. At the top, you'll find that nanny duties will not even include cleaning up after the kids or doing their laundry—nope, those elite employees are more like governesses than the caregivers you typically see hanging out in the park.

On the Books, Off the Books

Whether you will insist on handling that caregiving situation "legally" is a little tricky in cities where so much domestic employment is fulfilled by people without papers. For the employer, off the books is certainly cheaper, but then there are other complications: Your caregiver will have difficulty traveling outside the country, getting health care, even setting up bank accounts, and won't build up any Social Security benefits; you're technically violating immigration laws if you hire someone who's not in this country legally; and you can't file for child care tax benefits. But, for sure, the biggest issue is going to be taxes.

The rules are pretty simple. Federal and state tax laws require you to pay taxes on any household employee, unless they meet very specific exemptions. If you don't, and the IRS finds out, you'll be liable for back taxes, interest, and penalty (and because nonpayment of nanny taxes is technically tax fraud, your tax return stays open forever for purposes of any IRS investigation). Not that the IRS is likely to come after you for this (unless, apparently, you have some interest in political office), and in most cases, you and your employee will never look back. But there can be complications. Heaven forbid your employee is injured on the job and you haven't paid workers' comp (as happened to friends of ours). You could be in for some unpleasant times. Or, let's say, you fire your employee. We're seeing more and more cases of terminated employees popping up again, sometimes with their lawyers, threatening to expose an employer's failure to pay taxes unless more generous severance is forthcoming.

Going on the books is a lot easier than many people realize. Curiously (or maybe not; they do like to collect taxes), the IRS doesn't care if your employee is illegal. In fact, they have a special form, W-7, for illegal aliens who need an Individual Tax ID No. (ITIN), which serves as the caregiver's Social Security

Going on the Books

If you want to do things right, you need to be in compliance with immigration laws, tax laws, and workers' comp laws within your state. If you have an accountant, you can start there; otherwise, you have a few rounds to make:

1. Go to the Immigration and Naturalization Service, which has a booklet for employers dealing with immigration situations, including the pretty much mandatory completion of form I-9. You can get the booklet off the Web at http://uscis.gov/graphics/lawsregs/handbook/hand_emp.pdf.
2. Get clear on your federal tax obligations by calling a local IRS office and requesting IRS Publication 926 (Household Employer's Tax Guide), visiting the IRS Web site www.irs.gov, or calling (800) 829-1040 (IRS tax hotline).
3. Check with your state's department of taxation for state tax requirements; they may also want notification of any new employee. New York, for example, wants you to let them know within 20 days of any new hiring.
4. Call your state's insurance department to see if you have to pay workers' compensation and/or state disability insurance. If you do, they'll help you get set up for payments.

number for the purposes of both of you paying taxes. The IRS is forbidden to share this information with the INS, so supposedly you can square with the IRS without the risk of having your nanny deported. The paperwork is a drag, sure, but a relatively mild one. And the dollar cost to the employer? Maybe an additional 10 percent.

Ready to go on the books? One slight problem. Many city caregivers don't want to deal with taxes. Either they're utterly afraid of the INS getting wind of them, or they figure they're not going to be in this country permanently so why pay for the benefits, or they simply can't afford to have taxes taken out (the increase may not be so big for you, but it's probably a 20 to 30 percent reduction in their take-home pay). Your decision on taxes will make a significant difference in the size of your candidate pool, so be prepared to search a little harder if you plan to stay square with the IRS.

Culling Candidates

When you need to find a caregiver, you've got two choices: the agency route or do-it-yourself.

The agency route: Agencies are probably the least-used way to find a caregiver—maybe as little as 10 percent, according to one study. Most often, agencies are used for either the very high-end nanny hires or for live-in housekeepers.

If the agency concept is something you cotton to, here's a typical process. Your contact with the agency will be over the phone (unless you're looking to pay a lot of money or you have some star power yourself). You will undoubtedly have to sign some form agreeing to the agency's terms of payment should they find you an employee. You'll also have to fill out a form giving your specifications for the employee. The agency will search its files to match your criteria: whether you want to pay on the books or off, hours (except for live-in jobs, where potential employers are notorious for underestimating the actual hours their live-in will be working), personality, driver's license requirement. The agency will come up with a few candidates for whom it will, presumably, check references, and candidates that qualify will be sent to you for interviews. When you actually select a candidate, that's called a "placement." At that time, you'll get a written contract with a guarantee period (typically 90 days), during which time if you don't like the hire, you can get a replacement without paying a new fee.

Agency fees can vary from as much as 10 percent of the annual salary to a mid-range fee of maybe 1 month's salary to a low-end flat fee of something like $200. What are you getting for your money? "Elite" agencies claim to do rigorous screening of candidates, including medical and psychological exams, reference checks, and criminal checks (but usually only for the state in which you reside; you'd need to hire a private investigator to do more). They typically claim to have a more professional potential employee pool, with their candidates viewing child care as a career. They'll give you contracts to use with your nannies, which can be a great idea because they protect both employer and employee from misunderstandings by laying out in black and white things such as duties, vacation time, paid holidays, and insurance benefits.

We've heard a lot of agency horror stories, though, so if you want to go this route, be very, very careful of which agency you use.

- Big names or splashy ads are no guarantee of quality. Nothing surpasses personal experience, so get multiple references from people who've had successful placement experiences, ideally with the type of caregiver you are seeking.
- When you interview the agency, ask them in detail about their vetting process, particularly how they spot a phony reference—even ask to see their reference check sheets (they should be preformatted with a list of questions).
- Make sure the agency is bonded, has appropriate business licenses, and maybe is a member of a national nanny group like the International Nanny Association, which has some level of screening for membership.

Remember, just because you use an agency doesn't mean you have a guarantee of safety or quality. So for any candidate presented to you, ask for a copy of the investigative report, the references (which they may be reluctant to give you, but you can always ask), and, if the candidate is represented as being legal here, the supporting documentation.

CITYWISE WARNING

How Much Does Your Agency Really Know about the Nanny?

Interestingly, in the case of the really pricey hires, no one from the agency may ever actually meet your nanny because they're recruiting nannies from all over the place (in Los Angeles, they'll recruit in Boston).

The D-I-Y route: If you've got the time (and what better reason to make time than finding your child's caregiver), the city is a great place to do it all yourself. You have all the advantages of density at your fingertips. There are lots of places to look and people to get advice from. A survey from the Berkeley Parents Network in Oakland/San Francisco gives what we believe is a pretty typical breakdown of where you're going to find your caregiver: among the Berkeley parents, 50 percent found theirs through a friend or other

Mad for the Manny

So what if they only exist in tiny numbers. The newest status symbol among city parents with boys is the male nanny. Single moms, parents who travel, and moms and dads who want their boys to grow up rough and tough, not part of the urban effete, are all seeking a little testosterone in their child care. And the job can be very appealing to young men who find that, in good times, the pay is better than teaching at private schools and perfect if they just want to make some money during a year off. The experience is also not all bad for someone who wants to specialize in child psychology or education. What's a little different about the "manny" is you're less likely to find him cooking and cleaning; more likely, he'll be putting the hammer down on homework. It's a small trend that will probably stay small because of parents' fear of child abuse (which is disproportionately at the hands of men). But for some families, it really fits the bill.

Source: Harriet Barovick, "Super Mannies: They Cook, They Nurture; Who Says Being a Nanny Is Just for Women?" *Time*, March 4, 2002.

Berkeley parents, 18 percent had "other" sources, 13 percent were successful with advertising, just under 11 percent found care through a child care resource and referral agency (the much-loved Bananas organization), and 8 percent used agencies.

Paid ads: The best thing about placing an ad in a city is the volume of responses: You will get more than you ever dreamed. The negative, of course, is that you'll have to wade through them all, and the sheer magnitude of that task may cause you to shut down too early.

Most commonly, parents place ads in their local ethnic papers—*Polish Daily News* and *La Raza* in Chicago, the *Irish Immigrant* in Boston, and *Irish Echo* in NYC. You're not, by the way, just going to get respondents of that paper's ethnicity; they're well-known vehicles for domestic help placement, so they attract a lot of interest from all nationalities. Some tips:

1. Buy a copy of the paper(s) you're considering before you place an ad, so you can see what type of person it caters to and also get a feel for what you may want to say in an ad.
2. Don't use your home address in the ad. Too much information. Some people set up a temporary post office box to get responses. Or, if they go the phone or

e-mail route, they set up separate voice-mail boxes or temporary e-mail IDs to compartmentalize the nanny responses from the rest of the family business.

THE CITY PARENT RULES
Networking for Nannies

Rule #1: Talk to every parent you know, not just ones with caregivers. Even parents who use another type of care, or whose kids have outgrown caregivers, can still be in that great parent loop. Their kids' friends may have nannies they're ready to give up or their nannies may know someone. Caveat emptor: A nanny's recommendation has to be taken in context. We've heard of people finding nannies through the supposedly "fabulous," but somewhat new, caregiver of one of their friends, only to find that their nanny *and* that other fabulous caregiver revealed some pretty substantial flaws over time. What's key is the strength and length of relationships. Nannies who've worked a long time for one family have more credibility in our book than someone who's only worked for a friend for a year. Also, don't assume anything about the strength of the tie between the nanny and the person she's recommending. No ill will intended, but sometimes recommendations are made on a rather casual basis. Just check out how long and on what basis everyone's known each other.

Rule #2: Talk to all the good nannies yourself. If you don't know any, hang around a few playgrounds; the good ones stand out. We are such strong believers in the power of the "good" nanny network that a solid recommendation from a great nanny would be our first choice for finding good care.

Rule #3: Find child-centric bulletin boards on which you can post an ad (this is different than paid-for advertising). The best are at preschools and pediatrician offices, but independent retailers like local bookstores and coffee shops, which are really integrated with the community, often have boards, too. Additionally, most cities will have parent-oriented organizations like the Parents Place in San Francisco, run by Jewish and Family Children's Services, that will allow you to post an ad.

Rule #4: Check out the Net. A recent development, Internet city-focused boards *work* because there are so many people posting now, you can actually do some business. We love Craig's List, formed in 1995 by San Francisco programmer Craig Newmark (yes, there really is a Craig) as an e-mail list for local events. It has since morphed as *the* place for Gen Xers to find a job, a date, or a nanny in 17 cities. (Peruse the boards a little, and you'll actually find so much more from the million visitors a month—there's a heavy barter business going on, with people trading old pants for concert tickets, etc., etc.) It's a little narrow from the caregiving perspective because a pretty significant number of nannies don't frequent the Internet, but there's still a fair selection, augmented by employers who may post on behalf of their nannies. And if you're looking for part-time help, *this* is where you'll find that moonlighting preschool teacher. It's definitely worth a look, at www.craigslist.org.

Rule #5: Go to school. Colleges have begun to allow outsiders to reach their students through online job postings. Now, college kids are not always the most reliable of employees, and they usually want part-time work, but we do know people who rave about them. Call your local college and ask for their student career services or job placement office to get the details.

The Interview

You can find a lot of great articles on hiring caregivers on the Internet and in parent newspapers. Get a book if you're really flummoxed; we like *The Nanny Book: The Smart Parent's Guide to Hiring, Firing, and Every Sticky Situation in Between*, by Susan Carlton and Coco Myers. But just in case they don't give you that urban perspective (and they usually won't), read on for some city-specific questions for your interview.

THE CITY DIFFERENCE:
Questions for the Caregiver

1. How comfortable is the candidate with getting around the city? If your child has to be taken to doctors or school or classes that aren't within walking distance, ask what public transportation they would use. Don't be confrontational; you want to give them a chance to say they don't know. Then it'll be up to you to judge how big a deal it will be to teach them.

2. Ask about their daily commute. City caregivers rarely live in the neighborhoods of their employers, and 1- to 1½-hour commutes can be typical. If you require

long hours too, that may be too much to expect anyone to handle, however willing. And if they will be traveling home in the dark, you might want to see how safe their commute home will be.

3. Get a grip on their propensity for walking. Tell them you're big on pedestrian activities (no headphones).

4. Ask about their own upbringing, what they did for fun, how they were disciplined, what kind of manners kids were supposed to have—not to make value judgments, but you might tease out some potential conflicts in child-raising ideas that you'll have to address.

5. Of course, ask about their experience and get specific: names and ages of children, years worked at the last job or jobs, why the job ended. You'll need this information when you're talking to their references to make sure the reference isn't a setup.

6. Ask how comfortable the candidate is with setting up playdates. This may seem a little premature if your Nathaniel is only 3 months old, but playdates are the rule in most cities; it's not like suburbs where children run outside to play with the neighborhood kids. And if you're working, you need to make sure your nanny can handle the social calendar or else you will find your child is a little short on the friend front.

7. If the candidate doesn't speak English well, and you don't speak her language, we presume you have someone translating during the interview. Don't stint on questions just because of the awkwardness of having to deal with an intermediary. And, of course, make sure you discuss how the translation process is going to work on an ongoing basis should you hire her.

One important caveat about the interview, especially if you are talking to someone who's from another country: How the person "performs" in the interview may not be reflective of the person. Some people will have had no experience in an interview situation and may find it intimidating; others may have been brought up to be respectfully polite in such situations, which unfairly may appear at odds with the interactive, outgoing personality you're seeking; and still others may just not be that comfortable in English. Keep some perspective on this part of your evaluation. It may be the least telling component.

After the Interview: Checking It All Out

If a candidate survives the interview, you'll of course check references and may want to do some background checks. And since you're not living in Green Acres, where employer and employee have no more than 3 degrees of separation, every piece of information that can be validated becomes highly important. Reference scams are

The TrustLine Story

California's very popular TrustLine caregiver database was formed by an anguished mother whose daughter was abused by a caregiver who was eventually convicted of felony child abuse but not barred from being a caregiver again. TrustLine is a registry of caregivers and caregiver candidates whose fingerprints have survived a scan against its records database, an amalgamation of three nonpublic databases including the FBI Criminal History System. It costs $124 to process a caregiver; caregivers are only registered if they "clear," of course. All California employment agencies must run candidates they place through TrustLine. A potential employer calls TrustLine to get the individual's TrustLine status. If the employee has never registered, the employer can volunteer to pay the fee, assuming the potential employee is willing to provide fingerprints.

Is it effective? Since the database was created in 1993, more than 4,000 potential caregivers have been denied clearance—including convicted murderers and people with 10- to 15-page rap sheets, all of whom were seeking to be employed as caregivers.

Sources: Melissa Healy, "Lawmakers Respond to a Mother's Mission," *Los Angeles Times*, September 26, 1999; Vicki Haddock, "TrustLine: New Way to Check Out Babysitters," *Hearst Examiner*, November 16, 1997.

---

not uncommon in cities. The best way to sniff them out is to concentrate on the facts: Ask about names, ages of children, dates of employment, compensation, holidays, and reasons for termination to make sure that the information from the candidate and the proffered reference jive.

Other background checks—including criminal, driving, credit, and civil proceeding records—are becoming increasingly popular, but if you're hiring someone without a Social Security number, a lot of the normal methods will turn up zip. Still, if all you know about someone is their phone number, it would seem moderately intelligent to find out a little more about them. For not a lot of money, you can hire a private detective who can check past employment, court records, and past addresses (including overseas). To find a reputable investigator, check with any attorneys you know or the National Association of Legal Investigators (www.nalionline.org), which will provide you with member investigators in your area. If you don't want the extra expense, you can do *some* legwork yourself by calling current and old landlords, employers, and all references. If your potential hire won't provide these names, that should tell you something. Criminal record checking is going to be more difficult; you'll have to visit courthouses everywhere the candidate lived, so maybe that's when you'd bring in a pro. Finally, more and more employers are insisting their nannies undergo physicals (at the employer's expense, of course) including testing for TB and HIV. Some people are offended by this, but we think the request is legitimate; if you explain it as a natural precaution for any parent to take, it shouldn't be a deal killer.

Spying on Your Nanny

We never thought we'd feel this way, but after due consideration, we now can see the benefits of nannycams. What changed our minds? (After all, neither of us ever used one.) It all started when we talked to Naomi Siegel, a Manhattan-based family therapist, who told us that she recommends a nannycam to all her clients. It's not physical child abuse that she's so concerned about, it's the under-performing nannies—the daytime talk show watchers who plop their charges in a crib or playpen for hours; the nannies who can't be bothered to interact with their charges unless there's a parent watching; the caregivers who are sweet as pie until they're alone with the children and then they curse and call them names if disturbed.

How would you know if your nanny fits into one of those categories? Rely on your 2-year-old to tell you? Hmmm, we thought, that might be more of a problem than we'd realized, remembering all the suboptimal care that had occurred within our sights—at playgrounds and in parks where inattentive or disinterested caregivers allowed children in their care

to stumble into dangerous or naughty situations, or kept kids harnessed in strollers for ungodly amounts of time, or yakked on their cell phones while the kids sucked mindlessly on pacifiers or candy. The parents in these situations would certainly be alarmed if they saw what we saw, and betcha bottom dollar, nannycams in their apartments would turn up much of the same behavior.

Pressing the question a little further, we found many, many stories on Internet boards of people who installed nannycams, usually because some aspect of the caregiver's deportment had aroused their concern; almost inevitably, the nannycam proved their fears were justified, often stunningly so. For every comforting story where the nanny actually turned out to be fine, there were at least 10 bad ones. Now this data wouldn't be good enough to stand up in court, but it confirms our view that there are plenty of caregiving cases where what parents think is going on is a far cry from the truth. And it begs the question: Why wait till something gets your attention to in-

THE CITY PARENT RULES
Setting Your Caregiver Up Right

Rule #1: Analyze autonomy. Your caregiver is going to have a lot of decision-making power whether you want her to or not, so lay out the guidelines beforehand. If you plan on giving your caregiver each day's travel plans (what playgrounds, what playdates, where to get food, what errands to do or not do), then establish that fact

stall the camera? By then, some damage may have been done. If you're trying to protect your child, why wouldn't you use the camera from the start?

Is there a downside? Well, if your caregiver finds out that you've been spying on her, she may be furious at the lack of trust and the subterfuge on your part. That'd probably be our reaction, too. Or she acquiesces, but your relationship is irreparably tainted—an unhappy occurrence for sure. Another risk is legal: Capture audio without your nanny's knowledge, or put a cam in an obviously private place like a bathroom, and you'll be breaking the law. And finally, some experts think nannycams lull parents into security. Just because you don't see anything untoward in that room on that day doesn't mean everything's fine.

Our advice: If your nanny is going to be on her own for long periods of time, and neither you nor a close friend have had sustained exposure to her work habits, don't take the risk. Tell any potential hire that you will be using a nannycam—no reflection on her (blame it on us or Naomi

Siegel), but it's just the precaution of a careful parent until you get to know each other. There are some who will refuse to work under such circumstances, but maybe that's a good thing for you.

A couple of pointers: You can spend just over $100 to get a camera that connects to your VCR via cables, or go for much pricier cameras that are built in to clock radios, teddy bears, even potted plants and can transmit live to your computer, even your cell phone if you want. You will need to evaluate the risks of any wireless setup, however, since a popular new criminal activity is to intercept nannycam signals from remote sites up to a quarter of a mile away. We have no idea what they're doing with this "power," except creeping us out. Finally, remember to maintain some reasonable perspective on whatever you see; no one's perfect (think what would be captured if someone trained a nanny cam on you).

Sources: Sue Shellenbarger, "Skeptical Bosses Spy on In-Home Babysitters," *Wall Street Journal*, www.careerjournal.com/columnists/workfamily/20030509-workfamily.html; John Schwartz, "Nanny-Cam May Leave a Home Exposed," *New York Times*, April 14, 2002.

up front. We warn you, a lot of people start out that way and gradually fall out of the habit; it's a lot of work. A better solution, we find, is to establish basic rules for getting around (what to do, what not to do), but let the caregiver have the discretion to establish and change plans. That doesn't obviate the need for communication. A quick word on the plans for the day either in the morning or the night before, with a phone call alerting us to any change in plans, is mandatory in our homes. (And after 9/11, we became demons about knowing where our kids were at almost all times.)

While we're on the subject, this is a great time to emphasize to your nanny how excited you are to be bringing up your child in a city and how hopeful you are that she'll help your child take advantage of those wonderful urban offerings—which means trying different playgrounds, venturing to the museum every now and then, checking out the bookstore story hours, etc. She may think you're a little cracked, but eventually she'll get the idea; and if she's half as good as you think she is, she'll begin to take on the task of finding new adventures with relish.

Finally, you need to decide up front whether personal errands are okay on your time. The long hours caregivers spend working and in transit to the job don't give them much time of their own, so we think banning all errands is a bit harsh. But you may want to lay out what you consider acceptable (going to the bank, filling a prescription, picking up a few things at the drugstore) and what is not (clothes shopping, although we do know some people who allow their caregivers to shop, reasoning that they do it when the child is sleeping in the stroller).

Rule #2: Provide the two must-haves. Petty cash and a cell phone. Both of these should be standard issue for city nannies. Regarding petty cash, nannies are out a lot with your kids, and they shouldn't have to reach into their own pockets for bus fare or lunch money. Give them a little pot of cash (and if your situation demands taxis, you're going to need to leave more). It's absolutely fine to ask for documentation on where the money goes, but we don't think it's right for your caregiver, who's probably not exactly rolling in dough, to have to front the cash for caring for your child. If you're not sure what the amount should be, talk to your nanny and work it out together. We suggest having a week's worth of out-of-pocket expenses covered, and you can settle up at the end of the week. If your nanny takes care of a lot of purchases for you—maybe she gets the kids sneakers or does the grocery shopping—then petty cash is not going to be sufficient. Consider getting her a credit card tied to yours; maybe this isn't a great idea the first week out, but over the long haul, it really makes life easier.

Concerning the cell phone, if your nanny already has one, then you're lucky. If she doesn't, you should spring for one for her. It's a great communication device between parent and caregiver. Explain the terms of use. If you want to charge her for personal calls, that's fine and fair.

Rule #3: Talk about transportation. If your nanny will be driving young Cedric in her own car, you need to be absolutely firm about having an appropriate car seat. Some people buy one for the nanny's car, figuring it's more likely to be used if it's already installed. And make sure your nanny sets a good example and always uses a seatbelt herself.

If Nanny and Cedric will be taking public transportation, you need to explain what is okay and what is not. (Julia had an acquaintance who was so nervous about public transportation in New York that for the first year of her daughter's life, the little girl wasn't allowed to go anywhere that didn't involve a stroller.) Maybe you don't like certain subway routes at certain times of day; maybe you don't want your child in taxis (or maybe you do, in which case, you need to provide appropriate portable restraint devices). And make sure your caregiver takes the advice of Barbara Boisi, safety expert for the Parents League of New York: Caregivers should always sit near the front of the bus or in the car where the subway driver is sitting; these spots tend to be a little more protected from "incidents." In addition, if your caregiver is with your child and there is bad action developing (which can be very typical in cities in the afternoon when schools get off) she should know enough to get off at the next stop and catch another car or bus. Reducing the risk of having your child scared or actually being caught up in some melee is easily worth a few minutes' waiting time. Also, if your nanny is new to the area and will be expected to get Cedric to a doctor's appointment, you may want to tell your caregiver how much time to allow for transit between home and the doctor's office.

Finally, be sure and tell your nanny how it's good for the health of everyone concerned if Cedric walks as much as possible.

Rule #4: Play it safe with safety. You need to discuss absolutely every aspect of our safety concerns with your caregiver, including fire emergency procedures, emergency room choices and how to direct an ambulance; playground safety (which playgrounds, which equipment, which times); the absolute necessity of hand-washing; safe walking procedures (with an addendum for the nanny: no headphones or personal conversations while walking with your child); dealing with the elevator (this is pretty minor, but let her know how you think little Miranda should behave on the lift: no jumping, stay away from the door, no pushing all the buttons, no pushing the call button 12 times); other emergency evacuation info (if your child's preschool has a plan, your nanny needs to know, as do you); if there's some scary alert, which adult will be responsible for getting what kid, etc.

Rule #5: Get a grip on socializing. We've talked about the pros and the cons of nanny klatches. If your nanny has friends she can see frequently during her job, it stands to reason she will be a much happier person (you won't catch her complaining about the isolation that sometimes plagues suburban caregivers). Before you even have a clue as to the nature of her friends, you need to think through your feelings on the nature of those contacts. One woman complained that her nanny would always take her daughter out to lunch with a bunch of apparently better-heeled caregivers, and the meal bills were killing her. Forget about the bill: Why is lunching in a restaurant every few days appropriate for the child? And where were all the children—latched in their strollers? Another found that her apartment had become party central; while it wasn't like the nannies were swilling kegs of beer, Mom's grocery bill was climbing, and she found out she was feeding several other nannies lunch on a regular basis.

Now, you don't want to hammer your caregiver with a lot of prohibitions of things she may never have even considered. Take a positive approach and tell her you hope she makes friends in the neighborhood (caring for kids the same age as yours, ideally) and maybe drop a few hints about the types of social behavior you abhor (number one being kids sitting around in circles, strapped in their strollers, while nannies chat). You also need to make sure that she's venturing outside her circle for playdates for your child. We've seen nannies get awfully comfortable spending time with their friends when maybe the kids are not the best of friends— or maybe the kids love each other to death, but a little variety is nice too, particularly as the kids get older. If you don't mind her being the hostess with the mostest, let her know that, but tell her you'll maybe want the other nannies to bring their lunches. Finally, if you sense your nanny is getting into a rut, you can take a little action. Schedule a few playdates yourself, or ask your nanny to go to a new playground (then follow up to make sure it's done).

Ultimately, you will need to get to know your nanny's friends too because often care is shared. Certainly it should matter to you who's taking over Natasha's care, no matter how temporarily.

Rule #6: Be frank about food. It's not that we're health nuts, it's just that the practice of caregivers feeding the kids far more junk food than parents ever imagined is pretty widespread. Much of it is innocent enough: Kids like candy and junk food and fast food meals that come with toys, and caregivers like to give kids treats. That's one reason. But it's also a pacifier. "Duncan, if you leave the playdate now without kicking a hole in the wall, I'll get you ice cream." And it's a result of poor planning. Far from home, the playground was such fun, who knew we went past lunchtime? We'll just get pizza again. (We swear, in New York, some kids have pizza 12 meals a week; long-term effects still under evaluation.)

And whatever the caregiver's junk food tendencies, they're probably doubled by the parents. After all, we like to give treats too (and we aren't immune to the pacification and last-minute meal-planning virtues of junk foods). But you can't double up here; city kids are humongous and growing. Probably not yours, of course, but, just in case, you need to keep the junk food at a reasonable level, so set some firm rules. Keep in mind though, we're not talking about an absolute prohibition on caregiver junk food purchases unless you're prepared to take the same vow of abstinence. Those kinds of double standards wreak havoc on employee morale.

Rule #7: Be firm about no-nos. There are some relatively common city caregivers' behaviors that we would just dispense with up front.

- Leaving a child alone in an apartment. "What!?" you cry. "That's horrible!" It's certainly a bad, bad thing to do, but it happens more than you think and not for malicious reasons. A big one is laundry. If your caregiver has clothes washing in the basement laundry room, it's really tempting sometimes for her to run down and throw a load in while Cecily's napping. Address it and forbid it. Then there's smoking: If your caregiver smokes and you don't, you're going to have to deal with her habit, particularly if you live in an apartment. We know one caregiver who, having told her employer she was a nonsmoker, felt she'd be busted if she smoked in the apartment. Her solution was to step outside to the back freight staircase while she had her puffs, leaving the baby alone inside (always asleep in his crib, she said, but who knows).
- No telephone for social chats, no TV watching (unless they're approved kids' shows).
- Distractions while strolling: no headsets, no phone time. Sure this seems harmless enough when your caregiver's perambulating with a sleeping infant, but bad habits form and get worse. Caregiving is about focusing on the child, not a girlfriend's bad date or the latest hot song.
- Strollers off the curb. This should have been part of your transportation lecture, but we literally see this every day—caregivers waiting to cross a street: they're on the curb, the stroller's on the street. No, no, no, no, no.

Rule #8: Check up and check in. Since your caregiver will often be out of the house, you need to have some way of knowing what your child is doing. One nannycam purchaser found out that when her nanny told her she and the child had been at the playground all day (where everyone had a gay old time), in reality, they'd never left the house (trust us, only the nanny had a good time inside). Subterfuge like that becomes a little harder when constant communication is required. Here's what you can do to keep tabs on what's really going on:

- Make a chart for your nanny to fill out daily—maybe in 2-hour increments— that she can use to quickly jot down a couple of words about what transpired in those hours. It's not a huge chore, but it will give you a much better handle on Junior's day (plus, it does become increasingly difficult to cover up falsehoods).

- If a chart is too much work, or maybe in conjunction with the chart, set aside 10 minutes to talk about the day's events with your caregiver. Now the difficult aspect of this system is in holding to it without abusing your nanny's time, which means you need to get there before she's officially off the clock.
- Use that city density to your advantage. Enlist friends and neighbors to check in on the doings of your new caregiver. One friend we know asked her mother to "spy on" her nanny and her daughter at the park and report back on how the nanny was playing with the little girl. Our friend was able to take the information and gently make suggestions about how to play even better, and the nanny was none the wiser. We know more than one working parent who's asked someone with more flexibility to amble over to the playground on occasion to see how the caregiver was handling her duties. Maybe you have a close relationship with a doorman or a neighbor or another nanny who you can ask to stop by when you're not around—at least let them know that you want to be alerted if they see something about your caregiver that is problematic or worse.

Rule #9: Start your nanny off right. Your new caregiver deserves a full and thorough orientation—not just a list of the rules of course, but an introduction to lots of helpful things that will get her off to a good start. Ideally spend a half day, even a full day with her just to show her the ropes. Introduce her to your neighbors, tradespeople, parents of your child's friends, or anyone in your circle she's liable to often see. Take her around your neighborhood and show her any stores she'll be going to on your behalf (have a heart, help her find her closest bank branch and show her where she can pick up sundries) and, of course, all the kid hotspots—the playgrounds, museums, the local library branch, and bookstores. If she's new to public transportation, show her how to pay for her fare or get tokens or fare cards, and get her maps of the local transit system. And since you're going to be telling her about the particulars of your child's care (food preferences, naptimes, medicines, etc., etc., etc.), you may want to think about writing all this down. How much can one person absorb, anyway?

If, by the way, your nanny is from a different country, you want to take our earlier section on the impacts of immigration and language very seriously. That doesn't mean you need to discuss every little aspect with your caregiver now, but you should keep some of the differences top of mind as you go through your instructions, paying particular attention to the cultural differences in child-rearing and the impacts of bilingualism. It may cause you to cast your instructions a little differently.

PART TWO

OUT AND ABOUT

CHAPTER 6

PLAYGROUND NATION AND THE SPORTING LIFE

ere's how Kathy grew up as a city kid. Favorite group sports: Nerf ball and sewing. Nature knowledge: Could tell the difference between a squirrel and a rat. At camp, sporty Kathy was so averse to getting wet, she told her counselors she was menstruating the entire summer in order to get out of swimming. Admittedly, this avoidance of physical exercise is extreme. But parental fears are too, and those of us in the city expend lots of psychic energy fretting that our children will grow up to be completely sports-averse city slugs.

Let's face it, access to outdoor space is not a major city selling point. To the contrary, parents often have to struggle to find opportunities for children to just run around and be children. And if your child is in a city public school, you can just about kiss team sports goodbye because of the dearth of outdoor acreage and lack of funding for athletic programs. Sure, city parks can provide a wonderful antidote to pavement angst, but sometimes just the thought of how much effort is required to lasso the kids, get them outside, and actually find them something to *do* can freeze even the most nature-oriented of us right in our tracks (subway, of course).

Don't despair. City kids can be outdoorsy and active. But you have to want to make them so—and not shrinking from the challenge is half the battle.

THE GESTALT OF THE URBAN PLAYGROUND

If you're a city parent with kids under the age of 6, you will likely be spending a lot of time in public playgrounds—a thought that may make you either bubble up with visions of cherubic toddlers at play or quiver in horror (that would be Kathy). Julia, by contrast, is one of those parents who loves playgrounds. As a working mother, she adored the time outdoors with her children, especially the extended hours of summer nights. She'd regularly pack sandwiches for the kids, who would cavort for literally hours, often closing the playground down. And she greatly appreciated the opportunities to meet parents who were similarly marooned on a sandbox edge. Boredom was never a factor, because while living in a dense city means congestion to some, to Julia's clan, it means lots of playground options. And as far as kids are concerned, exploring different playgrounds is just about as cool as going to Disney World. So why doesn't everyone feel the same way?

Parents' playground issues fall, generally, into two categories. One is physical: discontent with the condition, cleanliness, or safety of the equipment and/or with the schlep to get there. The other is just a tad more emotional, so maybe we'll start there.

Playground Sociology

A while back, the *New York Times* ran an article quoting parent after parent discussing how much they hate, hate, hate the playground. For those moms and dads, the thought of another afternoon watching some completely undisciplined kid pull their baby off the jungle gym, or having to deal with the fact that the "cool mommy" clique has no interest in taking in new members, or engaging in one more conversation of whether so-and-so's sweetheart is really as G&T ("gifted and talented") as she says he is, carried all the appeal of jury duty.

We empathize with parents who absolutely dread the playground. They're not without justification. Public playgrounds are shared spaces, which means you and yours are in an environment that obliges constant human interaction (most of it among members of our species who aren't old enough to know what *interaction,* or even *human,* means). Baby brawls are bound to happen; they're a natural rite of passage for anyone just figuring out how to share or take turns. But adults who scuffle—what are their excuses?

Chances are, when an "issue" arises, especially a social one involving your child, your emotions are going to be aroused beyond any sensible level. How bad can this really be? We actually know people who've stopped visiting a playground because of some kid clash that resulted in an oh-too-memorable adult exchange.

Getting Along without Getting Arrested

One day when Julia took her youngest to a well-attended toddler playground near their home, she was startled to see a police car pulled up off the street to the side of the playground. Cops standing near the car were interviewing a mother who clearly had just stepped out of the playground. Fearing the worst (kidnapping?), Julia asked a parent sitting inside the playground what had happened. "You're not going to believe it," he responded. "A little kid was riding around on her tricycle and knocked over another toddler who bumped his head. No blood or anything; the toddler looked fine. But the mother of the bumped kid went ballistic and insisted that the police *and* an ambulance be called. And because the police were called, they had to file a police report. The only good thing about the whole brouhaha is that the hysterical mom will have to spend her whole day in the emergency room." Happily, there were no arrests in the playground that day, but suffice it to say, tricycle riding was severely curtailed for a while.

Playground Etiquette: FAQs

There's definitely part of us that intellectually appreciates the anthropological opportunity playgrounds present. Where else do you get the chance to see so many examples of parenting styles in evidence? Mostly, though, we just want to get out whole and, we guess, without an arrest record. Here's our mini-guide to playground etiquette, a little primer on how to handle those oh-so-common playground encounters without developing a migraine or spending a sleepless night cogitating on all the ways you could have handled some incident better than you did.

Q. Whenever we go to the playground, my child is always much more interested in other kids' toys than his own. How do I explain the concept of ownership to an 18-month-old?

A. Don't sweat it. From coast to coast, toys in city playgrounds are freely "shared."

Of course, when you're under 6, "sharing" generally means a toddler toy owner gets distracted by some other apparatus, temporarily leaving his lonesome toy to the devices of the next child who wanders along. Alternatively, the owner is

---

Beware the Playground Cliques

CITYWISE WARNING !

Nanny, stay-at-home mom, working mom—yep, you'll find cliques for each group at every playground you frequent, and they have caused many an intimidated outsider to dread passing through those playground gates.

Ignore them! Being a member of the playground pack is not something a parent should aspire to. For one thing, they're invariably lodged, semipermanently, at whatever post they've taken up, regardless of where the kids are—not smart, in terms of playground safety. Plus, the clique chatter tends to be more about competition than anything else. And heaven forbid you rely on the "park bench" for advice; playground gossip is absolutely the wrong forum for true guidance.

A better plan: Remember you're there to watch your kid, not to find your new best friend. So when you strike up a conversation, just try to keep the adult discourse on the light side, lest it so engross you that you take your eye off your heir. And a little perspective, okay? This is not your whole life, it's a few moments out of your child's toddlerhood, and you will look back on these moments with bittersweet longing when they're gone.

---

still in the sandbox but happily playing with somebody else's provisionally discarded toy. It's all fine as long as you observe a few ground rules (and by the way, if your child is one who is always most interested in some other child's toys, for goodness' sake, make sure to bring some especially cool toy to swap).

Q. What about those horrible kids playing combat games? They're loud, rough, and scare my little Fauntleroy.

A. Careful: In a couple of years, your little Fauntleroy could be Mr. Scary. First-time parents especially don't realize that there's a big difference between the physical style of a 2-year-old and that of a 5-year-old. Generally, the older kids are just doing what comes naturally, and while the evolution may be hard to appreciate when your child is but a toddling tot, do try to look a couple of years ahead. Unless the older kids are playing in a truly dangerous or offensive manner, either relax or move your play to a more tranquil section of the playground. On the other hand, if the play is intrusive (for instance, they kick over your tot's sand castle), then it's perfectly appropriate to turn in loco parentis

Make Your Kid King of the Playground

Bring this stuff and your kid's popularity at the playground is guaranteed.

A big shovel. Every kid should have one, but it's the big ones—or the uniquely shaped ones—that draw the most admiration.

Multicolored chalk. The big chunky chalk made especially for sidewalk art is almost unique among playground accessories for its ability to draw a crowd. Other benefits: Kids of all ages can have fun with it: The littlest can draw "trails" or make mazes; bigger kids can draw trucks or rainbows or their names; and the biggest can create a hopscotch grid (you'd be amazed how even 11-year-olds can get into chalk). Chalk's also great to kill time at a park or even play in front of a building (watch the cars); plus, passersby cannot help but stop to look.

Bubbles. Don't worry about the fancy guns and wands. Bubbles from old-fashioned plastic bottles and wands have just as much allure as the fancy electronically spawned ones.

What to resist: remote control cars, ride-in battery-powered vehicles, any other hot, expensive toys. Unless your child is happy to let every kid in the playground have a turn (and you're prepared to spend your afternoon policing the turn-taking), we'd limit play with this kind of toy to your home, Grandma's, or any area not populated by hundreds of envious 5-year-olds.

and give them the same firm but gentle instructions you would give to your own child. You may still have to move though. If another child's being truly disruptive and an adult fails to materialize, chances are that kid *was* poorly supervised, *is* poorly supervised, and will probably always *be* poorly supervised—which means your ability to remedy his ill behavior is probably close to nil.

Q. The last time we were at the playground, an older boy kept pulling my daughter's leg as she was climbing, despite my admonitions. I didn't see any adult with him, so I pulled him off the jungle gym. Did I do the wrong thing?

A. Warning! Warning! Warning! Never touch another person's child unless your child is in imminent danger. You have no idea what litigious city parents will threaten you with should you disturb a hair on Attila's head. Most child-to-child playground incidents don't rise to the level of bodily injury, so, generally, you'll be best served by getting the adult in charge of the misbehaving child to do the right thing (which often just needs some aggressive glaring on your part). If no one surfaces, or if the supervising adult seems disinclined to do anything, you are always entitled to act verbally to protect your child's comfort and safety—with these caveats. Abusive language or yelling is never in order. Don't forget that the person you're addressing is still a child. Try to think like a (good) teacher: Take on the behavior, not the child. Quite often, just a firm tone will be sufficient, but when it isn't, you may have to use your parental power to refocus or move your own child. It's not fair, but you can't really start screaming if the other child won't play nice.

Q. To pee or not to pee?

A. There are lots of strong opinions on both sides of the fence on this one—from the "oh please, don't we all have more important things to worry about than how and when a 5-year-old takes a whiz?" group, to those who are so incensed by adults who let their child publicly relieve himself that they just about break out in hives. It's not like you can avoid the issue. We've seen kids urinating on just about every tree, bush, and shrub by (and in) our favorite playground haunts, on fences, and inside and outside the grounds. The transgressors: typically 3- and 4-year-olds, the ones in the midst of conquering potty training; and predominantly boys (girls are either able to "hold it" or simply less likely to get permission from caregivers to let it all hang out in public). Their accomplices? Generally parents or caregivers who just can't be bothered getting them home, to a park bathroom, to a coffee shop . . . Oops, our predisposition is showing.

The "it's an emergency" excuse just doesn't do it for us. Most of us can recognize the early warning signs—the fast-stepping, crotch-grabbing routine of a kid who truly can't hold it anymore. And because we have never seen someone let his child pee in the middle of a grocery store, maybe we just need to convince people that playground peeing is not a good thing. Here's why we (and hopefully you) should make it an issue:

1. It's confusing to children on several levels. For starters, it contradicts the lessons of toilet training—which are, of course, controlling oneself and using a toilet. It also goes against everything you're trying to teach your children at this age about respect for others, persons and things. (FYI: We get pretty heated about littering too.)

2. It's unsanitary. Sure, sure urine is sterile—when it comes out of an infection-free bladder, that is. But release it on city ground and you've got a virtual petrie dish for all that bacteria lurking in wait.

3. It's illegal! Most cities have hefty fines for public urination—up to $500. Now, cops aren't generally going after toddlers, but occasionally you'll read about some hapless caregiver who was issued a ticket on behalf of a spraying and displaying child.

Peeing in public is almost always avoidable if you want it to be, and here are some tactics that'll help. Make a bathroom run before the playground outing starts. Find places close to your playground, either public facilities (if you think they're too gross, bring wipes to clean them or use toilet seat covers) or other places that will let you use their bathroom—coffee shops and kids' stores are good choices if you're far from home. Stick to playgrounds that have the most convenient access to restrooms if you're planning extended stays. And monitor your child frequently for physical signs of the need to relieve (even *ask* them on occasion if they need to find a bathroom), so you won't be caught with no time to spare.

THE CITY PARENT RULES
Sharing in Playground Nation

Rule #1: Playground etiquette demands that the adult in charge seek out the appropriate consenting adult to make sure it's okay to borrow the toy. If that adult seems a touch reluctant (or maybe you're the reluctant one), we'd pass. Your child may kick and scream, but it's not his (or your) right to take the toy. And don't dis the caregiver. Maybe it's a new toy or a special toy, maybe the child just goes crazy when another child touches his stuff, or maybe the adult just doesn't believe in sharing. (Please note: Sharing toys is definitely not the norm in much of suburbia, so you might get some strange looks if your child tries to poach in Greenwich or Shaker Heights.)

Rule #2: When the other child wants his toy back, sharing time is over. This means no staring helplessly at the other parent if your little Ashley wants to keep the cool bubble gun. And if Ashley's unwillingness to relinquish a borrowed toy creates too many scenes for you, then you'll have to forego the "sharing" until she's capable of returning borrowed goods without a fight.

Rule #3: Never, ever allow your charge to move the toy to another location. It's inconsiderate to the other caregiver, who will have to hunt down the toy when departure time approaches, not to mention distressing for the other child who may return to the spot where he left his treasure only to find it gone.

Rule #4: If a toy looks like it's been abandoned, it's okay to play with it, but not to take it home. Salvage rights may be the law of the open sea, but they don't apply in city playgrounds.

Rule #5: If your toys keep disappearing, put your name on them. Toys, shovels, and dump trucks have an annoying habit of all looking the same, and it's really easy to pack up another tot's stuff when you're scrambling to get your kid and his caboodle packed up for home. So if you put your name in big black letters on your stuff, it'll help prevent some other adult from taking your toys by mistake *and* help prevent you from doing the same.

Rule #6: Equipment is for everyone. You're perfectly within your rights to decide that young Jeremiah isn't ready to lend out his toys yet, but the playground equipment is public property, and it is emphatically not acceptable to let him hog community assets. And what a perfect teaching opportunity: Explain (even if it's the kazillionth time) the concept of sharing. Make sure your child waits his turn and uses the equipment for an appropriate amount of time.

And if the issue is other kids hogging the equipment, it's perfectly fine to encourage them to take turns. *Most* kids will melt away silently if an adult reminds them that others are waiting. Failing that, you can always appeal to the supervising adults, most of whom will be embarrassed into persuading their little monopolists to give other kids a chance. It only gets tricky when you're dealing with slug supervising adults who appear to have no sense of what makes a civilized society. In this case, you're best just ignoring that homicidal rage building in your chest. Instead, play it safe and tell your confused tot that "those people are just not well brought up" and move to another part of the playground where politer company hopefully prevails.

Playground Perils

In comparison to the social angst that playgrounds can generate, the physical issues seem much easier to deal with, except for the fact that the stakes are much higher—your kid's safety—and the odds of a physical incident having lasting impact are much greater.

Although there are well-documented, well-publicized design standards for public playgrounds, they're not mandatory in many places. You absolutely can't assume that because your playground is run by the city, it will win any sort of health or safety award. Out of more than 1,000 public playgrounds surveyed by the U.S. Public Interest Research Group, 75 percent lacked adequate surfacing and more than 50 percent had climbers and slides exceeding safe heights. But it's not just playground construction or maintenance that should draw your attention; you also need to focus on use. As many as 40 percent of accidents are caused, at least in part, by inadequate supervision. Many, many accidents occur because children are playing where they shouldn't, in ways that they shouldn't, and with "accessories" that they shouldn't. So if you want to do a reasonable job of keeping your child safe, you're going to have to pick where and how she plays, and you're going to have to make sure that any adult in charge of her understands your rules as well.

For the wee ones, the safest playgrounds are those that have a separate play area for 5 and unders. Besides the fact that toddler play areas are designed to have age-appropriate equipment, the separate nature of the space tends to minimize the number of bigger kids who come barreling through. But, even if you're lucky enough to find a toddler playground, that doesn't mean you're safe and sound. A comprehensive study by the U.S. Consumer Product Safety Commission (CPSC) analyzed playground-equipment–related injuries treated in emergency rooms from November 1998 through October 1999. Some of the findings:

- Eighty percent of the injuries occurring in public playgrounds were fall related. The falls, however, were not necessarily from great heights; in fact, nearly half of the falls from public equipment (including at schools) were from less than 4 feet. The biggest reason for a fall? The child losing his grip.
- For the 2-and-under set, the slide was the most dangerous apparatus; over the age of 2, climbers were the worst offenders.
- For children under 5, injuries to the face were the most common. One reason: Children this age are the most prone to walking in front of or behind a moving swing.
- Most dangerous times? From noon to 3 P.M. (when 42 percent of the public playground accidents occurred) and from 3 to 6 P.M. (when 27 percent of the accidents occurred). Maybe it's the crowding as older kids getting out of school hit the playground, maybe it's the mix of different age groups, maybe it's the fatigue that descends on kids in the latter parts of the day—the reasons are a little hazy, but the accident incidence is not.
- Climbing-related injuries appear to be on the rise in public locations perhaps, the report surmises, because of the increase in multiuse climbing structures (you know, slide, bridge, pole combos, and the like).

• More than half of the playground deaths involved hanging, from ropes, clothing, shoe strings, and various items "tied" to the playground equipment—everything from dog leashes to jump ropes—though deaths have a far greater incidence in home playgrounds than public ones. While the report doesn't make this generalization, from reading descriptions of some of the incidents causing death, it would seem likely that many of the kids involved were playing unsupervised. (One case involved a little girl who was hanged while pretending to be a puppy on the end of a bathrobe sash tied to the top of a slide; another involved a girl who had a sled rope tied to her neck as she climbed the slide. She fell and the sled caught on the railing, causing her to hang.) While we often see children who are not well-supervised in city playgrounds, there is always some adult presence, presumably with enough sense to curb some of the more dangerous inclinations of creative children.

City Playground Hazards to Avoid

Safety groups consider these no-no's. Judging from the playgrounds in our areas, these hazards are not uncommon.

Unsafe surfacing. This would be any hard surface including grass, dirt, and asphalt; and any loose fill surface (like sand or wood chips) less than 9 inches deep and/or tripping hazards (tree stumps, exposed concrete footings).

Inadequate fall zones. A cushioned, obstacle-free area should extend at least 6 feet in all directions from equipment, with 9 feet between adjacent structures that are higher than 30 inches.

Unsafe equipment construction. Here's our list of what to pay attention to:

• Height (highest platform or rung should be no more than 4 feet for preschoolers, 5 to 6 feet for older kids)

• Peeling paint (potential toxic risk from lead); pressure-treated wood (arsenic danger)

• Collision hazard from swings too close together (separation should be 24 inches or more and 30 inches from swing supports); hard or rigid seats

• Head entrapment (openings should be less than $3\frac{1}{2}$ inches or greater than 9 inches)

• Clothing entanglement hazards (open S hooks, gaps, protrusions)

• Elevated surfaces with no guardrails

• Inappropriate equipment like chain walks, swinging trapeze bars, rope swings

• Slides facing directly into the sun (don't underestimate the ability of a slide to give a burn)

THE CITY PARENT RULES
Developing a Safe Playground Game Plan

Rule #1: Scan playgrounds for any equipment dangers. Scrutinize all your options for hazards noted in the accompanying box, but don't panic if you see some; many playgrounds will have a few. Nonetheless, you'll want to eliminate from play any equipment that's inherently unsafe: too high, too complicated, or just plain scary looking. Obviously, banned structures should include pieces of equipment that exceed height guidelines or have other hazardous issues like peeling paint, inadequate fall zones, and the like. We would also recommend forbidding play on structures that the experts consider unsafe in their entirety: chain walks, multiple occupancy swings, swinging exercise rings/bars, and climbing ropes. Unfortunately, some of the most hazardous equipment is the most enticing to some kids. You're the parent. Put your foot down.

Rule #2: Deconstruct the demographics. Over the course of a day, *who* is in the playground can change significantly: That serene morning oasis can become a Wild West show after school lets out. When older kids hit the scene, the level of play will often become more frenetic and challenging. And while it's perfectly okay for 5-year-old Jasper to play on the swinging bridge when it's just his age cohorts around, prudence may dictate that he be limited to more sheltered pieces of equipment when the older kids take over.

Rule #3: Reconstruct what you know about age-appropriate equipment. According to the CPSC, 4 is the minimum age that a child is truly capable of using upper-body equipment, so if your 3-year-old monkey wants to use those horizontal bars, either squelch the urge or stand by ready to catch. If you have a very young child, your biggest source of concern should be the slide. While parents and caregivers might be reluctant to let toddlers go on climbers by themselves, they don't seem to hesitate at all when it comes to slides. Our suggestion: Keep a hand on the youngest ones all the way up and down the slide. If the slide is too high for you to do that successfully, it's too high for your child. And please, exercise

CITYWISE WARNING

Handling Multiples in the Playground

Keeping track of more than one small child at the playground can be aggravating, even mildly terrifying. On a crowded spring day, it is well nigh impossible to watch two active 4-year-olds if one wants to play in the sandbox and the other prefers a play area 180 degrees to the north. But consider this: If you do let them have their way, you are effectively deciding not to watch one of them. There is only one truly safe solution: Insist that they play in a relatively circumscribed area where you can eyeball both at the same time.

some judgment: A 2-year-old has no business on the big-kids slide or sliding down the pole from the tree house, no matter how grown up and coordinated you think little Persephone is.

Rule #4: Always keep kids in sight, if not under hand. Kids under 2 need an adult's physical guidance on just about any piece of playground equipment. Once they're 3, they can be a little more independent—on age-appropriate equipment only. But you do need to be watching them all the time: Their safety should depend on your judgment, not theirs.

Rule #5: Wash up. With new concerns about arsenic in pressure-treated wood, a hazard that may affect as much as 15 percent of public playgrounds, parents have another reason to make sure their kids are frequent hand washers. Arsenic, a dangerous carcinogen, is prevalent in the environment. In fact, we all encounter it daily. It comes from chromated copper arsenate (CCA) substances used in pressure-treated wood to prevent attacks by wood-boring pests. There's real concern for excessive dosage levels of playground arsenic—as a result of kids touching contaminated surfaces and then engaging in hand-to-mouth activity. Parents of toddlers, who may put their hands to their mouths as often as 30 times an hour, should be particularly concerned. The exact repercussion for children is difficult to assess because the impact of arsenic tends to be long-term and is mixed with the effects of many other cancer-causing agents an individual is exposed to over a lifetime.

Climbing Guidelines

Once your child is old enough to go on climbing equipment, you'll need to set some modest rules and regulations:

- Assess your child's climbing ability before you let him go on every piece of equipment. Kids' capabilities differ enormously, and from the CPSC's point of view, some of the newer multiuse structures have some pretty unusual and fairly difficult parts to navigate.
- Try and keep your child off the climbing equipment when he's tired. Many accidents happen during the afternoon when young kids are likely to be flagging, particularly if they've just moved out of the nap stage.
- Absolutely discourage improper use of equipment, particularly climbing on the *outside* of structures unless they were specifically designed for this purpose. Even if your child is an athletic daredevil, the next kid who tries to emulate him may not be.

Nonetheless, studies are clear: Arsenic exposure from pressure-treated wood is undesirable (and avoidable). Under a voluntary agreement with the EPA, the manufacturers of CCA-treated wood agreed to cease using arsenic in most consumer applications by the end of 2003.

What about what's already out there? States are reacting differently: California, for example, is requiring all public playgrounds be treated with a sealant, while other states have not yet reacted. And it's not like you can easily tell if the wood's been pressure treated. Often, pressure-treated wood has a greenish sheen and patterned indentations that look like the marks left by large staples. To be sure, you need lab tests. The EPA's advice: Assume that playground wood is pressure treated unless you know with certainty that it's not, and take appropriate precautions:

- Always wash your children's hands with soap and water after they've touched any wood that may be pressure treated.
- Don't let them eat food that has been placed directly on wood picnic tables, and don't let them use their hands to climb on benches and then eat their food.
- Don't let your kids dig in the sand near any equipment you suspect is pressure treated and certainly don't let them eat that sand.

GET SPORTY

Scads of newspaper and magazine articles, research reports, and TV specials make it impossible to ignore the growing incidence of child and adult obesity in this country. Are city kids more at risk? Hard to say. But it's even harder to argue with the fact that physical activity is tough to come by in lots of American cities. In fact, a joint study conducted in 2001 by Cook County Children's Hospital in Chicago and the University of Illinois Medical Center evaluated 525 healthy city children, ages 4 to 18, and compared them to a major reference study out of Canada. The results: 61 percent of the U.S. boys and 81 percent of the U.S. girls performed below the 25th percentile of their Canadian counterparts. Not good.

You do know whose fault this is, right? Apparently, a significant part of the problem is that city kids are almost totally reliant on their parents for opportunities to become physically active—they can't just walk out the back door to go run around in the yard—and their parents are not stepping up to the plate. If you are punting on this one ("she's only 4; we'll deal with sports when she's 8"), you may be making a big mistake. Study after study substantiates the value of early physical education; lifetime patterns tend to take hold in childhood. More particularly for younger kids, according to the National Association for Sport and Physical Education (NASPE), basic physical skills like running and throwing don't just happen. They develop from the interaction of genetic potential and experience. So, NASPE points out forebodingly, a toddler who doesn't bounce and chase balls may lag in eye-hand coordination.

This is not an iffy issue; you need your family to get physical. But, you know what? It's not as hard as you think.

The Walking Way of Life

In New York City, we walk and walk and walk. Our city has sidewalks just about everywhere. Routes to the grocery store, school, and the dentist are always interesting—people-watching, parks here and there, a movie shoot. Julia's family has made walking a major habit. They walk to school in the morning, including half a mile through Central Park. Could there possibly be a better way to start the day? Often they do their morning walks with friends; it's like starting the day with a playdate. In the summer, Julia's family makes ice cream cones and walks outside

---

How Much Activity Does Your Child Need?

Now that we've gotten your attention and you've committed to making sure that your child will not blob out just because he lives in the city, exactly how much time should he be spending running around?

The NASPE thinks that toddlers and preschoolers should have a whopping 30 and 60 minutes daily of structured physical activity, respectively, plus another 60 minutes of unstructured activity. [a]

Ouch!

Before you hyperventilate, let's put this into context. The structured play is adult-supervised activity that can help your child develop gross motor and manipulative skills and a sense of balance and rhythm. It can be broken up into increments of time: 10 minutes of skipping to the grocery store, 15 minutes of dancing to the Wiggles before dinner, 15 minutes at the playground kicking and throwing an inflatable ball, 5 minutes holding your child's hand as he navigates walking on park benches, 15 minutes of tag, and you're done. And if your child attends nursery school or preschool, chances are much of the structured activity is already in place.

a. "NASPE Releases First Ever Physical Activity Guidelines for Infants & Toddlers," National Association for Sport and Physical Education press release, February 6, 2002.

---

until the last drip has been devoured. When one child or another has a special problem that needs talking out (and with three children, there's always one), they get to walk it off with a parent. Likewise, every errand includes a parent and a child; it is simply unbeatable one-on-one time.

But is all that walking really doing anything for them? Urban planners at the University of British Columbia set out to answer just that question in a survey of more than 12,000 respondents. And, in fact, they found that people who live in dense cities like New York, Boston, Chicago, Seattle, and San Francisco are thinner than those in more sprawling urban areas like Atlanta and Phoenix. Why? Because they walk more.

Teaching Walking

Some kids are natural walkers. Julia's two oldest kids could walk forever. But her youngest? Let's put it this way, months before he could say "mama," he could say "taxi," and he would try hailing a cab the second he set foot out the door. With a little parental encouragement, though, even Malcolm learned to be a walker. Follow Julia's two-pronged strategy of distraction and deprivation, and yours will too.

Distraction involves:

- Games. "Crazy steps" is one where everybody has to do 10 specific silly steps (giant, scissor, baby, walk-like-your-brother, your dad, etc.); "red light/green light"; and "street find," where kids run to something "tall and green" or "with the number 2 on it" or any item in the forward field of vision, strategically chosen to keep the team moving in the right direction.
- Wall walking. Julia's crew knows all the buildings on their habitual routes

that have walls, cool steps to climb, and ramps that can be hopped on or run down. Anything is fair game, with the proviso that forward motion cannot be impeded.
- Landmark spotting (and you need not rely on the preservation society for ideas). One of the kids' favorites games was to guess what color lights some anonymous person living in a brownstone basement apartment would put on the evergreen in their window well.

Deprivation is more straightforward. "Yes, we can get soft ice cream on Broadway, but after we walk to get there." "Yes, you can have an ice cream sandwich after dinner, but only if we walk around the park with it." Come to think of it, ice cream played a pretty huge role in Malcolm's pedestrian education.

And eventually he learned: Walking is what we do.

We know it's wildly avant-garde, but walking can be done even in "driving cities." Look for every chance to park the car and walk between errands, or intentionally park a little farther away from your destination to allow a walk with your kids. It's great exercise, it's great talking time, and it's just fun.

Sports for the Tender Ages

Even though there are definite benefits to incorporating as much walking as you can into your lifestyle, walking simply can't compete with more aerobic activities on certain dimensions: greater fitness, the opportunity to find a lifelong hobby or passion, and the mental benefits of understanding how to function on a team. For these, you'll need to introduce your child to the world of sports. But while exposing your children to physical activity is crucial, it's also imperative to find something your child enjoys doing. This is just not the age to make her do something because "it's good for her."

Individual Sports

If you want to pay the price, you can get your little superstar coached in any sport at any age, especially in a city. For children not yet able to even walk, there are zillions of "swimming" classes. Once your little one can actually toddle, your sports opportunities are unlimited: tae kwon do for 3-year-olds, micro b-ball, peewee tennis, yoga for 2-year-olds. Ah yes, the options for spending your money are endless.

Realistically, most physical "instruction" at this age is about anything but learning the sport (remember NASPE's prescription for younger kids: a little gross motor movement, a little rhythm, some balance. . .). Sure there are the rare examples—Andre Agassi and Tiger Woods come to mind—of very young kids who were proficient at their sport, but most kids are simply not physiologically ready. So, if you have it in your head that learning to play tennis at the age of 3 is going to set Sarah on that road to Wimbledon, you're going to be sorely disappointed. (Probably, that is; Julia's mother always tsk-tsk'd the little girl in her class who was taking skating lessons for three hours before school each day. Her name was Dorothy Hamill.)

The rest of us will probably aim for a more reasonable goal: to gently introduce kids to the joys of physical activity. We've selected the following sports because we think everyone should know how to do them. Keep in mind that if your child is not yet 6, it's really quite all right for her not to become proficient at any of these. (Though with the right strategy, that, too, will come.)

Ice skating. You probably won't have a public pond to practice on, but many city rinks are just a couple of dollars a session, so it shouldn't cost much to take your child over enough times to get him comfortable on skates. Plus, you undoubtedly will have the benefits of Zambonis, supervision, and snack bars at your rink. We've seen children as young as 3 do wonderfully on the ice, though Kathy thinks 4, when Alice began skating, is the magic number. Kids at this age can physically handle the new movements and they're still young enough to enjoy (or at least not mind) falling down. And if you're considering group lessons (a blessing for your back, with the added benefit that your child may become a lot more adventurous when skating among peers), the slightly older age may be mandated by the rink, which will want to assure that the youngest students have enough maturity to stick with the group format.

Bicycle riding. We cannot tell a lie: Teaching a child to ride a bike is a royal pain in the city. There aren't any long driveways to practice on or a whole lot of pedestrian-free sidewalks or carless roads anywhere. And jumping out the back door for a quick 15-minute practice session just isn't so easy. No, for most of us city parents, teaching a child to ride a bicycle means schlepping child and machine over to a spot we hope won't be too densely occupied when we get there. That effort alone probably costs us at least 20 minutes before Ari even starts riding. And this doesn't include the added thrill when public transportation's involved. Still, Junior's got to learn, so there's nothing to be done but bite the bullet and teach him how to ride safely. A couple of city pointers:

- Kindergarten age, 5 or 6, is probably a prime time to teach this skill. It's great because they are physically up to the challenge, and, because you'll be doing this in public, you don't want a child who's embarrassed to learn because he already feels too old.
- Don't let the hassle of getting to a sheltered training area (away from traffic) let you stint on safety. Always have your child wear a helmet. It's the law, you know (and even if you're on training wheels, use the helmet).
- Try to schedule training sessions for early in the morning. Learning to ride a bicycle in the city comes complete with an obstacle course since it's tough to find a flat stretch of land that's not used by other people. Best places: unused basketball courts (either the outside perimeters or even the courts themselves if there's no game in progress) and grassy park grounds. And here's a surprising piece of information: The sidewalks of city side streets can work amazingly well if your child is an early bird or a night owl, allowing you to schedule practice sessions in non-busy hours—of course, this only works if the supervising adult is religious about keeping a hand on the tot at *all* times to prevent straying into the street. Worst places: playgrounds (too many kids; many playgrounds ban bicycle riding for just this reason).

- Always have your child walk his bicycle across streets. Most newly trained bike riders are not competent enough to keep control of their bicycles if they're startled. To be safe, make sure your child gets off his bicycle well before he reaches an intersection. (We saw one child nearly killed as he rode down a hill to a busy city street and didn't have enough strength to bring his bike to a stop. His panicked father, many steps behind him, screamed in despair because he couldn't do anything to rescue his son. Fortunately, a really quick-thinking passerby grabbed the boy as he entered the street and oncoming traffic. Really, really scary.)

Swimming. The American Academy of Pediatrics (AAP) doesn't think any child is physically capable of truly learning to swim until age 4, but that shouldn't stop you from having your child start lessons for other reasons: to get comfortable with water, to have something different to do one day a week, to get in some more physical activity, or, hey, just to cool off during the sweaty summer season. So by all means, go right ahead. Just expect more splashing than stroking.

The City Pool

Lots of people we know simply can't fathom their clean little pixies swimming in a city public pool, yet think nothing of tossing them into the comparable suburban one. We have no idea why or where this prejudice even comes from—particularly since we could find nothing to indicate that a city pool is any more likely to be poorly maintained or a source of dreaded diseases.

Still, not all public pools are created equal, and those that don't observe proper maintenance procedures can be dangerous. The biggest problem is fecal matter, usually from little kids; if *E. coli* is involved, serious illness and even death can result. So choose a pool that is well maintained and is health and safety conscious. Look for:

- Water that appears clear, not cloudy
- A setup that minimizes child "incidents"—for instance, one that has a separate kiddie pool or changing facilities near the pool
- Water-quality monitoring on a regular schedule, and a pool with a "fecal accident response plan" (call and ask; their willingness to respond may speak volumes)

Do observe safe practices yourself. Never change your baby by a pool; don't count on a swim diaper to prevent leaks; and if Zora has diarrhea, do us all a favor and keep her out of the pool.

There are tons of options. Most cities have for-profit groups that teach kids at private pools leased for the instruction period. There are also specialized facilities—sports complexes, even health clubs—that offer swimming for tots. And every city offers public options, although many are available in the summer only because most public pools are open-air. Private swim classes tend to run on a "semester" basis with fall, mid-winter, spring, and summer sessions. Public lessons vary by pool and program, but typically you'll be able to sign up kids as young as 3 for one- and two-week programs. The frequency may be significantly less than the private offerings, but it's age appropriate and, of course, you can't beat the price. Just call your local parks and recreation department, or check their Web site to get the scoop.

Organized Sports

In cities, as elsewhere, organized sports are huge these days. As the AAP puts it, "During the latter part of the 20th century, 'free play' or unstructured games gave way to organized sports. The starting age for organized sports programs has also evolved to the point that infant and preschool training programs are now available for many sports." We can see why. Even little kids benefit from an introduction to the rules of a sport, the concepts of coaching and teamwork, and a little time concentrating on gross motor skills. Plus, city parents have to work doubly, if not triply hard, to find space for an impromptu game of soccer or softball. For the most part, if you want to get your kids in the game on a regular basis, a group effort will be your only recourse.

But be careful. Some of these sports programs have clearly lost sight of what is appropriate for young kids—favoring goals that "are not necessarily child oriented," as the AAP notes. Problems include imposing demands on children that far exceed their cognitive and physical development, dependence on volunteer coaches (um, that would be us parents) who have no training to teach young kids, and inappropriate parental expectations. If you or the coaches get upset that pre-K'ers are not drilling goals or fielding flies, then you're going to destroy the experience for your kids and yourselves. (This is exactly what happened to a friend of Julia's. "What do little girls do when they're playing defense and the rest of the team is on the opposite side of the field chasing the ball? They do cartwheels. They braid their hair," said Julia's pal. Apparently this perfectly normal behavior infuriated the coach of her daughter's team, who was unhappy with his own daughter's performance as well as the lack of "focus" of the rest of the pre-pre-preteens. So one day, he had a screaming fit that reduced the girls to tears and caused the early termination of her daughter's soccer career.)

The real challenge here is to make sure *you* have age-appropriate expectations for this kind of exercise. If you can honestly say that you're into this for the right

A League above the Others

The American Youth Soccer Organization (AYSO) started in Los Angeles 40 years ago so that kids ages 4½ and up could learn the sport in a kind and age-appropriate environment. Today, AYSO sponsors 50,000 teams supported by 250,000 parent volunteers in cities and towns across the country. It's probably so popular for two great reasons.

First, its emphasis is on what's right for the children. All coaches are required to attend special AYSO training classes, which spend significant time on the particular physical, social, and cognitive characteristics of the age they're responsible for. Coaches are taught about what the kids are capable of (and what they're not) and how to best meet the needs and abilities of the age group. For 5-year-olds, for instance, AYSO says don't expect a lot of focus, coach more by demonstrating and less by verbal instruction, and don't be surprised if half the team wanders off the field in the middle of a game to watch an airplane go by. In other words, they have reasonable and realistic expectations.

The other great reason to go AYSO: It's largely volunteer-run, which means it's cheap relative to other physical activities in the city. You probably have to help out in some capacity yourself if you want your kid to participate, but there are loads of ways to do your share, so don't let that stop you. To find out more, call AYSO at (800) 872-2976 or check out their Web site at http://soccer.org/.

---

reasons—if spending a few bucks on what is, for this age group, only a touch above controlled chaos doesn't bug you, and if you're willing to give a few hours of your time (trust us, most of these programs rely on pretty serious parental involvement), then by all means go find a program with like goals.

Remember, though, that at this age, your objective is to initiate a love of sports, not perfect skills. Your standards for what makes a good program should be very different than what they're going to be when Junior's 14 and trying to sharpen up the finer points of his game. So how to find the good and avoid the bad? First, focus on sports where your little one has a minute chance of actually doing something (how many 4-year-olds do you know who can handle a basketball?). For us, that means softball (usually T-ball for this age group) and soccer. Also, look for programs that share your objectives, have a focus on fun, emphasize age appropriateness, and provide coaches some sort of training in child development in addition to the mechanics of the sport itself. And definitely ask other parents if their kids had fun in the program.

If your child is not a team player yet (so many preschoolers are not), and you're looking for something that's a little less drill and a little more fun than skating or swimming, cities offer loads of other physically oriented activities. Consider the plethora of "gymnastics classes" for the preschool set. They're really about jumping and movement, with a forward roll or two thrown in, and are excellent for developing balance and a sense of body awareness. Ditto for little kid "dance and movement" classes. Don't stereotype your son: He may love moving to music as much as the little girl next door. Or you can sign up for a kids' class at a facility with an indoor playground. These generally emphasize games involving play apparatus that painlessly develop your little one's sense of physical competence. If money is a concern, check out nonprofit facilities—neighborhood community centers, churches/synagogues, and as always, your parks department, are all good sources for low-cost kids' programs.

Cabin Fever Solutions

When inclement weather or just plain life gets in the way of your family's outdoor plans, you'll need to have a plan (and some equipment) to let off steam indoors. Of course, that's never easy with little ones, cramped spaces, or apartment buildings with poor soundproofing. But where there's a wired wee one, there'd better be a way. In fact, here are some indoor exercise options that make being cooped up fun and almost worthwhile—okay, almost.

Mini trampolines/inflatable corrals. Nothing like jumping to get the little ones hopping with excitement. The newest, coolest versions look almost like inflated playpens that surround kids with 30-inch walls (plus they can hold three kids at a time). When you're done, just deflate and store. Or you can get the more traditional tramp—just make sure it has a handle and stabilizing feet (might be a good idea to have the kids wear helmets too).

Tubular mazes. Fold-up tented tubes will have your kids scrambling with glee. You can buy a couple, reconnect them in different ways, even add a few tent houses (which also come in about every theme you can think of, from firehouses to castles to every licensed character who ever hit the small screen) for variety. The big fun for Julia's son Malcolm and his buddies was to move all their toys into the tents and then back out of them. We have no idea what the attraction was, but it took up several entire rainy afternoons, so we'll worry about the psychological implications later.

Kick ball in the basement. There is nothing that pleases kids more than being able to kick away with abandon indoors. There's just something so illicit about it. So, if you live in an apartment building and the weather's kind of shabby, take the kids to a basement hall with some rubber balls and let them kick or throw them around. If the halls are long enough, you can run crazy relay races, even let the little ones bomb around on their trikes.

Dance party. Turn on the music and start moving. Fifteen minutes of dancing burns about 100 calories, but most important, burns out those kids who are bouncing off the walls. Plus, it's fun and often you can get away with dancing to your music, not theirs. Yippee.

The 10-second tidy game. Here's a cleaning "game" we found on About.com's "Indoor Fun with Twins/Multiples," and really it's a win-win for everyone. The rules: Everyone has a room and spends 10 seconds straightening up (okay, maybe 15 seconds if you really want to get something actually picked up) before going to the next room. Make an assignment—for instance, "For the next 10 seconds your job is to put all the furniture back in the dollhouse." Then a quick break and on to the next task. Think of it as cleaning circuit training.

Play gym. Kathy was intrigued to find that the fitness craze has definitely hit the preschool set. Sports-Fun's KidStarts line offers scaled-down fitness machines—bikes, treadmills, and weights—for children starting at age 4. Check out sportfun.com.

Watch it. You can also try putting on one of your exercise videos and letting the kids try to do what they do best: mimic you. Or get tapes geared just for them, such as *Exercise Fun with Buddy Bird* and *Hip Hop Animal Rock Workout*.

SUMMERS IN THE CITY

Summertime and the living is easy—sometimes. The youngest kids may perceive no change in their schedule: more playground and outdoor time maybe, but the routine doesn't have to be so different if you have something that works for you. However, once your child enters any kind of regular school, by age 2 for some and 3 for most, summer stares you in the face like an oncoming train. Unfortunately, those of you who freeze at the thought of planning one more darn thing may well find that your child is frozen out of your top choices for camps by the time you actually have gathered your resources enough to act. You'd think all those kids leaving the city for the summer would make securing camp spots for your own citybound tykes a little easier, but we've heard many a sad tale of those who waited and found themselves wanting by the time summer actually rolled around.

Summer Programs and Day Camps

From an organizational perspective, enrolling your preschooler in some kind of summer program is the easiest route to take. The same daily routine means less work for you than trying to figure out a new plan every day. And some parents (Julia for one) like having the opportunity to get their kids into classes by themselves the summer before starting preschool. It certainly gives you a chance to work on those separation issues.

If you are interested in some kind of program, you have a couple of decisions to make:

Indoor versus outdoor oriented. Lots of parents are really interested in getting their kids outdoors in the summer for the physical activity, if nothing else. But there are other benefits as well: fresh air (depending on the city), Vitamin D (a big benefit for those in northern climes who need to build up their stores of it—this is a real thing; read the studies if you don't believe us), and simply the feeling of freedom from being able to run around in less constrained spaces. But invariably, the outdoor-oriented camps are dropoff, thus not suitable for very young kids. Another issue is location. There are certainly outdoor camps within cities—generally run by the parks department—but most others are out of the center city, requiring your kid to be driven or hop on a bus or van chartered by the camp. Many parents think the daily round-trip travel, without benefit of parent or caregiver, will be way too traumatic for little kids; but for the record, some children do the camp bus thing as early as 3 (Julia's son, Pearson, did) and many more at 4. It's not as big a deal as you might think.

Long term versus short term. Which way you go will depend on your intent. If you are looking for a one-stop solution to fill the summer school void, then a long-term camp that your child can attend throughout the summer may be just the ticket. On the other hand, if you're just testing out the camp idea, or are trying to find some cover for the weeks your caregiver's on vacation, or

Coolest Summer Activity: Ice Skating

It certainly wasn't our first thought for a summer activity, but now that we've been made aware of indoor city skating rinks that open during summer (sometimes with selected free hours), we think this is a fabulous idea. It's a great way to cool off, and they're far from crowded. The activity has become so popular that several city rinks even offer summer skating camps. Parents give five stars to San Francisco's Camp Freeze,[a] where children 4 and up learn to skate, play fun games on the ice, and take up ice painting.

a. Parent rating from GoCityKids.com, San Francisco.

Busing to Camp

If it's your child's first time being bused anywhere, the experience will be infinitely easier if he's going with a friend or a sibling. If none are in sight, call the camp and ask them for the name of another child of approximately the same age who will also be on the bus and arrange for the two children to meet ahead of time (if you really want to be on top of this, make sure the other child will get picked up first; then, when your son gets on the bus, you can point out his new friend).

simply want to get a range of specialty activities for your child (one week art camp, another week gymnastics), then short-term programs are a better fit. And if short-term programs catch your fancy, you'll have loads of choices because businesses that run kids' activities during the school year (i.e., music, dance, gymnastics, and/or outfits like Ys and gyms) are all trying to cover their summer overhead.

Price. If cost is a constraint, you might be unpleasantly surprised by how much money you'll have to shell out for the most obvious camp choices (i.e., those run by schools and the more well-known specialty camps). While many of these are capable of providing great summer experiences for your child, they are definitely not cheap, particularly if transportation's involved. If you're looking for a more economical solution to your kid's summer needs, camps attached to public, not-for-profit, or quasi-public facilities will probably be your best bet. Definitely check into any camp programs that your zoo, parks, and discovery centers may have; they're relatively inexpensive (many offer discounted rates to children of members) and their animal/nature focus is particularly appealing to younger kids. The highly popular Los Angeles Zoo camp, for instance, costs about one-third of the local private alternatives (even less for members). YMCAs and YWCAs are great sources for summer camps and, compared to private options, most are still somewhat reasonably priced. However, fees can vary dramatically from city to city, even within cities, depending on real estate prices, location, cost of upkeep, etc. Also note that some Y summer programs may be held in local public elementary schools or community centers rather than the main facility, which may increase or decrease the attractiveness to you.

THE CITY PARENT RULES
How Not to Screw Up Your Kid's Summer

Rule #1: Register early. Getting a camp spot for your child is much less anxiety producing than finding a school—unless you make the mistake of many first-time parents: waiting till just before summer to find a place. Then the bomb drops: You're told, "We're all full and have been for months (and months and months)." Sometimes there's just laughter at the other end of the line (try e-mail; it's much less humiliating when you ask what turns out to be an insanely stupid question). Many camps have priority registration for returning campers, siblings, or—in the case of Ys or schools—members or current students (in some cases, membership will even be a condition of admittance, as is the case with Boston's popular YMCA Camp Polliwog). All those people get to register early in the fall, while the newbies have a second registration later on (which could be as late as January). The point is, if you are interested in a particular camp, you may need to register as soon as you're eligible because spaces go quickly, particularly for 4- and 5-year-olds. The competition eases off considerably as the kids get older and specialty sports camp and sleepaways draw off a good portion of the camp-going population.

You will have to pay a registration fee, and many are nonrefundable if you are offered a place and choose not to take it. Some are even nonrefundable under any circumstances. We know of one popular New York City camp that charges—and gets!—$500 from applying parents, many of whom are denied a place when the dust settles. So read the fine print lest your out-of-pocket expenses climb into the six figures before you've even paid for a day of camp.

Rule #2: Pick the camp for the camp experience. There is a theory going around that getting your kid into a school's summer program ups their chances for admission to the school itself. Not true. Nor is it necessarily going to give you much insight into the school since, quite often, many of the camp counselors and campers are not even affiliated with the school. Sometimes the school doesn't even run the program; it just leases the facilities to a camp operator.

Rule #3: Consider your child's temperament. Kathy learned how important this is when she signed Alice up for two weeks at a local sports camp that her friend's sons Alec and Charlie had attended and adored. She was excited that Alice would experience a little athletic activity and some change from her preschool summer program. But after day one, her typically bubbly daughter came home depressed and actually begged not to go back. What went wrong? Coming off her intimate preschool program, this facility, while state of the art, was just too loud and large. Plus, it was impersonal, a characteristic that may be

Where to Find Camps

You'll be doing a lot of networking among friends and school staff to find personal recommendations.

- If you want your child to stay close: Call the private schools in reasonable proximity and ask if they offer a summer camp for your child's age.
- If you want to go further afield or are looking for more specialized activities: Call the editorial office of any of the family newspapers in your area and ask if they have a summer camp edition from the prior year that you could obtain. (Look online first; it may be archived.)
- Also, check parent organizations to see if they track recommendations. Julia used New York's Parents League files of parent comments to find her kids' first out-of-city camps and found the aggregate opinions were amazingly accurate.

Finally, during the late winter and early spring, many cities have camp fairs at Ys or local schools, sometimes hotels, where you can meet representatives from many prospective camps. Beware that these little get-togethers (not so little sometimes: The Atlanta Parent expo has more than 70 camps represented) tend to focus on out-of-city camps and have little or no representation from specialty camps in the city or from school-run camps. If those are what you're looking for, you may be wasting your time at a camp fair.

---

endemic to shorter term camps, which allow week-to-week signups. Such programs typically experience a large amount of turnover among the attendees from one week to the next (that's the point, actually), making it difficult for relationships and familiarity among counselors and campers to develop. If your little one is on the sensitive side and disturbed by a little extra rowdiness or disruption, she may be better off in smaller, more structured camps that require stints of at least two weeks from their attendees. On the flip side, some kids may be so tired of what they've experienced during the school year that they relish as much change as possible. For these go-getters, summer programs based on a lot of boisterous, physical activity may be perfect.

Rule #4: Check out the camp facilities in person. A very savvy doctor we know says she is astounded by the lack of due diligence performed by city parents on summer camps. While they're all over the schools, many pick a camp based on the merest of hearsay, mail off a check, and the next thing they know little Rina's on the bus, not to return till the end of the day. Her point? All of those parents

There'll Be No Summer Brain Drain for Your Tyke

Another benefit of winging it in the summer: You can save your money and hire an amazing "nanny." Many teachers look to make extra money during the summer months, and if they've taught at your child's age group level, they may be able to put together some absolutely fantastic activities for your kids. Some may only be available for a regular gig (say every afternoon), but others may be willing to work for the ad hoc assignments during the summer.

are completely defaulting on the health and safety issues. What good is it to be rabid about playground security for 10 months of the year and then turn a blind eye to where your children hang out for the other two? Even if the camp doesn't operate in the off-season, check out the physical facilities. You'd be surprised what questions even a fast look may provoke (where exactly do all those little campers go in the rain?). Most important, make sure you're happy with the medical care in emergencies (do they know CPR and how to handle a child after a fall, etc.) and the equipment, facilities, and counselors for your child's age group. And, of course, check the transport routine if your child will be taking a camp or third-party-provided bus, with special emphasis on safety routines, safety records, and driver screening.

THEY'VE GOT GAME:
HOW ONE FAMILY RAISED SPORTY CITY KIDS

Just in case you think we're not dead serious about everything we've written here, we will leave you with some actual evidence that, when it comes to the physical side of cities, proactive parenting works. "Not turning out city sissies, the kind of kids who scream when they see a bug or don't know how to swim" was paramount for Leslie Bennetts and her husband, Jeremy Gerard—the ultimate NYC power couple (she's a celebrity writer for *Vanity Fair*, and he's a top magazine editor). Self-avowed couch potatoes, the urbane couple went to great lengths to make sure their children would feel comfortable in the woods, have the skills necessary to participate and succeed in team sports, and be happy in their bodies.

From the time her son and daughter were toddlers, Bennetts says, "we planned the structure of their lives to make sure they were exposed to a different way of living than our urban life. Our feeling was that if we chose to raise our kids in the city, we'd have to go that extra mile. It took a tremendous effort but was well worth it."

Sports, for example, required organization and action. The couple aimed for variety. They took up tennis, capitalizing on their park's free courts ("do your homework to find out what hours are available and the rules, etc.") and joined local Little Leagues and basketball leagues ("city parents should definitely expect to be hit up at some point for coaching"). When their eldest was "really upset that they didn't have a Ping-Pong table in the basement," like his suburban counterparts, did Bennetts say, "Sorry, honey, no place for Ping-Pong in the city"? Quite the opposite. As Bennetts describes it, "I did research and found a little hole-in-the-wall

Secrets of the Athletic and Outdoorsy

Leslie Bennetts and Jeremy Gerard of New York City share their secrets to raising sporty, nature-loving children.

- Picnics—lots of them.
- Walks in the woods. Don't leave it at walking, though. Stay engaged with your child, observing and discussing what's encountered. Point out the trees, the leaves, the flowers. Your child won't necessarily pick up these things by osmosis; your words can make the outdoor details pop out for them.
- Small amounts of time away. A jaunt doesn't have to take an entire day or a weekend. Steal little moments. Take the kids to the local basketball court after dinner for a quick turn at the hoops. They'll have a blast just trying to reach the basket.
- Day camps out of the city. Sometimes even city kids need room to roam.

- Swimming classes, as soon as the Y will take 'em.
- After-school activities that include movement. Choose classes like gymnastics, tae kwon do, and dance; some are expensive, but plenty aren't.
- Schleps to everywhere there's "nature." Go to the aquarium, zoos, and science and natural history museums.
- Ice skating. Yup, from kindergarten on.

Use your local facilities regularly. Too many parents don't. In New York City, for instance, there are great public pools that are empty half the time because people don't take advantage of them. Says Bennetts: "It's silly. There's a huge opportunity, but you have to seek it out." When you're using public facilities, pick your times well and always know the "house rules" before you get there.

Ping-Pong parlor nearby that is run by a former professional player, and now my son is a killer Ping-Pong player. By the way, it was cheaper than sending a kid to a movie," she points out.

As a family, they went outdoors at every opportunity, even if it was just for an hour-long walk through the woods (there they'd talk about the plants and trees and bugs and animals). Or they'd picnic in the local park with the goal of nature study. "My husband and I were really conscious of the fact that the kids were not absorbing nature as a matter of course, so we took the time to recognize trees, study leaves, bugs, and flowers. And when the outdoors wasn't an option, nature study took place in a Native American–style teepee that was stationed in their living room in place of the more "classic" playhouse.

So committed were these parents to preventing their kids from turning into city slugs that, in the earliest years, even family vacations were planned around this overall goal. Instead of zipping off to London as she and her husband would have preferred, they'd go to Cape Cod and have a beach vacation or to the Adirondacks for a hiking trip.

The couple definitely didn't let their own interests limit their children's. "While my husband's and my idea of winter is sitting in front of a fireplace with a good book, we forced ourselves to ski in the winter," she adds. And in summer, the kids were on a bus by the age of 4 ("I know some people are afraid of this, but it turned out to be a fun experience for our children") going to day camp, where from 8 A.M. to 5 P.M. they played sports, swam, and enjoyed the outdoors."

Actually, swimming was key for the family. "Every year, you read horror stories in the tabloids about some urban class trip to a beach that ends in tragedy because some kid from the city goes in the water and doesn't know how to swim. I wanted to make sure my kids would be competent in this skill." How did she manage this? Swim classes at the local Y from the time they were 2.

So is it possible to raise sporty city kids or is that an oxymoron? Listen to Bennetts. "It's astonishing," she enthuses. "My kids are accomplished athletes. If you know my husband and me, who hate all forms of athletics and sports, that's truly amazing."

CHAPTER 7

FINDING YOUR URBAN BACKYARD

■ ■

Our cultural lives are so active, our cities so vibrant that it's easy to lose touch with the natural world—especially when "Do Not Walk On the Grass: Rat Poison" signs pass for greenery. For many city dwellers, interaction with Mother Nature is purely a question of seeing what wrench she has thrown into the day's transportation plans. "Nope, can't walk to preschool, rain's too hard." Or, "How is this stroller going to get through that impossible-to-navigate snow drift on the curb?" But surely you want your kids to see nature as more than an obstacle, don't you?

Well, we do! And as soon as you see how easy it is, we know you will too. We firmly believe that children benefit enormously from participating in and understanding the workings of the natural world. How they learn to observe and analyze and their ability to think outside of themselves can be shaped and sharpened by encounters with nature. And along the way, think of the sheer pleasure your kids will derive just from jumping in mud puddles, picking flowers, and watching tadpoles evolve into frogs. We think that all city children deserve such joys and lessons and that it is within reach. But you must venture out.

PERUSING YOUR PUBLIC SPACES

Too often when it comes to outdoor stuff, we think provincially. What's the closest park or playground? Is there a walking path that's within walking distance? It's time to think outside your neighborhood.

Most cities have acres and acres of protected lands managed and programmed for your pleasure. The only obstacle to enjoying them is your willingness to spend a little time to get there; and if you want to use these lands to the max, some pre-departure planning is definitely in order.

Strangely, urban wilderness resources are remarkably low profile. Maybe it's a case of those in the know wanting to keep their favorite haunts a secret—or those not in the know just assuming that nature and cities occupy different zones on the planet. Check it out, though. We guarantee that your local parks and recreation department will have lists of the parks, botanical gardens, zoos, and nature preserves in your city along with any activities and special events offered. We recently checked options in our city, and they included reptile walks

Park Places

When it comes to land, not all cities are created equal. Sure, New York's got the acreage, but on a park-per-person basis, San Diego's the city to beat.

NAME OF CITY	POPULATION	OPEN SPACE	ACRES/PERSON
San Diego	1,223,000	36,108	.030
Phoenix	1,321,000	36,501	.028
Portland, OR	529,000	13,006	.025
Cincinnati	331,000	7,391	.022
Dallas	1,189,000	21,828	.018
Minneapolis	383,000	5,694	.015
Washington, DC	572,000	7,504	.013
Seattle	563,000	6,194	.011
Houston	1,954,000	21,964	.011
Los Angeles	3,695,000	29,801	.008
San Francisco	777,000	5,916	.008
Philadelphia	1,518,000	10,685	.007
New York City	8,008,000	49,854	.006
Detroit	951,000	5,890	.006
Chicago	2,896,000	11,645	.004

Source: Extracted from charts from the report "Inside City Parks" (Peter Harnik, Trust for Public Land and the Urban Land Institute, 2000) as shown on the Trust for Public Land Web site www.tpl.org.

(with live specimens), hiking, fishing, flower pressing (at a tulip festival), investigating insects (like dragonflies, damselflies, and centipedes that make their home in one park pond), bike rides along the beachfront, a saltwater animal workshop, a spring birding session, a celebration of the return of the native shad (a fish) to the Hudson River (with free tastings!), more fishing, and an oceanography-made-simple lesson. *All that in just one spring weekend!* We also discovered that deer, red foxes, wild turkeys, and coyotes are all living within New York City limits. Who knew?

To locate the folks responsible for your city's parks, try the Internet first. Just type your city's name and "parks recreation department" on your favorite search engine. That will get you an appropriate link in many cities. If you come up empty (in Chicago, for example, the right body is the Chicago Park District), call your city's information line and ask for the number of the city department responsible for park events—and also for any nonprofit group that runs park events (like the Central Park Conservancy in New York). You can always hit up your local tourism bureau or visitor's center; chances are they'll have info on parks, local greenery, outdoor activities, and day trips.

There are also national organizations that keep track of local greens. The Sierra Club and the Audubon Society, for example, may have branches in your city; if they do, they're great sources of nature and wildlife info. For the most off-the-beaten-track prospects, we recommend contacting the Trust for Public Land. This San Francisco–based national nonprofit organization is aggressive in its goal of preserving natural lands for public use and enjoyment, and much of its work has centered on urban areas. Their tentacles are everywhere—from safeguarding the open areas surrounding Chicago that are threatened by sprawl to helping create and sustain community-managed parks, playgrounds, and gardens in many cities. Go to the national Web site, www.tpl.org, to learn about a variety of new and old lands near your city that are all for the people or e-mail them at webmaster@tpl.org.

CITYWISE WARNING !

Nature Dangers

It's great that you're venturing out to the local wilds, but remember that nothing is more tempting to an infant or toddler than the leaves of a pretty plant or flower. If yours has a wandering mouth and fast hands, we recommend calling your local poison control center to request a list of poisonous plants in your area and how to identify them (it's a free service). And heaven forbid your child actually does swallow that errant leaf; call 911 to get to poison control and follow their instructions. If you're told to go to an emergency room, bring a specimen of the plant with you.

THE CITY PARENT RULES
Getting Kids into the Nature Habit

Rule #1: Trek regularly and vary your venues. Make being outdoors a regular feature of your life. One weekend, visit a new park in a new neighborhood; another, visit a wetland area and look for waterfowl. You can get a lot of excitement out of smaller expeditions as well:

Breakfast in the park. Just pack up some doughnuts, juice, and coffee, and you're good to go. There's something enchanting about watching city parks get going for the day.

Farmers markets. Find one near your house and make it a regular family stop. They're fun environments, and the vendors are usually very happy to talk to kids about how the corn is grown or what they fed the cow to make that cheese.

Park events. Those great city parks departments sponsor lots of free outdoor events, including family fishing days, sports demonstrations, telescope viewing of the night sky, falcon flying, and art fairs. Don't assume your kids are too young to appreciate any of this—somehow life out-of-doors takes on a magic all its own.

The Picnic Plan

We bet we do loads more picnics than any of our country friends (okay, they do barbecue a lot, but a barbecue ain't a picnic). Here's why we like 'em:

- Cleanup is easy; we use paper.
- They can be as elaborate or as simple as you'd like. Even peanut butter has a little glamour when it's eaten al fresco.
- Seating is flexible. We use a rubber-sided blanket but carry an old sheet when the group is bigger than just our family.
- While the adults talk, the kids can run around or do whatever. One

time, our group of children, then between 3 and 8, spent the whole of one protracted meal watching ants go up and down a tree.

Our tip for extending picnic fun: Alternate feeding and activities. Think courses. Give the kids their main course, then send them off with some balls (if your park allows it) or chalk. When they return, give them dessert, then send them off again with a challenge (i.e. find enough sticks to make a wall or stones that can be painted later with watercolors).

Develop Their Inner Park Rangers

Make the family excursions more than just a trip. Put on that Sherlock Holmes hat and become nature detectives together.

1. Watch wildlife, bugs, butterflies, and bats. Check out what they're doing, how fast they're moving, etc.
2. Hunt for wildflowers and animal artifacts like feathers, bones, scat, and tracks.
3. Scout for animal homes like bird nests and burrows.
4. List things that wild animals eat, then see if you can find some.
5. Sit outside and just listen. How many natural sounds can you recognize?
6. Teach the kids to use a compass to find directions. Some parks will give orienteering tutorials. Even if the little kids don't understand it, they still like scampering over hill and dale.
7. Become tree sleuths. Try to identify five trees by the shape of their leaves.
8. Test out some binoculars; the youngest children will have trouble figuring out how to use them but 4- and 5-year-olds may be able to get the hang of it.
9. Use a magnifying glass to look at very small animals, plants, and their parts.
10. Learn which native plants attract butterflies. Then go out and see if it's true.
11. Find five different rocks; identify and describe their differences.

Sources: Suggestions culled from the Texas Parks & Wildlife Web site. For more ideas, check out www.tpwd.state.tx.us/adv/kidspage/oknature.htm. Also, we recommend picking up a copy of *City Kids and City Critters,* from the Houston Arboretum and Nature Center by Janet Wier Roberts and Carole Huelbig. While this lively activity book for "urban explorers" is geared to children 8 and up, parents can assist younger ones with the many creative suggestions.

Mud days. It's really a drag when your free weekend is mucked up by two days of solid rain. But all is not lost. Every so often, Julia will suit up her kids in boots, slickers, and clothes she could care less about, and they all go running, sliding, and jumping through the muddiest, most puddle-filled section of the park near their home. Even for a parent, there is something exhilarating about trying to get dirty. If you're a little far from a park and don't relish a muddy bus ride home, don't fret. Kids are just as happy to go puddle jumping on sidewalks and they can get just as dirty; we've seen the evidence.

Rule #2: Do your homework. Before venturing out to some city green space, brush up on your high school earth science and biology. Start researching the local flora and fauna at your library or on the Internet and then get the kids excited by giving them a couple of fun facts about what they'll be encountering.

Get enough of a grounding yourself so that when your observant 5-year-old asks what kind of butterfly she's looking at, you'll be able to tell her (truthfully for once) that it's a moth. Kids eat this stuff up if you're not too pedantic about it. Really, if you can't name the birds, mammals, reptiles, insects, etc. in your area, how can you expect your kids to?

Rule #3: Greet the seasons. Don't take Mother Nature for granted. Those glorious D.C. cherry blossoms may be old hat to you, but they provide a perfect opportunity to teach your children about seasons and life cycles—and that knowledge is guaranteed to surface every time they look at a cherry blossom for the rest of their lives. You don't even have to pick quite so spectacular a nature display. Even those five lone tulips popping up from the base of the nearest city tree can get a point across.

Rule #4: Go to anything and everything that has a nature component. This is so obvious we sometimes forget that aquariums and natural history museums

Nurture Their Nature Center

Nature centers should be at the top of every city parent's list of places to go. Typically, they'll have discovery rooms and touch tables and are staffed with rangers and/or volunteers who are knowledgeable about their particular area's ecosystem. Most of the activities are constructed with the goal of getting children to interact with and investigate nature. Many have a guided outdoor component as well.

Take Austin's Nature & Science Center, which offers a variety of activities geared to mini-nature lovers—all, like most nature centers, for minimal fees. For just $2 to $3 a pop, Austin preschoolers can "Meet the Animals" (where they'll touch a snake, smell a ferret, and listen to a quail while exploring skulls, feathers, bones, and fur) or become a "Dinosaur Detective" (which lets kids dig for fossils like a paleontologist in the "dino pit" exhibit while gathering clues about their favorite prehistoric beast). Or, check out the differences between insects, spiders, and other invertebrates and search outdoors for live critters using nets and magnifying glasses in the "6 Legs, 8 Legs, Many Legs" class. And that's just the beginning: Kindergarteners have nine other classes from which to choose.

are not just welcome diversions for that rainy day, they're really excellent ways for city kids to see, experience, and enjoy nature. Ditto zoos, botanical gardens, nature centers, and arboretums. All are fiendishly inviting to youngsters, and most have an assortment of interactive exhibits that will keep kids wanting to come back for more. And did we mention park tours? Most cities sponsor tree-naming walks, park history sojourns, and guided walks for bird-watching (don't expect to follow those tours slavishly; avid birders can happily watch one little feathered friend for an extended period of time, well beyond the attention span of a child). They're usually free, and no one is going to care too much if you dip in and out.

Rule #5: Join a local garden. Your child's interaction with the plant world needn't be limited to the grocery store, not when almost every American city has an active grassroots movement—every pun intended—in place for "greening up." Adopt-a-park programs, where local residents get together to turn unused paved areas into green viewing parks, abound. Many of these once-cement stations have flowered into mini gardens of paradise, often because residents went to local officials and asked. (Kathy's husband has led their city block's effort to turn a little traffic island into a mini-park. It's currently in process, and when it happens, daughter Alice will be among the volunteers watering the flowers.) Local community gardens are typically manned by volunteers who welcome newcomers. In many cases, they are hooked up with the local public school system, providing students with outdoor "class time." During summer months when school's out, the volunteers will usually be happy to "train" younger locals. It's a great way to learn about life cycles of the fruits, vegetables, plants, and flowers that grow. Maybe they'll even spot a worm or two.

Day Trip Ideas

Sometimes it's worth getting out of town to get back to nature. If you're in a driving city, then you likely have a car to get you out of town. If not, public transportation (through commuter rails or buses, or even some long-distance subway rides) should be able to get you there.

Some ideas to get you started:

Hike your heart out. "If they can walk, they can hike. And hiking is a great form of exercise for children and a way to enjoy nature," American Hiking Society president Mary Margaret Sloan reminds us. Contact local hiking groups. The Sierra Club can refer you to some, or you can find groups by searching the Internet for using the name of your city and "hiking" as search terms. Trails.com is a great Web source, with a database of 30,000 trails nationwide. With small children, unless

---

CITY SAVVY

Tips for Peewee Hikers

When kids enjoy themselves, they'll want to go back again. Herewith are some suggestions to make their trailblazing a pleasurable experience.

Choose short hikes with terrain that'll hold your child's attention. Don't blow it by picking a first hike that leaves your child crying with fatigue (and remember, however far you're going, you'll also have to get back). But that doesn't mean you need to stick to flat, easy paths. As the American Hiking Society points out, kids love to climb over rocks, so something short with a little scrambling built in, even a very gentle stream to cross, might be perfect.

Keep the kids well-fueled. Kids are often so entranced by new surroundings that they forget that they're hungry or thirsty and the next thing you know, you're dealing with a meltdown. Bring plenty to eat and drink, and make sure you schedule snack breaks.

Dress appropriately. You're probably aware that every hiker, even the littlest one, needs sturdy shoes, but lots of clothing layers are just as important, especially for kids, who can heat up and cool down a bunch of times over the course of a hike. You'll want the flexibility to add or subtract layers to keep them comfortable.

Give the kids control. At the young ages, it's all about that anyway, so here's an ideal opportunity to give them a little authority. Let them chose where to take that snack break or whether to take Trail X or Y.

Mix it up. There are lots of things to do to keep little ones engaged on a trek and using a variety of tactics may be your best bet. Try teaching (names of trees and plants, how you use a map, the concepts of trail markings and trail etiquette), playing games (I Spy works for any age), even singing.

Sources: American Hiking Society's (AHS) Family Hiking Fact Sheet and personal tips from AHS president Mary Margaret Sloan.

---

they're in a backpack (but who has the room to keep one of those in the house?), aim for the simpler, shorter trails. "Keep your expectations low," suggests Sloan. But that doesn't mean it won't be fun. "I've always found that when I hike with kids, I see things from a different perspective—looking at things from their lower eye level," she says.

Beach it in the off-season. During the summers, public beaches near cities tend to be packed (and loud and, yes, sometimes filled with litter). Feel free to join the throngs for some seaside play, but also consider a visit during the off-season when the young ones will actually have a little space to move around in.

Have a cow. Many local farms accept guests (expect to pay a little for admission). You can find the popular ones in guidebooks for your city; the local tourist bureaus also have listings. Of course, they'll likely be crowded, but even the most touristy farm will have animals to admire, pet, and even feed. You can also go a little off the beaten path by requesting a list of working farms that accept visitors from the chamber of commerce of an agricultural region near you.

Pick and treat. Harvest time means picking berries, peaches, vegetables, apples, and pears. Apples never taste better than when you pick them yourself off the trees. Halloween is that much more exciting if you all lug your future jack-o'-lanterns home after having picked them yourself. The local literature—freebie guides and city magazines (look up archival articles on the Web)—will tell you where to go.

See stars. There's nothing like a night outdoors to make your toddler "wild" in the ways you want him to be. You'll find national and state parks easily on the Web and even listed in the telephone directory. If camping is a little too much nature for you, many city zoos sponsor parent-child sleepovers. Also, local branches of the Sierra Club, whose national office is based in San Francisco, put together great inexpensive outings.

BRINGING NATURE INDOORS

Sometimes of course, you just can't get outdoors, and that's why you'll want some nature at home as well.

Pets: A Little Critter Goes a Long Way

Ever since you introduced *Pat the Bunny* to Chloe, you've been waiting for the inevitable "Mommy, I want a rabbit" (or dog, or cat, or bird, etc.). Of course, animals are to children as chocolate is to milk: a perfect combo that makes life that much sweeter. Unless, of course, you live in a city, where landlords don't want pets, where there isn't an inch of space in your abode for another *anything*, and where exercise is hard enough for you to handle, let alone manage for a

What to Say and Do When Your City Pet Dies

The death of a pet can be a special challenge in the city. Not only do you have to deal with the big issue of *death*, you've got to manage the sometimes tricky logistics of getting Barney to his final resting place.

What to say (Hint: Don't ever tell Ryan you're flushing the parakeet down the toilet; don't tell the super, either.):

Children can take the death of a pet very hard. The youngest children probably won't understand the concept of "gone forever," but older kids can be seriously affected by the loss of a pet. How do you tell? One good test: Play peek-a-boo. If your child still realizes you're there even though her eyes are covered, she will probably have lots of questions about where the pet has gone and will need to be dealt with in a safe, age-appropriate manner. Never tell the child that the pet has gone to sleep, psychologists warn. The child may keep waiting for the animal to wake up. Furthermore, it may be disturbing for a child to equate sleep with dying or not coming back. Equally harmful would be to flush a small animal down the toilet *with* the child's knowledge.

What to do (Hint: No park burials.):

But once you've negotiated the emotional sensitivities of a pet's death, what exactly do you *do* with the dearly departed? If a creature is small enough to be flushed down the toilet, the law generally won't get in your way; on the other hand, most cities have strict laws against the burial of animals, for health reasons. In Fort Worth, for instance, you can't even bury a pet on your own property, so don't bother trying to find a suitable grave at a local park. Furthermore, even if your city does not have a law prohibiting animal burial in public spaces, it will likely have rules against unlawful excavation; if you are caught, you can expect a handsome fine.

Instead, you must call your local dead animal disposal unit (look under Animal Control or the Department of Sanitation in the Yellow Pages), which will explain the local regulations on packing up animals (usually two plastic bags) and arrange for curbside pickups. Do ask what, if any, fees you'll incur. In some cities, the service is free; in others, there will be a small fee. You can also make arrangements with your vet for cremation or disposal (although you may want to inquire about where your beloved will go, as many end up at rendering plants that—sit down for this one— "recycle" the animal into pet foods).

Finally, your local ASPCA or humane society will probably offer pet cremations and memorial services.

four-legged friend. Still, there's that reverberating "Mommy, I want a . . ."

So what's a city parent to do? Get one!
According to the American Academy of
Child and Adolescent Psychiatry, pets provide a welcome connection to nature and so
much more. A child who learns to care for
an animal and to treat it in a kind, patient
way gets invaluable training in learning to
treat people the same way. Developing a
loving relationship with a pet can boost a
child's self-esteem and self-confidence and
can aid in developing nonverbal communication skills, compassion, and empathy. Sold!

Picking the Best Pet for Your Family (and Apartment)

Next step: How to make it work when city
living seems to conspire against having a
pet. Choose carefully. The animal you decide to welcome into your family should
be a function of the size of your home, your availability to provide the appropriate
amount of exercise for the pet, financial costs, and the pet's potential life span.

Often, parents of young children start small, on the theory that small
means less work (you can't really expect your 4-year-old to help out too much,
you know), and landlords will often accept caged pets even when they forbid
dogs or cats. But consider a few things: Small animals often have short life
spans, so bereavement may be an issue at some point. Also, young children are
often aggressive with animals, and their clumsy handling can be dangerous to
little creatures. This means adult monitoring at all times. (Julia always told her
children that they couldn't get a guinea pig until they were sure Malcolm
wouldn't flush it down the toilet.) Many small animals are nocturnal and will
bite when they're awakened unexpectedly during the day. Lastly, there are those
cages to remember. If they're not cleaned often and immaculately, don't run
crying to us about that foul odor permeating your digs.

Good smaller choices include a variety of rodents, rabbits, fish, and birds. Stay
away from the reptiles (lizards, snakes, and turtles)—the Centers for Disease Control and Prevention (CDC) warns that the slimy ones carry diseases (many reptiles
carry the salmonella bacteria) that can compromise the health of children 5 and
under. Besides, reptiles like to dine on live foods, which could make feeding time
not the most age-appropriate activity for our coddled youngsters. Other animals

(continued on page 182)

CITYWISE WARNING !

Pets and Your Kid's Health

According to the CDC, infants
and children under the age of 5 are
more likely than most people to get
diseases from animals (and are more
likely than others to get very sick). This
is mostly because young children indulge in a lot of hand-to-mouth behavior that is trouble if you've touched
a surface that's contaminated with
animal feces. Be scrupulous about
having kids thoroughly wash their
hands with soap and running water
after animal contact.

The Lowdown on Smaller Pets

THE BEAST	THE GOOD	THE BAD
Guinea pigs an excellent choice.	Super gentle and cuddly, they love attention and petting. Side benefit: They're great role models for good eating habits since they love veggies, fruits, and grains (they need their fiber!) and drink lots of water.	Usually they're sweet as can be, but when they bite it hurts, and they don't like to be grabbed from above. Gotta be prepared to clean the cage. They poop a lot!
Hamsters not recommended	Besides being little, and cute to some, not many advantages. Hamsters are hoarders; we call them the little rodents with obsessive-compulsive disorder. They love to store their food finds for safekeeping, which will, at least, keep your little ones entertained for hours.	Nowhere near as nice as guinea pigs, so it's important to go to a reputable breeder to find one with a good temperament. Skip the pet shops, which breed for cute appearance rather than kindness. Handled too quickly or roughly they can become vicious.
Gerbils eh, there are better rodents.	They're little, relatively inexpensive, entertaining, and fairly easy to maintain.	Little escape artists, ya better keep those cages locked, otherwise beware: They'll chew up anything in sight. When provoked, they can bite.
Fancy rats first pick of the rodent litter!	These domesticated vermin are adorable and smart. You can teach them to recognize their names, respond when called, and even do a few tricks. Like cats, they are amazingly clean and groom themselves several times a day; like dogs, they're friendly pack animals who thrive on attention and form real bonds with people.	If you let them loose, they'll need constant supervision because they love to nibble on everything from material and cords to walls. Imported Gambian rats started monkeypox, and the CDC is currently investigating the import of exotic pets. Stick with the domestic versions.
Rabbits not recommended for kids under 7.	They are quiet and can learn near-perfect litter box habits. They're kind of like toddlers: love to run around the house, poking their noses into everything that's new.	In reality, they hardly live up to their cuddly stereotype. They'll bite if not held properly; they chew on things like electric cords; and they need a lot of exercise to boot. Not to mention the fact that they do need to be potty trained and possibly neutered. For all the work you'll encounter, you might as well get a dog. Or a rat.
Birds Cockatiels' size and sweet dispositions are particularly great for kids.	Huge variety of sizes and personalities from which to select. Many can be trained; many can talk. Highly interactive. Budgies/Parakeets and Cockatiels are lowest maintenance.	Hope you're neat freaks: Birds need daily cleanings. And the larger birds need more attention and time. Some birds will bite, and the very small ones are pretty delicate. Some can carry psittacosis, a disease that is dangerous to the young or immuno-compromised.
Fish pretty and soothing, if you can deal with the upkeep.	They're relatively inexpensive, low maintenance, and easy to feed.	Not a lot of one-on-one interaction, unless you know something we don't.

SPACE PLANNING	LIFE SPAN	WORD TO THE WISE	DID YOU KNOW?
They need 2 square feet of living space and a cage with high sides.	6 years	They're social creatures, but without a constant companion they become depressed. Get two (same gender, otherwise they'll reproduce like rabbits)!	In post–18th century England, ladies of the court had their servants carry their pet guinea pigs alongside them on a silken pillow (the *Golden Age of Guinea Pigs*, apparently).
A cage measuring 24 × 16 × 12 inches is the minimum recommended size.	2–3 years	They like to dig so an extra layer of peat moss is nice in the cages. Experts say cages must be cleaned at least once a week, but we've found that you really should plan on tidying up more.	They've been bred up the wazoo, so they come in lots of different colors. They're solitary; don't keep two of the same sex in the same digs or they'll fight to the death.
Same space needs as their cousins, the hamsters.	2–3 years	They need playmates, or they can get depressed and live shorter lives. Best combo: a pair or trio of males from the same litter.	Females who come from the same litter may fight until one is no more.
A cage the size of a 20-gallon fish tank works just fine.	2–3 years	Social, they also like a friend of the same gender. Easy to care for, cages need cleaning only once or twice a week, although they'll need food, water, and attention daily.	So many fun varieties: Siamese, Manx (tailess), Sphynx (hairless), Dalmatian (spotted), Rex (curly fur), and on and on.
You'll need a cage that's at least 30 × 30 inches or 24 × 36 inches. The cage will need to be away from TVs, stereos, or high-noise areas and cleaned frequently—at the very least twice a week.	8–12 years	Just like toddlers, rabbits need routines and don't respond well when you change them.	Peter Cottontail, Bugs Bunny, and the Easter Bunny are mythical figures. The real ones love fiber and actually digest it twice by doing it once then (yeech) eating their own droppings and doing it again.
Space needs depend on the bird, but you're going to need a cage at least 1½ feet wide. Also, many birds like to be able to fly daily—and they can get lost even in small apartments.	Varies by breed. Parakeets can live 7–12 years; cockatiels 10–18 years. Some parrots can live for 50 years.	Try to buy a baby, 1–3 months old, that is still being hand-fed. This allows the bird to learn to trust the hand that's feeding him. Birds need specialty grooming every 3 to 4 months.	Parrots and profanity: Once a word has been uttered for 21 days, it'll be part of Polly's eternal vocabulary. Also, some birds have predispositions for other inelegant sounds: burps and belches; coughs and sneezes.
Aquariums vary, but size is not generally a big issue and kids love *furnishing* them.	Unless your aquarium is well maintained they have a way of dying frequently.	Aquarium management is practically a science: You need to maintain the proper pH, temperature, and nitrogen level to keep your fishies swimming.	*Finding Nemo* was one giant fishie PR campaign. Have your kid watch the movie and then surprise him with a fish of his own. You'll be a hero for at least a week.

on the CDC no-no list: amphibians (frogs, toads, newts, and salamanders), baby chicks, and ducklings.

When Only a Dog Will Do

Small space be damned, your kids want a *real* pet. Does that make any sense at all when you're living in the confines of a city? It can.

We all know that dogs love people, but they're just so much more complicated. The daily walks; the potty training; the barking (and the neighbors' complaints); the shedding all over your apartment; the sucking up to the landlord; it's all a little daunting, isn't it? But, for a family, there are some huge canine benefits (they provide companionship, demonstrate compassion, can help a shy child feel more secure, teach responsibility, they can even get sedentary kids on the move). It's obviously a personal decision. Kathy has one and wouldn't have it any other way. While Julia says not a chance (she told her older kids it was either a new sibling or a dog). But, just in case you're so inclined, we'll give you the list of dogs that work well in apartments and are great with little kids.

In general, the younger the child, the larger the dog you should be considering—though space considerations may pre-empt all the advice in the world. Bigger four-leggeds are usually less sensitive to pain, so when toddler terrors give Pugsly's tail that inevitable tug, they may not even react. Inflict that same poke or pinch on a smaller pooch, however, and even the sweetest little love puff will transform into a pint-sized warrior. Big or small, though, it's important to always supervise your child in their dog interactions.

For all things dog, we always consult with Bash Dibra, the author of *Your Dream Dog* and dog trainer to the stars. Dibra—who counts Sarah Jessica Parker and Matthew Broderick's Border Collie, JLo's Chihuahua, geez even Henry

If You're Thinking Feline . . .

Independent and the most hygienic of animals, cats *are* great indoor pets and can adapt readily to small spaces, plus they could care less about that daily walk. All in all, they are pretty much in the top ranks of city pets. On the kid-friendly front, the verdict's a little more mixed. Some cats are beyond independent, actually downright unfriendly, even edgy; so if you're getting one as a family pet, you have to get one that's calm and likes to be handled.

Kissinger's Labrador Retriever among his many privileged students—points to several traits a city family should look for in a dog: trainability, easy grooming, and flexibility. Flexibility? "You want a dog that can adjust well to a variety of activities, that can handle an old lady in the elevator, a busy intersection, and the antics of kids," he says. Biggest mistake city dwellers make? "Getting a high-response dog. They start barking at any little noise. You want a dog that's energetic but not bouncing off the walls."

Here are Dibra's top 10 picks for the best city *and* kiddie-friendly breeds.

Affenpinschers: These dogs are tiny but they still do very well with children. Plus, they're smart, highly affectionate, and need little grooming.

Basset Hounds: Low to the ground, happy-go-lucky dogs, they do "vocalize," but if you get a female and train her at a young age, barking is less likely to be a problem. A stocky medium-sized breed, basset hounds lumber about apartments without a care in the world—except for their human young 'uns, whom they love and protect with abandon. They'll usually permit some rough play and rarely bite. If they get their daily exercise, they can be pretty low-key indoors, but they'd probably be a little happier in larger apartments.

Bichon Frise/Havanese: Members of the bichon family, both sub-breeds, are sweet little furry things that resemble poodles and make excellent city pets. In fact, they're just about perfect for city kids with asthma or allergies because they have hair, not fur, in which case the fact that they need frequent grooming is actually a plus, says Dibra. "The more you bathe them, the healthier their coat gets and you're regularly brushing away the mites and pollen." On the other hand, these animals are very sensitive, he warns, so wait until you have a child who is old enough to know not to abuse them.

Cavalier King Charles Spaniels: Hands down, Bash thinks these regal beasts are the best of city/kiddie breeds. "Those you can start at one or two," he says. "They're so mellow, so sweet so loving." They're not big shedders either so if you manage to give yours a weekly grooming, you should be okay.

Collies: Remember Lassie? "These are wonderful family dogs," says Dibra. "You can't go wrong." They do need to be walked regularly, but if you make walking the dog part of your child's day, you'll be benefiting both kid and dog. The real payoff? A collie, bred to herd, will just think your child is part of his flock. He'll be your little one's steadfast guardian angel.

Golden/Labrador Retrievers: These are the most lovable of creatures, and Dibra thinks they really want to be kids. "They're particularly great for the town and country lifestyle that so many city people have," he says. Yes, they're big, but they are amazingly laid-back with little kids, and as long as you have a good dog run or park nearby (these guys do like their runaround time), they'll

Safe Ways to Deal with Pooches on the Prowl

Urban dogs, like their owners, are often out and about town—seated by their masters at an outdoor café, playing in the park, strolling on the sidewalk—lots of opportunity for kid-dog encounters. And little kids invariably want to pet Rover, which may be why children make up 60 percent of dog-bite victims. Very few bites happen without provocation—though it's not obvious to humans, especially the youngest ones, what's provoking to a dog, so precautions must be taken.

- Watch for warning signs like growling and disinterest.
- Never allow your child to approach an unfamiliar dog without first asking the owner if it's friendly and likes kids.
- Kids love to pet dogs' faces and look 'em in the eyes—behavior that can be highly threatening to the dog. Teach your child early on how to approach a pooch properly. Let the dog sniff your hand first before trying to pet it and leave its face alone.
- Never disturb a dog that's tied up, sleeping, or eating.
- Never scream at or run from a dog.
- Pit bulls and Rottweilers seem to be pretty popular in cities. Some are sweet, but many are trained as guard or attack dogs. Be very careful approaching a guard dog breed, even with the owner's approval.

be just fine in a city. Goldens do need to be brushed a lot, which means a little extra work, but it can also be a great responsibility to give to a slightly older child.

Poodles: They're plus-size Bichons. "People shy away from them because they often have that puffed-out look," notes Dibra. "But you can always keep their coats short. They don't need to look froufrou." Did we mention their brains? Everybody always says that poodles are the brightest of dogs, and there's a reason for that. Smart, trainable, fun—what's not to like? Of course, if you forget to give them enough outdoor exercise, they might be a little frenetic indoors. Take care of that, and you'll have a paragon of a pet.

Portuguese Water Dogs: Comical and endearing, they have a Labrador look with a poodle coat, just like the new "in" dogs, the Labradoodles. These, however, are members of a long-established purebred. They do need exercise but are trainable and particularly great if you alternate between city and country.

Pugs: "They snore and make that constant stuffed nose sound that makes everyone sleepy," says Dibra. But you know what? This may be a benefit if your little Thumbelina is sleep-challenged; pugs are delicious cuddlers and will take naps with your little one. Plus, they're small but sturdy enough to withstand the fumblings of small children. And they barely need any exercise. On the negative side, they do shed, so keep a dustbuster handy.

Schnauzers: These distinguished-looking small- to medium-sized terriers are really fine with children and adapt easily to apartment spaces. A little heartier, perhaps, than some of the smallest breeds, their sweetness and loyalty to their families are undeniably appealing.

In addition to these top 10 breeds, keep in mind two favorites of older children:

Boston Terriers: The all-American breed is best suited for children 6 and up. They're good watchdogs and come in a convenient, easy-to-manage size. At times a little hyper, they're still great with kids. Dibra calls them "big dogs in little bodies" that adore their owners, are tolerant of other pets, need minimal grooming, and seem perfectly content in even the most claustrophobic of apartments.

Border Terriers: These guys also do better with the older child (6 and up). People-oriented and eager to make their owners happy, they can be real kid-pleasers. Another positive: They shed very little, although you do need to plan a weekly grooming.

Greening Up Your Home

Every time we see those design magazine houses stocked to the rafters with foliage and flowers, it makes us want to bring a little green into our homes. Easier said than done. Apartments do not make the most hospitable environments for plants, especially for tropical varieties that require high humidity and lots of sunlight. Now for a double whammy: "Most plants suitable for apartments are

Baby-Safe and Apartment Hardy Plants

It's kind of a tall order to find plants that are kid-friendly and able to thrive in the somewhat inhospitable environment of the typical city apartment. But we do have a few thoughts. FYI, we've used our editorial license to go right ahead and eliminate those plants that are particularly attractive to mealy bugs since you have bigger bugs and mice to worry about.

- African and flame Violet (not good for cold climes)
- Aglaonema (Chinese evergreen)

- Begonias
- Cast-iron plant
- Coleus (does need enough light)
- Corn plant
- Geranium
- Pothos
- Snake plants
- Spathiphyllum
- Spider plants
- Wandering Jew
- Yucca (needs high light intensities)

toxic to children," according to the specialist manning the plant information hotline of the New York Botanical Garden. That's seriously scary news, considering how tempted toddlers are to sneak in a nibble of a leaf or a lick of the sap when Mom isn't looking. Apparently far too many parents are unaware of the dangers of apartment plants (we know we were). Poison control centers around the country receive more inquiries about bad actor plants than any other sources of poison.

We couldn't track them all down, but a few plant families to be *very wary* of include: the poinsettia family (do your families and pets a favor and find another way to celebrate the holidays—and we don't mean with mistletoe since that's poisonous too); the cactus family; the tomato family (the leaves and stems, that is); and the dumb cane and philodendron families, both of which have parts containing oxalate crystals that can cause the tongue to swell so severely that breathing stops after ingestion. But the plants that scare us the most: castor bean and oleander plants; when eaten, they can be deadly.

We know what you're thinking: This is too much brain damage. You'll just get plant pictures. But don't give up so easily. That one plant can provide a fabulous and cheap way to teach your child how to take care of something, and watering has got to be about the easiest, most fun way to introduce Lolabelle to the world of chores. Want more? That little greenery can also become your child's first "organized" science lesson as well—with a little help from you.

Developing Your Child's Inner Gardener

Have you ever watched a child stare in fascination at a plant that is just sprouting roots? We have, and trust us, tracking the rise of plants from "nothing" to tiny seedlings can be a source of great pride for any youngster who has done the planting (with your help, of course). Margaret Blachly, a preschool teacher at Manhattan's prestigious Bank Street Family Center, believes that plants also provide invaluable instructional experiences. "Watering plants" is an entry that always appears on her classroom job charts. "Kids learn that plants are living things that need to be taken care of," she explains. "What's more, at 3 to 4 years of age, kids are starting to talk about growing up—moving on to kindergarten next year, getting bigger—and through growing plants, they can relate their own experience to the thing they're taking care of."

To do this at home and ensure a happy result, you'll want to stick with varieties that germinate, have large seeds, and can grow readily. Pumpkins work: You can actually grow them from seeds left over after Halloween, although at some point they'll need to move from your small flowerpot and be replanted outdoors.

With large seeds that are easy for kids to handle, sunflowers are also excellent choices for indoor growing, according to a volunteer we called at our local botanical garden. The sunflowers get quite large before they flower; eventually they will have to be replanted, so first the kids can watch the stems come up and then they can learn about repotting. Equally sweet: carrot tops and sweet potatoes. You probably have them in your house already. Both can be planted in a clear glass container. They have large seeds and tend to grow readily indoors. Kids will adore watching nature take its course.

Teacher's Tips on the Best Growing Plants for Kids

"In the city, we've got an extra responsibility to show kids that food doesn't come from the store, that it actually comes from plants/farms," says preschool teacher Margaret Blachly. So she'll tell her class, "We've made popcorn all year, and now we're taking kernels and sprouting them into plants. Kids get the experience of seeing something grow from seed to plant. They get to see the process." Popcorn is one of the many plants that draw kids in to understanding nature's cycle. In fact, there's no lack of growing options for city kids. Her other faves:

Spider plants. Kids can cut sections of a larger spider plant, place them in plastic cups filled with water, and then watch the roots grow.

Bulbs. They grow quickly, and kids can see how the bulb transforms into something different. Want to add some math and manipulatives? Chart the growth with Cuisenaire rods.

Beans. You can sprout any bean (don't get castor; they're poisonous). Just place them in a wet paper towel until they sprout, then plant in a pot and watch the bean plant grow. Blachly recommends *One Bean*, a colorful book by Anne F. Rockwell that walks kids through the process of growing a bean plant.

CHAPTER 8

GETTING BABY UP TO SPEED

We bet you just can't wait to get out there and introduce your child to that great, big, exciting city. But no one ever told you what a hassle it was to get such a little baby outfitted for the urban outdoors. (Stocking the diaper bag! Preparing for inclement weather! Even just getting the darn stroller to move on those lumpy sidewalks!) We know what you're thinking. Leelee doesn't even know the difference between the outside and the inside. She can just stick indoors for a while. Or maybe Leelee's older now. She's a real walker, so no more stroller! But she hasn't quite got that toilet-training thing licked yet, and who wants the stress of finding out where she can go when she's got to go? Not you, certainly. Maybe it's a good idea to minimize the travel for a while.

Stop right there. It is our strong view (another one) that if you don't get out and about with your city kids right from their first breath, you will find yourself locked into a pattern of behavior that will be mighty hard to break. And you know what the repercussions of that foot-dragging are, don't you? Kids with limited experience in their city who might as well be growing up in the suburbs. What a shame.

It's not so hard to get your young family perambulating. And there are pretty decent benefits if you do—lots of little city things that you and your babe can enjoy together, even if she's not yet ready to critique that Gauguin exhibit. We're here to help with advice on how to choose a city-smart stroller and create a transportation strategy to make your outings go smoother. We'll also give you some tricks to deal with those logistical sticky wickets like breastfeeding and outdoor expeditions with kids-in-training (toilet, that is). Once you're familiar with how to get up and go, we'll even provide you a bunch of places to go that are tailor-made for you and your young one.

MOBILIZING THE CITY FAMILY

Whether you're venturing out with a newborn, twins, or just one who feels like three, city fun will be that much more fun if you get the transportation thing down.

Suburbanites get to carry enough stuff in their cars to outfit a day care center, but urban dwellers must rely on that lean machine, the portable stroller. Successfully navigating a day's worth of errands and activities with kids in tow requires planning and strategy: what wheels to use, what routes to take, what items to bring along, and even where to go. Says one city mom who's been there, "If stores have stairs, I'll think twice about going." Another parent frequents a grocery store five blocks away (not the cheaper one next door) because it has wide aisles.

Your Stroller Personality

Picking a stroller is not just an exercise in checking out hardware. Now maybe this is a little Zen for you, but it does appear to us that there are some distinct parent personality traits, even divisions, that really dictate a lot about how you'll move around the city with your kith and kin. Some say the divide is one of preparedness; others see it as a fundamental philosophical rift. Either way, you can't avoid it because consciously or not, you will end up (more or less) as:

1. A pared-down proponent of stoic parenting. (Kids getting a little hungry and you have no food? Hey, it's good for them to get off of that immediate gratification thing. Buddy has a booboo and you are without Band-Aids? Aahh, it's only a scratch; we'll let it get some air.)
2. A self-sufficient survivalist, who plans and provisions for every eventuality, from missed meals (you carry three courses) to temperature changes (you have sweatshirts and bathing suits) to medical emergencies (antibacterial ointment and bandages appropriate for the seven most common childhood injuries).

Of course, we suggest you confront your psyche now because your personal orientation should be a significant factor in figuring out which stroller to buy. Maximalists, for instance, should check out prams for all their extra cargo space; minimalists, meanwhile, will want to look for only lightweight strollers. (Either persuasion works just fine, by the by, as long as the mobility test is passed: Can you, vehicle, and child still get on the bus and/or push the many miles you may cover in a few hours running city chores?)

Choosing a Stroller for the City

Time was, buying a stroller was as simple as Sears: Just run down to the local branch and pick from one of a whopping two, maybe three, models on the floor. Not anymore. Today, we have *choices*. From stripped-down to Porsched-up, you'll find a baby vehicle for every taste, with every option combo, and at more price points than a cell phone plan. With all the makes and models (apparently that '80s Beemer lust was *redirected*—to the carriage trade), you'd think that finding the perfect city stroller would be a snap and go. It's remarkably not.

Despite the rather frightening amount of stroller literature out there (who are those people posting daily on all the stroller message boards, anyway?), city issues are only tangentially addressed. What good, really, is knowing that the Miranda character on *Sex and the City* chose the Frog by Dutch maker Bugaboo or that

Find Your Stroller Style

	MINIMALIST MOMMY	MAXIMALIST MOMMY
Characteristics:	Values mobility above all else. Relying on her quick wits, this mom is often a parent of multiples more prepared to wing it in case of emergencies and less prone to worrying that the impromptu snack is a street vendor's pretzel rather than some nutritious snack from home.	A survivalist, this mom is ready for anything. Either the super stay-at-home whose every focus is on parenting or the workaholic who doesn't want any of that precious bonding time cut off by an emergency dash home.
Motto:	"I can buy whatever I need."	"Armageddon, here I come."
Advantages:	She may be a mom, but she still rocks and guys think she's hot.	The hit of the playground because she often bails out lesser-prepared parents.
Disadvantages:	Like flying without a net—a great chance of aborted trips due to mutinying progeny (too cold, too wet, too hungry, etc.).	More prone to backaches; hazardous on steep hills or potholes; children less likely to "go with the flow."

Sarah Jessica Parker favors the posh British Silver Cross carriage if *you* can't get *your* status stroller to even fold up in your spatially challenged apartment? And given the cost of urban real estate, surely you have better uses for your precious square footage than housing nonperforming strollers.

Learn from Kathy's sad tale. How proud her husband was the day he took it upon himself to buy the lovely Alice a "big girl" stroller. How sad he was when he realized it couldn't make it up a sidewalk curb. How annoyed Kathy was when he wouldn't part with the monstrosity, despite how much space it occupied. (Hey, it hurts to chuck out a perfectly intact stroller with one outing's use. And a word to the wise: Don't throw out that box until you're sure, *really sure*, you won't need it.) If someone had only pointed out to Kathy's husband that negotiating sidewalks can be problematic for some strollers, he probably would not have made that expensive mistake. With the aim of protecting your pocketbook, we pinpoint some essential city needs to consider when picking your kid's first transport.

THE CITY PARENT RULES
Wheely Important Stroller Stuff

Rule #1: Measure maneuverability. Primo, guys. Your city baby is going to be spending a lot of time in the stroller going on errands, to the park, to stores, restaurants, friend's houses. The stroller better be capable of going over many terrains—sidewalks, stairs, cobblestones, grass, and, those stroller busters, potholes. Maneuverability is all about the wheels. Tires better move easily—sideways as well as forward and backward—so look for front wheels that swivel. Also, keep in mind that small wheels do make for easy navigating while big ones are more shock absorbent; air-filled tires gives a smooth ride and are great over bumpy sidewalks, but have a tendency to pop in hot weather.

Rule #2: Give weight its due. Somehow the fact that kids can grow pretty quickly doesn't always penetrate the craniums of parents considering a new stroller. But every pound counts when you need to get up and down stairs with that quarter-pounder of yours. So it's not enough that your potential purchase handles fine with your little one's current weight: You need to think about what life will be like 5 or 10 pounds down the road when you're trying to carry kid and carrier up or down a couple of steps. That's when you'll curse yourself for buying the 22-pound carriage instead of the 18-pound one or the 11-pound stroller instead of the 8-pounder.

Rule #3: Check for collapsibility. How easily the stroller folds—do you need one hand or two?—is seriously important if you're going to be in and out of cars and a serious benefit if you frequent a lot of crowded places that require you to fold it when it's not in use (think apartment halls, kid locales like Ys, birthday parties, and schools). You don't want to find out the hard way, like the unhappy mom we read about who couldn't get her stroller folded quickly enough to get on a bus and ended up sitting down on the dirty sidewalk in despair when the impatient driver pulled away.

Rule #4: Think ahead. If a second child is in the stars for your family, consider purchasing a stroller that either has a standing ledge (basically a metal shelf attached between the back wheels that a tired child can hitch a ride on) or can handle a buggy board attachment. The latter is an ingenious platform on wheels that attaches to the rear axle of a stroller, allowing older kids to stand on it. There are a variety of models that work with many different brands and types of strollers, but not all.

Rule #5: Remember sizes—yours and that of anyone else who'll be a frequent driver, that is. Your stroller's got to work for all pushers, and if they are of vastly different heights, you need to figure out how to make it work for all of them— whether you pick a stroller with adjustable handles or buy extensions that can be attached and unattached with ease.

Rule #6: Conveniences count. How much basket space does the stroller have and how accessible is that space? How large are the hoods? What type of harness does it have (does it go over the head or just sideways)? Does it come with a rain or snow attachment? City kids live in their strollers, so such details matter.

Rule #7: Evaluate your ability to clean. When you consider the grime of city streets and the fact that urban urchins can spend extensive hours (including mealtimes) in their stroller, no one should be surprised at the filth that can accumulate. The surprise is the fact that not every stroller has fabric that detaches for cleaning or is even eminently washable. If crud buildup is likely to offend you, make sure that every inch of fabric can be easily and thoroughly cleaned.

One parting thought. Since most stores don't let you test-drive the merchandise, you'll probably have to rely on the experience of others to make your final decision. Definitely ask the advice of friends in your city (and not in others because the particulars of a locale add up quickly—driving cities necessitate different strollers than walking ones; older cities are different than newer ones, etc.). Amazingly, you don't need to know a soul with a child to get a thousand opinions on strollers. If it were us, we'd probably start by checking out www.consumersearch.com, an aggregation of reviews from sites such as Consumer Reports and Baby Bargains. The best news here is the editing: You're not going to be looking at a thousand tiny message

Other Stroller Strategies

Here are a few alternatives to the traditional stroller:

Multiples choice. There are two types of double strollers: the tandem style, with seats one behind the other, and the side-by-side style. Tandem styles are well suited for a baby and an older sibling (the baby in the back seat because it reclines fully, the toddler in front for more leg room) and are definitely slimmer than the side-by-sides. But city parents tend to prefer the side-by-sides because they maneuver over curbs more easily. Plus, now you can find some models that fit through standard exterior doorways (although you'll still grit your teeth trying to maneuver them through small, crowded aisles).

But think a bit before you jump on the tandem; consider a buggy board attachment. The older sib can hop on when he needs a ride (and, hey, he really should be walking most of the time anyway).

Big wheels keep on turning. Baby joggers needn't be for athletes only. They're great for long walks over potholes and provide shelter from inclement weather. We've noticed more parents using double jogging strollers as their main get-around-town gear, not just for that morning run. Why? They tend to be narrower and more maneuverable, a big deal in tight city spaces.

The stroller/backpack. It doesn't look all that comfy and will not be good enough for use as a primary stroller, but this modern-style hybrid does make travel easy and is great for mass transit. Kids perch comfortably on your back when it's in the backpack form. Then in one quick motion, the whole apparatus converts to a stroller (the wheels are built in). It's a bit closer to the ground and more upright than regular strollers, but just fine for tooling around. Of course, there are a few shortcomings: First, you probably won't be able to get a child out of the backpack on your own unless you have a table to lean back on. Second, as a stroller, there's virtually no support for a sleeping child. Finally, the stroller wheels hang out when it's in backpack mode, so you either have to cover them with the stroller booties provided with most models or run the risk of having tire treads on your back.

board postings; whoever is doing all that synthesis seems to know what he's doing. But if you really want to get into it, you can check out the vast national network of parents populating the almost inconceivably detailed stroller message boards on epinions.com, parentsplace.com and the Web site of Denise and Alan Fields, authors of *Baby Bargains*—windsorpeak.com. Read past the many boasts and busts, and you will pick up some city-specific nuggets. Your eyes may glaze over in the process, but if you can organize the thoughts, you will be informed.

UH OH, GOTTA GO

In 1898, a pamphlet distributed by the Citizens Union complained of the lack of public toilets in New York City. More than 100 years later, the Big Apple still lacks adequate public loos, as do many other cities across the country. The dearth of public toilets in the "most advanced nation in the world" leaves city parents scrambling, especially when time is of the essence for a toilet-training tot. It's true that most city parks have public restrooms, though not all do. But are you going to take that chance? And if you do, can you get past the cleanliness? (Word to the wise: Always, always bring wipes on city outings of any kind—not just for cleaning but also as a stand-in for the often nonexistent toilet paper.)

Even in progressive San Francisco, which a few years back placed a couple dozen toilet kiosks modeled after the European "pay as you go" system (25 cents buys 20 minutes of privacy, and the toilets clean and disinfect themselves after each use) in well-traveled areas such as Fisherman's Wharf, citizens complain that the kiosks are used for illegal activities—drug use, prostitution, and other not-so-family-oriented stuff. Naturally, there are exceptions. Kathy went pee-green with envy when visiting her family in Phoenix. Not only were there sparkling clean public lavatories everywhere the family went, but in one children's park, parents even let their small children traipse into the bathrooms *by themselves*, so sure were they that the kids would be safe. (FYI, we're New Yorkers: We would never recommend that.)

Say your city is not as restroomed up as Phoenix. What d'ya do? Use a little

---

The Web to the Rescue!

Virtual restrooms may not yet exist, but the Internet and wireless technology have plenty to offer families in need of assistance.

The Bathroom Diaries: Forget the *Nanny Diaries*—this is what we call a must-read for any city parent! Our new favorite Web site, www.bathroomdiaries.com, allows users to plug in their city, even neighborhood, to obtain listings upon listings of local public bathrooms. It's easy to follow, includes all the relevant details about cleanliness, aesthetics, safety, and hours available. Facts like celebrity sightings and best public bathrooms are thrown in just for fun. Comments from other users are excellent and helpful (for instance, pointing out when ladies' rooms have no lines, exactly how to find them, etc.).

Attendants Please

Public bathrooms with attendants, experts say, are generally better maintained and safer than unsupervised ones. But can someone tell us where the heck they all are? We haven't found many.

foresight, a little schmoozing, and a little planning. Herewith the tried-and-true bathroom antics of savvy city parents:

1. Frequent your neighborhood stores and restaurants, suggests Leigh Anne O'Connor, New York City mother of three young kids. "The stores in my neighborhood know me," she explains. And when the need arises, they are always happy to lend their facilities to her brood. This strategy may work best in smaller stores, but even in chain stores, you can make friends if you go often enough. Whenever one of Julia's kids had the urge at an inopportune time, her nanny was always able to get ready access to the bathrooms of their local grocery store. Of course, she was friendly and polite, which gave her a substantial leg up in our tough city.

2. Hotels all have bathrooms in their lobbies.

3. Retail establishments are a mixed bag. Kid stores are more likely to have bathrooms that you can use, and bookstores tend to be bathroom-friendly. But women's clothing stores? Not likely, unless you really chat them up. On the other hand, some of the big retail chains will let potential customers use the employee bathroom (after all, a brand is at stake here).

4. Local community centers and public libraries (they're usually just adequate but will do in a pinch) are also options, as are places of worship, police stations, some post offices, municipal buildings, arts centers, some banks, colleges, and universities.

5. Department stores. They often have terrific restrooms, but getting to the right floor and right corner can sometimes be time consuming and thus defeat the purpose.

6. Movie theaters. Give them a sob story, and they may let you in to use the facilities. You can offer to leave the stroller with them, so they'll know you're not just trying to sneak in to see a free flick.

7. Coffee shops are, by law, required to have bathrooms, and if you buy a cup of coffee at the counter, they really can't say no to you.

BREASTFEEDING ON THE RUN: LOCATION, LOCATION, LOCATION

While the Supreme Court made it perfectly legal to breastfeed in public places, ignorance on the issue is still pervasive. We've heard plenty of instances where nursing moms were told to "take that outside" by security guards in public buildings or retail establishments. Notwithstanding the fact that they are squarely on the right side of the law, many city mothers, especially those living in more urbane towns, often feel uncomfortable breastfeeding in public. Even those mothers who couldn't care less what others are thinking sometimes just want to nourish their offspring with some degree of privacy. At the very least, cars honking and the din of people in perpetual motion can distract from the bonding experience.

Best Bets When Baby Hunger Strikes

Naturally, like everything else about living in the city, you'll benefit from the tried-and-true strategies of other parents.

1. Residential neighborhoods rule but others do not. Some parts of town are obviously better suited for the act. In a residential part of town, go for a park bench in any park or playground. Chances are, you'll find another breastfeeding mom already there (remember the power-in-numbers theory). In cold weather, try a local coffee shop booth or one of the other ideas below. As for the commercial and business districts, assume you won't find a great outdoors option.

2. Department stores. Their restrooms often have lactation/changing areas, and dressing rooms are a fave for their privacy and convenience (you most assuredly will find a chair there). Handicapped rooms are often nice and spacious, mothers report.

3. Places of worship. Again, just like with restrooms, it's hard for a clergyperson to turn you away. Also some churches have private family pews, a perfect spot to nurse.

4. Starbucks and Barnes & Nobles. Breastfeeding moms in our mini survey voted first for the coffeehouse (for their comfy couches and chairs) and second for the bookstore chain, where as one parent put it, "You always see moms breastfeeding at them."

5. Just do it. Take it from city dweller Nancy Ede, mother of two: "People have seen everything. It's not a big deal. But it could be your attitude. I just don't care. I even nursed once while I was getting a pedicure. And I had no problems."

A final note: If you're among the less uninhibited, lots of city mothers swear by slings like the Maya Wrap. They conceal and are ideal for nursing moms.

STEPPING OUT WITH MY BABY

In our parents' day, social outings with very young children were really kind of limited; kids didn't generally make the scene much before the age of, hmmm, 20. My, how times have changed. Today's kids can be seen pretty much anywhere anytime. Not that it's always good. Two-year-olds bouncing off a restaurant ceiling next to a couple celebrating their 30th wedding anniversary strikes us as a clear example of poor parental judgment. But the good news is, if you like the idea of having a family social life, cities provide a cornucopia of choices suitable for even the youngest members of society.

Classes for Lil'est Lasses

The number of city "activities" for babies as young as 3 months is sometimes remarked upon with derision—with classes such as French for pre-walkers, baby yoga, and toddler theatrics held up as yet more proof of hyper-urban-parenting. Not so, we say. In our view, activities for 0s to 2s were always less about learning and more about the adult socializing that these activities allowed. Sitting in a circle with 1-year-olds blowing bubbles may seem a little silly, but it gives the attending grown-up a chance to get out of the house and meet other adults taking care of children the same age as theirs—a perfectly great reason for doling out extra dollars for a baby-and-me course. And if you are otherwise spending all day cooped up in a small space with a small human being, getting out to that toddler group activity once or twice a week may be the one thing that keeps your sanity intact.

There isn't a city in America that doesn't have an abundance of baby and toddler classes. They're in every neighborhood, price range, and theme and even offer time slots well-suited to the working parent. Lots of places schedule evening classes so Mom or Dad can enjoy the bonding time and meet other neighborhood parents, without taking a day off from work. Find out about your city's trove through the usual suspects: local parenting books and free giveaways, city magazine articles and Web sites. All regularly list classes and the like.

Cheap Tricks

Not that you have to spend a fortune for Tatiana's first classes either. Community/rec centers and all those religious institutions (the Ys—YMCAs,

YWCAs, YMHAs, YWHAs—and JCCs, for instance) offer reasonably priced classes, which can be everything from the general parent-child structured playgroup to specialized playgroups (we found a Mommy and Me Torah for Tots program at one place). By the way, if you're not of an institution's particular religious orientation, don't let that dissuade you from considering one of its infant and toddler classes or playgroups. All of today's Ys (et al.) not only are completely family-oriented but offer plenty of nondenominational classes/activities too.

Libraries shouldn't be discounted either. While they don't all offer formal kids' classes (although some do and they're free), those that have children's sections often have weekly or monthly gratis programs geared to the youngest children. Even if they don't, they're still great for socializing. Usually, the children's area is outfitted with toys as well as books, and there are always plenty of other children around to play with. It's essentially a free playgroup—with the huge benefit that it's not at your house, so the only cleanup is whatever your child played with. Of course, you do need to be a little careful with the toys: It's unlikely that the public library playthings are being cleaned or disinfected on any kind of regular basis. Many parents choose to wipe them down before their child plays with them, especially if everything Lily touches goes in her mouth.

Working Out Together

Sometimes baby classes are not even about the babies! Today, there's an entire cottage industry dedicated to helping new moms get their bodies back in shape without losing precious baby bonding time. "Mommy and Me" workout classes, now in every city, offer exercise geared to postpartum bodies that incorporates babies into the routine. At San Francisco's popular Baby Boot Camp, for instance, sit-ups are much harder with Rufus on your belly providing extra weight resistance, and "Push-up Kisses" make all that hard work worthwhile. Meanwhile, stroller-based exercise programs like Strollercize and Stroller Strides (they or their variants can pretty much be found now in every city) get moms together in city parks under the leadership of a fitness expert who engages them in a variety of strengthening and cardiovascular exercises using the stroller as prop (complete with baby, of course). And there are many local versions now, some of which are based on jogging strollers for the more running oriented. New York City–based family therapist and parent educator Naomi Siegel strongly recommends these programs to her clients. They get postpartum moms out of the apartment, exercising and socializing with their peers, and provide ready-made support groups in about the healthiest way possible. What could be better?

Mom/Tot Culture Klatches

Let's face it, you're tired, maybe even suffering from a little postpartum angst, you feel fat, and suddenly the town you're so used to conquering—*your* city—is scary and isolating. And sure, you get some adult face time in at your baby's music and movement class, but maybe that's not enough. It was only a matter of time before some crafty entrepreneurs realized that it absolutely was not enough and, glomming on to the almost desperate need of new moms to socialize together, built a new industry.

In the latest urban social phenomenon—mom/tot cultural gatherings—city moms and their charges can be found at the movies, in gab sessions, and whining and dining together. It certainly makes sense: Moms were going to movies, eating in restaurants, comparing their lives, and running to lectures way before baby came along. Why should they have to give it up now? (Well, maybe because movie patrons don't usually take kindly to colicky 3-month-olds, and spit-up is not the most appetizing of sights while dining.)

But in this newborn class of events, the antics of infants and young children are not only *not* frowned upon, they're the raison d'etre. There are myriad new parent support groups and expert lectures across the country that are directed at new mothers, who are welcomed with baby in hand. At New York City's twice-weekly New Mothers Luncheon, for instance, food is just the appetizer and babies and burping are the main course. There are similar formally organized, informally run get-togethers all across the country.

The mom/tot gatherings have expanded of late. At Reel Moms movie screenings, held in cities all across the country, kids can spit-up, crawl till they drop, and scream to their hearts' delight while mothers breastfeed and dads change diapers. And nobody thinks twice about it. The brainchild of Loews Cineplex Entertainment marketing vice president John McCauley, who found as a new parent that he and his wife were not exactly welcomed with their infant at the movies, Reel Moms is a joint effort between Loews and Urbanbaby.com that allows parents and their young charges to come to select Loews theaters once a week for a morning or matinee viewing of first-run flicks. Youngsters are happily accommodated: Lights are dimmed, not darkened, and the sound is turned down from its usual loud volume. There's valet stroller parking, and, blissfully, there are no kids' movies. And since the kids aren't exactly watching the movie, their admission is free, while adults pay the regular ticket price.

The test program in Manhattan was so successful that Reel Moms has already expanded to San Francisco, Santa Monica, Baltimore, Boston, Chicago, Cleveland, Detroit, Indianapolis, Seattle, and Dallas; plans are under way to bring the weekly screenings to Atlanta and Tucson. Movie buffs should also be on the lookout for variations on the theme. Reel Moms is considering adding father-daughter days, weekend events for working moms, and a special version for parents and toddlers. To find out more, you can go directly to the "events" tab of www.loewstheaters.com for current movie listings and locations. Or register at http://reelmoms.urbanbaby.com, and you'll be sent regular updates for your area.

Playgroups, Big and Small

Even more rampant than mom/tot culture fests are playgroups. Some are highly organized, led by social workers and psychologists and offered at various institutions like places of worship, Ys, community/rec centers, even pediatric offices. Others just seem to arise organically—one mom knows another who has a baby the same age, they get together, another duo joins, then one more, and soon a playgroup is born. At Brooklyn's Tea Lounge, caffeine is the tie that binds. At this low-key neighborhood joint with comfy couches and a friendly atmosphere, new mothers regularly gather over lattes to swap their ideas and strategies in an "it takes a village to raise a child" kind of way. Many of the parents who come in feeling undersupported and overwhelmed find comfort in others and say these get-togethers are their only moments of sanity and stability. How do you find these groups? Typically word-of-mouth—pediatrician offices, local baby or maternity stores, and the playground (of course).

And then there's the Internet. Apologies to Al Gore, but *we* think the Internet was developed by a mom who wanted to connect with other mothers for playgroups. Message boards at parent and city sites are filled with people looking to hook up. We've seen playgroup solicitations for every type of person, neighborhood, and scenario—from mothers who want to walk and those who just want to talk to young moms, single moms, laid-back moms, creative types, working moms (weekend-only), stay-at-home moms and dads, mothers of color, Greek, Vietnamese, Italian, and German moms—and even Hungarian caregivers.

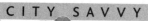

CITY SAVVY

You Can Always Find Playmates

Try a Google search using the name of the city and playgroups and you will find loads of fellow city dwellers for exercise, coffee klatches, and playgroups.

There are also quite a few Web sites and services devoted entirely to setting up your new social life. Matching Moms, at www.matchingmoms.org—with some 1,000 playgroup listings and tens of thousands of members nationwide—is one great site for locating new friends in your city. The Mommy & Me Association, at www.mommyandme.org, is a subscription-based membership organization started by child development specialist Cindy Bunin Nurik, Ph.D., that aims to support and provide resources for playgroups nationwide. Members can find like-minded socials through the huge nationwide directory and also find tons of ideas to enhance the experience. Even Meetup.com, whose claim to fame has been its ability to use the Internet to marshal support for political candidates, has gotten in on the

Special Look at the Urban Playdate

The idea of playdates, social planning for toddlers, used to be strictly an urban phenomenon. But the practice of kids just playing outside in the neighborhood is disappearing even in the most sedate of suburbs. Playdates have become a national practice.

That said, there are still a few urban distinctions—chiefly, what happens when an indoor playdate is taken outside. Not a big deal for younger kids, where there's always adult supervision from both sides. But it can become an issue for 4- and 5-year-olds who are mature enough to be dropped off at someone's home.

Here's where problems arise: You have, we hope, set up rules in your own household for acceptable playground play (even acceptable playgrounds), modes of transportation, outdoor snacks, etc. But those rules may or may not be what's in force in the playdate's family. If you have any bugaboos, make them known. In fact, we've known parents who requested that their son not be taken outside his playdate's apartment because they were unsure of the caregiver's ability to handle two active 5-year-olds crossing streets and running around a very busy playground. And we've also known parents who found out after the fact that their child was traipsing all over the city with his playdate's caregiver, who had to pick up various siblings. Now the caregiver was really attentive, so safety wasn't an issue; but for quite a period of time, the parents had no idea where their child was.

So, set any ground rules, ask what the plan for the playdate is, and request to be notified of any changes before the fact. Oh, and get the cell numbers of the responsible adults. You never know when they'll come in handy.

act. At www.moms.meetup.com, interested parents can post and sign up for play-groups in some 100 cities.

If you are going to initiate a group, do it safely. Do not use your real name on the posting and always meet in public places first—bookstores, playgrounds, etc. You want to make sure that you will all be compatible and, most important, that you're not inviting any psychos into your or your child's life. The latest in urban etiquette? Playdate cards to be handed out by you or your caregiver to likely playmates encountered at the park or a playground. It sounds effete, but it sure beats scrambling around for pencil and paper when Lola makes a new friend in the sandbox and you want to get the budding buddies together again. You can get cards made anywhere. Smart parents list the child's name and phone number or parent e-mail address only; never a home address—you never know who's going to pick up an errant card.

CHAPTER 9

THAT'S ENTERTAINMENT

■ ■

Culture. Cuisine. Now here are topics every city parent can feel superior about. Compare our entertainments to the ersatz events of suburbia. Would anyone actually pick a ridiculously priced "Blues Clues" spectacle over avant-garde puppeteers, authentic Indonesian shadow plays, or "Green Eggs and Hamadeus" (the new hot kiddie show)? Or how about family dining? While the rest of the country is stuck with the local family commissary—that chaotic purveyor of Wonder Bread cuisine—we get evening activities as varied as a cocktail and hors d'oeuvres jazz hour at the local art museum (kids welcomed and encouraged to dance), a noshing jaunt through an exotic ethnic neighborhood, and dining at a hip restaurant, pre-"scene."

City parents adore passing on their sophistication to the next generation, basking in pride when they feel their darling's imagination is sparked by a storytelling hour (author present, natch) or a trip to a local landmark or outdoor sculpture garden. And, frankly, our cities' rich leisure offerings are a big part of why we put up with all the other nonsense, anyway. So grab up the kids and go out and enjoy it all. You deserve it.

RAISING LITTLE CULTURE VULTURES

Once your child goes beyond the toddler stage, you'll surely want him to be a slightly more active participant in all those fabulous city goings-on. So why, pray tell, do you end up doing the same things weekend after weekend? If you're like many city parents, it may be that you're just stymied by all that choice, not to mention the thought of crowds, long lines, and the process of getting everyone to the same place—a combination that has stopped many a city family cold. But once you get over the initial hump of cultural forays, you'll find it's so much easier than you ever dreamed.

One good way to start is by adopting a visitor's mentality. That's what you'd do if you went to some other city, right? You would gather, gather, gather (ideas, books, articles, pamphlets, friends' recommendations) and then hunt, hunt, hunt (for great new spots, new museums, neighborhoods, the works). This strategy works wonders for hometown jaunts as well.

Your first order of business should be a trip to the local visitors' center or tourist bureau (be truthful now, you've never stepped foot in yours, right?) for some guidance and loads of free pamphlets, maps, and info booklets. Chicago tourism czar Dorothy Coyle suggests you discuss your child's particular interests with the staff. Specialists on hand will undoubtedly tell you about things in your town you never even knew existed, she promises. "Typically, people come having read an article. They'll know about the usual things. In Chicago, it's the aquarium or children's museum. But we can also design a visit according to any interest: a sports theme, a certain ethnicity, or neighborhood," she says.

Wherever you go to get info, we highly recommend you start a family fun library. Include all the usual suspects: tear-outs from the local parent magazines and any family guidebooks. Most city newspapers have a kids' calendar (often posted on the Web as well) that usually appears on Fridays or Saturdays in time for the weekend. Their selected highlights can be particularly helpful. Despite our repeated warnings about taking what you read on the Internet with a grain of salt—especially in the parent message boards—as far as entertainment listings are concerned, the family-oriented city Web sites should be considered among your regular touch points.

The quality and quantity of local Web sites vary fairly dramatically from city to city. You're going to have to do a little experimenting here. If you have no clue what's out there, try a search using various combinations of the following words: (the name of your city), parents, children, kids, family, entertainment, fun, leisure. You'll discover quickly which sites offer plenty of listings and local tips. Don't forget to check out your city's official site, as well. There should be a section for recreation and leisure, and often within it is a family portion worth viewing.

THE CITY DIFFERENCE:
The Inside Scoop on Urban Entertainment

Now that you're pumped up with family possibilities, you still need to know how to do it up the city way. And in a refreshing change of pace, when it comes to culture, almost everything that's different about the city is a benefit rather than an issue to sidestep.

Freebies and cheapies abound! We promise that no matter what your financial situation, you will find tons to take advantage of. Each city (through the mayor's office, cultural affairs bureau, department of tourism, not-for-profit arts groups, and corporate sponsors) hosts free or inexpensive events all year long that are suitable for, if not specifically targeted to, youngsters—arts festivals, food fairs, parades, movies, classes, and more. Some cities are better than others at publicizing their assets (Chicago, we love you!), so you may need to take your research seriously. But the payoff is well worth the "price" of admission: an endless supply of free or nearly free events to entertain and even educate your brood.

Don't forget to include parks and public libraries in your cultural quests. Parks are home to many family activities that make for an entertaining (and educational) day—bird watching, nature hikes, regular music events (some participatory), and in a relatively recent development, outdoor movie theaters, with family-friendly offerings shown nightly during suitable seasons. Every city also has at least one public library that offers children's programming like movies (many times classics you won't find elsewhere), story hours, and arts and crafts classes.

Worse comes to worst, you can always fall back on those insidious retail events designed to make your 2-year-old aware of the power of a brand. If you can get

Great Entertainment Site-ings

Your city may be one of those covered by our two favorite kid activity sites, GoCityKids.com and UrbanBaby.com.

GoCityKids.com began in San Francisco and now covers Atlanta, Boston, Chicago, Denver, Los Angeles, Miami, New York, Philadelphia, Salt Lake City, San Diego, San Francisco, Seattle, and Washington. For your sake, we hope they'll be coming soon to your city, if they're not there already. For about $19.95 a year, they send a weekly e-mail newsletter that outlines a fairly extensive selection of the week's family fun activities. Members also get access to the site's ultimate online calendar. While you can find all the information contained on the site elsewhere, the time it would take to do so is well worth the yearly fee.

UrbanBaby.com, another site with plenty of family fun ideas, currently has local outposts for Austin, Boston, Chicago, Los Angeles, New York, San Francisco, and Seattle, with more on the way. The entertainment material is far from exhaustive, but it's well-organized, user-friendly, with a between-us-parents feel. If yours is an older child, don't be put off by the children-2-and-under orientation; there are plenty of listings applicable to children up to 6. You can also opt in for daily kid-oriented announcements, but they are typically very retail oriented and not local enough.

away without buying something, there's no reason not to go to in-store events too.

Moral of the story: Never assume you can't afford to do something fun and special with your child even if you're on a tight budget.

The early bird gets to meet Big Bird. Okay, the city does have one or two drawbacks on the entertainment and activities front, and competition for in-demand spots is one of them. The stakes are obviously not as high as what you're contending with in terms of school competition, but cities are nonetheless still dense and filled with kids who presumably want to do everything your tyke wants to do. Buy tickets in advance—especially to events that are infrequent, like the circus or the hot theater troupe. If you're considering after-school classes or Saturday morning activities, for instance, do your research a few months before they start and sign up as soon as you're allowed to. The good news: Little Elmo will always have something to do, but the seats at the circus may be pretty far back or the available times inconvenient or the class not the exact one you had in mind.

Family fun doesn't have to stop at sunset. Cities stay up later than suburbs. It's not uncommon for streets to be hopping well into the night. Not that we're suggesting that your child forfeit his sleep; it's just that on occasion, those rollicking dusk-to-evening hours can come in handy, especially in summer months when you can get away with letting Luke wake up later than usual. Be on the lookout for activities that have evening hours—many museums stay open late one night a week (and are blissfully underused during those times) or check out outdoor evening concerts for an after-dinner boogie-down. Why not go to the 5 P.M. viewing of the next DreamWorks movie and *then* have dinner? The change of schedule won't kill your child, but it may provide a new perspective on the city, and it certainly will extend your precious time together.

Ethnic diversity provides depth and dimension to family outings. We feel this is so central to city living and one of the finest benefits that we devote an entire section to it (see "Making the Most of Diversity" on page 220), with enough ideas and points of interest to turn every city child into a cultural anthropologist. The ethnic ethic permeates all aspects of city life—dining, museums, parades, off-the-beaten-track venues, freebies, and more. After all, there are children in every culture, and they have fun, eat, create, read, and play with toys, just like yours do.

You can wing it. Unlike health, unlike education, unlike so many other aspects of life in the city, this is one area where you absolutely can afford to, on occasion, just get up, get out, and see what happens. Since you're never more than a few blocks from some source of entertainment, amusement and bemusement can take place anytime, anywhere. Maybe the hoopla will be centered on a heated sidewalk chalk contest. Maybe it will occur at that particularly touristy part of town where street performers are working hard for their hatful of coins. Maybe it's in the wonderful exchanges that take place at the nearby farmers market or street fair or parade or café. Which brings us to . . .

Even street life is an activity. It only takes a tiny bit of effort to turn a regular day into an event. The yogis call it mindfulness. Just being aware (and sharing your perspective) can spark your child's imagination. That unexpected encounter with a mime is the perfect occasion to play "mirror mirror" together, discuss face paint, even introduce her to the work of Bill Irwin (he was the original "Mr. Noodles" on *Sesame Street*). And what about the blues band in the subway, the impressionist who is painting a traffic scene, the juggler by the museum—all excellent fodder for conversations that could take a million different directions. The performance is not just by performers; it can be anyone or anything—the guy with the python around his neck, the foreign sailors in town for Fleet Week, the white-haired gents playing bocce in the park. Don't just hurry by; slow down, look, listen, learn, and share.

And don't forget the less-spontaneous events. Every city organizes cultural activities all year long, though summers and holiday season usually have the most. The latest "in" thing to do is go to outdoor kids' movies, but all the old faithfuls still abound: children's musical performances, puppet shows, and games.

Bookstores are the best! You already are aware that the local and chain bookstores make more than respectable venues for nursing and bathroom runs, and it turns out they've also been elevated to an actual, viable "activity" among city dwellers. For the younger set on rainy days, they're almost indispensable. The good news is bookstore staff members don't generally seem to mind kids under foot. Many shops, in fact, actively encourage it by organizing story hours or creating an environment conducive to kid hang time, with batches of toys and semi-mutilated books on hand for kids to play with. But to be honest, we have seen too many parents and caregivers abusing this privilege. When your rambunctious toddler takes down a shelf of books at a time, try to put them back (alphabetized). It's the right thing to do.

Of course, you may end up making some purchases while you're there (and when it's the board book that spent the past hour in Derek's mouth, we think you should). If you do, you may want to consider some books about life in the city. Kids love to read and see pictures about circumstances that relate to their lives, and most kids' books seem to be set in the 'burbs. Luckily there are enough that aren't. See "The City Parent Book Club" on page 208–209 for some of our favorites.

Tourist Attractions: Why Should Visitors Have All the Fun?

Remember the visitor's mentality we suggested you adopt when investigating your city's cultural opportunities? Well, don't stop there. Go that extra mile and

(continued on page 210)

The City Parent Book Club

Another great way for you and your child to get to know your city is to check it out from a new and fun point of view. So skip the guidebooks and head for the children's section of your favorite bookstore. Kids' books offer a great adventure to hold your child's attention, along with amazing illustrations of the city's best spots—sure to spark interest in exploring outside your apartment walls. Here's a list of recommended reading from booksellers in cities across the country.

San Francisco

City by the Bay by Trisha Brown

San Francisco never looked so good. In a fun-filled whirl around the city, the Golden Gate Bridge, cable cars, and Chinatown are just some of the many landmarks we get to see along the way. An extra "explorer's guide" at the end of the story, just adds to the fun.

—Recommended by Alexander Book Co.

Denver

Pigs over Denver by Kerry Lee MacLean

It's a Rocky Mountain high as this ABC-style picture book depicts all the sights and activities of the Colorado city. Schoolchildren helped the author Kerry Lee MacLean by choosing what each letter would stand for. And don't forget, "K is for kayaking," and "M is for mountains."

—Recommended by Bookies Bookstore

Seattle

There Was an Old Lady Who Swallowed a Trout by Teri Sloat

The old lady has been given a nifty face-lift in this bright and breezy rendition of the classic rhyme, set anew in the Pacific Northwest. There's no dark ending here: When the old lady finally swallows the ocean, it just makes her laugh and laugh and, as she does, out pop all the animals she swallowed.

—Recommended by All for Kids Books and Music

Chicago

A Field Mouse and the Dinosaur Named Sue by Jan Wahl

You wouldn't guess that Chicago and the largest T. rex ever found would be center stage in this tale of a tiny field mouse. One day the little critter finds that his home—a well-chosen, robust bone in the dusty hills of South Dakota—is missing and off he goes to find it, all the way to the halls of the world-famous Field Museum in Chicago where he "meets" a 67-million-year-old dinosaur named Sue. Fun story and stunning illustrations.

—Recommended by Children in Paradise Bookstore

Boston

Bus Route to Boston by Maryann Cocca-Leffler

This sweet story of two young girls who go shopping with their mom in Boston paints a vivid picture of the city's old North End, the Italian enclave that to this day has the feel of another time. One tiny gripe: a small picture of a large woman trying to stuff herself into a dress at Filene's Basement. It's supposed to be humorous, but Kathy—who was once the editor of a magazine geared to plus-size women—thinks that children's book authors especially should be sensitive to the messages they are sending, even the minor ones.

Journey around Boston from A to Z by Martha Zschock

Another delightful alphabet book packs in info about the many historic sites of Boston, Cambridge, and outlying suburbs.

Make Way for Ducklings by Robert McCloskey

The old favorite about Mr. and Mrs. Mallard's struggle to find a safe place to bring up their ducklings is just as good as we remembered it. When the ducklings take a break in Boston's Public Garden, they find a welcoming, duck-loving policeman, and a great spot to call home. Creator McCloskey won a Caldecott award for his lovely illustrations of Boston hot spots traversed by the ducklings on their search for housing.

—All Boston books recommended by Children's Bookshop

New York

Madlenka by Peter Sis

Madlenka wants a dog so badly she imagines one. And when she takes her invisible mutt for a walk around her New York City block, she meets all her worldly neighbors: the French baker, the Latin American fruit vendor, the Asian artist. It's urban and diverse and so are the many dogs who end up following her home. Julia actually gave this to Alice for her third birthday, and she asked to read it every day for a month.

Uptown by Bryan Collier

All of Harlem's jazz, and culture, and street life come to life through the eyes of a little boy living there as expressed in Collier's poetic text and beautiful illustrations. We get a glimpse of the neighborhood's landmarks too—the renowned Apollo Theater, historic brownstones, and the bustling stores of 125th Street.

The Garden of Happiness by Erika Tamar

This book's message is about finding beauty anywhere, and the story line is not so far off from what happens in New York City's gritty Alphabet City all the time. In this case, the neighborhood people work together to create a lush garden from a lot filled with litter. Marisol, a young girl, plants a seed that becomes the most surprising plant in the Garden of Happiness.

Moo Moo Goes to the City by Jo Lodge

The excitement of the Big Apple is captured in this book filled with all the gizmos: pop-ups, lift-the-flaps, and pull-outs. Moo Moo the cow hops a train into the Big Apple, where she goes Rollerblading, joins other sightseers on a boat ride, and even stops to feed the pigeons.

—All New York books recommended by Bank Street Books

actually *take in* the loads of attractions your city undoubtedly has. It's embarrassing, but here are just some of the classic things out-of-towner kids love to do in New York City that Kathy has not yet introduced to Alice: a sunset Circle Line cruise around Manhattan (despite Alice's enthusiasm "I l-l-l-love boats, Mommy" every time she's on one), a visit to the Statue of Liberty, a double-decker bus ride for that special view of the city that only pigeons and tourists are privy to, and a slew of other local landmarks. Shame on her, and shame on you if you don't at a minimum go to what everyone else seems to find absolutely fascinating about your own city.

In every city there are plenty of touristy opportunities your child will enjoy. They're so easy to skip when the city beckons with plays and music fests and the myriad other entertainments, but you'd be selling your child and city short if you do. Herewith some more city fun:

Landmarks. Think interesting architecture, lots of stairs to climb, historical or period elements, military themes, and wax museums.

Outdoor art. According to Dorothy Coyle, director of the Chicago Office of Tourism, her city's many outdoor artworks are particularly attractive for youngsters. Wee glee is what you see as kids of all ages slide down the giant untitled Picasso sculpture that's planted in front of the Daley Plaza, she says. Coyle isn't entirely sure the activity is encouraged, even legal—but no harm, she says, it happens all the time. "The kids love the sculpture and its scale," she reports. "They love to guess what it is. Some say it looks like a bird or a woman." Another favorite outdoor piece that Chicago kids enjoy is the enormous Duboffet sculpture at the State Building, which kids run in and out of. But every city has its offerings. How many New York City kids learned about Alaska because they climbed the Balto statue in Central Park? Check out your own city's public artworks, both stationary and changing (the traveling Cow Parade was a big hit with Julia's clan a few years back). You can make an afternoon tour of them or just a game of spotting them during your daily travels. And don't forget to include murals on your jaunt. Those brightly painted panoramas of local familiar scenes are magnets for the little ones.

Bridges. Okay, so the Golden Gate might be a bit long for children to tra-

Be a Good Guide

Always make a point of reading landmark or art plaques to kids. Kids are surprisingly interested, and they remember even when you don't.

verse, but there are plenty of city suspension bridges that are absolutely walkable or rideable (that's what kid seats are for) and whose views make for a fun venture.

Horse and buggy rides. Sure it seems a little cheesy, but kids absolutely love them, and they're just as fun at night or in the cold as they are on that balmy (probably crowded) spring day.

Boating adventures. Ferry rides, cruises, and other waterway activities all count. If it's your first time out, bring a Dramamine just in case.

Factory tours. A dying breed, maybe, but you can still find a few urban factories that open their doors to the public. It's worth the hunt to let your kids actually see something physical being made. They'll think it's pretty cool and will get a sense of the effort involved in making a product—not a bad thing all in all. Many cities have at least one choice (the Brown Bear Factory in San Diego and San Francisco, the Mary Kay Cosmetics Factory in Dallas, the Steinway Factory in Brooklyn, Eli's Cheesecake Factory in Chicago), but if yours doesn't, think small: The noodle and fortune cookie factories in your city's Chinatown, artisanal bread bakeries that serve your city's restaurants, and specialty chocolate makers are all possible bets. Two tips on the tours: Always wear closed-toed shoes (it may not be a requirement, but it is a good practice); and, if the tour is long, ask ahead about the temperature, as some places are kept cool either to protect food or machinery (a chilly kid is an unhappy kid, you know).

Star gazing. A local university or other research institution may have an observatory open to the public during specified times. If the real Milky Way is a treat for Copernicus Jr., get thee to a telescope. In our town, Columbia University's observatory is free and open to the public two Fridays a month, excepting summer months. And check your local planetarium to see if they do a family "night sky" exhibition where they show what stars you can see at night in your own city. You won't see many because of the light pollution, but kids are pretty content just to be able to pick out Sirius.

The Total Tourist. If you want the super-duper family indulgence, book your brood into a local hotel and really finger-paint the town. During weekends, when business travelers evacuate, many city hotels try to make up for the loss in business by offering reasonably priced family-friendly packages. Boston's Le Meridien, for instance—which is within walking distance of the New England Aquarium, Children's Museum at Museum Wharf, Fanueil Hall, and Downtown Crossing—has a "Kids Love Boston" program that offers many special amenities for families. Those include: children 12 and under staying for free; special children's menus that come with crayons and games; a Saturday afternoon Chocolate Bar Buffet (September through May), where kids can sample from among 25 different creations; the kids' corner at Sunday brunch; and did we mention free pool use?

Getting the Inside Skinny on Museums

Family programming is usually part of a museum's education department. Call to ask about any demonstrations, workshops, ongoing classes, family exhibits, or special viewings—even parties that may be available for your child. We've seen many fine examples. We've even found live animal visits offered (at the Dallas Children's Museum, for one). Ask for suggestions as to the exhibits that'll best catch the fancy of kids your child's age and for tips on how to approach viewing those exhibits.

ARTISTIC ENDEAVORS

Museums are among the city's greatest resources, but parents don't nearly make full use of them. Sure on a rainy day, we join the throngs of other desperados seeking shelter at the local children's, natural history, or science museums. But did you know that just about every museum—"adult" ones included—sponsor loads of excellent family activities, most free with the price of admission? Houston's Museum of Fine Arts has gratis "Family Days," filled with storytelling, performances, a creation station, and drop-in studio workshop. Atlanta's High Museum has its "Toddler Thursday" classes that beckon children ages 2 to 5 to view works of art and then create masterpieces to take home. At the San Francisco Museum of Modern Art's monthly "Family Studio" Sundays, kids can spend 3 hours in hands-on activity linked to the museum's collections. Why spend your hard-earned money on costly arts and crafts classes when you can get free instruction from experts in programs such as these?

Okay, sometimes all this good stuff is not completely free; there is that matter of admissions. But talk about value. At most museums, children (typically under 5) are free (except for children's museums; they usually start charging kids at a pretty tender age). And many museums are also free to adults on certain days of the week or month. Even if they're not, admission prices are often flexible, though usually they insist that you pay something. Those that post "suggested donations" mean what they say: You're allowed to give what you can (but please, since your donation goes to cover museum operations as well as all those wonderful special programs, be fair and actually give what you can).

Family Museum Memberships:
The Best Deal in Town

Find a museum that your child is particularly drawn to, and it'll be more than worth your while to check out the family membership deals (usually including up to two parents and all non-adult children). At first glance, the fee may seem steep, but when you do the math, it generally pays for itself within just a few visits. Plus, along with entry, family memberships include perks like parent-child workshops and children-only classes, priority entrance, a godsend, and those special members' viewings that can make the museum experience infinitely more pleasurable. Galleries are less crowded and exhibits are easier to see, making navigating with kids all the smoother. Julia's kids really get a kick out of the special openings the American Museum of Natural History has every time a gallery has been renovated. Because the openings are often held at breakfast or at night, they always have a tinge of glamour and excitement. The museum is particularly good at explaining what work has been done ahead of time, so Julia's family discusses it before going to see what's being unveiled. It might sound geeky, but it's anything but. The kids feel cool because they get to see something first; they have a sense of ownership of the museum because they have this special kind of behind-the-scenes knowledge; and they develop an understanding of the scholarship and effort that goes into the museum. Want more perks? Discounts at the gift shop, kiddie pizza parties, or just the ability to throw birthday parties there.

THE CITY PARENT RULES
Making Museums Work for Your Family

Rule #1: Choose frequency over duration. Go fast, but go often. It is one of the great luxuries of city living that you don't have to drag your kids for hours through some great museum because it's your only chance. Ah, the virtue of proximity. Museum-going for you can be as ad hoc and abbreviated as the mood strikes. And in the case of little kids, less is truly more. Sure, the more children are exposed to museums, the more comfortable they'll feel in them, the more memorable the experience, and the more everyone, including you, will get out of it. But, as precocious as 2-year-old Tonya is, she probably won't acquire that passion for Picasso if she is forced to stare at one for any extended period of time. Go in short doses and don't try to see everything. And don't fret if your entire museum visit barely tops 15 minutes. Fifteen minutes one time will turn into a half hour the next, and eventually you'll be begging them to leave! Be on the lookout for signs of a tiring child. And plan a break. Sometimes a trip to the museum cafeteria can perk up flagging attention, and you can sneak in a little more viewing afterwards.

Rule #2: Go early, go late. You really want to avoid the most crowded times (usually weekend afternoons). You have to keep a tighter rein on kids when there are a lot of people around, out of courtesy for others and concern for your kids' security, making the experience tenser for you and them. No fun. Best bets are when the museum first opens or late in the day if they have night hours. Many museums now run Friday or Saturday night specials, supposedly geared to adults with music and cocktails—but these are just fine, we say, even desirable for kids. Most of the grown-ups are clustered around the bar, leaving exhibits free for the viewing (although not every gallery may be open).

THE URBAN A-LIST
Museums Your Child Will Adore

These work every time, just in case you've forgotten. . . .

Children's museums. An obvious choice with enough kid-oriented interactivity to last a lifetime. Only problems are the crowds and somewhat limited age appeal; if you've got a range in your family, the older ones might be bored.

Natural history and science museums. Obviously these are a favorite among older children, but younger kids will be intrigued by dinosaurs and dioramas. Plus, so many of the exhibits are interactive these days with cool buttons to push or short movies to see.

Transit museums. Think trains, planes, automobiles, and fire trucks, and do ask your

local port authority if they operate a museum. And sometimes . . .

Modern art museums. Big ones will have numerous special exhibits. Keep an eye on them: Some of them will be particularly appealing to kids because of their color, crazy designs, interactivity, and multimedia aspects.

Design museums. Check the temporary exhibits. Often they will be interactive or in some other way tremendously appealing to kids. New York's Cooper Hewitt, a branch of the Smithsonian, has had exhibits covering futuristic designs in furniture and vehicles that even little kids could like. Just expect to go at their pace and skip the parts that leave them cold.

Rule #3: Hit the bathroom right away. If you're museum-hopping at peak times, there may be lines (especially the ladies' rooms so maybe Dad can take this one), and bathrooms are generally not located on every floor. But the most crowded bathrooms are likely to be nearest the entrance, so pick a more interior bathroom (preferably located near something you actually want to see). If you can't force the issue up front, at least know the loo lay of the land as you walk about the museum.

Rule #4: Let the kids run around. Kids need to move, and thankfully most museums are well-constructed for a little action. Try incorporating the building itself into the visit: Let the kids run up and down unoccupied stairs or ramps to let off steam. After all, you want them to appreciate and enjoy the whole experience of going to a museum, not just a particular exhibit. "Museums usually have interesting floor surfaces," notes Shantras Lakes, head of Family and Community Programs at the High Museum of Art in Atlanta. Her game: "Ask the child to compare the floor surface with texture of the pieces. Does the paint look smoother or rougher than the floor? How are they similar or how are they different? Is one made of a different material than the other? It's also good because you can touch the floor, so sometimes it satisfies the child's need to touch something."

Rule #5: Check out children's programming and exhibits. If you have time for advance research, call the museum's education department or just stop by the information desk to inquire about any children's itineraries, specific exhibits, galleries, or permanent installations that your kids might especially enjoy. Tell them about Jenna's newfound fascination with tea parties, and they may point you to the fancy china display; if Jenna's in her medieval phase, it's off to the suits of armor.

Rule #6: Let them guide you! Please get off the "gotta do everything, life's an agenda" routine. It's bad enough that we schedule kids up the wazoo. But to enjoy a museum, it's essential to let children guide you to the things that they like the best, experts agree. So if Tobey's agenda turns out to be different than yours, give in gracefully and let him stop and see what HE wants to see.

Rule #7: Talk, talk, talk. Here's how important this is. Even the official Web site of Art Institute of Chicago encourages parents to chatter away. "People think they have to whisper in the Art Institute, but this isn't true," the collateral material explains. Discuss the works you visit and relate what the children see to what they already know. "A suit of armor, for instance, is all about protecting the body, similar to a catcher's mask or elbow guards and bike helmet," the site points out. Lakes concurs: "You should also pick out details that make what children are seeing relevant to their world view. If it is a piece of furniture, maybe choose one that looks like something that is in their grandparents' house, maybe one that they are somehow familiar with, and talk about the different uses for the table or chair."

Rule #8: Take home a memento. It is always nice to have a takeaway piece to remember the experience. Let your kids choose a postcard, small toy, book, or magnet that will help continue the experience after they leave. Museum stores often have terrifically edited selections of kids' arts- and crafts-oriented toys and games. Even a floor plan, a ticket stub, or those cute little entry pins (if they're used) will do. The goal is to keep the kids talking about their visit. If a museum visit was particularly successful, try checking out its Web site. Many have "kids' corner" sections, and you just may find a piece of work your child has seen. Many museum Web sites also have fun, age-appropriate, interactive games to play.

Rule #9: Move off the beaten track. There are so many more museums you absolutely must consider. But the only way to find out about them is to open your scope and do some digging. Any specialty museum that coincides with your child's interests—i.e., coin, doll, or naval—is a good bet. Ethnic museums, too, can be hidden treasures. At Chicago's Swedish American Museum in Andersonville, for instance, an entire floor is devoted to kids where they can pretend they're working on a Swedish farm, go into a Swedish house, and climb aboard a small Viking ship. When Pearson was in preschool, his class went to the Jewish Historical Museum—a big mistake, Julia thought, before she watched the twenty 4-year-olds absolutely spellbound for an hour as they handled thousand-year-old dishes and learned about artifacts and historical digs. It's all in the editing, she decided then and there.

Your Toddler, The Art Lover

Okay, you say, we'll go along with the idea of kids at the transit museum and the natural history joints, but art museums? Really, my child would rather do our taxes. You're not alone in your sentiments. It's truly a shame, but art stumps far too many parents of young children. They fear that they just don't know enough about it to be able to share the experience. Or they assume their tykes can't or won't appreciate art. Hogwash.

No child is too young to appreciate art, experts say, and in the process of developing that affinity, there are so many benefits. Judith Lynn Shupe, founder of Art Smart Adventures, which runs children's tours of New York City museums, reports that even the 3-month-olds who tag along at her "New Moms in Museums" tours "perk up in front of the shiny and bright objects." Further, she says, "Parents don't need to know about an artist or period to begin a conversation with a child. Art is very intuitive. They just need to stop and pause and take the time to digest what they're seeing."

Because viewing art uses different mental "muscles" than those that are traditionally developed in school and elsewhere in our culture (visual, not verbal), it provides a built-in and potent opportunity for parents to stretch their children's brains and deepen their understanding of the world around them. Says Shupe, "Museums are filled with objects and paintings that came out of people's passions and beliefs. Religious icons, for example. So you say, 'People back then believed in blank so strongly that this is how they lived or what they emulated. What are you passionate about? What do you think is right, wrong?'" It's just this kind of dialogue that the modern family needs more of. "As we live more complex lives, juggling playdates, and managing the family dynamics, it's even more crucial to be able to have these kinds of simple conversations," Shupe reminds us. "They are another way of establishing that core foundation of open communication."

The Children's Medicine Principle

The way we see it, children should ingest their art experiences just like they do that flavored antibiotic: in small, easy-to-swallow doses. Structure a quick art viewing around some common themes that you know children will be inspired by. You can't go wrong with animals, folk art pieces (that look like they're made with materials the child is familiar with), and things that move (look for a mobile or something big and colorful), according to Lakes.

At the youngest ages, it's really about basics, the shapes and the colors, and talking about what the child is seeing, Lakes points out. She recommends that parents have a few simple questions to inspire conversation about the piece. "Ask about shapes, colors, and lines. How many circles do you see? Name all the colors. Count the people. Sometimes it helps to stop by the gift shop and get a postcard of the piece so the child can hold it at the same time that he is looking at it," she says. "You could take a few basic shapes or toys that the child likes from home and then wander through the gallery finding all the matching shapes. Take a ball and see how many round things you see, or a block and find the squares."

Toddlers and preschoolers can spin a good yarn, so have your child imagine herself in the piece of art and let her tell the story—making this kind of personal connection to the piece enhances the experience. For the 4-year-olds and up (maybe 3 if your child is accustomed to art museums), definitely take advantage of the scavenger hunts so many museums now offer (inquire at the information desk). Basically, they're a series of themed clue sheets that take kids through a number of different galleries to find the artworks that satisfy each set of clues. The hunts are generally not complicated, but they do require participants to look at and think about art (though in a wholly painless way). This highly interactive level of engagement is not just fun: As kids find and check off items on the list, they experience a real sense of accomplishment.

If you're still doubtful about your own ability to nurture your child's inner connoisseur, you can always put the little guy in group classes like the Art Smart tours offered by Shupe. Feel up to a challenge? There's no reason why you can't construct your own theme adventure. The topics Shupe has found particularly enticing to preschoolers and kindergarteners include safaris (kids look for claws and jaws, scales and tails in African, Ancient Egyptian, Medieval European, and Southeast Asian works); memorable mummies and famed pharaohs; cool knights (from medieval tournaments to samurai warriors); the silly squiggles of modern art; and lions, tigers, and oliphants. If you need a little help, go to Shupe's Web site at www.ArtSmart.com for more ideas.

Make Your Outing a Game

These suggestions came from the Chicago Art Institute's Web site but can be enjoyed at any museum.

Postcard games: Buy some postcards at the museum shop. Then turn your children into detectives and ask them to find the pictured items. Not only will they enjoy the hunt, they'll be thrilled to discover the real thing. Later at home, the cards can be arranged for a home exhibition.

I Spy: Have youngsters choose an object in a gallery and describe it to other family members so that each one can take a turn guessing what the object is. For example, "I spy a work of art that is red and brown with sharp angles."

Seek and find: Ask your child to find pieces of work with favorite colors, shapes, or objects in them. This teaches children to look very closely at the artwork and gives them a sense of accomplishment when they successfully identify everything asked of them. Ask your children to find something in the gallery that is very old or soft or hard or strong or shiny.

Museums at Your Fingertips

For even more ways to get your child excited about art, play with some museum Web sites. The larger ones are likely to have a kids' corner filled with interactive games. At Washington's D.C.'s National Gallery of Art's Web site, for instance, youngsters are drawn in by an online version of hide and seek using the work of James Jacques Joseph Tissot. They can also count the colors and shapes in Wassily Kandinsky works and learn about Native American culture through the artist George Catlin. Plus, once kids see a work online, they kind of get a kick out of seeing it in real life.

The Performing Arts: Cosmopolitan, Please!

Possibly the most singular aspect of city kiddy arts is the sophistication. We have children's theater productions winning Tony awards in "adult" categories (in a first ever, the Children's Theater Company of Minneapolis took home the 2003 best regional theater award for the musical *A Year with Frog and Toad*). Even heady movements like the theater of the absurd have been made available to children (who think that way anyway, so why the heck not). Then there are the weekly family disco nights at restaurants that have cottoned on to the value of the family trade to perk up business in the early evening hours. The food is good, and the kids are introduced to the glory of Gloria Gaynor as well as hip-hop and reggae dance moves upping the barre for children and adults alike.

Live music for children has been one of the loveliest developments of the last few years, as performers of the '70s, '80s, and '90s discovered the joys of parenthood themselves and turned their talents to composing and performing family music. Not for city kids the dulcet strains of the Barney theme song. Nope, they get real music. New York's Wendy Gelsanliter is a perfect example. Having grown up in a bunch of cities herself, she really gets the city swing. As a longtime folk performer (compared by reviewers to Shawn Colvin and Suzzy Roche), she's played at some of the top spots in the city. And as a teacher and parent, she really understands kids. Put it all together and you get tot tunes that are witty, musical, and easy on the ears of parents and kids alike. Ditto former rocker Laurie Berkner (whose musician-parent followers include Bruce and Madonna). Maybe the biggest of them all is Dan Zanes, formerly of the

A Cool Class with Mass Appeal

Inspired by the birth of his son Ezra, David Weinstone, a former punk rocker, came up with a laid-back, groovy children's music class in Manhattan. Five years later, his "Music for Aardvarks and Other Mammals" has one of the hippest word-of-mouth followings in Manhattan. What's so special about it? The music works for both children and their parents, technically bringing in different music styles and eras and lyrically engaging the kids. Alice attended a class 2 years ago, and she's still singing the Taxi song:

Taxi, taxi riding in the back seat/ Roll the window up, roll the window down/Put the money in the slot see ya later thanks a lot/ Sure beats walking cross town.

Weinstone has plans to take the classes across the country to Chicago, San Francisco, Philadelphia, Los Angeles, and Boston. In the meantime, you can order tapes and CDs at www.musicforaardvarks.com.

del Fuegos, whose family-friendly music is so popular that he plays at major venues in cities around the country (with a portion of proceeds dedicated to charities like Heifer International). If you want to give your family a treat, check out his Web site, www.festivalfive.com, and see when he's coming to your town.

Many of these musicians also perform for free at playgrounds, parks, and city festivals. Keep a lookout.

MAKING THE MOST OF DIVERSITY

It's not like one has to travel afar these days to reap the benefits of distant cultures. As centers of immigrant commerce, our cities are filled with people from every walk of life and every country, with vibrant ethnic neighborhoods reflecting all this glorious diversity. Some places are more organized than others—think Little Italy in Boston's North End, the Chinatowns of San Francisco and New York, Chicago's Polish sector—but all showcase their unique cultural identity in some form, and certainly enough to get your 5 and under excited about other people and ways of doing things (and if your family is of ethnic descent, making the effort to learn about your ancestors' way of life and heritage is a wonderful way to instill familial pride in your child).

Check Out Different Neighborhoods

One of Kathy's best writing assignments was a travel story about taking the no. 7 train in New York City. Get off at any stop along that subway line, a kind of "immigrant express" that goes through at least two dozen ethnic communities while traversing Queens, and you'll find myriad authentic restaurants, clothing stores, music halls, pharmacies, playgrounds, and ice cream stands. It's constant culture—Hindu temples, Argentine steak houses, quaint old-world parks full of bocce-playing seniors—and everywhere kids: kids flying kites, kids in playgrounds and parks, kids in restaurants, and kids munching on exotic-looking treats.

We know your city may not have an immigrant express (or even a decent subway system, for that matter), but it will have plenty of kid-friendly exotic spots to discover. What child wouldn't enjoy venturing off to Los Angeles's Mariachi Plaza, a colorful corner in the heart of the Latino barrio, where mariachi bands, costumed in the requisite ruffled shirts, colorful embroidery, and bolero jackets, are happy to entertain passersby. Or there's St. Louis's kitschy Hill section, where the traditions of the turn-of-the-century Italian immigrants who settled it are still in evidence everywhere: mom-and-pop trattorias, Italian grocers and shopkeepers and residents who all seem to know one another—along with some new touristy touches like fireplugs painted in green, white, and red, the colors of Italy.

If your kids are truly patient (or young enough that they won't care), you can try an organized walking tour. New York City has the popular "From Naples to Bialystock to Beijing tour"; Chicago, too, offers the ethnic perspective on foot of the city's many different cultures—Polish, Mexican, Italian, and Irish, among others. But for the young'uns, the do-it-yourself approach is best so you can linger where you want, take a bathroom break at the moment when it's absolutely needed, or pop into the local bakery for sweets from a different country of origin. Now we can't all be as lucky as Philadelphians who can go to their city's visitor center, press a button, and select any ethnic identity to receive a computerized itinerary with appropriate local sites and streets. But all cities celebrate their ethnic heritage. Be sure to keep any articles from newspapers or your local city magazine that cover the ethnic or cultural history of neighborhoods. You'll find plenty over the course of a year. Ethnic jaunts are so hot in Boston, that *Boston* magazine even publishes an annual guide on the subject.

If you want the experience to be remembered, put a restaurant, or at least some form of ethnic food, on the itinerary (see kid-friendly culinary suggestions in "Ethnic Eating" on page 231). Who knows, that Mexican flan just may turn out to be your child's Madeleine. If that can't be arranged, a keepsake will certainly do the trick. Alice has a pair of beautiful little beaded pointy shoes she got in "Little

India," and every time she pulls out her "Indian princess slippers" from her dress-up box, she talks about the time when . . .

When we started working on this book, we decided to start a culture club for our families. For the first installment, we chose to visit an area of Manhattan known as "Little India," partly because it was very accessible and partly because it was small and contained and we figured a safe start. Both families met up around 6 P.M. one summer evening to go browse the many authentic establishments in the neighborhood. An Indian grocery store was the first stop. It was bursting with enormous burlap bags of every rice imaginable, a fine array of teas and spices, exotic cooking devices (to our Western eyes, anyway), oils and soaps, and Indian magazines. Julia's daughter Katherine immediately pulled out a Mendhi tattoo kit to take home, while Alice went for the spicy-scented Indian soaps. The shopping spree culminated at a sari emporium, where Alice scooped those slippers and Pearson scored a mortar and pestle (perfect for all those home chemistry experiments, ka-boooom). The salespeople were charming and friendly—and so enamored that we "foreigners" had made the trek that all the children were rewarded with on-the-house baubles: bangle bracelets and little elephant key chains.

By this point, the crew had all built up an appetite. So it was off to a vegetarian all-you-can-eat restaurant that turned out to be great for kids because it was decorated to look like an Indian village with bamboo roofed huts, a succession of elephants beckoning us in, and village scenes hand-painted on the walls. We climbed onto benches piled high with kilim cushions, rested our feet in wells beneath the table, and were treated to a royal feast. Julia was certain her children would go home starving (vegetables are not their strong suit). But the format of the presentation—big Indian platters for each guest with small portions of maybe 8 or 10 dishes for each course, including plenty of breads and rices—was so exotic and intriguing that even the pickiest of the group found plenty to eat. The event was so successful that Julia's kids started fighting over who would get to choose the location for the next outing. Oh, and by the next day, apparently every uptown 9-year-old girl was demanding a Mendhi of her own.

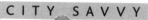

C I T Y   S A V V Y

Festivals.com

One of our favorite new Web finds, festivals.com offers a pretty exhaustive listing of every festival in the country, with search capabilities by city. Just plug in the name of your city to find the smorgasbord of ethnic festivals near you.

Ethnic Celebrations

If walking tours and family culture clubs are not for you, there's still plenty of culture to be enjoyed at your city's ethnic festivals, parades, and holiday celebrations. Whether or not such events are specifically geared to children—as are the

THE URBAN A-LIST
Keeping Festivals on Your Radar

1. Look out for Norwegian fests (kids love to watch the authentic line dancing), traditional Irish celebrations (did someone say folk dancing?), polka parties, Caribbean family days, and anything that features Klezmer, Cajun, or Zydeco music.

2. Holidays offer the perfect opportunity to learn about other cultures. Maybe it'll be the Kwanzaa celebrations at Los Angeles's Leimert Park Village or the Chinese New Year, which in NYC is a month-long celebration that usually begins in late January and ends with the Golden Dragon Parade, firecrackers, and yummy Lin Go cakes.

3. Thanksgiving isn't the only holiday celebrating the fall harvest. This time of year is ripe for an array of international festivities: the Chinese Harvest Moon festival, the Jewish holiday of Sukkot, and the Korean *Chusok*, (purists refer to this kind of Thanksgiving as *Hangwai*).[a] At Chusok, people feast, honor ancestors (by leaving fresh fruit, dried fish, and rice at simulated tombs), and consume massive quantities of *songpyeon*, the delicious crescent-shaped rice dumplings filled with a sweet mix of ground beans, chestnuts, or sesame seeds that are as prevalent as turkeys on Thanksgiving. At a recent Chusok festival in New York City, the largest Korean gathering outside of Korea, families were everywhere, eating, dancing, watching tai kwon do demonstrations, even enjoying the pageantry of a Korean wedding fashion show.

Just keep your eyes open. Some of the coolest activities are in unlikely places. On warm-weather weekends, eastern European folk-dance enthusiasts gather in New York's Central Park by the impressive statue of King Jagiello (the 15th-century Polish-Lithuanian warrior-king). A dance is selected, some recorded music begins, and away the group goes—and grows, as newcomers are welcomed and encouraged to learn the latest step. It's absolutely entrancing for little ones.

a. Sandee Brawarsky, "For Koreans, Feast and Thanks," *New York Times*, October 4, 2002.

Pittsburgh International Children's Festival and the Seattle International Children's Festival—there's plenty of excitement for the young'uns. Music, dance, food, theater, even toys and games—there isn't a country or culture that doesn't have them. Go, explore, enjoy. Just beware of celebrations with corporate sponsorships. You may not want to bring your little innocent to that beer-sponsored Cinco de Mayo festival (or arrive early before the alcohol has totally taken over).

DINING OUT: BEYOND MCDONALD'S

Dining can certainly be one of the sweetest treats about living in any city. So why not take the time to turn your city kid into a culinary adventurer. But even if you're 1000 percent certain that Oscar's palate isn't expanding anytime soon, he can still become a pro at the art and etiquette of eating out.

Reluctant to venture out with your little handful? Think of the benefits. First, there is the chance that he actually might develop a taste for something besides chicken nuggets. Studies have shown that repeated introductions to different foods is key to developing children's taste buds. "Repeated introductions" may seem like an oxymoron but it's not. On average, it takes 10 times before some children will even try the new food, let alone enjoy it. It worked with Alice. Every time Kathy's parents take Alice out to dinner, they just marvel that the munchkin regularly asks for salmon teriyaki and miso soup—tofu cubes, seaweed, and all (on the other hand, it did nothing for Julia's kids, who apparently are programmed to subsist on white food—macaroni and cheese, bagels, and pasta—until they reach the age of 9, when some previously dormant taste buds kick in).

Which brings us to the second benefit: Even if your kids don't take advantage of an expanded menu, you will. Let them have plain pasta while you ingest more refined items. Everyone will be happier. Of course, your kids will have to behave a little—and that's the third benefit. There are lots of tricks to this eating-out thing, which we'll tip you off to, but fundamentally, you will need to work with your kids on eating in a public place, respecting other people's desires for a nice, quiet meal, not leaving a holy mess for the busboys to clear away, and saying please and thank you when talking to the waitperson. So dining out also becomes manners school, and what, exactly, could be wrong with that?

Kid-Friendly Is No Longer Just "Kiddie"

Just in time for your family's dining expeditions, a wave of new family restaurants is washing across cities from coast to coast. These eateries welcome the under-3-feet set (though admittedly are not as kiddie-centric as their crayons-on-the-tables counterparts) while serving up enough ambience and edible food to satiate both parent and child alike. Could a soft economy (kids are always more welcome when there's no queue at the door) have spurred the trend? Or perhaps a recognition by savvy restaurateurs that a significant number of time-deprived parents wanted to trade-up from the obvious "family-friendly" choices to options they'd like as much as their kids. Probably both.

For sure, some credit goes to restaurateurs with kids of their own. Many thanks. The story is a classic one: Restaurateur doesn't think about kids until he has them and then suddenly realizes there's a huge need for an establishment that dishes up high-caliber food in an environment that is attractive to adults without freezing out kids. That's exactly what happened to Joachim Splichal, the chef/owner of Los Angeles's popular Patina Group restaurants. He decided that if his 2½-year-old twins, who dined regularly at his Patina Bistro, were satisfied with the adult menu, then other kids would be as well. Now, at all six of his Pinot restaurants, kids under 12 can eat anything off the regular menu—for free! And when Boston-based sisters Cary and Sarah Wheaton started raising children, they didn't think they should have to abandon the family tradition of fine dining even if the kids took all of two

Kids' Menus Grow Up

California here we come. The foodie capital leads the nation in upscale kids' menus that adults will want to pick off. Skeptical?

Consider the kids' menu at San Diego's El Bizcocho restaurant. It is so "advanced" that it comes with an "education card" explaining each dish and its exotic ingredients. Some offerings on the menu: Salmon Snappers, which are smoked salmon roulades with tomato, dill cream cheese, a cucumber "baton," and frisée salad. And for an haute variation on the chips theme, the prekindergarten set can gorge on their popular Cheesy Chips, parmesan potato chips with white truffle oil.

Then there's LA's Fuga restaurant at Studio City, which has designed a special children's bento box happy meal. Instead of the grown-up versions that come with the usual mix of sashimi, teriyaki, salad, etc., the Japanese restaurant fills up the dish's many compartments with kids' favorites, among them edamame, tempura, cucumber roll, and fruit. And in their twist on the "Happy Meal," a toy comes with the meal too. Only in this case, it's usually some kind of Pokèmon item or plastic monster.

Source: Jessica Strand, "Baby Food Go Bye-Bye," *Los Angeles Times*, April 24, 2003.

seconds to finish their meals. But they couldn't find a place where both kids and adults would be happy either. Their answer was to open Full Moon in Cambridge, where the tots can play with a smorgasbord of "smart" toys while their parents finish their meal at their leisure.

Restaurants That Work

Too many city parents are still under the misconception that adult restaurants won't welcome them. A restaurant needn't have high chairs (our kids do just fine on phone books, even kneeling if the chair or banquette is comfy) and kids' activities on hand to make your short list. All that really matters is that kids can blend in with the environment and that the waitstaff doesn't run for cover when they see kids coming. Here is what to look for in dining spots that will help your kids and other diners peacefully coexist.

Pick loud for your crowd. Any restaurant that has a noise level that can drown out your gang's racket is a restaurant worth considering. Establishments that cater to groups, especially, are a good starting point. Chances are, if you're seated next to a raucous klatch of mojito drinkers, Karla's little table tantrum won't even register.

Go for lots of room, back rooms, and corner spaces. Restaurants with ample room to move around in make all the difference when having to get through that exasperating tight squeeze with strollers (not to mention trips back and forth

Group Fun for Some Adventurous Moms

When Jane Rae and her adorable infant, Simon, were living in Washington D.C., the duo regularly dined in a Lebanese restaurant with a group of similar two-somes who they'd met through a parent-baby yoga class. "We would charge in there with our strollers, and they were kind enough to let us use a back room that was ordinarily empty during lunchtime. It's a VERY popular place, so that was great of them," Jane recounts of the wonderful experience. "It was sweet how they watched our children grow from babes in strollers to needing high chairs, booster seats, plastic forks, and a place to explore when they started walking. We ended up celebrating the kids' first birthdays there and only stopped convening weekly once all the moms started back at work." And the real kicker? One of Simon's favorite foods is chicken shwarma! Take that Micky D's!

Catering for Kids

A recent trend among time-starved parents is to use a caterer for family dinners. A step down in price and luxury from the personal chef, the food comes from catering kitchens or freelance cooks, the latter of whom can shop and cook for you once a week, preparing any number of complete family meals in your kitchen or theirs, which are then frozen or refrigerated until you want them on the table. Voilà—everyone's eating better, and Mom and Dad have more time to relax with the kids.

To make this work for your clan, menus should be conceived with a family of palates in mind—generally a kid-friendly entrée with some vegetable and starch sides, plus dessert. Simpler dishes may be more successful with kids and probably easier on your pocketbook too. New York City's Tartare does a fabulous roast chicken family dinner with seared spinach, garlic mashed potatoes, Caesar salad, and homemade cookies for $25. Sure it's more than you'd spend if you cooked it all yourself, but when you factor in the preparation time and the taste (not all of us are quality cooks), it's the bargain of the year—and no doubt lots healthier than ordering pizza or Chinese. One smart parent finds using a caterer every other week cuts her culinary burden to a manageable load. She also suggests that with little kids as diners, two full meals can actually cover the entire workweek.

Wanna try this? Check out neighborhood catering and/or take-out establishments and ask for their meal menus. If you want to find an individual cook, call the local cooking schools for names or even try placing an ad online at www.Craigslist.org, if that message board runs in your city.

to the bathroom) and stressful situations when kids need a little mobility to get through the meal. A few years back, *New York* magazine actually voted a restaurant "best kid friendly (but not kiddie)" that had a clientele that leaned more to the singles-with-roommates scene than the parents crowd. Why? Because of its cavernous space and nice staff. But even restaurants with tighter quarters may have back rooms that are not always in use and perfect for parent/children klatches. Another good alternative is a table in a corner. Often there's enough room to put an active 2-year-old on the floor (between the table and the wall) where he can happily play with crayons, LEGOs, or trucks without disturbing the traffic flow, the diners at the next table, or your own attempts at adult conversation.

Al fresco is besto. Outdoor space usually means room to run around or people watch. Your child isn't interested in people watching? How about vehicle viewing? Julia's youngest son loves an outside table at a restaurant near their local firehouse. Every time he hears the alarm, he runs to the front to wave at "the guys" as they head out for action. And when he was smaller, he was quite content to look for cool trucks and cars while the rest of the family kicked back with their meals.

Think little food and lots of action. You don't need a theme park interior for insta-fun. Think small, like tapas, dim sum, and any kind of serious interactivity such as picking out your own ingredients for a pizza or a Chinese dish. Any place where food is prepared in front of you is bound to distract your little guys. Watching sushi chefs in action can keep Alice occupied for 20 minutes at a time. Julia's crew thought the table-side guacamole making was pretty cool at one Mexican restaurant. Other kid favorites are open pizza ovens, hibachi grills at the table, and food that comes out '50s style on conveyor belts.

Institutionalize them. Some of our favorite restaurant finds are in museums, hotels, and retail establishments. Quite a few have great food, and they're set up for crowds, noise, and kids. Plus, there are usually lots of distractions and places to step out to if the kids get a little antsy between courses.

Look for chefs with kids. If they haven't created kid-suitable environments, they've at least trained their staff to be amenable to kid-oriented requests like warming up a bottle or preparing a special order for those tender palates.

Choose casual joints. Any restaurant with words like bistro, trattoria, or café is by nature more relaxed and family oriented.

Go for broke. Expensive means service. But it also means other customers are paying a pretty penny for that fine dining experience. If anyone has ever applied the words "manic" or "out of control" when describing your kids, skip the white tablecloth places. On the other hand, if you think your child is past the stage of pounding silverware on the table, give a good restaurant a try, but start with an off hour (or an off season—maître d's who would turn up their noses at you in the middle of winter will greet you with bells on their toes come the dog days of summer).

Strategies to Be Invited Back

All this is dandy, but only if you dare to go. Understandably, many parents fear the spectacle that accompanies a little cherub going ballistic when, say, that errant vegetable touches the pasta. There's nothing like a stressful eruption to take away your appetite. We're here to say, that's true, but go, do anyway. Only now, do it smartly.

Choosing the right times and the right places, and bringing along whatever accoutrements are necessary to keep Spike occupied between courses are key. And by all means, heed the warning signs of the truly inhospitable restaurant. You have plenty of options, so just skip those establishments that post No Strollers signs or have a dimly lit dining room or a clientele of either suits or couples gazing deeply into each other's eyes.

THE CITY PARENT RULES
Eating Out

Rule #1: Become regulars just about anywhere! Frequent a place enough and chances are the owners and staff will recognize you and repay your patronage with tolerance when your child acts up. What's more, says Sanna Delmonico, M.S., R.D., a San Francisco–area nutritionist, "When kids are in a comfortable environment, they are more willing to try new things. It becomes a home away from home." Of course, tipping well is essential. That way, the staff won't mind (as much) any extra cleanup and will happily accede to your request for extra cherries in the Shirley Temple.

Rule #2: Use the off-hours. Lunch is a great way to make restaurant going palatable while working on your child's palate and public comportment. A restaurant that may be fancier at night will often be more relaxed during the day. Alternatively, going to very hip restaurants before the crowds come makes everyone happy. The management gets more business, parents and kids still get good food, and no one's annoyed by anyone else's presence. (Julia's family frequents a jazz restaurant that really doesn't get going till 10 P.M.—allowing them plenty of time to eat a respectable dinner without having to resort to early-bird specials.)

Rule #3: Accelerate the plate. They say timing is everything—definitely the case with meal timing and children. Lots of times, parents will be asked if the kids' food should come right away. That's fine to agree to, except then they're done eating before your main course has even hit the table. On the other hand, if you're okay with them having dessert while you eat your entrée,

---

CITYWISE WARNING !

Never Ever Let Them Wander without Supervision

There's nothing that drives waitstaff crazier than a little imp bumping into them while they're carrying a tray full of dishes. Tripping a server or hurting a patron is just unacceptable. The temptation at a restaurant, especially one filled with activity, is to let George take off to let off steam—only a good trick if you're willing to escort the little tyke. Even then, be mindful of the serving staff corridors. Don't hang out by the kitchen or any of their main routes around the restaurant. T'aint fair.

then accelerating the kids' meals will work just fine (except you won't get dessert, but maybe that's a good thing). Also, know when to quit. As a rule of thumb, pay early (like right after you get the main course). That way, if you have to get out of Dodge, you can just bolt with impunity.

Rule #4: Be selective about seating. Booths are great. The kids are trapped for one, but they also have more space to squirm around on than a high chair or regular chair would allow. We also like tables near doors in case a fidgeting kid needs to be taken out for some air. And remember our tip about corners: They're great places for toddlers to hang out sight unseen.

Rule #5: Bring some entertainment. Even if you're the ultimate pared-down parent, make an exception for restaurants. Before courses arrive, and in-between, there's always downtime when children will need to be occupied. Bring books or small toys for the youngest kids; by the time the kids are 2 or 3, most will be able to scrawl or play with stickers. Slightly older kids can do mazes or puzzle books (older than that and goddangit they'd better be conversing).

Rule #6: Don't let your child starve. To avoid the excessive crankiness that comes with true hunger pangs, ask for bread immediately or bring a bag of crackers or cereal for your child to munch on. It'll take the edge off his hunger without completely destroying his appetite and keep him occupied for a bit.

Rule #7: Clean up after your child. We certainly know some adult slobs, but face it: Your kids are probably messier eaters than the typical diner, so have a heart and mitigate the mess. If Chachi throws half the bread basket on the floor, get a couple of napkins and clean it up. And explain to Chachi why you're doing it (in fact, make Chachi help too).

Rule #8: Consider a bribe. Julia, as you may remember, resorted to bribes to entice Malcolm to walk, and we think that the promise of an ice cream cone for good table manners seems fair (best purchased somewhere else; they've probably been at the restaurant too long already).

Rule #9: Be prepared to make amends (and an exit). Sometimes all your planning, preparation, and careful selection is for naught: What starts out to be a delightful dining experience turns into the Hundred Years War. If other diners are giving you dirty looks because little Fifi will not stop singing "Itsy Bitsy Spider" in a voice that could reach a mezzanine, you need to admit defeat. Get the check and make a fast getaway. And if you really think Fifi's antics have disturbed your fellow diners, you might consider offering to buy them drinks or dessert by way of reparations.

Ethnic Eating

Just because your child will only eat pasta doesn't mean you have to completely forgo dining out on exotic fare. "Every cuisine has a plain starchy food that kids can fall back on if the other foods are too intimidating—plain rice, breads (like Indian *nan*), potatoes, tortillas," notes Delmonico. Of course, we're all for ordering something a little more adventuresome for your child, but in a pinch . . .

If you don't have a good handle on what your child will actually eat, ask the waitress for her suggestions (and do see our menu suggestions below). Kathy and husband, Jim, tried this with Alice at their local Japanese restaurant and were surprised to learn that the small "flying" fish roe is popular among Japanese-American children. She thought her daughter would never go for it, but when she received a little mound, placed oh-so-delicately in a scooped-out piece of cucumber, Alice giggled, "It's soooo cute," and proceeded to play with it a bit before giving it a try. Don't forget drinks. Fresh guava, mango, and the nectars of other exotic fruits are healthy and fun to introduce to your children. Also, many ethnic restaurants have their version of a sweetened milk drink, whether it's a Greek yogurt smoothie or Thai coconut milk extraction.

And while you're in Rome, Ethiopia, Greece . . . by all means, dine the way the Romans and Ethiopians and Greeks do. It'll add to the experience. Take chopsticks. Your little imp can master them, you know. Asian cultures rig them up by wrapping rubber bands around the tops to make it easier for their children to learn. Just ask the waitstaff to prepare your child a version. She'll probably get such a kick out of it, you'll end up with them at home.

Starting your own restaurant club? Here's our dinner cheat sheet of the ethnic foods kids love to eat.

Greek

Avgolemeno soup: There's a chicken noodle soup in every culture, and this one's sweet and lemony and served with rice.

Pastitsio: Think of this as Greek lasagna made with beef, béchamel sauce, and big noodles. FYI: The top often gets dark and crunchy, and Greek parents often flip it before serving so kids don't see it and refuse to eat it.

Falafel: Omnipresent in Middle Eastern restaurants, these fun balls of deep-fried chickpea puree can be rolled in peanut-buttery tahini sauce (actually made from ground sesame seeds, so no problem with allergies) or stuffed into a pita pocket.

Souvlakia: Children who prefer their food to be plain might go for these grilled skewers of lamb that often come with vegetables—plus your child can usually pick what goes in them.

Kourabiedes (or Kourambiethes): Baklava may be the most popular Greek dessert among adults and non-Greeks but not so with kids, who instead prefer these thickly powdered sugar cookies.

Indian

Chicken Tikka: According to the Bollywood Café in Los Angeles, kids particularly like this chicken dish because its creamed spice sauce is kind of like barbecue sauce without being too spicy.

Saag Paneer: A comforting concoction of spinach and cheese. Ask for it without sugar, and it tastes just like creamed spinach.

Samosas: Various deep-fried veggie and meat items; fun to pick up and eat with your hands.

Nan: There are many types of Indian bread, but this doughy and fluffy one is the preferred bread of choice. Order it plain, or there's a kind of sweet one that's stuffed with chicken, coconut, and raisins.

Kulfi: Indian ice cream comes in mango or almond flavors (there's pistachio too, but most kids don't like that one). If your darling becomes a fan, it's fun to make at home. No need for a fancy ice cream maker; the mold of choice will do.

Japanese

Edamame: Kids really love the now ubiquitous soybean pods. It's a great way to start the meal. Just think of them as soy toys—kids have fun popping out the beans, and they get all the healthy benefits at the same time.

Miso soup: Another appetizer to consider is this brothlike soup with floating pieces of tofu and seaweed (you're not obliged to tell the kids what it is).

Tempura: This shouldn't be a big stretch since they're battered and fried, and most kids love that treatment. Los Angeles's Sushi Masu recommends asking for pumpkin and sweet potato.

Katsu: These fried pork or chicken cutlets are also no-brainers, though not terribly adventuresome.

Gyoza: Japanese versions of dumplings. Kids will eat them without even knowing what's inside.

Udon noodles: Thick, white, and slippery, they look like worms and come in broth served with either chicken, vegetables, or fish. Or try soba noodles (thin and brown), or the even thinner ramen.

Sushi: Certainly the cooked sushi pieces are possibilities, like the eel that is so buried under the sweet teriyaki sauce. Also, egg custard, fake crab, and fish roe and California rolls seem to go over well with small children.

Tempura ice cream: These rock-hard frozen scoops of ice cream (yam, caramel, and vanilla seem to be the kiddiest flavors) are dipped in tempura, then deep-fried—always a hit. They're yummy and an ongoing source of wonderment: "Mommy, how do they get the outside so warm and the inside so cold?"

Mexican

Tortillas: This thin flat bread made from cornmeal and cooked on a griddle is what most Mexicans eat instead of bread.

Tacos: Take a tortilla, add a rich sauce, cheese, and some chicken or ground beef and many kids will gobble it up.

Quesadillas: Just like tacos, these Mexican grilled-cheese sandwiches can be eaten with your hands. They're formed by filling two tortillas with cheese (usually Monterey Jack) and grilling or frying until it's all soft and gooey. If your kids are really into plain food, just ask the waiter to make sure to have the quesadillas prepared with cheese only (no peppers, no spices, no sauce).

Fajitas: Basically, a mixed grill of thinly sliced meats, chicken, and/or vegetables rolled up in a tortilla, this simple dish is a good alternative for kids who don't like sauces. Plus they get to roll their own, which adds to the entertainment quotient.

Flan: According to Casa Antigua in Los Angeles, kids love this pudding-type dessert, not just because of the creamy caramel taste but also because it's slippery and just jumps right off the spoon.

Korean

Korean barbecue: A platter of thinly sliced raw meats, poultry, and vegetables brought to the table, where you get to cook them in a hibachi-style grill that's either built into the table or rests on top of it. Small children must be guarded carefully, but with guidance, this interactive dish is fun for everyone. It comes with spicy side sauces that should definitely be avoided—unless, of course, your child is one hot tamale.

Mandu: Dumplings are another dish Korean children love. Either circles or cute crescent shapes of wheat dough seal in a mixture of tofu (remember, no one's forcing you to tell them what's in it), minced beef, pork, and mixed vegetables. The dumplings are then steamed, fried, or simmered in stock and typically served with kimchi and soy sauce on the side (just make sure that crushed red peppers haven't been added to the soy sauce before your child dips in).

Japchae: This is a dish with mixed vegetables and noodles, light-years more exciting (and fresher) than ramen noodles. Often part of Korean celebrations and parties, japchae can be made with any vegetable—seasonal varieties are preferred. The veggies are fried on their own in a small amount of oil. Vermicelli-style potato noodles are then cooked and cut into short pieces. And some variations of the dish include thin slices of beef (also lightly fried). All the cooked ingredients are then quickly sautéed together to marry the flavors. The finishing touch is a dash of soy sauce, sesame oil, and sugar.

Bibimbap: A bowl of hot rice topped with a kind of vegetable sauté is another dish to keep in mind, though make sure the spicy sauce comes on the side.

Yeot Gangjeong: Koreans usually eat only fresh fruit for dessert. But they do have a chewy rice treat made from a mixture of *yeot* (sticky rice sugar) plus sesame seeds, beans, walnuts, or pine nuts, cut into bite-size pieces.

Peruvian

Roast chicken: Their version of rotisserie chicken is flavorful with a light chili powder spicing but still simple enough for any child who eats chicken.

Cancha: A side of roasted corn kernels is another favorite.

Arroz Con Leche: This rice pudding is a popular kid-friendly dessert. And for a fun twist, try *Mazamorra Morada*, a version that's made from purple corn.

CHAPTER 10

FROM SIN CITY TO MAYBERRY

O ne thing you get used to as a city parent is fending off jibes about the person your child might turn out to be. Why would you raise Olivia in the city? She'll end up so jaded, so fried by the pace, so dehumanized by the multitudes who surround her at every turn. Why, indeed, you sometimes wonder. If it isn't your pesky in-law making you feel guilty about your choices, then perhaps it's your own fears. Are you doing her a disservice? Won't she have more of a chance to be a child outside the city? Is there any way you actually *can* control how she's being raised here?

Come to think of it, as much as you love the idea of bringing up a cultured and tolerant city baby, visions of her possible 18-year-old self dance before your eyes: a chain-smoking, eyebrow- and naval-ringed club kid morphing to a Cavalli-wearing, skin-bearing party girl. Oh great, you're thinking; let's book the movers now, honey, we're going to Montana.

Relax. Your child doesn't have to turn out jaded or insensitive (or too sensitive, for that matter); nor does she have to grow up so overprotected that she's terrified by the world around her. But we won't pull any punches on the problems you'll encounter. Shaping your child's psyche is no cakewalk in the city. As the parent, you'll need to find the delicate balance between those urban highlights and lowlifes. Exalt the good and mitigate the bad, we like to say.

And just in case you haven't noticed, the city *is* helping you raise your child, for better, but sometimes for worse. Since there's no way to escape its influence, you will need to *manage* the city experience for your child. And you'd better be prepared for a daily effort. Exposure (over and under), stress (the noise, that too-close-for-comfort togetherness, the high velocity of city life), finding a place in a city of millions—these will be constants in your child's life. And watching over it all? This must be part of your daily parenting routine too.

PARENTING IN A PRECOCIOUS WORLD

You know you're not in Kansas anymore when a simple little stroll through the park puts you on a collision course with all sorts of urban fauna and flora—random acts of public urination, high-fashion photo shoots with more skin showing than any beach your kid has ever been on, and amorous partners manifesting their obvious strong affection for one another. Managing the very graphic and immediate reality of a city for its younger inhabitants is clearly one of the most important and hardest things an urban parent must do—but it's also one of the best because the great big untold secret is that city living provides some rather impressive tools for parents to use in the psychological aspects of parenting. Think about it. Every day, Ramon *is* going to encounter people in need *and* people helping out. Every day, Ramon *is* going to witness rudeness (and probably acquire a virtual United Nations of swearwords just while ambling down a city block) *and* graciousness. That's not of issue. The real question is what will you do about it? You can filter or magnify or censor or shade how the city and your child interact—and your proactiveness in that regard will make a world of difference in how Ramon incorporates all that city "life" into his consciousness.

"T" Is for Teaching

Family therapist Naomi Siegel, who counsels parents in and outside of New York City, makes an interesting observation. In the suburbs, she believes, kids come under the influence of their peer group far earlier than in the city. "Kids as young as 3 go out on the block" to hang out with the neighborhood children. Slightly older children, quite often, "go out immediately after school to play, sometimes not returning till dinner." While it's great they're getting all that runaround time and free unstructured play, Siegel sees an underside: At very tender ages, children are becoming substantially influenced by the "values" of the groups they're spending time with (including almost inevitably, the slightly older kids in those groups), to the detriment of their parents' influences.

City kids, in contrast, are under adult supervision till much older ages, which means that *your* interaction and influence can loom pretty large in your child's development. That's the good news. Take advantage of it, and it's *very* good news. The close contact that being a city parent requires gives you enormous opportunity to impact your child's moral development, convey your sense of ethics, explain right and wrong, discuss standards of behavior, and develop consciousness and self-awareness. And you will do this whether you plan to or not, simply by the way you react to the many, many experiences you and your child, or your child and his caregiver, share. So be careful how you respond to city life; your child is watching.

"C" Is for Character

If you think about the nature of character development, you begin to see the advantages of city living. William Damon, director of the Stanford Center on Adolescence and one of the country's leading experts on moral growth in children, explains that character development is an incremental long-term process in which parents as the first source of moral guidance are responsible not only for a matter of conveying the "do nots," but also for emphasizing the positive. Don't worry; the city will work with you on this one. Here's what you need to do:

Start early. Teaching your child to be a moral person doesn't come in one giant "lesson" when your little one turns 16; it happens as soon as the babe is talking. All those endless conversations with your toddlers on waiting their turn at the swing and why people should throw their ice cream wrappers in the garbage and why those people are marching around with signs—keep them up. This is where moral development begins.

Be constant, be consistent. As Damon reminds us, for that moral guidance to be effective, "children must hear the message enough for it to stick." It's not a once-a-month homily or even once-a-week; it's a continual give and take. And keep on point with your own behavior. It's not going to facilitate your kid's development if every time you get caught in some contentious city situation, you violate half of the principles you've been trying to convey.

Use your environment. With all the evidence of humanity and humanity's effects in a city, you will have more than enough fodder for discussion even at the level of a 3-year-old. And don't just focus on the bad messages like littering, a poorly parked car, and playground roughhousing. There are plenty of good examples you can use to enlighten your child: someone helping an elderly person across the street or giving directions to tourists or calling to report a broken traffic light. It almost doesn't matter what message you want to convey. The richness of your city environment will give you plenty of live examples to make your point.

"R" Is for Resiliency

Ah, the "R" word! If you've even remotely kept up with the latest parenting literature, then you know that "resiliency" and "self-reliance" are the buzzwords du jour. Why? Because these important character traits, which our kids are going to need in order to successfully navigate life, seem to be in especially short supply these days. Many experts believe that we the people are currently turning out the wimpiest, most handheld, most entitled group of youngsters the world has known. There are lots of causes—the drive to turn out A-list children, guilt-ridden parents compensating for their lack of time by overindulging and under-demanding—and city parents aren't alone in succumbing to them. But when you throw into the mix the tendency of city parents to monitor *everything* their youngsters do, you end up with an even *higher* risk of overcontrol in urban locales.

It's what clinical psychologist Wendy Mogel, Ph.D., author of the best-selling parenting book *Blessings of a Skinned Knee*, calls "viking parenting," where "city parents . . . come charging in, and maybe it's all the constant supervision, but the tendency is to always want to make everything right." And *that's* not right either, Mogel warns. Fail to step back and your child will end up with the "Teacups and Crispies Syndrome," the name that dumbfounded college administrators and educators all across the country are giving to students who are so fragile that at the first sign of a problem they crack (ergo "teacups") or are so burned out from being overscheduled that they're plain old fried ("crispies").

Loosening the Lead Line

Giving kids the chance to make decisions for themselves and learn from the outcomes may seem a trifle tougher in the city than it actually is. You just need to look for opportunities. You don't have to go overboard here, says author and clinical psychologist Wendy Mogel, and *never* be reckless. Just stretch a little: "Maybe two degrees more than your intuition tells you is safe because our perception of danger is greater than the reality." Family therapist Naomi Siegel advises parents not to rush in every time there's an altercation in the sandbox. As long as no one's getting hurt, you can afford to let little kids try to figure it out for themselves.

And look for ways for them to feel independent. When Julia's two oldest kids were 5 and 3, they wanted to go across a big enclosed expanse of park by themselves while their parents walked the perimeter. The kids were never out of sight, certainly never in danger, but they did have to figure out a route and wend their way through picnickers. The kids were immensely proud when they came out the other side intact and at the same time as their parents. Now, we're not talking about giving 4-year-olds $20 to take a cab to preschool by themselves; for little kids, freedom should come in little ways, but it needs to be there.

On the other hand, you *can* choose to turn out a resilient and self-reliant child—and the city will even help you, if you let it. "Consider the small act of taking your child shopping," says Irwin Redlener, M.D., former president of NYC's Children's Hospital at Montefiore and current head of the Children's Health Fund. "While you're busy negotiating the streets, public transportation, crowds, and different people—and of course, making sure your kids are safe—they are learning rules: how to be and act in public, how to stay safe, and more. Kids get more capable, more street savvy more readily, and in cities it starts happening relatively early." The psychological upshot, he says, is significant: "It contributes to a potential greater sense of resiliency."

So don't short-circuit all that fabulous life experience the city offers your child, stresses Mogel, because that "broad swath of life is not just invigorating, it can be humbling." With so many outside influences and people to contend with, a child who's acting bratty or super-entitled will have a much harder time getting away with this type of behavior on a city street, she explains. And that's an advantage. Give children the freedom to make decisions for themselves, and they'll learn from the outcomes, she promises. Even if that freedom leads to some poor choices, well, that's okay too; mistakes are the ultimate teacher.

MANAGING EXPOSURE WHEN YOUR CITY'S NOT RATED G

Many aspects of a diverse urban environment will be great, interesting, exciting, and invigorating. And then there will be those that you'd just as soon your kids didn't embrace. So how do you manage a child's intake of city excess? Well, as often as you can, through distraction and avoidance. And when those tactics don't or won't work, you tread very, very carefully.

Reacting to Rudeness

One of the really annoying things about raising kids in the city is that just at the time *you're* trying to instill in them the most rudimentary of social graces, *they're* starting to take in all the blatant rudeness that abounds in an urban landscape— all those instances of random swearwords, people fighting for a cab, another outburst of "checkout rage" at the grocery store. And what makes this particularly tough terrain is not just the confusion this causes for little Jessica (why should I be polite if no one else is?), but the fact that, as Yale professor Stephen L. Carter, J.D., points out, in many ways, rudeness is a perfectly practical response to living life in a crowd. After all, we can't possibly nod good morning to everyone we pass on a busy D.C. sidewalk the way we might in a small town in Georgia. Brusqueness,

Parenting Horror Stories

It's not just the adults that are a problem, you know. Manners take a beating on the playground too. Take these incidents from anonymous moms who posted online for advice on how to handle rudeness on the playground.

> . . . four or five boys were teasing a girl under a jungle-gym and were actually TEARING HER CLOTHES OFF. She wasn't screaming, just whimpering, and many adults around didn't even notice. A nanny (not hers, the nanny was with a toddler) pushed the boys away and picked up the girl. One of the boys fell to the ground and called the nanny by the N word.

***

> A boy, dressed all in fatigues and carrying a toy AK-47, was pointing the gun at a bunch of smaller kids. I told him to stop, and he told me to shut up. I can't even imagine who or what his parents must be like, so we just left that area.

***

> Two 8–9-year-old kids in a McDonald's Playhouse area. One was behind the other and told his friend to hurry up the tunnel. The friend replied, "I'm trying but these $%^&*! kids are in the way" (one of which was my son). I said sternly, "First of all, you're too big to be up in there." He said, "Shuddap!"

***

> A 5–6 y/o decided it'd be fun to pull my son around by the arm (who was 2.5 at the time). I calmly said to him, "No, no—don't pull him by the arm like that." He said, "Shuddap." I said, "Don't tell me to shuddap." He glared at me and went back to playing.

Source: Urban Baby New York Message Board, anonymous posters, October 23, 2002.

shoving, a dearth of pleases and thanks yous—that's what gets us through an urban day. The only problem is that our pragmatic city conventions are "morally inferior" to the ones they replace.

So what then? We just let that urban fallout be soaked up by our beautiful little sponges? No, the answer is not to give up: It's to shape up. We regard manners as an absolute necessity when you're living in a crowd. Think of all the fringe benefits teaching manners will bestow: a sense of self-restraint, awareness of others, and the concept of fairness. There are important lessons here.

Rule #1: Make your expectations known. Greetings and goodbyes to neighbors, acquaintances, building staff, and the like; pleases, thank you's, and excuse me's to everyone when the situation demands it. Give your child lots of chances to practice. Let him give the money to the delivery guy, ask for a newspaper at the newsstand, or question whether he can borrow a toy in the sandbox. Don't always do it for him.

Rule #2: Explain why manners are necessary. "We live in a crowded city" and "We need to respect others." Talk about why we have laws, the concept of public goods, that we all share the park, the air. Kids soak up this stuff at a young age when your every word is gold to them; they won't later on, so take advantage while you can.

Rule #3. Be a role model yourself. Remember what we said earlier about the consistency of your message. What's Tristan going to think if you politely thank the super for holding the door and five steps later yell "f—you" to the limo driver who cuts you off in the crosswalk? We're not suggesting you never get mad, but we are strongly advocating you adopt a consistent policy on how you behave in your outdoor life. Controlled anger would help, plus an explanation about what the person did that was bad. You can even try channeling some of your rage into a proactive solution that you share with your child—like calling the police and reporting the bad guy's license number.

When Strangers Get Too Close

Of course, if safety is at stake, we say, let manners take a back seat. In close encounters of the city kind, you really never know what you're dealing with, so you must proceed with caution. In most of the more dubious situations, avoidance is best. That man muttering on the park bench? Probably no harm to you and yours, but don't take a chance.

Here are some other suggested responses to common city situations:

- The stranger reaching into your newborn's stroller: Absolutely block the pass and say "please don't" firmly.
- The irate person on the bus who your rambunctious toddler just grazed: "We're terribly sorry, sir/m'am" (we've found obsequiousness and overpoliteness to be an excellent defensive maneuver).

- The resident panhandler who tries to chat up your 5-year-old every time you pass by: It's your call whether you give money. We're wary types, so we do not encourage friendship (why exactly do we want some guy we don't know anything about to know our kid's name?) and tell our kids that we prefer to give money to shelters (which we do).

How to Talk about All the Bad Things They See

On a positive note, all those "bad" encounters you anguish over? Think of them as teachable moments. In her hometown of Los Angeles, for instance, Mogel sees a lot of decadent spending. And when she's with her daughters, she uses it as an opportunity to talk about what's important, values, and how money buys things but is not a measure of an individual's worth. "You point out someone you know who doesn't have a lot of money and you discuss all that person's fine attributes." And by the way, the time will come when you won't be able to ignore these "moments" even if you try, says Brooklyn mom Laura Broadwell. For years, her daughter Eleni apparently didn't notice the occasional unpleasant city scenery—the transients sleeping on benches, the occasional ranting passerby. But by the time Eleni had turned 5, that all changed. "Now," Mom reports, "Eleni is very curious about people coming up to us asking for money." While Laura always handles panhandlers with a "no, sorry I can't," she still has much explaining to do. "Eleni wants to know what they're asking, why they're asking for money. Why the woman can't just go to the bank. She's doing a lot of processing right now and has taken to collecting money in her piggy bank so that she can give the money to those people on the street who don't have money."

CITY SAVVY

Helping the Homeless While Making Them Seem Less Scary

Here's an intelligent way to work with your child's perception of homeless people while introducing her to the concept that she can really make a difference. Familycares.org recommends you create "Sleepy Snack Sacks." Lots of kids in shelters go to sleep hungry because their big meal is in the late afternoon. Your child can create a bedtime bag for people in shelters that is filled with healthy snacks, books, toothbrushes, stuffed animals, soaps, a written goodnight wish (or, for the youngest contributors, a colorful picture). Then all you do—together, of course—is drop it off.

THE CITY PARENT RULES
Starting a Dialogue

Rule #1: Elicit your child's views. "When I talk to kids about negative occurrences, I always ask them what they think is going on there," says Mogel. "I like to just say, 'Wow, what do you think?' You want to start at their level and to know what it is exactly that they understand." Often a child has misperceptions, and all you'll have to do is clear them up simply and straightforwardly. "Mommy, I know why that person is sleeping on the bench. It's because he doesn't like to go to sleep at night either" (sound like someone you know?). "No, honey, that person is sleeping on the bench because he doesn't have his own bed." "Oh."

Rule #2: Make the discussion age appropriate. As your child gets older, the discussion will get more complex, particularly as he starts exhibiting (and you're reinforcing) greater capacity for empathy, compassion, and the ability to problem solve. He's going to want to figure out ways to fix the situation. When the kindergartener learns that a homeless man doesn't have a place to live, for instance, he might say, "Let's take him home to our house." "Part of the fun of being a parent is to hear a child's charming and distorted sociology," says Mogel. But fantastical thinking aside, you'll need an alternative "fix." Your response: "Well, we can't do that, but here's something we can do about it . . ."

Rule #3: Express your views. And do it, as Damon says, with "clarity and conviction." That way, they'll understand what you think and why. With enough force, it will register as an important view that they might want to incorporate into their own thinking. And with enough repetition, they will.

Putting Media in Its Place

As if the human element were not enough, city parents also have to deal with a completely media-saturated environment. Sure, sex is big everywhere, but not as—how shall we put it?—robust as the Adonis in the Calvin Klein briefs plastered on billboards at every corner. Most parents today are aware of the concerns psychologists and educators raise about our children's overexposure to media, but in a city wallpapered with ads, you'll be working overtime to address the problem. And if you think little Ottavio doesn't notice the commercialism he passes at every store, subway, bus, taxi, even newspaper kiosk (he doesn't read yet, after all), you're dead wrong.

It can all get to be a little too much for impressionable young children. When Mogel was raising her children in Los Angeles, a media city if there ever was one, she worked especially hard to undermine its effects on her kids' psyches. "From the time they were born, we've been deconstructing the media," she says. "They knew about airbrushing when they were very little." Now maybe that's a little technical for your 2-year-old, but given everything your child will be exposed to, encouraging a little healthy skepticism seems completely in order. So when the opportunity presents itself:

- Talk about what's real and what's not (yes, dear, it looks like Spiderman's climbing up the building, but even if he were, he couldn't climb it like that).
- Address misinformation (no, those sneakers will not make you faster than a car).
- Point out stereotypes or how unrealistic certain images are.

And work in a little bit about why the media portrays something in a way that's less than accurate or fair or desirable. They'll get the message.

CITY SAVVY

Parents Can Take Action

More parents than we anticipated really do worry about the effects of all those non-PG-rated posters "decorating" so many city storefronts. So we thought we'd share one NYC mom's crusade against them. This can-do mother makes it her mission to personally discuss the issue with any shopkeepers she thinks are stepping over the line. When she sees an egregious example, she brings one of her little cherubs with her when she petitions the owner or store manager to be more considerate of her impressionable children. This personal touch she says is foolproof: Invariably, the stores remove the offensive advertisements. It works best, she says, in your own neighborhood where shopkeepers recognize you.

On a national level, nonprofit Common Sense Media is spearheading a grass-roots movement to improve all media for the benefit of kids. Its charismatic founder, James Steyer, one of the country's leading experts on the impact of media on children and the author of *The Other Parent: The Inside Story of the Media's Effect on Our Children,* is convinced that the collective power of concerned parents can dramatically reshape the content kids are exposed to in movies, music, magazines, books, and eventually even advertisements. Steyer says, "Parents can fight back. You can start by joining up with other parents, bringing the issues to your schools and local parenting organizations." If parents start to "Just Say No," he contends, the media will have no choice but to respond with better, more age-appropriate choices. For more information about what you can do locally and to check out Common Sense's excellent media reviews, go to www.commonsensemedia.org.

THE ROAD TO TOLERANCE

As city parents, we tend to believe (or is it rationalize?) that the natural consequence of all that city exposure is tolerance. But just because Michaela is surrounded by diversity does not mean that she'll grow up color-blind or otherwise immune to the effects of racism or ageism or sexism or any of the isms. To the contrary, because of the way children's brains and reasoning develop (we're getting to that soon), the isms can happen anyway. It's tolerance that must be taught—and much earlier than you'd think.

The Need to Teach

The good news: It may be pretty darned embarrassing, but the first time Annika shows off her developing awareness of the world around her—"Mommy, that woman looks like chocolate" or "Look, the fat man's on the swing"—is not prejudice. Your child is just doing what's she's developmentally programmed for: trying to make sense of the world around her. Hey, haven't you spent the last year pointing out differences—colors, shapes, big/small, boys/girls, people/animals? Now she's just putting it all together and responding to what she observes.

New research is debunking the old thinking that prejudice is learned; in fact, bias may be the more natural progression. Sara Bullard in *Teaching Tolerance: Raising Open-minded, Empathetic Children* is not alone in pointing out that a child's proclivity for the familiar, along with his ability to rank things and draw quick conclusions, can lead to intolerance later on. And the research of Rebecca Bigler, an associate professor of psychology at the University of Texas at Austin, has shown that children can become biased without being taught to be—and over the most trivial of things like the color of T-shirts assigned to them.

Fortunately, there's plenty of time to counteract any prejudicial tendencies. But city parents need to be especially alert to what's going on in their little ones' heads. Many experts pinpoint 5 or 6—when a lot of kids start school and thus broaden their encounters with people—as the magical age when a child's social sense starts kicking in. But since most city kids have been enrolled in some sort of structured out-of-home program well before kindergarten—and experience an enormous numbers of social contacts just about from the day they're born—there's good reason to believe social judgments on peoples' differences may start even earlier than that in the city. So be alert to your child's thinking and be ready to step in if you detect some developing misconceptions.

There's much you can do now to make sure your child develops into that tolerant, open-minded adult you've been hoping for. So instead of running for cover because your loving cherub sounds like some close-minded racist, take it as a loud and clear cue that it's time to start your child's diversity training.

How Kids Understand Difference

Here's an age-specific guide to cultural awareness:

6 months:

Babies this young can discern differences in such physical characteristics as skin color and hair texture.

Age 2:

Children are starting to become aware of gender (distinguishing men from women) and more conscious of physical attributes in general.

Ages 2 to 3:

Children begin to use the differences they see to describe people's appearances. They begin to tell it as they see it: the girl with the orange hair, the boy whose skin is "so white."

Differences may begin to frighten some children. Some may even exhibit what experts term pre-prejudice by avoiding a child they perceive to be unlike themselves.

Ages 3 to 4:

Children begin to organize the information they gather, which may result in them grouping people by their physical characteristics but in terms familiar to them (chocolate people, vanilla people, etc.). They may start making assumptions about gender differences (girls play with dolls, boys like trucks).

Of course, to give parents a run for their money, around now the charming *why?* pops up. So along with your child's many observations come a litany of questions: "But why is that man wearing the funny cap?" "Why do their eyes look so funny?" "Why is her hair so straight?"

Ages 4 to 5

Children start to associate social values with physical characteristics. They might start to perceive, for example, that skin color has a greater-than-cosmetic significance; stereotyping may begin.

Simultaneously, they may begin to attempt to figure out where they fit in.

Ages 5 to 6

Children begin to understand the factual basis of physical differences.

Their knowledge of the social implications of difference continues to deepen.

Sources: Stephanie Irby Coard, "Preparing Children for a Multicultural World," www.aboutourkids.org; Kelly Burgess, "Teaching Tolerance: Closing the Book on Hate," Preschoolers Today Web site, www.preschoolerstoday.com; Caryl M. Stern-LaRosa, "Talking to Children about Diversity: Preschool Years," 2001, The American Defamation League Web site, www.adl.org; Matt Alderton, "How Not to Raise a Racist" *Chicago Parent*, July 2003.

THE CITY PARENT RULES
Teaching Tolerance

Rule #1: Examine your lifestyle. Are the only people you socialize with of your same color and religion? And what do you think Fiona will make of the world if the answer to that question is yes?

Rule #2: Never allow harmful comments to pass uncorrected. If a family member or good friend makes an ethnic joke or slur in front of your child, deal with it immediately.

Rule #3: Set a good example yourself. Children are highly attuned to their parents' perspective on race, even when beliefs are unspoken. If you're intolerant of others, even subtly, your child is going to pick up on it. Lindsay Friedman, director of A World of Difference Institute, the anti-bias arm of the Anti-Defamation League, recalled to a reporter how when she was young, her mother would squeeze her hand tightly when they encountered someone on the street with a darker complexion than they. Not that her mom said anything to her. She didn't have to. Friedman got the message loud and clear. With her own son, she told the reporter, she plans on being very careful.

Rule #4: Answer your child's questions. Do it in the most straightforward way possible. You don't need to inject more than she can handle or go off on a diatribe about religion or culture. "Yes, people have many different skin colors. Look how yours is even different from mine." Or, "Some people believe it's important to keep their heads covered." And if you can give information about the reason for certain customs or beliefs or ways of doing things (what Kwanzaa is, why Catholics wear ashes, etc.), that's even better. By the way, if you're in public and don't feel comfortable responding right then and there, say, "That's a great question; let's talk about it at dinner later tonight." Then make sure that you do.

Rule #5: Focus on similarities, not differences. "Yes, Joia is in a wheelchair, but look how she loves to play puzzles just like you do." "Yes, Ming's eyes are different, but she has bangs too." Julia's kids think all nations are united by powdered-sugar-covered cookies, a recipe that got Julia through a multitude of seventh-grade social studies projects (think about it, Greek Kourambiedes, Mexican wedding cakes, Austrian Kipfel, Russian tea cakes).

Rule #6: Appreciate family backgrounds. Help your child take pride in his own family background as a way of getting him to appreciate the backgrounds of others. Talk about where your ancestors are from; point to the country of origin on a map,

Making Lemonade Out of Lemons: A Game They'll Remember

There's a great, 15-minute children's exercise, courtesy of the Anti-Defamation League, that you may want to try with a small group of your child's friends or ask your child's preschool teachers to do it in class.

Lemons are distributed to kids who are told they have 10 minutes to get to know their lemons. Each child studies the lemon's shape and texture and can play however they want with it, rolling it, throwing it, whatever. The lemons are then put in a bucket, and the kids are asked to pick out their lemon. Amazingly, they almost always do. When asked how they knew which was theirs, they point out specific features, like lines or bumps or bruises, differences in size, etc. Next up, the lemons are peeled and again placed in the bucket. This time, after giggles about the naked lemons, when the children are asked to find theirs, they can't. "But they all look the same," the children inevitably respond. And the door is opened. The leader of the exercise tells the children that people, just like lemons, can be different on the outside (and once you get to know them, you always find something special about them)—but on the inside, they are all the same. It's a fun game, notes Caryl Stern-LaRosa, director of educational programs for the Anti-Defamation League and co-author of *Hate Hurts*, and a lesson that stays with kids for a long time.

and tell stories about how people live there or how it was different back then, or even how it's different today. Talk about elements of that culture, traditions, even concrete items like clothing, decorative objects, or pieces of furniture that come from another culture. Use books, museums, or movies to bring your points alive. When they get older, start a genealogy tree.

Rule #7: Respect differences. Demonstrate your regard for ways of life that are different from yours. Make a point of experiencing others' traditions; make those ethnic jaunts we suggest in chapter 9 and find occasion to celebrate holidays from different cultures. In fact, celebrations are a great way for young kids to learn about different cultures, countries, and ethnicities. There are invariably lots of colors, exotic foods (to a 4-year-old's eyes, anyway), music, dance—all things that little ones will find wildly fascinating and attractive.

Rule #8: Debunk the media myths. Get in the habit now of pointing out stereotypes in the media. Your children are going to be affected by the media over a lifetime, so you can't start too early showing them how to scrutinize what they are being fed. That sweet children's cartoon has the fat boy who can't keep up or the girls who won't play with boys or the disagreements that are always won by the most powerful. Point out the fallacy, discuss why it's just not true, and if there's any inappropriate behavior involved—taunting, for example—explain why it's hurtful (and we'd consider banning the show from future viewings).

Rule #9: Bring home diversity. Talk about the issues of diversity and tolerance at the earliest ages. Use books and pictures to talk about differences—not just skin color differences but also disabilities, sex, religion, culture, and politics. Make sure diversity is reflected in your choice of books, dolls, games, paintings, and music.

The City Parent Diversity Book Club

Barnes and Noble and the Anti-Defamation League (ADL) sponsored a "Close the Book on Hate" national campaign to "help children celebrate diversity through reading and discussion." At the ADL Web site, www.adl.org, you can download "101 Ways to Combat Prejudice," a document with great ideas about what you can do in your home, schools, and community. While much of the material is relevant for an older child, there is an extensive book list at the end, which is well worth the few minutes it'll take to download. Here are some of their picks, plus a few of our own too.

The Colors of Us by Karen Katz
Ages 4–8
Lena and her mother take a walk though their neighborhood, meeting all sorts of people who prove Mom's contention that there are many different shades of brown—and each one so yummy: from honey and peanut butter to ginger and pizza crust. What makes the strong multicultural message particularly touching is that the story is in honor of the author's adopted Guatemalan daughter, Lena.

Beegu by Alexis Deacon
Ages 3 and up
A young alien crash-lands on Earth and struggles to find her way back home. In only 150 words, Deacon manages to address prejudice and tolerance while still telling a lovely little story. The *New York Times Book Review* called the book "something much richer, more real and more honestly humane than anything your standard overblown sci-fi epic has to offer."

The Keeping Quilt by Patricia Polacco
Ages 3–7

Great-Gramma Anna comes to America wearing a brightly colored babushka and dress, which later become part of a multihued quilt passed down through four generations of the same family. The striking contrast between the quilt's colors and the rest of the illustrations, which are rendered entirely in charcoal, make up part of the fun; the quilt's travels provide the rest. And there's a nice underlying message: Customs and fashions may change, but family is a constant.

It's Okay to Be Different by Todd Parr
Age 3–8

Parr uses bold colors and funky style to exalt individuality—say a fuchsia elephant against a zingy blue background ("it's okay to have a different nose")—encouraging kids to be happy with who they are. It's simple and makes the point fun.

Hair/Pelitos by Sandra Cisneros
Ages 3–7

This first children's effort by well-known author Cisneros, the story describes each member of a Hispanic family by the characteristics of their hair. Mama's is the best, as it smells like fresh-baked bread. Preschool teachers say that their students are enraptured by the way the book describes things that are different and things that are the same.

STRESS AND THE CITY

We know older kids are not immune to stress—homework, social pressures, parental expectations, etc., etc., etc. Even little kids, sadly, have stresses of their own—the anxiety they face when a caregiver changes, worries about the first days at school. But generally, as parents, we're more or less primed for those, which are more in the nature of rites-of-passage concerns. What we sometimes fail to recognize, however (even in ourselves), is the stress that builds up from the mere fact of living in the city. Not to scare you, just to prepare you: All that city excitement does have a downside. The research is compelling but doesn't say anything you wouldn't suspect if you could slow down enough to consider it. Frantic environments cause stress, and stress has real physiological and psychological impacts on children. The important point, though, is that there is plenty you can do to mitigate those effects, and your entire family will be better for it.

Urban Stressors, Human Impacts

Oh yes, the city does have its share of stressors. And while you are undoubtedly aware of many of them—heck, you're subject to them too—you may not have put the whole picture together for your kids.

Let's start with noise. Of course, it bothers people (in 2001, 83 percent of the complaints to the NYPD's Quality of Life Hotline were about noise), and yes, it does have real physiological effects besides the obvious impact on hearing. Now, a long way back, when our ancestors were tooling along in the brush, those physiological effects were probably a good thing. In those days, anybody who didn't get a pretty massive jolt of cortisol (the stress hormone) when a loud noise erupted out of some cave probably ended up getting eaten. Today, we're not so worried about carnivores attacking us; yet, when we're exposed to excessive noise, our bodies still respond much the same way as Great Uncle Cave Guy's did. And that stress response on a daily (or greater) basis is not a good thing—which begs the question for those of us who live in less-than-silent cities 24/7: How bad is all that noise for our children, let alone big, tough adults like us?

Scientists have only recently begun to address that issue. Although there has been a lot of work on the negative repercussions for kids who live in high-intensity noise areas, typically by airports, the first study to focus on children living in less-intense, but still chronically noisy, conditions (like that arising from city traffic) was reported on in the March 2001 *Journal of the Acoustical Society of America*. That study on Austrian fourth graders found distinct effects on the kids living in the higher noise areas: higher resting blood pressure and overnight cortisol levels (both indicators of stress reactions). Even these limited consequences, said the researchers, have potential long-term negative health implications.

Other noise studies have demonstrated a host of deleterious effects on children, including feelings of helplessness (especially in girls) and negative impacts on learning and motivation. One oft-quoted study by New York psychologist Arline Bronzaft, Ph.D., found that children whose classrooms faced an elevated subway track had, by sixth grade, fallen as much as a year behind their peers who studied on the opposite side of the building. And a litany of physical effects have been linked to chronic noise exposure as well: increased blood pressure, upset stomachs, sleeping difficulties (even after the noise has stopped), and fatigue. Noise may even affect how people interact. Researchers in one study examined how passers-by responded to a woman with a broken arm who dropped her books. When a lawnmower was running at full volume, no one stopped to help. When the lawnmower was turned off, people stopped to help. Too much noise, then, may actually make people ruder.

Living in a noisy home is no picnic either, regardless of whether the noise is internally or externally generated, or both. A study of children living in an apartment building near an expressway found that the kids living on the lower floors, where they were more exposed to the traffic noise, performed more poorly on tests of auditory discrimination and reading achievement than those on the higher floors. Psychologists Theodore Wachs, Ph.D., MSC, and Gerald Gruen, Ph.D., found that internal home noise could significantly hamper the development of language and cognitive skills, and such homes were notable for the lack of interaction between parents and children (what *we're* now calling the lawnmower effect). While Wachs and Gruen were primarily concerned with low-income inner city communities, other psychologists point out that affluent homes can be just as noisy, with huge excesses in ambient noise levels caused by the surfeit of computer games, TVs, loud toys, and stereos—all of which seem to be constantly on. To make matters worse in city homes, all that electronically generated noise, not to mention the human din, reverberates in a pretty compact amount of space.

Of course, the effect of living in small, close quarters is stressful on its own, and it may be particularly so from the vantage point of a 3-year old. It's not just that there's not a whole lot of space to let off steam; it's also not being able to jump or run or raise a voice because the neighbors might complain. Or maybe it's the neighbors' noise that keeps your little one awake long after his peers have fallen into undisturbed slumber. All that with the oppression that comes if there're simply too many people crammed into too few rooms—the rats in a cage syndrome—would make anybody crazy.

Just for good measure, we'll throw in one more city stressor. Think about the information processing necessary just to get through the day. It's just a much bigger deal in the city, whatever age you are. Simply walking around means negotiating pedestrian and vehicular traffic ("hold Mommy's hand," "don't run ahead, that driver might turn") and reacting to the constant visual stimulation and distractions, conversations, and shouts. According to Frances Kuo, Ph.D., and William Sullivan, Ph.D., assistant professors at the University of Illinois, all those inputs "take their toll, resulting in mental fatigue, a state characterized by inattentiveness, irritability, and impulsivity." And in children, mental fatigue is associated with more problematic social behavior. Why? Mental fatigue impacts cognitive processing, which is important in dealing with tougher social situations. Complicated social situations—whether at the adult level or the child level—require reasoned, effortful behavior to get through, and the ability to expend that effort is reduced in someone suffering mental fatigue. In such states, as Kuo and Sullivan point out, social behavior is more likely to be thoughtless or tactless, "allowing conflicts to spiral out of control."

To parents, their kids' antics may just look like crankiness, jumpiness, or normal fatigue. But maybe all that unhappy behavior is just a kid stressed beyond his capacity to cope.

The Antidotes

Now, we really don't want a lot of stressed-out 3-year-olds running around our cities, do we? Noooooo. So, some stress reduction activities are in order. Unfortunately, we don't have the power of Julius Caesar who, when irritated by the noise (and dust and congestion) of his citizens' chariots, banned their use during daylight hours in Ancient Rome (and we're sure the littlest Romans were the better for it). But there is so much you can do to reduce the stress your child and you are under. Like Caesar, we'll start with controlling the noise, then help you find nature and other ways to destress in the city.

Turning Down the Volume

It's clear that too much noise too often should be avoided. Do a noise audit on your children's lives and figure out where you can make a difference. Where to start? We'd vote first for the home. It is unbelievable how loud a small space can get when you throw in a couple kids with a couple different activities: The noise level spirals into the stratosphere as everyone competes to be heard. What about your kids' travels: Where are they experiencing noise, and what can you do to reduce it? How about school? That's a little trickier; you may have to enlist some other parents to take action. Want some ideas?

Consider interior windows. If your home gets heavy traffic noise, that extra glass layer can make a world of difference—or at least consider beefing up the window coverings. Put your child's bed in the most interior room; children can adapt to sleeping with a lot of outside noise, but that doesn't mean they aren't being affected by it.

Keep the home noise level down. That means a ban on multiple simultaneous electronic outputs. Make your family choose: one computer game going or the TV or Nintendo or the stereo, but not all of them at the same time. Too drastic a change? Well, at least try to segregate the noise producers so they're not competing with each other. By the way, if your family is used to a lot of noise, it's also likely they're used to having the volume on any individual sound source up way too high for their tender ears. Get them to reduce it.

Pick your routes. If you walk your child to school, to a class, even just in a stroller, take the quieter path. There are always blocks with less traffic noise or less construction, so just keep an eye out.

Nix the loud movies. The volume in movie theaters today, particularly for action movies, is at disturbingly high levels. You can ask that the volume be reduced. Chances are, if it's disturbing you, it's disturbing other people too. Even better, bring earplugs for everyone (ones from an ear doctor or audiologist are best; failing that, drugstore versions are always better than going completely unprotected).

Stop buying noisy toys. Some are incredibly loud (up to 130 decibels) and can do real damage to little children, particularly given kids' propensity to hold them up to their ears.

Take quiet breaks. Every couple hours, make your family take a 15-minute "quiet" time-out; you'll be amazed at the calming impact.

Monitor schools/day care. If your child is in a noisy classroom, either get him moved or enlist the other parents to see what kind of noise reduction measures can be put in place (their kids are at risk too). Certainly, if your child is in day care, you need to consider this a big deal.

Getting Green

Nature can apparently work magic to soothe the injured psyche, and it deserves a prominent position in a city kid's life. No, this is not mellow, back-to-nature talk; there is both really impressive scientific evidence to back up our claim and a multitude of ways to put it into effect.

Here's one cut at the science. Humans have both voluntary attention (which is directed and deliberate, the type used to complete tasks like doing homework or coloring in the lines) and involuntary attention (which is easy and effortless, where we're kind of taking in stuff but it's not taxing us to do it). All of the information processing demands of the city require prolonged use of voluntary attention, which essentially uses it all up and causes mental fatigue (and all those other behavioral issues we mentioned earlier). At that point, the body needs a spell of involuntary attention to restore the capacity for voluntary attention.

Confused? It's all part of Attention Restoration Theory, which basically holds that exposure to natural environments works wonders in alleviating the fatigue induced in demanding environments like, ahem, cities.

There is a forest's worth of research attesting to the validity of this theory for adults. One recent study was conducted at the University of California at Irvine on young adults who were purposely put through stressful activities and then let loose in either a natural setting or an urban one. The results showed substantially positive, and surprisingly immediate, physiological effects among the test subjects who were exposed to nature after the activities, versus those who were not.

What's really interesting is the impact of attention restoration on kids whose attention-paying abilities are significantly less developed, making it harder for them to fight off distractions that use up their voluntary attention capacity. Several studies have focused on using green settings to reduce ADD symptoms in children.

Serenity Now

The desire to find a natural sanctuary in (or shall we say from) the city dates as far back as our metropolises do. In the 1800s, the local cemeteries provided that much-needed respite, prompting Frederick Law Olmsted, the prominent architect who later designed NYC's Central Park, to pen: "The rural cemetery, which should, above all things, be a place of rest, is too often now . . . a constant resort of mere pleasure seekers, travelers, promenaders, and loungers."[a] A century later, during World War II, public gardens became the number one haven from city living—the place for contemplation and winding down.

In the days following the 9/11 attacks, there was a dramatic rise in visitors to any place that could remotely be considered a sanctuary according to a report in *U.S. News & World Report*.[b] Religious institutions reported increased traffic, but people flocked to off-the-beaten-track venues too, particularly to serene spaces. The glorious Brooklyn Botanic Garden had people lined up at its gates the morning after the attack, and in the ensuing seven weeks (during which time the garden's entry fees were suspended) in excess of 90,000 men, women, and children moved through its Children's Garden, butterfly exhibit, and Zen-like Japanese garden, seeking—as Botanic Garden President Judith Zuk wrote on the Web site,—"to be touched by nature's healing hand."[c]

a. Anna Mulrine, "City Sanctuaries; Take a Look at New York City's Spiritual Places: The City May Never Sleep, but It Does Take a Break," *U.S. News & World Report*, December 3, 2001.
b. Ibid.
c. Judith D. Zuk, president Brooklyn Botanic Garden, "President's Message," Brooklyn Botanic Garden Web site, www.bbg.org

---

Researchers at the University of Illinois demonstrated that such symptoms are significantly relieved after kids are out in green settings—with results such as improved ability to concentrate and follow directions. The greener the setting, the more symptom relief was seen, although even placing a child at a window looking out onto green had an improved result versus no green view.

You don't even have to spend time in a garden of Eden to get the benefits of nature. Studies have shown physiological and psychological benefits from relatively low doses of vegetation. In one study, having a few trees outside a housing project (versus none) made a big difference in residents' levels of aggression; and, as the ADD studies demonstrated, benefits can even be obtained just from looking out a window onto trees.

Our take on all this: Finding time outdoors should be a must for every city family every day. Sometimes, it'll just be a quick walk on the most tree-lined street you can find or a fast winter jaunt to the nearest park playground; other times, you'll have a chance to do more.

City Stress Busters

Kids need calm as much as any of us, but where to find that serenity in the car-honking city—where a child can actually enjoy himself without ticking off every adult there who's also looking to zone out? No worries, it's easier than you might think.

Get flowers. Apart from the obvious wilderness portions of parks and refuges (and your city probably has more than you think), public gardens should absolutely top every city parent's list of accessible city sanctuaries. Rufus is a little more hyper than usual? Botanical gardens have a remedy: beauty and serenity at a very reasonable price. Most are located on plenty of acreage, with winding paths that kids can trot down and around (it's great if the gardens are particularly lush; 3- and 4-year-olds love the concept of being in a jungle). After you've visited the requisite butterfly exhibit, get some ice cream and find a quiet family spot. The kids tend to lick in silence anyway, and in the garden environment, they'll actually get some downtime without even knowing it.

By the way, horticultural scientists have been documenting the effectiveness of gardening as a tool for teaching nurturing and for moderating stress and depression. The success they've noted is stirring some action in city schools. Members of Kansas State's horticulture department helped develop a 1-acre garden for an elementary school in Manhattan. Each class gets a plot in which to grow flowers, vegetables, and herbs during the school year. The students learn how to be responsible, they get a sense of pride from their growing efforts, and they actually try new foods. Plus, they get all the relaxation benefits of spending time each week in nature. You might want to think about starting a garden for your kid's school. You don't need a lot of space to get most of the benefits (and if you're really strapped for outdoor acreage, you can start an indoor garden). Kansas State provides a lot of good tips on how to bring gardening to the classroom at www.oznet.ksu.edu/horttherapy.

Touch stone. For other child-friendly "mental refreshments"—precisely what Olmsted hoped visitors to Central Park would experience—think stone, sculpted stone. A unique blend of nature, art, and often history, statue gardens present a wonderful opportunity for children to experience calm. When children come to the Isamu Noguchi Museum—a magnificent, almost otherworldly outdoor sculpture museum in Queens—in no time they "find serenity," observes Olga Hubard, head of the museum's education program. "Adults bring so much into the experience, societal expectations of what knowledge should be. But kids, they just react based on their own experience, so it is always fresh." The very nature of sculpture is soothing to children, she suggests. Not only is rock cooling, but it is also totally stable, she reminds us, and as such "naturally attracts children." Add to this the art component "which on some level demands that children observe carefully and focus their attention, the combination is irresistible."

A sculpture garden is nice, but it can be just as appealing to kids to weave a path among sculptures that dot our cities' well-used parks. Get a list of the sculptures and the history—who or what the sculpture is of, who's the sculptor and what his story is, and who the donor was. There are plenty of facts that will entrance your kids.

Blow bubbles. Stress reduction through bubble blowing—who would've thunk it? You know how everyone always tells you to take deep breaths when you get upset? Well, slow, even breaths can reduce your stress levels. Sometimes, it's not so easy for angry little kids to figure out exactly what that means, so a technique used by Edward Christophersen, Ph.D., a clinical psychologist at Children's Mercy Hospital in Kansas City, Missouri, is blowing bubbles. If you blow too fast or too hard, no bubbles. He has kids practice with bubbles daily, gradually moving them

A Little Story about Bubbles

Ten days after 9/11, Julia and her family were leaving to go out to dinner when Malcolm decided he absolutely had to have bubbles. Whatever put this into his head? No one thought he even liked bubbles. Rummaging through the house, Julia scrounged up a bottle and wand. As they walked, Malcolm contentedly puffing bubbles, a man fell into step with them as he exited a synagogue. Addressing himself to Malcolm (Julia's radar went on high alert, but the man was well-dressed and certainly showed no outward signs of insanity), he told Malcolm how cool bubbles were and how much he enjoyed them. The man continued to walk with them down the block. Then at the crossing, as they started to go their separate ways, he spoke. "My wife died in the World Trade Center. She always loved the beauty of bubbles, so at her service we had 700 people blowing bubbles." We talked about how odd it was that Malcolm had wanted bubbles that evening and how fortuitous it was that the man left the service the moment we walked by. Was it a sign? None of us could know, but we promised the man that whenever we saw bubbles from then on, we would remember his wife. And so, Sareve, we still think of you.

to blowing without bubbles—and then when they get upset, their parents are to remind them to "blow bubbles."

Adopt a new frame of mind. Sometimes all it takes to find calm is a mental leap. British acquaintances of ours are big family hikers. From the times the youngest ones were out of booties, the family regularly embarked on marathon walking tours through the English countryside—the relaxed pace through field and vale and the chance to talk made the hikes a welcome respite from the hubbub of their daily lives.

Improbable as it may seem, we have a city version. Make a family game of getting lost in your own city. Set some time aside to walk, with no destination in mind (go where the WALK lights send you). Try to consciously observe your surroundings and the changes that pop up as you meander. Think of it as a kind of walking meditation. We promise you the excitement of not knowing exactly where the next light change will send you can be exhilarating and liberating for your youngsters. A lovely grace note would be to follow the advice of Alice's nursery teacher: See who can spot a "random act of kindness." Surely children will find a sense of peace in noting good in others, and if you find a lot of them, even you might find a renewed faith in mankind.

Practice yoga. Had yoga not originated in India 5,000 years ago, we'd have bet serious money that it was the latest, greatest brainstorm of some crazed, but capitalistic, city mom. The sport/discipline/practice—depending on who is speaking—is the perfect cure for city kiddie stress and, not surprisingly, has taken the country by storm. Today, there's yoga for every age and price range, from one-on-one private classes with personal meditation masters and family yoga retreat vacations, to "Mommy and Me" yoga intro courses at the local Y and free yoga in the park (or on the beach) during summer months. There are studios geared only to kids, schools that incorporate yoga workouts and practices, yoga Web sites, books, and videos.

But there's good reason for all the fanfare. Yoga for kids is an impressive form of fitness that's way fun. As much about play as it is about "the practice," youngster yoga adapts adult poses (*asanas* in Hindu) to the muscular and skeletal needs of children's bodies, which means not holding poses for long periods of time and eliminating questionable moves like inverted positions such as headstands. Then they're given fanciful animal names to spark the imagination. But there's much more to it. Yoga enthusiasts across the country laud its many benefits. Teaching kids early on to "listen to" and control their bodies through breathing techniques and exercise promotes coordination, flexibility, and strength while relieving stress. The mix of physical mastery with the noncompetitive nature becomes an important tool for building self-esteem. And the inward focus, they say, provides their aspiring yogis with a much-needed time-out from city stresses.

"Instead of being someone who is just going through a day of chaos, it's all about watching and letting go," explains Betsy Appell, who leads the children's program at the San Francisco Zen Center. At first, kids will often come down with a case of the wiggles, but soon yoga's meditative aspects take over and children do find that inner calm. Through breathing and other techniques to encourage kids to pay attention to everything and focus the mind (apparently amazing for children with behavioral and emotional issues), yoga helps kids "not to live in their heads or be ruled by emotions," adds Appell, lessons that translate well to everyday life. "When kids are sitting in the classroom or when they're taking a test, instead of hearing the car honking outside or passers-by in conversation and losing

Om Schooling

Some kindergarten and elementary schools are now integrating yoga into their physical education programs, even their general classroom routines. And surprise, surprise, California is leading the way. In the Golden State, yoga is now taught in hard-core inner city public schools of Los Angeles and in tony private schools in San Francisco (including the Cathedral School for Boys, no less).

Teachers especially like to use yoga tools after recess to calm kids and before tests to help focus them. "The changes in children are subtle over the course of the day," reports Kevin Sved, codirector of the Accelerated School in the heart of Los Angeles' inner city. "There is a difference when they go into the class and when they go out. The children are centered and focused and more positive. But over the course of the year, the changes are incredible. Kids grow to appreciate the time and opportunity, and some of the

toughest kids are the biggest advocates." In fact, Sved was so pleased by the results of the trial program that he upped the ante and now offers yoga to the whole school twice a week. To make sure that all students and their parents feel comfortable, the classes stay away from any religious stuff, he says. No chanting, no Sanskrit names.

True, it does sound a little amazing that you can actually get a group of wired-up kindergarteners to calm down enough to hold a pose. But they do. And if you start kids in a yoga routine that early, you will not only introduce a few more periods of serenity in their lives (and what could be wrong with that?) but you will also up the probability that the practice of de-stressing becomes as regular a part of their lives as brushing their teeth.

Source: Julian Guthrie, "Schools Reach for Yoga to Calm and Collect Students," *San Francisco Chronicle*, February 25, 2002.

concentration, they know how to hear it, then let it go," she adds. Now if it'll only work at bedtime.

FINDING THEIR PLACE

Our children are growing up in a small town. Okay, so maybe a population of 8 million people makes it a *big* small town, but notwithstanding that little detail, our kids have the same intimate relationship with their town, the same sense of connection with shopkeepers, neighbors, firemen, and the same sense of plain ole belonging that you'd come across in a *Mayberry RFD* rerun. Except in our case, the shopkeeper is the deli guy, the neighbors live in a high-rise, and the firemen are from three firehouses not one. In fact, cynics that we are, the coziness of the relationships that can form for city families would seem completely improbable but for the fact that it happens. When Julia's nanny shopped for groceries, the cashiers always babysat Malcolm behind the cash registers so Alreka could pick up a few items unimpeded (Malcolm was prone to grabbing sugared-up shelf products as they wended their way down the aisles). Sounds slightly scary and completely unwise in our crowded, forbidding city; but if you were there and saw it, it would seem perfectly natural, totally safe, and completely right.

Why City Kids Need Connections

To say that kids need connections to their community is not just more blah-blah-blah "can't we all get along" stuff. The latest scientific evidence is proving that it's truer and more important than you probably ever imagined; and for city kids, who are growing up in a pretty unique environment, social ties and the sense of belonging they foster are essential for healthy emotional and psychological development.

In fact, we're now finding out that humans are actually biologically programmed to seek and form social connections, and if the necessary relationships are not made, it can wreak havoc on your potential for happiness and on your future mental health.

Here's the back story: Astonishing numbers of American children have been displaying emotional and behavioral problems—get this: twenty-one percent of all children from 9 to 17 have a "diagnosable mental disorder or addiction." Needless to say, docs and children's advocates are concerned. So Dartmouth Medical School, the YMCA, and the Institute for American Values teamed up to create the Commission on Children at Risk—a group of nationally eminent children's doctors, research scientists, and youth service professionals—to figure out what exactly is going on. The commission's report, "Hardwired to Connect: The Case for Authoritative Communities," suggests an answer. Our children, it says, are growing up today without the fundamental attachments, the social connectedness, the sense of moral and spiritual purpose which they are *biologically* mandated to find, and the absence of those are causing the significant psychological damage the statistics connote.

Examining volumes of research, the commission synthesized and integrated neuroscience and sociology to address the biological underpinnings of "attachment." They identified parts of the brain, genes, and chemical mechanisms involved, as well as what happens when attachments are not formed, as a result of poor or nonexistent maternal or other nurturing relationships. Turns out a nurturing environment is so powerful an influence on brain development and genetic activity, it can actually neutralize genetic vulnerabilities to a host of stuff we don't want our kids to have: depression, anxiety, and alcohol or drug abuse. By contrast, when that nurturing and support aren't there, watch out: Brain and gene functioning can be altered in significant negative ways. Similarly, hundreds of studies examining the impact of "social connectedness" on the psychological well-being of children demonstrate strong correlations between high levels of social connection and positive child development.

The problem today, say the commission's experts, is that many of the vehicles that used to provide children with the support and the connectedness they need and even crave, have weakened. Two-parent homes are no longer the norm, religious institutions have lost members in droves, and no one can find the time to get to the community centers or the bowling league or the Rotary Club anymore.

The options for our children: Get connected to others and community or risk turning into a bunch of psychologically impaired young adults. As parents, we have but one course to follow: Make sure our offspring grow up feeling/being part of something (preferably with a sense of "purpose" as well). You need to find, support, and strengthen any group or institution that'll help make this happen.

The Extra Challenge of Cities

All that connectedness stuff makes a lot of sense, but can it work in a city? Our own experiences notwithstanding, the widely popular view of cities as cold, hard, heartless, and sterile environments is apparently the reality for lots of people. Take the many, many sociologists—from the late, great Emile Durkheim on forward—who, in countless studies, have found "dehumanization" and isolation to be inherent attributes of urban living.

There are loads of sociological forces in play. Not without cause, of course:

Most city residents lack proximity to their families, once the backbone of support for American parents. And the sheer numbers of people stuffed into most urban centers means that most city encounters tend to be abrupt and anonymous, hardly the "productive" contacts social scientists like to see. Worse, our natural self-defense to life amidst a million strangers is to view others as objects, not human beings, allowing us to comfortably "remove ourselves" emotionally. Hmm, that may be a great adaptive shield with which to brazen your way through city chaos, but it ain't exactly the homey "We Are the World" mentality you want your children to develop.

There's more (there always is). Kids who grow up in those conditions see so many more of these unproductive contacts than they do the warm and fuzzy ones. They also may suffer from their parents' inability to find a support network. The result? Isolation and lack of connectedness become the norm for such city kids because, scientists theorize, their busy parents just can't find the time to socialize them through other means and in other ways.

We already know what the Hardwired to Connect people would think about these social shortcomings. But they're joined by any number of people who've studied the city, and we can tell you they're chomping at the bit to let you know just how devastating the failure to develop those relationships and sense of place can be when it filters down to the level of a single child. It's not enough that studies abound describing the extraordinarily high rates of psychosis and psychosis-like symptoms among city-dwellers. Now we have even creepier reports from Dutch researchers, who believe that there is something about being *raised* in an urban environment that may create an "enduring" liability for adult psychiatric health—a "psychosis proneness" (they say most of those displaying psychosis-like symptoms, such as persecution complexes or "auditory hallucinations," will never actually become diagnosed with a mental illness; it takes more than hearing a few voices to qualify you for that in the city, we guess). The presumed causes of all these urban psychotic tendencies? Same old, same old: the deprivation and social isolation of childhood neighborhoods and all the psychosocial stress associated with just growing up in the city.

We're not scientists and we don't discount the importance of all the cutting-edge research, but we just can't find any good reason why cities have to be scary or chilling or isolating, or why they can't provide all the community and support that any one person could possibly stand. We certainly don't intend on raising any future sociopaths and don't think you have to either.

We'll go further, in fact. We believe the city can be a great, maybe even the greatest, place to find all the support social scientists suggest kids need. Certainly, you and your children may not fall as easily, as automatically, into the networks that you would have if you were born, raised, and died in some small town. But you can easily match the power of all those relationships, connections, and affiliations with city versions. In fact, we're willing to argue that with the Mayberrys of the world so few and far between these days, your chances of raising your children with a sense of belonging and a sense of importance to his community are a better bet in the city than most places. It's all yours for the taking.

Redefining the 'Hood

Remember that small town our kids are growing up in? You're not going to locate it on any map. In cities, community isn't a place: It's a state of mind.

To us, it's all in the definition. City communities are not built-in; they must be built. So what if Aunt Bea isn't next door baking your little ones pies. If you have someone like Jonas at Payard who makes up little packs of cookies for Julia's kids to smuggle into school, that's pretty fine too. As a city parent, your concept of neighborhood will need to be broadened. Stop thinking of it as contiguous or even geographic: Your child's community is defined by your child's travels. Where Nadim goes to school may be all the way across town, his best friend and Suzuki violin class miles in the opposite direction. Don't let those be isolated destinations; let them become part of your child's urban neighborhood.

Social ties can be developed in every pit stop on your child's schedule. That will make him feel part of a city that's not strange or frightening, but full of people who smile when they see him. So think about your child's travels. Instead of rushing home for a snack after swim class, have one at the Y's snack bar or the coffee shop across the street, or read together at the bookstore down the block. Over time, your child will come to think of these different quarters as his own. And imagine how much more exciting it must feel when he can share his swimming exploits with Mr. Papadeas at the diner, who rewards him with a lollipop every time.

To those of you who are shy, fear not. You have a secret weapon: Children bring people together. Stranger anxiety aside, their natural inclination is to talk, be open to others. They don't know from privacy (don't we *all* know that?) and typically have no compunction about starting conversations with absolute strangers. But even if it goes against every ounce of your adult posturing, we say go with it— you may find that your children guide *you*. Take the case of one New York City mom who for years happily walked around her part of town anonymously. No such luck now that her daughter is on the scene, she says. "Basically, I have no choice but to interact with people. If I don't start talking, then she will." The good news: "I clearly know so many more people now. It's like all of a sudden, you're part of this club," she marvels.

The People You'll Want in Their Lives

You obviously can't befriend the world, but as a city parent, you will need to cultivate at least a few choice friends in your immediate vicinity. Studies have shown that when people know their neighbors, they're more likely to develop a sense of community and ultimately be more satisfied. If for no other reason, consider safety. If you wind up with a 2 A.M. emergency, you'd better be able to quickly intrude on at least one neighbor (and needless to say, if you're leaving a child with that person, you need to know ahead of time that the couple in 2B are not ax murderers).

In terms of making your city a *Sesame Street* kind of place, establishing ties to the many people whose job it is to keep your children safe can also be vastly comforting to the little ones. From the vantage point of an imp, doormen are strong and powerful and spend their whole lives keeping an eye on the neighborhood. You can pass by a doorman without a nod, or you can take a moment, inquire after his health and family, and ask him to fill you in on any exciting local goings-on. Obviously, policemen (though we don't know any on our "beat") and firemen (a much better bet) have a built-in allure: their swell garb and vehicles. Maybe you don't want to go into detail with your child on the horrors of fire and crime, but you can still get the point across that these people are vital to the city; even the tiniest of tots can appreciate their protection. Plus, there are added benefits. Eventually, you will start introducing the idea of your child contributing to the community (read on), and having already established a semipersonal connection to a fireman or policeman is a wonderful place to begin their citizenship training. Also, should your child need help (when he's older and out on his own, or when the supervising adult is out of commission), there'll be a whole lot of friendly faces he can turn to for assistance.

Creating a Sense of Belonging

Perhaps the most far-reaching prognostic of the "Hardwired to Connect" report is its call to find and strengthen institutions that not only give a sense of connectedness but also impart a true purpose. The commission calls these bodies authoritative communities—groups of people who are committed to each other over extended periods of times and have the will and the way to show children "what it means to be a good person." The beauty of the city is that there are lots of these "communities," in every shape and orientation; you can surely find one that'll suit you and your kids if you open your mind.

Spiritual communities. In the old days, organized religions and extended families provided guidance for the spirit. Today, it's much more common for parents to seek the wisdom and viewpoints of "the experts" over ecclesiasts or uncles.

Apparently, there's still a void. In a bizarrely modern twist, clueless parents are turning their teachers into spiritual advisors. As Dr. Mogel explains, "It takes great effort to carve a community, and city parents often feel like salmon swimming against the tide," so what they do is glom on to "the closest thing that seems like a community—turning to schools for all their spiritual and emotional needs," she says. And the educators are none too happy about this.

So where should the modern city parent turn for help? How about back to the real experts of the spirit? Not surprisingly, religious leaders highly recommend city families get involved in some kind of organized religious community. For one thing, such groups already take the job of values very seriously, and a big part of their mission is to assist parents in educating their young about values. Furthermore, spiritual communities have a built-in screen that makes the big city just a little smaller; in so many ways, it's the great equalizer in the city of diversity. "Whether churches, synagogues, mosques, etc., you're dealing with a limited community of people with like-minded values," says Monsignor Thomas Hartman, half of ABC's popular *God Squad*. The fact that most religious communities incorporate some form of doing good into their basic agenda is the icing on the cake to Hartman.

After researching this book, Kathy—an atheist since the day she was allowed to prematurely quit Sunday school—is starting to come around to the idea that maybe joining a congregation will have something special to offer Alice. Julia and her husband joined a church when children were still but a gleam in their eye because they figured that when those kids did arrive, membership might bolster the family's protection against intrusions by the seamier side of the city. Not that they were without trepidation. Julia's memories of ruler-wielding nuns and stultifying services were not a small hurdle to get over. But times have changed.

City religious institutions seem to have gotten a lot more open to change and a lot broader in the opportunities they offer congregants than ever before— possibly because they've suffered huge membership losses over the last three decades. Seattle, for example, is a hotbed of new religious institutions that aim to combine spiritualism with creativity, flexibility, and slightly more modern outlooks than maybe most of us grew up with—with a range of styles and theologies to appeal to the most conservative or liberal, the most esoteric or traditional of religious tastes. Many of these newer churches are tremendously appealing to families, with flexible hours (Mars Hill Church runs morning and late afternoon services, both with children's ministries, allowing families to go to church *and* soccer practice) and an emphasis on tolerance and inclusion. Quest Church, which operates a 4,500-seat coffeehouse/community center, espouses to become a "multiethnic community" whose main thing, says Pastor Eugene Cho, is "relationship, relationship, relationship." To our eyes, this is great stuff.

The bottom line: City houses of worship really want members, and as a result, many have become more understanding of modern lifestyles. It's not that they want any less of a commitment to the values they espouse, of course. But there are many that won't expect you every week and, just as important, many that offer tremendous opportunities for families, outside of the traditional main service, that will greatly support you in your efforts to raise good kids.

Sporting and other interest-based communities. If religion doesn't speak to you, there are plenty of other ways for little Ricky to feel like he belongs. Look for groups that foster a sense of community with common goals—sports teams, for instance, or active community centers. "You don't need a church to be part of a community," Monsignor Hartman says.

Here's one example. When Julia's eldest son, Pearson, decided to start fencing, she and her husband thought the exercise would be a pure flash in the pan ("not what you think, honey; there're no light sabers involved here"). Were they wrong! Not only did Pearson develop a passion for fencing, but when he joined New York City's Fencers Club, he also became part of a phemonally supportive community. As Fencer's Club Executive Director Rita Finkel says, "If someone gets sick, I can walk out on the floor and find a specialist in any branch of medicine . . . or in immigration issues . . . in just about anything. That's the benefit of being in a city."

But there's more. Earlier, we wrote about those "authoritative communities" that teach a child what it means to be good. Well, Fencers Club has got what it takes. Values like treating people with respect are strongly upheld. Kids are pro-

Making a Lasting Commitment

Pick out a few places of worship (they mostly all advertise now, but ask friends and colleagues for recommendations too) and go to a service, pick up their literature, check out their Web site. See if they're family friendly. Is child care offered for special events? Are there child-oriented services around major holidays? What about the institution's role in the community? Do they provide plenty of ways for your family to contribute (besides money, of course)? Go to a bunch of services and don't stint on the outside events; even if you're not a member, many will let you attend Bible or Koran or Torah study sessions or let your kids come to the religious pageant or choral performance. Finally, do you like the other congregants? Do they seem to hold important the same things you do? Take your time. See how it all suits you and your family. After a while, it just might feel like home.

tected here; there's no swearing allowed if little ones are around. Students are also taught quickly about their own responsibilities: self-control, sportsmanship, and respect for coach and peers. For one thing, they're playing with weapons, so Little League–like outbursts cannot be tolerated; for another, that stuff just doesn't belong in the kind of place Fencers Club aspires to be. And early on, kids get the message that this is a community. Experts welcome novices with open arms, teach them, and buck them up when they feel like they're not making progress.

Now we don't mean to say that every sports lesson your little tiger has will introduce him to a community like this. But, we would say that rich and enveloping communities lurk in the strangest city corners. And if you're on the hunt, groups with a common interest are a good place to start. Maybe it's stamp collecting or chess or bocce—hey, there's no thicker community than the dog walkers at the local city dog run (though there your child will be known as part of his dog's family). Or maybe it's a playgroup that grows with its members. It could be the community that forms around the peewee soccer league (a great place because there are always kids and parents at the weekend games, and the nasty tone of excessive competitiveness has yet to creep in at the young ages). So when you're considering a choice of affinity group for you or your child, consider its community characteristics: It may make the difference as to which one you go with.

"Alternative" family therapy. If yours is one of those "alternative" units—whether that be families of single parents, gay dads/lesbian moms, families with mixed ethnicity, families with adopted children, biracial children, foreign adoptees—you're likely to be able to find great family-oriented support and networking groups in your city. If you're under the impression that these groups are purely parent support groups or advocacy oriented, they're not; most have regular family events, social activities, and kid-friendly seasonal celebrations.

Take raising an interracial or bicultural child. The city can be fundamental to your effort to be a good parent. Chances are, you've already picked your city and neighborhood because of the diversity it offers. When there's a choice, many parents prefer racially integrated neighborhoods over a better standard of living.

Laura Broadwell, a single mom who adopted a daughter from China (and chronicled their life together in the yearlong "Raising Eleni" column that appeared on Parentcenter.com), says that she doesn't know whether she would have taken the leap to adopt if she hadn't lived in a city. "One of the reasons why I felt I could do this is because I lived in a neighborhood with a fair amount of diversity. Eleni sees children who look like her all the time and sees a wide range of things. And I'm surrounded by people who think like me. As a single parent, I definitely feel less isolated."

Experts recommend to "alternative" families that they live in areas where their children will get to see people of various races and cultures as well as have role models who look like them. The current theory is that adoptees will have a great sense of self-esteem if their families embrace the "birth culture." And again, no better place but a city.

Broadwell would agree. "When I started going to Chinatown, it was just amazing how people would gravitate toward Eleni. Even the Korean grocer who never spoke four words to me now is friendly. This whole Asian culture has adopted us." She says she doesn't frequent local chapter get-togethers of the Families with Children from China groups, but if she lived in a less-diverse neighborhood she probably would.

GOOD BEGINNINGS: LEARNING TO GIVE BACK

One of the best ways to give children a sense of belonging is to make them feel that they contribute to the place where they reside. Much time and many resources have been spent on examining this phenomenon, which now is pretty much the consensus among top child psychologists.

On his website, Robert Brooks, Ph.D., co-author of *Raising Resilient Children*, says he's found that when children are asked to participate in what he terms "contributory activities" (actions that help others or the community), it lessens their anger, maybe even reducing incidences of violence. When an adult asks a child for help, he further explains, "it conveys a sense of trust," which in turn enhances a child's confidence, motivation, and self-esteem—all necessary ingredients to foster compassion and caring. In other words, children who think they can

Helping Others Starts at Home

To feel good about helping others, experts say, kids must first experience success themselves. *Raising Resilient Children* co-author Robert Brooks, Ph.D., has a plan that's easy to adopt.

- Start at a very young age.
- Give children tasks you know they can accomplish. But make it more about their aid and less about the actual chore. Say

"Mommy and daddy need your help doing . . ."
- Ask your children to participate in household activities like preparing a meal, setting the table, or putting away laundry.
- Don't forget to tell them how much you appreciated their "contribution."

Source: Robert Brooks, Ph.D., "Fostering Responsibility in Children: Chores or Contributions? Part 1," www.drbrooks.com, Nov. 1999.

Lead by Example

You're their major role model. So make sure they see that you're involved—as a volunteer, good neighbor, part of a local community-oriented group, a block association. And by all means, take the kids with you when you're voting.

have an impact and better the lives of others develop better self-esteem and positive self-image.

But if this is too loosey-goosey for you, then consider some hard-core research that shows feeling valued and contributing to one's community are actually critically important for children—maybe the only thing that'll keep them alive through those scary teenage years. The Search Institute in Minneapolis has surveyed one million kids to identify the "assets" that influence kids positively and that act as a check on their propensity to engage in risky behaviors (drugs, alcohol, violence, early sexual activity, and other scary stuff city parents worry about). Of critical importance is the feeling that you are valued by your community and that you contribute to it. A conference on developing citizenship in young Americans, hosted by the Stanford Center on Adolescence, affirmed that kids who serve their communities have less chance of engaging in risky behaviors, "greater interpersonal development," better ability to relate to diverse cultures, and are more motivated learners.

When to Get Young Kids Interested in Helping Others

Psychologists are quick to point out that children have an inborn desire to assist others. They are capable of thinking of, and feeling for, others from the youngest ages and are never too young to engage in charitable activities. In fact, the Search Institute insists that your teenagers will be much better off if you start developing the sense of empowerment that comes from helping others when your kids are tiny. Making sure your toddler shares toys or asking him to come with you when you deliver that holiday fruit cake to your friends in Apartment 2B—these are things a little one can do as soon as he can walk. And as the American Psychological Association (APA) reminds us, acts of caring don't have to be grandiose. They can be as simple as doing a favor for a neighbor or taking a stray animal to a shelter. The whole concept of service should be woven into your regular family conversations—as natural as, say, discussing school, work, and weekend plans.

By around 3, the "no" stage has already helped children begin to separate from their parents, so now they can begin to demonstrate more formalized concern for others. You may be surprised to learn that children as young as this can participate in structured volunteer activities, as long as you're doing it with them. Helping to put together a holiday meal or celebration for the needy can be a festive way to get started. Plus there are lots of appropriate jobs, even for the youngest kids, who can help put out napkins and silverware, straighten chairs, etc. Dr. Brooks believes little ones can also join you on any walks for hunger, AIDS, or multiple sclerosis.

The experts, of course, don't know *your* children, and parents differ in their assessment of when is the right time for their child to venture into organized volunteering—especially in cities where they worry the scene is too alarming or big or dangerous. You'll certainly need to keep your child's sensitivities in mind when making the decision about when to get started. The key is to pick a service opportunity that's appropriate for your child (or at least not inappropriate). Is your daughter most comfortable in one-on-one encounters? An adopt-a-grandparent might be ideal. Maybe your son is too energetic for those tête-à-têtes; then running around delivering meals could be the solution. Jessica

Volunteering's All in the Family

According to a new study, if you start your children on the right path when they're young, it can positively impact the rest of their lives. "Engaging Youth in Lifelong Service," released by INDEPENDENT SECTOR and Youth Service America, reports a strong connection between youth civic involvement and lifelong volunteering and philanthropy—and that was across all groups and income. Of the 44 percent of American adults who volunteer, two-thirds of them began volunteering when they were young, the study showed, and those who did start service work early on also gave more time and money than those who came to volunteering later in life. (Apparently youth involvement is also a family sport: Nearly 60 percent of adults who volunteered in their youth had parents who volunteered. And 70 percent of adults who volunteered as youth now volunteer with their children.)

Source: "Engaging Youth in Lifelong Service," report sponsored by INDEPENDENT SECTOR and Youth Service America, November 20, 2002; for more information, go to www.independentsector.org.

is artistic and detail-oriented; planting flowers in the community garden could be a good match.

Good Works in the City

Of course, if you thought developing your child's sense of belonging might be tough in the city, you're probably going to think it's even trickier to get him to feel that any of his efforts to "make a difference" won't be swallowed up in the vastness of his urban surroundings. Maybe your kids aren't going to save your entire city, but if you want to teach them the value of helping one person at a time, with all the millions of people surrounding them, they'll find ways to contribute every day and feel great about it. Here's how to get started.

THE CITY PARENT RULES
Making Charity Cool

Rule #1: Add a service component to whatever you do. You're baking cookies together? Wonderful. Talk about how those in need don't even get basic foods and then make a little extra so you can bring some cookies to a soup kitchen or shelter. If those places seem too frightening for your little one, look for a transitional housing center, which provides temporary living space for down-on-their-luck families. There'll be lots of kids there, helping to make the experience a touch less daunting.

Rule #2: Keep 'em happy. On a group volunteer activity, there are often wait times—which can blow the whole exercise if the kids become bored or kinetic. Come prepared for lulls in the action with stuff that your kids can do, ideally that relate to the mission at hand. Maybe they can decorate something to leave behind—place mats, for example, or cards for whomever's being ministered to. Prepare your child ahead of time about what she should expect—and in the most concrete terms. "For an hour it's this, then we'll take a break, then . . ."

Rule #3: Celebrate a job well done. Just as important as letting children know you feel strongly about their unkind acts is to let them know how highly you regard their kind ones, says the APA. "It made Mommy proud when you took care of the boy who fell down." Or after a hard afternoon's work cleaning up the park, treat the whole family to a sundae and replay your good works together.

Rule #4: Capture the action. To foster a sense of pride, a picture is worth a thousand words. Take a picture of your kids engaged in their charity activity. Or, if that won't work (say you're just dropping off some home-baked cookies), ask an appropriate person to take a snapshot of people enjoying whatever your kids contributed. You can leave behind a disposable camera with a stamped envelope (And depending on the circumstances, you may want to leave a neutral site address like your place of work).

Easy Ways to Improve Your Community

Here are some of our favorite ideas for you and your child to work together to make your city a better place—and have fun doing it:

Take care of your own "backyard." Working to beautify your environs— say your apartment complex or block—is easy and immediately gratifying. You and your child can venture out weekly to find trash and toss it into a garbage can. Everybody wears plastic gloves and can pick up soft items like empty cardboard food containers and candy wrappers; just don't pick up anything that might be unsafe like broken glass bottles. Make sure your little one is past the stage when she likes to put everything in her mouth! Maybe they want to help beautify the 'hood in other ways, like planting or scrubbing the walls. The action should be something they can tackle. Block or neighborhood associations are also good bets. If your street or area has one, you should join in and enjoy it. These are almost invariably family-friendly groups, and having your kids join in on block cleanups, flower planting, or good old-fashioned block parties is about as fine a way of being part of a city as we can think of.

Beautify your parks. City parks are a great and nonthreatening avenue to get youngsters involved in structured programs since most have volunteer opportunities for parents and young children. At Seattle's Adopt-a-Park program, for instance, volunteers join with park employees to restore and care for the city's

---

CITY SAVVY

Read to Understand Need

Books can send powerful messages to young kids. *A Chair for My Mother,* by Vera B. Williams, really helped Alice get into the spirit of giving. In this story, a child, her waitress mother, and her grandmother lose all their furniture in a fire and save their dimes to buy a comfortable armchair. In a lovely scene, each of their neighbors come together to donate one of their own possessions to get the family back on their feet. After being read the book for the first time, Alice went to her bookshelf to find a bunch of books she no longer read to give to children who didn't have them.

Park Scoop

To find out about a park's volunteer program near you, go to your city's parks and recreation Web site and find the volunteering link (if you can't find a site, check your city government's main site, or call 311, if your city offers that omnibus help number). It's often under "Activities." There are usually schedules of volunteer activities and names of people to contact if you want to get involved. You can always call the volunteer coordinator directly for more ideas.

green spaces. Families can help plant trees and pick up trash. New York's Partnership for Parks program sponsors fun one-day events like the "It's My Park Day," which turns into a giant feel-good party as volunteers work together to plant trees and clean up parks and playgrounds throughout the city. The Chicago Park District has Nature Stewardship workdays all throughout the year dedicated to maintaining the ecological health of Chicago's green spaces. For example, Chicago families can volunteer to help create a landscape that provides food and shelter to Chicago's wild bird population.

Befriend an elderly neighbor. Take your child to check on him or her regularly, and offer to run errands or just stop in to keep the person company. This could be especially helpful in hot weather, when elderly people are vulnerable to overheating. If your child doesn't have grandparents nearby, this could also provide an opportunity to establish a nice bond with an older person.

Get the kids involved in simple projects they can do at home that benefit others. Their job can be to round up loose change and put it in a jar. When they're dexterous enough, they can help you stack the coins. But at any age, they can be the ones to choose who the recipient should be (lest you want it to go to their teacher or best friend or even the dog, have a choice of three outlets you find suitable). Of course, gathering unused items for children's charities is a lovely way to raise their compassion quotient—that is, if you can get them to. When Kathy brought this up to Alice at age 3½, she was utterly appalled (well, it was more like a temper tantrum, if you must know). But half a year later, she's coming around, now that she's starting to understand that some kids have no toys or books or coats of their own. While you're at it, you should have an adult "charity chest" too; put in canned goods, books, used clothing, etc. Your kids should see that you live what you preach. And make the trip to donate goods a family effort. You have plenty of places to choose from in a city, so pick one that will send the right message to your little one without terrifying her.

Create a fund whose proceeds will benefit a local children's charity. Enlist the little ones to raise money at a lemonade stand. How about a family pot where miscreants (including parents) have to donate a portion of their money as payback for some prespecified offense (bickering is always good). A local (and receptive) pediatric ward could be a great destination for the funds you raise—and it won't be hard to find one among all the city hospitals. Visit it first with your kids (prearranged, of course) to check out what toys are needed, are in disrepair, etc. Get the children involved in the conversation, and then start a family collection with which to buy toys every now and then. When the family accumulates a couple, you all stop by to deliver them in person.

Befriend your local fire station and make a point of taking over little gifts every once in a while (a crayon drawing, homemade brownies). For some reason, firemen (and women) seem to be especially convivial types, and they usually respond very enthusiastically to kids. Your child, who already will know from you the importance of giving back, will bask in the warm glow of their attention—a great way to reinforce a charitable habit.

PART THREE

EDUCATION

CHAPTER 11

GETTING OFF TO A GREAT START

■ ■

School. Don't you just envy those suburban parents who blissfully register their kids for the local "good enough" public school and then that's it—one-stop shopping, no sweat, no pain? It just doesn't work that way in the city, any city. Wherever you live, and whether your predilection is public, private, or parochial, you can pretty much assume there'll be an army of parents out there who are competing with you to get their own beloved progeny into the school of your dreams and theirs.

It truly pains us to feed the frenzy that surrounds the quest for a good city school, but there is simply no evading parental responsibility in the matter of urban education. You will have your work cut out for you. If you don't do the research on your public school system, you may find Niall relegated to an overcrowded, dirty, scary-looking classroom. Step out of line during those private school tours and Courtney might not even have a school to go to.

How do you do right by your child? You learn from the mistakes of those who came before you. You take the time to understand the lay of the private, public, and parochial school landscapes, and, when it's time, you get your feet wet in the educational waters by finding a fitting preschool for your tot. Accept the challenges involved, and we promise you, Melissa will get an education that's at least as good, if not better, than what she would've received in the 'burbs.

THE MISTAKES PARENTS MAKE

For all the energy that urban parents expend on the schools issue, it's a crying shame how much of it is wasted. Wrong actions, wrong emphases, missteps, and omissions are endemic in the search and all because of the deluge of misinformation—even disinformation—to which city parents fall victim, sometimes consciously, sometimes subliminally. The mythology about city schools has the ability to twist parents' perception of educational realities—presenting some of the greatest stumbling blocks to obtaining a successful city education for your child. Let's set the record straight.

Thinking There's Only One Road to Oz

A distressingly large number of parents believe that getting their child into some particular elite private school or the top gifted public program is going to set them on some immutable course in life. You know the drill: High Five Nursery School, Big Time Ongoing Institution, then Ivy League for sure, and at each institution along the way, that child will develop connection after connection, assuring him beaucoup fabulous business and social opportunities for the rest of his life. Say it with us now: Connections don't guarantee happiness. Your child's life won't be over if she has to go to your second, third, or heaven forbid, fourth choice for nursery school.

These days you really can't afford to think that way, anyway. There's just too much random error in the process: the press of competition that causes nice kids, smart kids, great kids not to get into schools that would've been a slam dunk 10 years ago; or the unanticipated forces (school's too easy or tough, too quiet or wild, too expensive or not expensive enough) that cause a school and child to part ways post-admissions. So, given how imprecise the whole process has become, why in the world would you make one school your heart's desire? Be broad-minded and generous: Find the good in lots of schools.

Confusing Their Needs with Yours

Wait, how could this be a common mistake? Isn't this whole thing *all* about the child? Yes . . . but . . . maybe it's the constant surveillance of kids demanded by city life, the nonstop effort to move and mold them—however it happens, something blurs the boundaries between city parents and their kids, and never more so than in the school search. Ponder for a moment just how many parents you've heard discussing the admissions process in terms of where "we applied," where "we got accepted," and the slightly more frightening where "we're going" ("we're" not psychologists, but we do foresee $200-an-hour therapy sessions in Eldridge's future if you keep trotting down this path).

Or when Eldridge doesn't get in to that most esteemed toddlers program, how many moms and dads go off the deep end—feeling like failures, wondering what exactly is wrong with their sweet child, or simply brooding over the fate of their tarnished family? We've seen divorces occur over this, and *we* know it's *sooooo* easy to get caught up in all this. Been there, done that. When Alice was applying to nursery school, Kathy and her husband, Jim, were having second thoughts about the somewhat noisy school to which Alice had been accepted. Well, Jim started mentioning some of his second thoughts to the schools' powers-that-be . . . Word to the wise: Don't do this! Because, waddayaknow, Alice was suddenly *unaccepted*. Stunned by the reversal of events, Kathy reacted the only way a city spouse could: She accused her husband of ruining their child's life and theirs.

The slippery slope that parents start sliding down on their descent into complete lunacy? Confusing a name-brand school with a "good" school for their child. The disheartening modern phenomenon of the trophy child—the irresistible desire to say your kindergartener attends the crème de la crème private school or gifted and talented public program—causes far too many parents to become myopic when it comes to their child's strengths and peccadilloes. Too many parents push their kids toward schools that are unlikely to be successful experiences for them—wholesale mismatches between the school's expectations for academic excellence, classroom performance, social maturity, and the child's ability to deliver.

And it simply drives early childhood educators crazy. How, they wonder, can parents *not* recognize the implications of ignoring their child's needs? At the very least, this may result in a heart-stopping search to find a last-minute opening at the end of the summer when all those "best laid plans" come to naught. But far worse is when parental deception actually does succeed, because a miserable school experience is in store for the child.

So please, listen to those who know and concentrate on the "fit," as they refer to it in the biz. That means making an appropriate match between school and child by understanding who your little one is, how he seems to learn, and meshing it with your own educational philosophy and desires. You'll all be happier in the long run if you do.

Forgetting to Fact Check

Unquestionably, the competition factor causes city parents to do desperate things. Embellishing the truth is one of them. At every step in the hunt for a good school, you'll hear background chatter from friends and acquaintances whose kids scored in the 99.999th percentile on their Stanford-Binets or WPPSI tests. We can't stress this enough: Take everything you hear with a grain of salt. Apparently, we all lie about our incomes, our ages, and our children's test scores. We've even heard of cases in which the best of friends fib ("just a little one, so it's okay").

We're not saying that other parents can't be superb sources of support, guidance, and valuable information. Just know whom you're dealing with and try to gauge what their insecurities or agenda may be. If Adrienne's future really is at stake (not that it is, since attending a top nursery school does not guarantee admission to Harvard any more than admission to Harvard guarantees a happy life), we'd double-check whatever "facts" you're given.

Succumbing to the Testing Crazies

A most distressing aspect of the forage for city schools is the feeling that your child is being judged in a fundamental and sometimes lasting way, often before he's even toilet trained. Since tests are required for admission to many private schools, top parochial schools, and public gifted and talented programs, the stakes feel unbearably high. In competitive cities especially, slots are hard to come by—and for

Park Bench Poison

In the good old days, lots of parents relied on info they gleaned while on playground duty or in any of their casual interactions with other parents. Today, with the new improved "park bench"—Internet message boards—parents have even more opportunity to gather thoroughly unreliable information. Professionals in the field rail against park bench gossip and question the sanity of all of us parents who rely on casual acquaintances (or in the case of most Web postings, complete and utter strangers) for unsubstantiated information. But it's so seductive.

Julia remembers quite clearly the weight she and her husband gave to hearsay. It's amazing what one can concoct from all the comments of people who at the end of the day don't know jack about a school. In her case, those comments became hurdles to overcome—and they were, through in-teraction with the prospective schools. But what if the director of admissions at one school hadn't been so personable? Or if the parent of a child attending another hadn't been so thoughtful and articulate? Would Julia's brood have ended up elsewhere? Possibly. And that would have been a big and stupid mistake.

Should you ignore park bench gossip in its entirety? Well, maybe not everything. It certainly can be useful for identifying schools you'd never thought of, or to point you in the direction of parents whose child is actually attending a particular school you're interested in (whom you can contact for hopefully more reliable information). But the speculative, third-hand stuff—which is generally negative, by the way—is just as we said, poison. And you will find it hard to let go of once you've heard it.

Collateral Damage

Because for some parents, the verdict they see in the test results is just not acceptable, someone has to be at fault. The babysitter let little Tootie stay up 10 minutes too late or *Rugrats* was too exciting last night. The tester was a meanie; the office too dreary; a cold was coming on. The more unpalatable the result, the more blame there is to go around because the score must be wrong.

Some parents can't let it go. One therapist told us of a child, a nice, normal kid, who delivered solid, but not spectac-ular, scores on an admission test. The incredulous parents decided to go for a full-blown evaluation because they could not accept the child that the test described. The therapist's fear? That a complete battery of tests and interviews was bound to identify something "wrong"—you know we all have strengths and weaknesses—and then these particular parents would not rest, employing whatever therapy required, no matter how long or how intensive, until they got the child of their testing dreams.

gifted and talented, impossible—without more than acceptable results on the relevant test.

Here's the educational skinny: Test results do matter because they're the only standardized indicators with which to compare different children. For public schools, which typically have to submit to test cutoffs, they matter a lot; in private schools, administrators have more leeway and often look to other variables when assessing a child's fit with the school. You should know, however, that educators do pay close attention to low scores, substantial variations among subtests, or words of warning that might be contained in a tester's comments—all signs that there may be an issue that impacts a child's ability to learn. And while this is clearly not happy info for the family involved, with all the evidence of the benefits of early intervention to address learning issues, in a weird way, it may be the best news the parents could get. So, if your child is the one with the disappointing test results, look at this as an opportunity to help your child be the best he can be, not as the end of the world.

And the emotional fallout? Real damage can be done to children when out-of-control parents turn preschool testing into some sort of life event—and then take actions that give this little, little moment in a kid's life a much bigger impact than it ever deserved. For many, test scores provide some immutable fact about their child that they just can't shake. Andreas is not the little genius they thought, so they never feel quite as bright about him again. Or Andreas is a little genius so every other piece of info in his life is made to fit that picture. Andreas gets a bad mark or acts out in kindergarten? That's not his problem: They're just not challenging him enough.

Then there are the parents who can't seem to stop themselves from giving their kids an edge before the fact—even feeling it's their parental duty to hire tutors or play endless word games with their bored out of their gourds tots. But trying to change your child's natural outcome is a bad, bad thing. Here's what happens when you open the tutoring door: (1) you are putting forth test results that don't really reflect your child, which means you may succeed in getting Tabitha into a school that she will not be able to handle with unfortunate repercussions down the road (was that really your dream?); (2) you are telling your child and yourself that you have no confidence in him; (3) you are teaching her that you think cheating's okay (and of course she'll know it's cheating because you're telling her not to tell anyone, aren't you?). And if that's not enough, don't forget you can get caught. Administrators are completely on to the fact that test prepping is rampant; they are on the watch. As one said, "Kids just love to tell you that they already know how to do something." Quite often, the tester will figure out a kid's been tutored; other times, it will become evident when test performance doesn't jive with school reports or the child's interview at the ongoing school. And when your cover's blown, it'll get nasty. The results will be questioned, you'll be interrogated by your preschool director and/or admissions

The Whole Country's Gone Berserk

No city is immune to the completely out-of-whack attention on the efforts of 3- and 4-year-olds. One Los Angeles tutor discussed on Salon.com her experience training preschoolers to produce perfect performances in their kindergarten evaluations. Sometimes, parents would hire her for their 3-year-olds, to give them *a full two years* of tutoring before they face the music.[a] Even parents in the torpid Big Easy feel the strain, retaining speech therapists to beef up the vocabulary of their entirely age-appropriate 2-year-olds and trying to buy purloined copies of admissions tests off the Web.[b]

a. Theresa Heim, "Cramming for Kindergarten," www.salon.com/mwt/feature/2000/09/06/private_tutor/print.html.

b. Juliette Guilbert, "Cramming for Kindergarten," November 27, 2001, www.bestofneworleans.com/dispatch/2001-11-27/cover_story.html.

people, and if you're really busted, you'll find out your little darling's rejected from every school to which he applied.

The upshot: For most people—maybe 95 percent (or maybe it's 99.9999 percent) of the parents and kids out there—the tests won't tell you a whole lot that's truly meaningful in the scheme of things. You're going to be no closer to knowing whether your child will be a politician or a plasterer, a parent or a hermit, a criminal or a saint. All that stuff is still unwritten. Your child is still the same child that you adored before the test; his possibilities are still endless. So don't blow it by responding to the score like it's some day of reckoning. It's not and it won't be, unless you make it that way.

PUBLIC + PRIVATE + CATHOLIC = THE NEW EDUCATION EQUATION

To our way of thinking, it is completely appropriate to start mulling over your city's various educational systems before baby is even burping. It gives you loads of time to collect information calmly, more accurately, and with less emotional distortion than will surely occur if you wait until events force you to act. Even if you're thinking this is not your problem because either public school is your only option or you have the dough and you're going private all the way, we highly recommend you look at all three kinds of schools.

In fact, many alert parents, intent on getting the benefit of their city bargain, already treat education as a kind of Chinese menu: a little bit of public, a little private, with some parochial on the side, please. Public school parents contend with systems that invariably have one stage that seems especially lacking (in Washington, D.C., the dreaded years are high school, while in New York City, middle school is the abyss). They have the most practice at this game: choosing public when the educational offerings are ripest and then switching to private when the going gets tough.

Every parent could take a leaf from that book. It's surely not a bad strategy for families that can just barely afford private school to consider a combination of public and private schools. This will stretch your funds and even stretch your child's horizons. But we wouldn't stop there. Even financially unconstrained private school parents might want to at least investigate the mix-and-match approach. Fact is, none of us can make cavalier assumptions about what will happen with our children or our lives. Maybe those private school plans don't come through, or there's a layoff in the family and that bill's suddenly looking really large, or the public gifted program is more accommodating to your smart little kid. Wait to find this out until after the fact and you might be out of luck.

Timing Challenges: When You're Looking at Public and Private Options

In many cities, there's a swath of kids, especially boys, who will apply at one age for public kindergarten and a year later for private. If your son (and now sometimes your daughter too) has an August or later birthday, chances are he won't be *applying* for private kindergarten until after he's actually turned 5. Most public schools, on the other hand have later cutoff dates and would expect him to apply the year before. (Dates are converging however. In Miami, Pittsburgh, and Chicago, public schools require you to be 5 by September 1, just like many private schools.) That makes it a little tricky for those who are applying to both. If your child has a summer birthday and you're considering both public and private schools, here are your options:

1. Apply to both public and private schools on the private school schedule, but go for the first grade in public. Of course, if you're on the hunt for gifted and talented or other special programs, first-grade admission is generally on a space-available basis, so your chances are much more limited than if you'd applied for admission to the kindergarten.
2. If your child is small or on the young side emotionally, you can see if the public school will accept him into the kindergarten even though he's technically too old. Many will accede to your request.
3. Send your child to public kindergarten on their timetable and apply from there to a private school kindergarten, where he can repeat the year if he gets in. This gets a little tricky since obviously the public school has no interest in trying to get your child admitted to the private school, plus you're talking about putting your child through three different schools in three years (preschool, public kindergarten, private kindergarten).

It's not just kindergarten that pops up the timing question. It'll be an issue down the line if your October birthday public school daughter wants to go to private middle school, or if your 6-foot August birthday private middle schooler decides to go to that fabulous city public school. Will he feel out of place if he's that much older than all the other boys? You'll need to get a grip on how best to make the switch, not just emotionally and financially but also from a purely educational standpoint since private, parochial, and public school curricula don't necessarily correspond. Your child may be light-years ahead of her class or have much catching up to do down the road.

Bottom line: Knowledge of your options won't hurt you, and it just might open your eyes to opportunities you didn't even know existed.

Lest we forget, there's another option entirely, especially for those families leaning toward the public alternative: Catholic schools. As you'll read ahead, many are well suited to students who don't even follow their faith, and they're much more affordable than private schools. We're probably not ready to go as far as novelist Tom Wolfe, who's advocated turning the *entire* New York City public school system over to the Catholic Church (and he's a lapsed Presbyterian, so no agenda there), but they sure do fill a void in urban public education.

Now for a close-up on each educational category. Mix-and-matchers (and that should be you) will want to know the advantages and the disadvantages of each type.

Private School: What You Get and What You Don't

So what's the hook? After all, these places are not cheap. City tuitions range from $3,500 for bare-bones parochial education to $14,000 for full frills (almost $30,000 in the most expensive cities). Obviously with this price tag, there better be some darned good reasons for a private education. There are plenty.

What You Get

Here's where your money goes:

Lots of options. For starters, in a city of any size you can find a school to meet just about any educational philosophy and pedagogic preference, from Chinese Immersion to Waldorf to traditional British. You can find schools that focus on sports and music, are child-centered, or strictly structured. And if you're interested in the option of single-sex education, with the exception of the rare rogue public school, you have to go private. This won't be a guessing game for you: Schools are generally pretty good about defining what they think their educational niche is. So read through all their materials carefully.

Smaller class sizes. According to the U.S. Department of Education, the average self-contained private school classroom has 18.9 students versus 20.9 students in public, not a hugely meaningful difference. But much as we hate to reject data in favor of personal experience, those numbers do not reflect our reality—where private elementary classes run about 20 kids, watched over by 1.5 to 2 teachers versus public classes hovering nearer to 30, presided over by one very busy teacher who is lucky to have an assistant teacher. Don't assume anything anywhere, of course. Get the real numbers from whatever school you're considering.

Lots of extras. The rest of the presumed private school advantages include: varied curriculums; strong offerings of, and emphasis on, nonacademics such as art, music, and sports; neat, if not downright spectacular, physical plants; and safety and security, although like everything, there is considerable variability from school to school.

What You Don't Get

But there are certain things that are in short supply at private schools:

A whole lot for students on either end of the spectrum. With all the assets that private schools have and the prices parents are paying to access them, it often comes as a shocking surprise to discover how poorly equipped private schools are to deal with kids who don't fall squarely down the middle of the performance curve. Most private schools are geared to a high middle performer. Highly gifted kids or children with more than minor learning or behavioral issues will often find that their needs are not squarely addressed. In fairness, most schools don't pretend to have the special, often highly individualized, curriculums such kids need. If you have an inkling your child may fit into one of these categories, you are going to have to search harder for a school specially suited to him, or at least have a plan for what kind of supplemental resources that you, not the school, are going to bring to bear to meet his needs.

Economic diversity. While there are lots more non-Caucasian faces in private school yearbooks these days, in the lower grades, these are mostly the children of affluent professionals—all colors and all nationalities. If you're looking for economic diversity too, you're not going to see much of it (although without a doubt what scholarship money there is appears to be almost entirely devoted to low-income minority children).

An active role. Parents should know up front that their involvement in the school may not be terribly welcome. Private schools are not like public schools, which absolutely depend on active parental support to work. There is a range, of course. Some private schools welcome a great degree of involvement, even in terms of influencing the direction of the school. Others pretty much like to do things themselves, relegating parental involvement to the occasional field trip or book fair. But even in the hands-off schools, don't ever make the mistake of thinking that private schools are not big on volunteering; it's expected and noted. Heaven forbid you're the parent who never volunteers for any committee or shuns field trips and library duty. Schools' assessment of your willingness to step up may follow you from institution to institution. (And your job is no excuse; work on phone trees, do class e-mail lists—anything as long as it's something.)

Objective information on the schools. One big thing you won't find in private schools is a lot of objective, comparative information. Private schools escape much state regulation, although those that belong to a private school body, like one of the local affiliates of the National Association of Independent Schools, are periodically run through a certification regime. Regardless, you generally won't find test scores, matriculation rates, diversity stats, or detailed scholarship numbers when you're checking out private elementary school options. In fact, when *U.S. News and World Report* tried to rank private schools for academic excellence, independent school organizations recommended to their members not to participate in the survey.

Financial aid. Paying for school tuition is not a happy topic in many cities. The fact is, that while there is more financial aid available than ever before, as one school administrator put it, "There's no question the middle class gets squeezed." The biggest portion of scholarship money that is available goes to further diversity objectives—and you're more likely to see a school's financial aid pool give substantial aid to a few very low-income applicants than moderate aid to a bigger number of more affluent, but still stretched, parents.

You're In, Now It'll Cost You (Tuition, Donations, and Volunteer Work)

Most parents are prepared to lay out a hefty chunk of dough for their kid's tuition: $10,000 to $28,000 a year depending on the city. What really frustrates those parents who are squeezing every penny to make the next tuition payment are the "extras" that seem to appear out of nowhere—lunch, uniforms, books, field trips, physical education. By the time you add them all up, you can easily be paying 10 to 15 percent more than you'd budgeted. Be prepared to shell out for a few extras.

The good news on the financial end concerns donations. We know a lot of parents who just about go nuts trying to figure out how much they'll be expected to shell out for annual operating fund drives, capital campaigns (trust us, there will be at least one major building project in every child's K–12 career), auction nights, theater nights, book fairs, and on and on (in LA, we hear they like sample sales). But unless your donation is for a new library, the only one who's going to care if you can't free up more than a fiver is you. Sure, you'll get pitched for a contribution, and ideally the schools would like to see everyone give something (it helps when they're applying for grants), but they're completely realistic about financial capacity. If you're rolling in dough and are penurious, you will get a lot of evil eyes because people will not understand how you can cheap out your children's school. If you're stretched, they'll want you to do what you can, but no more.

If financial aid is a necessity, you will undoubtedly be required to file certain additional forms as part of your application process. Often the forms belong to the National Association of Independent Schools, which runs the School and Student Service for Financial Aid (SSS), a service to which many private schools turn for guidance on financial aid awards. SSS recently revamped its financial assessment formula to generate more aid awards for families with incomes up to $125,000—which may be an extremely comfortable income in many parts of the country, but not if you're living in an expensive city and have kids going to private schools. If your income is much higher, you'll get sympathy but no relief. No matter where you live, spending more than 25 percent of your gross income on education, which the SSS formula can require, will put a serious bite into spending on discretionary items like food, shelter, taxes, and the college fund.

Public School: What You Get and What You Don't

Ah, public school. Another beast entirely. Urban public school systems are perpetually faced with too many students and too few funds, and chaos rules about every large public school system we've examined. There's a dearth of attractive, state-of-the-art facilities, few have all the lovely amenities that come with private schools, and frankly there's no guarantee of institutional civility either. Then there's the whole "teaching to the test" phenom. With standardized test scores one of the few empirical measures of "quality" in public schools, teachers can spend large parts of the school year prepping kids with rote, canned, drill-heavy work for an upcoming state exam, a tendency not likely to abate with the passage of "No Child Left Behind." Still, our children are perpetually getting educated in public schools, and plenty come out just fine.

What You Get

Public schools deliver a number of great benefits:

A pass on tuition. Surely it's impossible to monetize the value of an education, but we'll try anyway. Parents can expect to fork out up to $200,000 for a K–12 private school education—even more in the really high-cost U.S. cities. Public schools are, of course, our free and inalienable right. So while you're getting your tax dollar's worth, you're also living proof of our country's lofty ideals.

Better qualified teachers. Another lovely plus for public schools: teachers are generally better qualified and certainly better paid than their private school colleagues. A broad study of San Antonio, Texas, schools found results that mirror the country's other cities: Public school teachers were more likely to hold master's degrees or to be certified, and had more teaching experience, than those in private schools.

That exciting city diversity. Maybe the single most voiced asset of city public schools is that their populations reflect the diversity that so many city parents welcome, cherish, and praise. "[Public] school opens kids' minds. It helps them realize that the viewpoint espoused at home is not the only one in the world. It helps them to see people of different races and socioeconomic backgrounds in a setting that isn't Wal-Mart," writes one parent on a Salon.com message board. A person on another family site was equally enraptured by her son's color-blind experience. The child had attended a posh, private Manhattan school, but when his family's situation changed he had to leave. Mom was hesitant at first, but not anymore. "I think my son is a better person for it," she writes. "He has friends of all different colors and economic backgrounds and seems to have a sensitivity and generosity beyond his years."

What You Don't Get

But public schools fall short in a number of ways:

Small classes. While study after study has found that smaller classes yield higher achievement, you can forget about finding them in most city public schools. Increased immigration over the past 20 years, the numerous children, even grandchildren of baby-boomers now of school age, and a renewed interest in city living mean that competition for choice school spots just got that much tougher. According to a U.S. Department of Education report, "America's cities are plagued with a burst of enrollment and not enough schools to accommodate all the new children." This pattern is likely to continue, the report states.

Don't think this is minor stuff either. While already some 15,000 schoolchildren in Los Angeles's Unified School District must ride buses each day because there is no room at their home school, the district has a projected shortfall of 85,900 desks over the next decade. At Miami's public schools, which have seen a 32 percent increase in enrollment over the past 10 years, 41 percent of schools are at least 150 percent over capacity and some 84,000 students (out of approximately 368,625) attend school in portable classrooms. There are equally disturbing stats in city schools across the country.

Regular physical education. City youngsters, who need that exercise more than most, are going to have to look elsewhere because in the public school domain, PE is treated as the "ugly stepchild" of education. The minute a budgetary crisis hits, it's the first program to suffer. Notwithstanding that the National Academy for Sport and Physical Education recommends that elementary school kids get 150 minutes a week of PE instruction, state requirements can be as low as

30 minutes a week. PE is not the same as recess. PE enhances all sorts of developmental functions, strength-building, flexibility, endurance—not to mention those wonderful endorphins! So find out exactly what your child's school is offering and be prepared to supplement physical activity after school and on weekends.

Safety and security. Dare we mention the danger that lurks in the corner or even on the front steps of many city schools, where metal detectors are not uncommon even in elementary schools? It's a reality, and you will need to deal with it if it becomes the reality of your child too. Even if your child is never actually in physical danger from fellow students or visiting miscreants, constant behavioral problems from a hefty percentage of the school population is a sad given in too many urban public schools.

Strong, consistent educational records. When you put together outrageously large class sizes, uninterested students, and crumbling facilities, can you really expect excellent performance? No way, not in most schools, but there are exceptions (quite a few) in every city. Seek and ye shall find.

A lot of attention to your child's needs. "My husband jokes that my kids are homeschooled in the Oakland public schools," muses mom, Susan Bower. She spent half an hour in the classroom every morning for a few weeks, getting her daughter Emily up to speed when she wasn't reading very well. While not every school permits parents in the classroom, all public parents should anticipate a need for supplementing their child's education in some way. There ain't a public school in America that has it all, and your job will be to know what your kids are getting and what they're not, and to make up for what's missing.

Catholic Schools: The New "Public School" Option

A whopping 85 percent of American private school students are in religiously based schools. However, many of these schools are pretty much geared toward serious religious instruction, generally of interest only to families seeking such specialized curriculums. We won't examine them all here, but we're going to make an exception for Catholic schools, which not only account for about half of all these private school kids but also, we believe, merit a special focus for city parents reviewing their children's educational needs.

What's the draw? Julia, who's on the advisory board of a Catholic girls high school in a gritty section of South Bronx, knows exactly what the attraction is. To the parents of girls in St. Pius V, that school is a godsend, literally. Nearly 90 percent of the girls go on to college, a screaming distinction from the local public alternative where most of the kids don't even graduate. City Catholic schools show some striking advantages over their public compadres. Dropout rates are one-quarter the level of those in public schools, disruptive behavior much less common, and the gains in performance for minority students, in particular, have been shown to be substantial. A 1990 RAND study on a composite group of schools in New York City, for instance, showed that only half of entering seniors in the public schools graduated at all versus 95 percent of those in Catholic schools. Similar results have been observed in cities throughout the country. That's a stunning difference, wouldn't you say?

Be assured, the differences cannot be explained away by demographics. On the whole, the mix of students in city Catholic schools tends to mirror that of their public counterparts. However, someone had to take the initiative to get the child enrolled and pay the tuition. The support of a committed adult is telling, of course, and also reflective of perhaps a greater degree of parental involvement and interest than might be found in the typical public school. In fact, many city parents who are dissatisfied with their public school choices and/or can't afford or don't get the "value" of paying $18,000 a year for an independent school find solace in the Catholic school system—which charges a fraction of the tuition charged by non-sectarian privates.

But would a non-Catholic be comfortable in one? Apparently, yes. In Washington, D.C., for example, 51 percent of Catholic school students are not Catholic. Surely the commitment to character and academic endeavor are appealing to families of all religions. Possibly one reason for the nonecumenical draw is the reduced focus on religious education and greater emphasis on the dignity of the person, on community, on social justice—themes dominant in the wake of Vatican II, which is said to have revolutionized Catholic education. Whether the parents who line up outside Catholic school doors are aware of the impact of Vatican II is somewhat suspect, but they clearly will understand the school's orientation. In your own case, what you really have to decide is whether you are okay with having your child listen to Catholic doctrine in the religion classes that are surely part of the curriculum. If you're on the fence, talk to the head of the school; they'll either be welcoming to a non-Catholic or not.

What You Get

Catholic schools provide:

Clear educational mandates. As researchers in one study noted, Catholic schools have much in common with special purpose city schools like magnets because of their plainly articulated curriculum goals ("academic and college preparatory") and clearly defined expectations for students, particularly regarding moral values and character. One study said Catholic schools appeal to "families for whom college attendance is a prominent goal."

Traditional curriculums. You may not see a lot in the way of extras at your local Catholic school, but there will be a strong emphasis at the lower levels on reading, writing, and 'rithmetic. The relatively narrow focus can be quite attractive to parents who are terrified by the number of kids growing up in this country without acquiring even the most basic skills. Interestingly, some parents also choose Catholic schools for their "mildly learning disabled" child because they want a strict, rigorous curriculum. Reportedly, such children can succeed in Catholic schools, losing their "disabled" label in the process.

Structure and discipline. Catholic schools pride themselves on their ability to maintain a sense of order. There is an emphasis on manners, addressing teachers with respect, doing what you're asked, when you're asked. Enormous attention is given to the concept of student accountability and responsibility for one's own actions. Kids are expected to toe the line. And to assist children in keeping their eyes focused on the right goals, Catholic schools are big proponents of uniforms (the focus is on education, not fashion) and discipline. Violations are just not tolerated, and kids who can't get with the program are kicked out. To a freewheeling individualist, this all may sound a tad fascist, but we can tell you it plays very well to parents seeking a haven from overcrowded, dangerous, academically underperforming public alternatives.

What You Don't Get

You are unlikely to find the following in Catholic schools:

Flourishes and frills. Catholic schools, which charge maybe 25 to 50 percent of the tuition of their private school counterparts, simply can't afford to offer much in the way of extra-academic activities. You won't be seeing a lot of sports or music or the arts except in the few well-funded big urban high schools, like Manhattan's legendary Cardinal Hayes, or independently funded Catholic schools like those in the Sacred Heart system, which function like full-fledged independent schools with tuitions to match.

Absolute stability. A large number of Catholic schools struggle financially. The rate of closures has accelerated over the past decade because the generally lower income parents cannot support the rate of tuition increases that would be necessary to keep up with spiraling urban costs. That's not likely to change. Of course, that's also why you see such heavy support among blacks, in particular for the use of vouchers, most of which have been used to fund attendance at Catholic schools.

Our view on all this: If your money is tight, and your public school option is not spectacular, Catholic schools may well be worth a look.

THE CITY PARENT RULES
Practical Principle for the School Hunt

Rule #1: Do thorough research. In some ways, what we're talking about is a mind-numbing amount of work, certainly compared to what your parents had to do for you. But if you're trying to exercise your right to choose, you need to figure out what you want and why *and*, since no one's guaranteeing that your top choice will choose your child, you need to research some backups too. Developing that short list of schools requires a little more than picking a name out of a hat. You'll need to define what you're looking for in a school, philosophically, physically, locationally, and every other way. That will involve talking to lots of people, reviewing any objective information around (which isn't always much)—including the obligatory parent-authored books on local schools—contacting local parent groups (à la Chicago's Northside Parents Network or the Parents League in New York), and evaluating the material provided by the school (or school district). You will be busy.

Rule #2: Get started early. For so many reasons, it makes sense for you to jump on this ball early. God help you if you suddenly realize some August that your 3-year-old needs a preschool in a month, your choices will probably not be pretty. Lots of people don't do enough of the preliminary work, which means they miss out on some great options for their child because they didn't know about them, they missed some deadline somewhere, or they relied on dubious sources of data for their decision. Don't let that be you.

Rule #3: Organization is everything. It may be dreary, but being methodical can help enormously in minimizing everyone's stress and in keeping you in good graces with the schools to which you're applying. Keep folders of info on your schools. (We love those expandable law files.) Track the application process, and if you're not sure what the deadlines are, ask until you do. Then honor them. A surprising number of people seem to find it excruciatingly difficult to follow a school's or school district's timetable. We're sympathetic. Parents have day jobs, households to run, lives to live; to devote so much family energy to the education of a toddler does seem silly on more than one level. But don't slack off unless you're prepared to live with the consequences.

Rule #4: Be helpful; be nice. All things being equal (and they never are), all schools want kids from nice families where the parents are committed to and involved with the education of their child. Public or private, administrators prefer parents who are willing to help out, so establish a track record of helpfulness when and where you can—and not just because it may make the difference to Delphina's getting the nod from The Goldman Sachs School for Girls or Public School #1. You should be willing to help. It's a key part of being a parent. And mind your manners, all the time. Because what schools don't want are obnoxious, rude moms and dads, even if they're rich and obnoxious. Being nice may not get you in, but we can assure you, not being nice will keep you out. And for those for whom being polite is not a habit, be very afraid. Even big cities are surprisingly small towns when it comes to gossip. In the school game, your reputation will often precede you.

NURSERY, PRE-K, AND YOU

At some point you have to get beyond mulling over the very broad strokes of your city's educational options and actually participate in the system. For most of you, that will mean a foray into what experts call "early childhood education."

When we were growing up, nursery school and pre-K were not only optional, they were nearly nonexistent. But today's city slicker wouldn't be caught dead in kindergarten without having attended school for 1, 2, even 3 years prior. What could possibly be the big deal about school for 2- and 3- and 4-year-olds? If nothing else, it's important for the reason that, with very few exceptions, nearly all private school kindergarten entrants come from a pre-K program. And it's not so different for public schools either, considering that two-thirds of all American kids now attend preschool (up from only 5 percent in 1965).

What's more, the benefits educators perceive from early childhood education should not be taken lightly. Good programs teach children how to work in groups (standing in line, taking turns); how to take direction; how to take care of themselves and their things; how to follow a schedule; how to transition; and how to manage pre-academic curriculums like learning to count, forming letters, and learning letter sounds. All of these are not only great skills in and of themselves, but with the stepped-up requirements of many kindergarten programs, they're actually prerequisites. If your child doesn't have that stuff under his belt by the time he enters an ongoing program, he may well be behind his cohorts—not an auspicious beginning. For those of you who wonder when exactly the beginning begins, the classic city timeline is often: a twos program of sorts (so you can at least tell preschool admissions people that your frenetic little Olivia has already been socialized); then 2 to 3 years of preschool, depending on the birthday; then on to kindergarten.

What's Available?

The supply of preschool spaces lags the demand. In the public realm, universal pre-Ks are seriously few and far between—maybe they don't even exist in your city. With budget constraints hammering many city coffers, expanding public pre-K programs is, for now, more dream than reality. City parents used to having lots of choices have suddenly hit the preschool wall.

This leaves you with two basic strategies. Either choose an organized program or create one of your own. For parents who make a conscious choice not to send their lovelies to nursery school—and for parents of children who somehow fall through the admissions cracks—cities offer plenty of one-off classes in art, music, gym, language, and on and on. An enterprising parent can easily devise an exciting, rich "school day" from these offerings. We know parents who did it just this way, on purpose no less, and did just fine when it came time for kindergarten admissions later on.

But the freeform, do-it-yourself prekindergarten experience is not exactly typical. The bulk of early education offerings are in *private* preschools. And what a great introduction to city school systems because the effort you'll have to make to get your toddler into an early childhood program will be great training for the big move into kindergarten. Getting into preschools could even be a little tougher in some ways because whatever high-falutin' name your favorite early childhood school goes by legally, these places are all "day care" establishments, regulated by your state's Department of Health (which, FYI, is why you'll be filling out that DOH day care medical form even if you're at a posh preschool with limos lined up

CITY SAVVY

Check the Decibel Levels!

City nursery programs housed in lofts may suffer from poor acoustics, and loud does not a learner make. So, if you're considering one of these schools, visit during peak noise hours.

outside). That means they have to honor the hard and fast state regulations for number of staff members and amount of space per child. Hence they lack the ability of private kindergartens, which being outside the daycare fold, can and do add an extra class every now and then when their acceptances greatly exceed their available spaces. Thus competition, especially at those schools that parents believe are the most "influential," can end up being fiercer than that for kindergarten entry. As one Chicago parent lamented, getting her child into preschool was "worse than her college sorority rush."

Fortunately, perception is not always reality, and certainly not in this case. Cities have many, many early education programs—not just the names you read about in whatever acronym rag is profiling your city, but layers and layers beneath them. And there's no dearth of educational philosophies and program structures from which to choose—everything from 2 to 3 days a week and half-day sessions (mornings tend to be the most desirable) to five times a week with extended days. Some will be "academically" inclined; others follow a particular teaching method like the individually oriented Montessori or developmental Emilio Reggio.

THE CITY DIFFERENCE:
Considerations in the Nursery or Pre-K Decision

You've probably run into lots of good thoughts on how to evaluate a preschool, from how they handle discipline to the mix between academics and play. And many of these generic concerns are as right on for city parents as they are for everyone else. But there are a few differences.

1. Check out the staff's training and qualifications and tenure/turnover. That urban cost of living can be pretty hard to handle on a preschool teacher's salary, so staffing can be tough, tough, tough. At a minimum, the director should have substantial early childhood background; hopefully many of the teachers do as well. Ask where their teachers come from, how they're trained, and what sort of ongoing teacher ed programs they have.
2. Investigate the physical activity of the program. Without acres of room to run a program in, city schools often have to be creative in the use of limited indoor and outdoor space, to make sure students get enough running-around time. If children travel outside the school to a nearby playground or park, ask how they keep all the critters safely corralled in transit.
3. If you're in an older city (think East Coast, Midwest) or an older building in any city, really scan the physical plant. Schools are supposed to be closely regulated, but stuff falls through the cracks. Peeling paint? Insecticide smell? Wouldn't make us happy.

Program Types

We separate preschool programs into three categories of schools: public, parent co-operatives, and private. Of course, like just about everything we've found for city schools, nothing fits neatly into anything. Case in point: Some public schools charge for pre-K. We're not including full-time child care centers in this section, even though many of them have become real factors in early childhood education, ranking up there with the top preschool-only programs in certain cities. Some centers even belong to their city's independent schools' association and offer parents a limited-use option, which mirrors typical preschool hours and operates similarly to the schools discussed below. However, since their reason for being is to offer education within the context of a full-time care operation, we cover them separately in chapter 5.

Public Preschool

The surprising news for city parents is how likely they are to find a pre-K program: 45 percent of city schools offer pre-Ks compared with roughly a third of schools in non-urban areas. Even better, city pre-K teachers are slightly more qualified than those outside: fully 91 percent have bachelor's degrees or higher, compared with a national average of 86 percent. But the sad, important truth is there are still too few places to go around. Many of the spaces that do exist are in special programs created for at-risk children: low-income, LEP (limited English proficient) kids, and children with special-ed needs.

To ascertain whether you're lucky enough to be in a city or a neighborhood with a public preschool program that's actually open to everyone, follow our

Finding a School That Fits

So much of finding the right school consists of weighing the emotional issues—i.e., how your child does with separation, strangers, toilet training—with the educational ones—will your 2-year-old be a child-oriented or pre-academic learner? None of these issues are city per se, so we'll leave this to the many wonderful experts who have offered tome after tome on the subject. We particularly like the information provided by the National Association for the Education of Young Children (NAEYC) and the Department of Education–funded ERIC clearinghouses, which aggregate early childhood education articles on just about any subtopic you can imagine at www.eric.ed.gov.

guidelines on finding your way through the public school system in chapter 13. And by all means, expect to get in line during the wee hours of (or in some cases, even the night before) the day of registration in order to secure that coveted spot.

Parent Cooperatives

Parent cooperatives are not-for-profit establishments that depend on significant parent participation for the operation of the school. Willing moms and dads actually have to sign lengthy contracts outlining their roles and commit themselves to supporting the school rules. Given the level of parental involvement required, co-ops tend to appeal to progressively oriented folks who are happy with being part of a shared value community and can deal with the good (the intimacy of the family relationships that develop) and the bad (the sometimes in-your-faceness of it all and the divide that can develop between the hard-core participants and those who don't have as much time to devote). It's excellent preparation for the parents who will be looking at public school, where the needs for parental involvement and for tact in dealing with lots of different kinds of people are not dissimilar. Furthermore, having been a co-op parent is a valuable chit when trying to sway public schools with some discretion over admissions to give you the nod.

Because they use parents so heavily in their operation, co-ops can be less pricey than other private school options. However some co-ops also like to give out a lot of financial aid, which means the tuition they charge to non–financial aid students

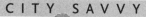

CITY SAVVY

If You're Going Public, the Pressure's Off

Parents who know their children will be moving on to public school have the benefit of not even having to consider the more competitive preschools. Instead, they can concentrate solely on finding the most appropriate venue for setting their child up for a life-long love of learning. Of course, that's not to say that the Triple AAA Power Nursery won't turn out to be that venue. But as you're investigating your options, keep in mind that whatever preschool Sierra attends won't make a lick of difference when you're registering her for the local public school. As a result, many public school parents buy out of the hard-to-get-into nursery schools. Also to consider: Preschool directors at establishments that service mostly families bound for private school can be unfamiliar with the ins and outs of public schools—save for that one neighborhood shining star, which your child may or may not be eligible for.

may be as high as private school options. If you're comfortable with the concept, you can find parent co-ops in most every city, although maybe not more than one or two. Identifying and joining them is a quirky word-of-mouth process. Knowing folks who attend or who are alumni definitely helps. On applications, parents will be asked what special talents they have that they can bring to the school. Our advice: Enumerate *all* of them. If you're an accountant and can help with the books, say so; if you're a carpenter and can work on the space, let it be known.

Private Schools

Private nursery schools range from the top-dollar, brand-name versions, with the attendant competition in admissions and exmissions (the process of exiting a school for a new one), to the low-key rolling admissions schools on the corner—and there's a fair range in between. The preponderance are freestanding early educational entities, though some are attached to religious or other institutions, as you'll read a little further on.

To obtain a listing of the private preschool programs in your 'hood, check out the National Association for the Education of Young Children, www.naeyc.org, for links to your local independent school association. A goodly portion of private schools belong to these associations. Lots of cities host preschool fairs, which we recommend attending. At these events, representatives from freestanding programs that are typically clustered around a particular neighborhood or zone band together for an afternoon of talking to parents and passing out school brochures and other interesting literature. Your local resources, such as the parenting newsies and associated Web sites, typically publish the whens and wheres of these get-togethers; early fall seems to be the most common time of year for the fairs. The parenting papers, by the way, will also have lots of ads from preschool programs—another good place to get names.

And while you're perusing those papers, keep in mind our take on a couple urban private preschool myths and legends.

Getting religion. Joining a church or synagogue with an affiliated preschool has become a very popular back channel for getting your kid a place in a sought-after preschool. It's not dumb thinking because many, many private pre-K programs are affiliated with religious institutions, which started them as a service for their congregation members. Most of these programs are fairly well established and staffed by experienced pros with extensive knowledge of kids, education, and the ongoing school process. And despite the religious connection, the majority are open to all comers, accommodating members of different religions quite comfortably.

In toto, these schools rank among the most desirable of the options for city parents—with one small glitch: They do tend to give significant preference to the children of congregation members. In response, many city parents are reestablishing their religious roots or even discovering the wisdom of some new religion, just as the concept of preschool enters their consciousness. We think religious affiliations can be wonderful for a family, so if it suits you, why not? Just be aware that religious institutions are tightening up their requirements—they want real members, you know. Quite often, they will require parents to have joined the congregation and attended services well before any preschool application is due; 2 years is not uncommon. Additionally, membership is supposed to be *active*, which means volunteering to help out for church/synagogue events and projects as well as being financially supportive. We're told by individuals monitoring such activity that donation expectations are completely relative: "If you have a big apartment and a country house, and you're giving $500 a year to the church, that doesn't sit too well" with the powers that be.

Checking into ongoing schools early. Another gambit city parents are employing is applying to an early childhood program contained within an ongoing school (a colloquial terms for schools that "go on" after preschool to varying endpoints: some go up through 12th grade; others end as early as 5th grade). These parents don't avoid the pressures of the preschool process, of course; but when other parents are scurrying around with kindergarten applications, they can just kick back and relax.

There are a few problems with this strategy. Indeed it's true that this used to be a remarkably effort-free way of finessing the whole private school ordeal. But so many people have cottoned on to this tactic that the early entry is now just about as competitive as waiting till the kindergarten year. And, of course, that early entrance is only an advantage if you plan on staying at the school. If you don't, it can really work against you because no one in an ongoing school's administration actually has an incentive to help you find a place in another institution. If it's still something you're interested in, keep a couple of things in mind. Entry points differ, with some ongoing schools running their own preschools for 3- and 4-year-olds (although they always accept more kids in kindergarten) and some just starting with a "junior kindergarten" class (that's "preschool" for the rest of us) for 4-year-olds—a typical scheme in Chicago, for instance.

The feeder school facts (or fictions). Did we mention the continuing fixation on the legendary "feeder" schools? You know, those schools that exist in every city and are reputedly conduits to the hot ongoing schools, whose heads horse-trade their students, mixing and matching kids and available places—all the while making the parents think that where they end up is where they wanted to go in the first place.

Lydia Spinelli, renowned head of Manhattan's hot, hot Brick Church School, believes the hype is unwarranted. She says the feeder school construct hasn't been valid for years. Referring to a well-known boys' school that had regularly taken a few Brick graduates, now there are years "when I won't have a single boy going there," she comments. In fact, the influence of any particular preschool head over the admissions decision of any ongoing school is greatly overrated these days. So when you hear stories about a particular preschool having a "lock" on slots at some fancy private kindergarten, don't believe them. There's absolutely no incentive for any decent school to hold places these days.

Which isn't to say that preschool heads don't have a role in the process or that conversations between them and kindergarten admissions directors don't happen. To the contrary, in some cases, those talks can be integral to admissions decisions as everyone tries to get a fix on whether a particular kid belongs at a particular private school. Is he too young or too boisterous? Do his test scores signal a learning issue, or is it just that random variability? Does the family really "get" the school? In super-competitive cities, these conversations even dance around first-choice letters, with preschool heads trying to divine whether one might be wasted at such and such an institution, and ongoing schools trying to tease out whether they're going to get that letter from a particularly "desirable" candidate.

For sure, such conversations are more direct and the opinions more heavily weighted when the discussion is between an admissions director and a preschool head who've known each other for years, rather than between first-time phone correspondents. But so many other factors come into play in the admissions decision these days that dilute the importance of that connection, however strong it may once have been. As Spinelli points out, parents should realize that "there are many, many good early childhood programs out there" that can serve children and families very well on the education front, and all good, proactive preschool directors are pretty much making and taking those admissions calls these days. If *your* director is not quite as dynamic as you might have hoped and you need a little help, just ask—nicely.

Nursery School Admissions: Let the Follies Begin

Because of the perceived dearth of spaces, lots of city parents are pretty frantic about getting their little ones into a threes program (God forbid you make the mistake of waiting to apply for the lone space that may exist in a fours class, the thinking goes). Actually, it's even worse than that. Nursery schools that have twos programs rarely have openings for threes, parents complain. "People have figured out that it's easier to get in at two—sort of like early admissions to colleges," reports one parent. In Los Angeles, landing a child in one of the perceived prestigious preschools has been likened to "plotting a military campaign"—with parents trading tips with "the paranoia of passing Pentagon secrets." LA is quite possibly the worst city in this regard, with its parental antics dwarfing even those of their Big Apple cousins. No joke. It's so bad there that one desperate LA parent broke out in a full-fledged panic attack when she couldn't get into a class on the topic of coping with preschool because it was full.

The anguished cries of parents who diligently set out to sign up their child for preschool or kindergarten, only to find out they were months or years too late, reverberate from coast to coast. Most programs maintain an admissions' cycle with a pretty rigid fall-winter applications season. Woe to those who miss the window. Even noncompetitive programs fill up quickly, so it pays to be among the first in a first-come, first-served regime.

Schools that run twos programs, which often consist of two or three short morning sessions a week, typically require the child to be 2 as of the day the program starts. Applications are generally accepted in the early fall of the year preceding the child's planned admission—which means that unless you like the idea of operating in panic mode, you need to start gathering information, say, 18 months before your child will actually begin. Want to start with a twos program? Do the numbers, and you will find that you might be in the hunt when your baby is only *6 months old*. Well, at least it's not during childbirth.

Probably the greatest number of preschools start with threes programs, nearly all of which are 5-day schedules with morning or afternoon sessions. These programs often will allow kids as young as 2 years and 9 months (or 2.9) to enter in their starting year. Once again, 18 months or so *before* the September you want your child to actually start is the time to begin checking out the requirements in your city. Maybe you live in a more low-key town, in which case you can put your feet up for a few months. But never assume anything.

By the way, for those of you who are budget conscious, you might develop some age consciousness as well. Ongoing independent schools (those with post-preschool classes) usually require kids to be 5 by September 1 (sometimes earlier) to start kindergarten. And that official guideline is often overridden by an unspoken bias toward taking older kids who are more likely to be "ready" for demanding kindergarten programs. In some cities, boys with summer birthdays are regularly "held back" and not allowed to move into kindergarten till they turn 6; these days, even girls with summer birthdays are getting held back. If tuition dollars matter to you, be sure to factor in the cost of three years of preschool if Sumner is born in the summer.

For many more guidelines on the admissions process—everything from what you should wear to the "interview" to how many schools you'll need to apply to—please refer to chapter 12. All those gory details about getting through the private school admissions battlefield in one piece are relevant for nursery school, since the preponderance of early programs are, in fact, "private."

CHAPTER 12

THE AGONY AND THE ECSTASY: A PRIVATE SCHOOL PRIMER

No pain, no gain, as they say. You are submitting yourself to more than a moderate amount of stress if you plan on putting your kid in a city private school. The competition, the interviews, the wondering whether your child's good enough, whether you're good enough—the strain of it all has been known to bring grown men to their knees. Accept it. But in the interests of making your life slightly less miserable, we'll give you a few pointers to ease the pain at every step along the way.

A LITTLE BACKGROUND

Dip a toe into the search for a city private school and you'll find yourself pounded with urban myths—from the fish stories of just how tough the competition is (every year, applying families hear that *this* is the toughest year ever) to the whispered rumors of backdoor ways to secure a space. The experience is enervating enough without hyperventilating over the wrong things for the wrong reasons. So let's take a minute to separate fact from fiction. It may clear your head just a bit.

Sparring for Spaces

For decades, the competition for spaces in city private schools was hardly intense enough to raise your pulse. Ongoing schools X and Y filled their classes with kids from preschools A and B, a process driven as much by geography as anything else; people just didn't expect to have their little ones travel to elementary school. Shutouts were rare; in fact, even good schools sometimes struggled to fill their seats. Today, however, it's a different story. Washington news rags report that Georgetown Day and the Maret School get 8–10 applications for every one space. In

Chicago, the Latin School accepts 250 applications for 60 spots, half of which are held for sibling and legacy (children of alums) candidates. Whipping up the frenzy, the *New York Times* reported that 2,221 kids had taken exams for admission into the kindergartens of NYC private schools against a supply of only 1,700 places. Hapless parents were left to assume that *one out of every four* of them would not be finding a place for their child. What the heck is going on?

There are more kids applying. A number of factors are contributing: The baby boom "echo" produced more children; the widespread improvement in urban quality of life has encouraged more parents to raise kids in the city; and the affluence of the 1990s created more parents who could afford private school. Put 'em all together and many schools have been happily hanging out No Vacancy signs at the end of every admissions year. But that doesn't mean, as some inferred from the *Times'* stats, that droves of kids are getting left out. A survey taken by early childhood educators in New York indicated there were actually only 40 kids who were shut out of private schools that year. So yes, the absolute numbers are less favorable to applicants these days, but that's not the whole story.

The process has been "democratized." Parents intent on the best for their child no longer limit themselves to their neighborhood. If that highly desirable school is all the way across town, then 5-year-old Dahlia will just have to weather the commute. There is little doubt that the in-vogue schools are seeing greatly expanded demand for their few places—and they're thrilled. One admissions director excitedly discussed her ability to put together great classes from the very wide range of applications she now sees. Kindergartens, which maybe had kids from 5 to 10 preschools in other decades, now happily announce their new students come from 25 or more different preschools. This change, while a positive one, does mean that

CITY SAVVY

Don't Do the Hype, Do the Math

Before you bust a gut about how many applications per place your top choice school has received, think about what the numbers mean. If you have 100 kids applying for 100 places in 10 schools, that's a 1:1 deal. However, if each kid completes five applications, that gets you to 500 applications in total or five applications for every place, which sounds horrible. In reality, though, there's still a place for every child. Where it gets tricky is if all those applicants want to apply for the 50 spaces in the hot five schools, ignoring the others. Those in-demand schools would then get 10 applications per place, while the out-of-favor (but maybe just as good) schools get none.

traditional paths from nursery to ongoing school are much less defined than they used to be.

Sometimes it's just about bad luck. City parents are responding to the greater uncertainties of the process by tapping on the doors of a whole lot of schools. In the good old days, kids would apply to 4 or 5 schools; now 8 or 10 are not uncommon. Beleaguered admissions officers are responsible for evaluating huge numbers of candidates (250? 300? 400?). And when you think about their selection process—we're talking about very young children, limited data, compressed time—how precise can the differentiation be? As one educator remarked, it's not just kids with problems (or kids with *parents* with problems) who are getting closed out. These days, nice kids can and do slip through the cracks. And those are the horror stories that keep parents up at night.

But you need not become an insomniac. In reality, only a very few kids don't get a place anywhere. If you're diligent about your part of this whole process—whether it's expanding your horizons to find the right schools or just making sure you get the application in when it's due—you and your child will in all likelihood be satisfied with the results when it's all over.

Gaming the System

The sinking feeling that the school odds are greatly stacked against them makes more than a few city parents look for shortcuts in the whole process. For the monied crowd, it's "heck honey, we'll just buy our way in." For others, it's the hope that a few bucks forked over to some consultant with whispered connections will do the trick.

Does Money Talk?

In the fall of 2002, it seemed every paper in the country trumpeted the price of NYC preschool admission: $500,000 per head and no discount for twins, according to those who followed the saga of Jack Grubman's preadmission "discussion" at Manhattan's exclusive 92nd Street Y Nursery School. The stories that passed from parent to parent about seven-figure pledges for kindergarten seats could've filled a year of *National Enquirers*.

We'd like to say this type of thing is a complete fabrication, but you know, sometimes where there's smoke, there's fire. During the roaring 1990s, it dawned on some of the more worldly city school heads that a mounting number of their applicants had outrageously wealthy parents who could potentially be persuaded to donate a boatload or two of money to the school. And *some* of those school heads were widely reputed to be courting the rich. But two factors mitigated the absolute power of money to gain access.

Your Wish List

Parents could stand to expend a little less energy on aimless worrying and a little more on figuring out the schools to look at. The biggest source of names? Often other parents going through the very same school search process. Bad idea; you miss a lot of good schools that way, ones that would be good for your child too. Our advice:

Start with your child. If you don't decipher your child's learning style at the beginning of the process, you may never actually get to it. There are lots of materials from psychologists and educators that can help you out. Your child's current and past teachers will likely have points of view on this, such as whether Cameron is better in structured or unstructured environments, in child centered or traditional. And then there are his test results. Without wanting to overemphasize the importance of admissions tests, we will tell you they do carry weight with admissions officers, so understand what they mean.

Consult your school head. If your child is in nursery school or preschool, take advantage of the director's knowledge of the system, of the school universe, and of your child. The director has a vested interest in seeing your child happily placed too. Yet, as helpful as these conversations can be, we've heard a considerable number of stories from preschool directors about parents who wouldn't take their advice and ended up badly. If you don't like what you hear, make sure you understand the reasons for what you're being told before you summarily reject the suggestions.

Open your mind. At the early stage, you want to broaden your choices, not reduce them, so make a conscious effort to add a few names to your list. Go to school fairs and open houses, talk to everyone you know with school-age kids. We're not suggesting you apply to every school that hits your radar, but you'll be surprised what turns up if you dig.

Don't ignore your own comfort level. Even though it's your *child* who's going to school, *you* will be part of a parent body, and in cities, these tend to have very distinct identities. A mother we know had her child at a fabulous school, with unbelievably impressive resources, and the kids seemed nice. The parents, though, were very social compared to our homebody friends. "It's okay," said our friend at the time. "It works for my daughter." She ended up pulling her daughter out after a couple of years, moving her to a much more under-the-radar school. We're not suggesting you have to be best friends with everyone you meet, but your ability to interact with the parents of your child's classmates will be of real importance. If you get that fish-out-of-water feeling every time you enter a school's lobby, maybe you should rethink your choice.

First, there was—and still is—so much money out there. Billionaires apparently are not such a rarity (an often quoted statistic holds that 41,000 NYC families are worth more than $10,000,000 each—the new middle class). So if money is to be your ticket in, you need a whole lot of it to stand out. Second, as the role of donations became more prominent on the school scene—with gargantuan gifts noted in annual reports and seats on the boards of trustees increasingly held by very well-heeled parents—whispers of bought places or heirs receiving favored treatment in school activities grew louder. Administrators began seriously worrying about the potential backwash on their schools' images. In fact, parent bodies of more than one school were rumored to revolt against swaggering money, causing their institutions to adopt lower profiles.

There are plenty of stories of families ready to write any size check to secure their child's admission, only to be denied. The reality is money can't buy everything. But sometimes, those who are prepared to be very generous *and* who have friends or, better, heads of facilities (i.e., preschools, museums, religious institutions) who will vouch for their donating habits do receive the preferential treatment of the uber-connected and wealthy. Our view on this? Live and let live. Neither of us is prepared to donate a building, so if someone else is able, and their kid can do the work (and is not totally obnoxious), then we'll live with that as the way of an imperfect world.

The Consultant Rap

While we're on the subject of money, did you know that $4,000 will buy you your own personal advisor who will stand by your side as you wend your way through the process of getting into a school? Too much for you? For a more modest $600, you can buy a little help just with the application. Today, there is an educational consultant for every need and every pocketbook.

In yet another demonstration of the wonders of a capitalist system, an entirely new industry has sprung up as individuals with all kinds of backgrounds set up shop to help desperate parents finesse the city school process. Think about the attractions of the job. The profession clearly pays (the *New York Times* quoted one consultant on the *seven*-figure annual income she brought in from advising nervous Gotham parents on the ins and outs of private school applications) and apparently you don't need any specific credentials. Nor is there any licensing or regulation involved. Overhead costs are minimal (a room in which to receive clients, a phone line that's open 24/7, a desk to edit your client's thank you notes). And since nobody gives references anyway (you know "client confidentiality" and all), no one will ever know if you're any good before that retainer fee gets plunked down.

What do consultants do for the money? Most of the time, really, really basic stuff: make appointments, help formulate a list of schools, and give interview pep and prep talks for parent and child. They'll even help cull cute little stories that moms and dads can use to wow an admissions director. And they all have lists of do's and don'ts—mostly don'ts.

The view from the other side? Admissions directors are just about unanimous in their negative reactions to consultants. First, they heartily resent hearing from consultants, whether they're calling to make an appointment or asking a question about the applicant pool. "We want to hear from the parents," said one admissions director. Second, some of the advice given by consultants flat out contradicts what educators think is in the best interests of parent and child. As an example, experienced preschool heads are telling their parents to apply to maybe six well-chosen schools. Any more than that and the parents forget which school is which, while the kids melt down at even the whisper of another interview. Consultants, however, almost invariably suggest more, even 10 to 12. One has to wonder who really benefits from plastering the waterfront with applications.

One last beef. They often don't have real qualifications—in education or in school admissions. "They're not going to really know how we do things," asserted one admissions professional. A lot of consultants don't have any background in psychology or child development either, which doesn't seem to stop them from "evaluating" your child's strengths and weaknesses and school needs.

Then again, let's not be too hasty. Robin Aronow, an NYC-based family therapist and educational consultant, describes two benefits that a consultant can legitimately provide for jittery private school–oriented parents. The first, somewhat surprisingly, is knowledge about the vagaries and mysteries (zoning! variances!) of

the public school process. Since even the most diehard private-school-or-bust parents are now told to check out a public school alternative (just in case), it may well be worth a little money to tap into someone else's research on all the intricacies of getting your child into a good public school. A second aspect of her services is therapeutic; it's what other consultants have termed "keeping parents off the ledge." Aronow describes one father who called her once a day, every day, during an entire admissions cycle. Did she have anything particularly scintillating to share with him in all those phone calls? No, but he "needed" to make the call—part of what a former top tier admissions director calls the desperate attempt to "control the uncontrollable." We say, better that call went to the consultant than to a less-receptive admissions officer.

> ### *Buyer Beware*
>
>
> Don't get sucked into paying a lot of money to someone who preys on your terror of being shut out. Avoid at all costs the scare tactics employed by some consultants who take out full-page ads admonishing parents against the certain failure they face if they go it alone. Chances are, all you'll get for your money are a lot of canned tips, obvious advice, and the chance to view schools and your child through that consultant's filter.

We are, therefore, of two minds about school consultants. If you're hiring someone to be your human sticky pad, reminding you of every interview, application deadline, and thank-you note requirement, we warn you that this wholesale dependence on some hired hand may become apparent to admission officers who will not be impressed by your neediness.

On the other hand, if you're new to a city and/or taking on both the private and public school system for the first time, you may well benefit from someone with ready access to accurate information about schools and the process. Ditto for those who truly believe they'll have difficulty getting through the admissions cycle without coming off as a raving lunatic. Admissions directors are full of foolish parent stories. There's one about the mother who actually asked if she could charge her cell phone during the interview. That poor mother's question marked her as self-centered and clueless. But we know better, having been immersed in stories of overstressed parents, fighting the barely winnable battle to hold on to a semblance of a work presence and/or manage a family while making three or more visits to every potential school (all, of course, done with the knowledge that they could very well fail in their first quest for their child). That kind of pressure could make anyone a little stupid. So if you're one of those who just feels like you can't hold it together, then it's probably cheaper to hire a hand-holding consultant than pay for the professional help you'll undoubtedly require after your nervous breakdown or divorce.

When You Really Should Ask for Help

There is a subsegment of school consultants who focus on special placements—kids with learning issues or highly gifted children. Most of the ones we've encountered have strong education/developmental psychology backgrounds—true professionals, in other words. If your child has any kind of special needs, consultants such as these can be very, very helpful. One place to look is to search by zip code at www.educationalconsulting.org, the website for the Independent Educational Consultants Association (IECA).

AND NOW . . . GETTING IN

Admission into a private school, whether for preschool or kindergarten, requires parent and child to pass through a series of hurdles—testing, parent interview, child interview, applications, essays, letters of reference. All of this is tough enough to do, but is even harder when the hurdles change from city to city and school to school.

Starting the Process

The cycle for applying to ongoing schools (which may admit children as early as pre-K, depending on the city and school) can start well before applications are even printed. One big reason: Many schools offer spring tours to prospective parents whose kids have not even entered their final year of preschool—a full 18 months before kindergarten even begins. So, check in with any prospective schools in the spring before you actually apply. You'll have a heads-up on what's required from them as well as the chance to take advantage of any early reconnaissance activities.

The Application

The school application is key. Don't look at it as just the piece of paper you fill out with a few items of personal data. That's simply the start. The completed application is really a dossier, full of your child's past schools records, evidence that you paid any required fees, recommendations, test scores, and whatever else the prospective school requires to check out your child. And woe to those who screw it up. Here's what you need to know.

Each school has its own process. Some schools start with a tour or open house, giving applications out to those who attend; others require a filled-out application before you ever step foot through their doors. Sometimes you can figure this out from a school's Web site (although if you're looking at early childhood education programs, you may find them less than Web-friendly). Or you can call the school and ask which steps they require (tour? open house? child interview? parent interview?) and in what order. The application package itself should take you through the rest of the process, laying out what the school wants from you, key dates and deadlines, when they give out acceptances, etc.

The costs can add up. Figure about $50 per application, even for preschool (and pity parents of twins who may have to do 20 sets if they're looking for schools that will take both kids). Here's a sign of the times, though. We've seen some schools waive the fee if you submit your application online. We love that and you should too (just be sure you read everything really carefully before you press the Send button).

You can't win if you can't play. It's bad enough you're not assured of getting a place in a school you're interested in. These days, you may not even get an application. Annoying, isn't it, to be rejected *before you've even applied?* But many admissions offices have seen applications literally double over the last few years, and their spare staffs simply cannot handle unrestricted volume. As a result, schools have adopted varying policies to manage the flow. Some have strict quotas, only taking, say, the first 350; other schools are going with application

CITY SAVVY

Don't Let Writer's Block Hold You Up

It's not enough to *get* the application; you have to submit it in a timely fashion too. Increasingly, schools are only accepting a certain number of applications, which may be something less than the number they've actually given out. If you're looking at an application with a lot of essays or other requirements, don't freeze. You can just fill out the data section, leaving the more time-consuming stuff out, and send in the partially completed application—*with* the required check *and* a note that the missing pieces will follow. That way, you have more time to work on your writing without missing any deadline the school has imposed for receiving applications or for giving out tour slots. And who knows, you may decide before you finish the application that you don't want to go through with the process for that particular school.

lotteries where they literally pick names out of a hat. Some schools use cutoff dates. If you ask for an application in October, and they've already been distributing them for a full month, they figure you couldn't have been that serious anyway.

In the face of all this uncertainty and variability, we highly recommend the better safe than sorry approach of obtaining and returning applications as soon as possible within the school's own application regime. But please, don't allow yourself to be terrorized by all those war stories of parents setting up dialing teams to break through the telephone logjam on the day applications are available or of applications running out only 1 day after parents were allowed to request them. There is a little room here, at least a couple of weeks from when the process officially starts—even in the hottest of years with the hottest of schools. It is certainly worth your while to check to see which schools let you download an application off the Internet. There'll usually be a date specified before which applications will not be accepted, but at least you'll have the forms in hand. For schools that distribute applications by mail or by tour, start asking for the application or tour appointment as soon as they allow (which is often right around Labor Day). And for any out-of-towners reading this, who've found out late in the season that they've got to deal with getting kids into school in another city, don't panic. Admissions directors are inclined to bend rules for parents transferring into a city; they're not heartless you know.

Restrain yourself. Although we have suggested that you cast a wide net when looking at schools, at some point you need to make a short list. Whatever school level you're applying to—nursery, preschool or kindergarten—try and limit your completed applications to five or six per child. Any more than that and you will completely exhaust yourself and your child in the process. Plus, you

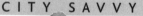

Checking Out a School's After School

Private schools run the gamut in their after-school offerings for elementary-age kids. Some schools have full-fledged programs: Children can stay late attending classes in art, drama, chess, music, and sports. Some schools will even schlep kids back and forth to swim or skating lessons. Other schools have nothing. Personally, we like the programs. They'll cost you extra, of course, but it can be far more efficient and easier than trying to get the same experience for your child on your own. Plus there's a big socialization factor, as these types of programs tend to be very popular among the younger kids.

literally will not be able to distinguish between any of the schools by the time you've taken all the tours, done all the interviews, and attended all the open houses.

Make sure you're actually done. The application package will list everything the school requires to evaluate your child. Incomplete submissions will be ignored, and it's up to you to make sure the school has all the pieces. Do yourself a favor and check with every school, several weeks before the application deadlines to see if anything's missing.

The Tour

The tour should be a really important part of your investigation. After all, it's your chance to get a firsthand sense of the school's personality, the tenor of the kids, and the pace of the classrooms. But if you don't gear yourself to really focus on what you're seeing, you'll join the legions of parents who say that all their school visits blurred together.

You won't have a lot of time to gather your impressions. Typically, you walk the school with a bunch of other parents; sometimes you'll only see the lower school facilities (you are applying for kindergarten, after all). You may spend a little (we mean little) time in a couple of classrooms; if this doesn't appear to be a stop on your tour, ask to see some—it'll give you a perception of the school you can't get any other way. Often, there's a question-and-answer session with someone from the administration—possibly the director of admissions, maybe the head of the lower school. Most of your questions, though, will be answered by your tour guide, who could be the director of admissions or a parent or student volunteer. As a result, the quality of information and insight you'll get from your guide will vary considerably.

As cursory as it all may seem, you still need to wring out of it what you can. You want to look for everything—climate, teaching methods, facilities, interactions, examples of student work, the demeanor of the kids. When you get home, without fail, write down your impressions and significant comments made by tour guides and school staff. Notwithstanding your razor-sharp mind, by the time you have to make a decision maybe 6 months hence, your memories of individual schools will have merged into one big hazy mess. If that's not enough reason to commit your impressions to paper, think how helpful it will be having those notes to refer to when you're prepping for your interview or writing a thank-you note or first choice letter, if you go that far.

Everything You Always Wanted to Know about Admissions Testing but Were Afraid to Ask

Not all schools require admissions tests, and it's certainly not typical for admission to preschool. But at some point during the kindergarten search, it's more than likely that your child will be spending some time with a professional tester.

The Testing Experience

Admission tests differ from city to city, although most private schools within a given city use the same test (if they test at all). Popular ones include the Detroit Tests of Learning Aptitude, sometimes used for evaluating entrants to preschool, and the WPPSI-III (the newest revision of the decades-old WPPSI exams), a multi-part exam that takes a child about an hour to go through. These tests, and others like them, usually consist of a series of different exercises or subtests, designed to evaluate specific aspects of your child's cognitive makeup: listening skills, memory, persistence, ability to express himself and follow directions, ability to understand concrete and abstract concepts, and ability to process information.

Because they're geared to pre-readers, the tests are given to children individually by a professional tester. Your child will find the experience to be quite interactive: He'll be listening, talking, looking at pictures, manipulating puzzle pieces, and possibly engaging in some limited pencil-based activity. Typical tasks might include simple puzzles, copying shapes, being asked to characterize similarities between two things, looking for differences or missing elements in pictures, and answering lots of questions geared to discerning simple math ability, reasoning skills, and even auditory processing. Every tester is instructed to try and put the child at ease; most will explain to the child that some of the activities he'll do will seem easy and some will seem hard, and that's okay. Generally kids like the one-on-one attention and don't find the test boring—although many do tire by the end of the session and that will show up in the scores.

Where to Take the Tests

Although some schools prefer to use their own homegrown evaluation procedures, in cities like Washington, D.C., Houston, New Orleans, and Seattle your child will likely be taking a test with an outside professional. Some schools provide a list of testers with whom you can make an appointment. Others arrange for your child to be tested at their school; all you have to do is show up. Wherever you go, you can count on picking up the tab: $75 to $300, depending on the city.

The Scoop on the Scores

With all the money that parents are asked to blow on getting their children tested, you'd think they'd end up with a good understanding of what it all means. Not so. The customer here is really the school, and parents often get a lot less data on the test results than the school does (not to mention that most parents don't have the expertise to interpret what little information they do get).

Here's the most reliable overview we can give you. From the admissions director's perspective, tests scores and tester comments (to the extent the latter are provided) are both important. Educators really love to see scores all tracking within a similar range—it just makes their lives so much easier if they can sort of peg the child. And written comments from a tester can do much to shade the significance of the test scores, positively or negatively. Testers have their own code words so the import of seemingly offhand remarks is sometimes not apparent on the surface. (Admissions directors will be very interested to read, for example, that little Josie needed to be "refocused" or "redirected," a comment that would blow by most parents.) Do note that admissions directors today are all much more

The New York City Difference

In New York City, testing is handled by the Educational Records Bureau—hence the tendency of many parents to refer to that city's admission test (actually the WPPSI-III) as the ERBs. And in that city, by custom, certain preschools try and accommodate parents by arranging for testers to come to the school. Parents who don't have that luxury often feel at a disadvantage, thinking that in-school testing is easier on the child and that a tester assigned to a specific school is more likely to give high scores. As far as the former concern, whether it's a benefit really depends on the child. If your child has difficulty transitioning, you may well want him to test outside of the school so he doesn't get ticked off at the tester who's pulling him out of block time (that happens a lot). As for the latter, there are certainly differences in testers, although we expect that bad testers get weeded out of the process: Parents don't recommend them; schools don't ask them back.

careful about comparing the perception of a child gained during his interview with both test results *and* preschool reports, so they can rule out any, shall we say, artificial scores.

For your part, you can try, with the help of a willing preschool director, to assess whether your child's scores are in the ballpark for whatever schools you have in your sights—though even this is problematical. We know kids who've gotten very, very low scores and still gotten into reputedly tough schools. And there are no slam dunks: High scores don't guarantee admission anywhere. Second, you should ignore all the gossip on cutoff scores, school requirements, and the weighting of one subtest versus another. The rumor-mongering is invariably wrong; don't go there. Third, you can address any less than par test results by focusing on schools that don't require high scores. Some schools may believe in less academically tough environments; others may just be skeptical of the relevance of tests. And if there is any indication that the results signal a learning or behavioral problem, get an expert into the picture.

Getting Your Child in Top Testing Condition

You say you'll do anything to have your kid ace his admissions test? Okay, it won't be easy; it won't be fast. In fact, it really should take his entire lifetime, short as it is. Read all the early childhood literature and talk to educators, and you'll find what really make a difference are things like bringing them up in "linguistically and cognitively rich environments." You know what that means, don't you? Read to your kids every day. Give them lots of opportunities to imagine and create with LEGOs and paints and crayons and puzzles and trains and dolls and dress-up and the like. And have many, many conversations with them.

So that was the big picture. Now we'll move disturbingly quickly to the nitty-gritty of admissions tests.

Test scheduling. If you have any say in the matter, don't do it before (or after) Lisette goes to the circus; she'll be too excited to concentrate on any test questions. To the extent you can, it might be wise to schedule testing for the time of day that she's at her best. And if you're not given much choice, which is often the case, it's up to you to manage your child's activities before and after the test so that she's rested and relaxed.

Test prepping. This is what we consider *appropriate* test prep: sufficient rest, sufficient food, and a little calming explanation. Tell your darling that she's going to do some special work with a special teacher. (If the test is conducted at the potential new school and you have any doubts about what's going to happen, ask them what to tell your child. They will undoubtedly have very good advice.) Don't harp too much on any reward that'll be forthcoming. We've heard of kids who were

Test Prepping the Urban Way

You want to talk about cognitively and linguistically rich environments? Well, just step outside. Walk down the block and you've got a thousand things to talk about: fire engines, newspaper vendors, cars being towed away, a demonstration here or there. A summer day in the park brings out hippies and Frisbee players, dogs and street performers. You've got museums dedicated to the celebration of aspects of history and culture you probably didn't even know existed. You've got parades, street fairs, puppet shows, and probably thousands of music, theater, and art performances. Fun for you, fun for them, and good for you both. It is really the most fantastic part about being a city parent: the wealth of experiences that you can share with your child. Look, you can flash cards at your child till your hair turns gray, drill him in analogies and similes till you both can't stand the sight of each other—and it may help Caleb's test score, but just his test score, not his brain. Share your city with him on a daily basis. That will expand his mind.

so excited about what was going to happen after the test that they couldn't concentrate on the tasks at hand.

The clingy child. If you think Lisette is unlikely to be able to tear herself from your side, ask your spouse, a caregiver, or a friend to take her. It'll be easier on both of you.

Interviews: Yours, Mine, and Ours

You and your child may never even have to suffer through an interview, but if you're applying to a number of private schools, chances are good that one or all of you will be doing some talking.

Grownups First

Let's start with you. Don't make the mistake of thinking you're in the driver's seat when you go in to meet with the director of admissions or the head of the school. Treat it like a job interview in a depressed economy, and you'll have exactly the right attitude. You want to find out about them, and they want to find out about you and your child, so everyone should be on their best behavior.

The most prevalent interview situation is for the child's parents to meet with the director of the admissions office; less frequently, families are interviewed together. Sometimes you meet the head of the school or the lower school as well. The format and style of these little meetings can range tremendously. Some schools conduct very structured conversations with set questions. Others run more informal conversations. Don't be lulled either way; they're still checking you out. And you'll be best served if you understand that admission officers go into interviews with some very clear objectives. We'll explain.

Talking about your child. The admissions office's number-one objective is to find out more about your child. They're trying to triangulate all the information they're collecting to come up with an accurate picture of who this kid really is. In fact, a quite typical question is the wildly open-ended "Tell us about your child," so be prepared for that one. If nothing else, prep yourself with anecdotes and a more cogent description than the not particularly illuminating "He's a really happy guy." Another common, also obvious, school query is, "Tell me, why are you interested in our school?" You'll often get questions about the daily routines of your child and your family—pretty predictable stuff, but it's not at all unusual to get inquiries that frankly sound a little weird, like what was the birth like (an attempt at ferreting out whether there may be any learning issues lingering) and when did he

CITY SAVVY

Dressing for Success

What to wear to a school interview is yet another one of those things that people get way more stressed about than they should. Since everyone talks about "fit," it's pretty hard not to want to dress to fit in; but really, there's a lot more latitude than you think.

Kids wear. Conventional wisdom aside, even traditional schools certainly don't expect your little boy to be in a blazer or your little girl in a party dress when they come for their interview. Nice play clothes are absolutely fine, and the kids will probably feel and act more like themselves if they're not dressed for success (although washed faces and brushed hair would be nice).

Adult duds. The best advice is to be understated (unless that's really not you, in which case, let it all hang out up front). If the school requires uniforms or a more formal dress code, chances are the administration dresses more formally too. Nice pants and top for mothers, maybe a blazer for the dad would be sufficient, unless the parents dress more formally as a matter of course. In a clearly casual school where the teachers are in jeans, the parents always in sweats, you can probably lose the jacket and pearls. But we wouldn't dress too far down; maybe your best casual pants.

walk and talk. Be assured there's always a method to the madness. Well, usually. We know of one admissions director who's fond of asking people if they have a country house; we haven't quite figured out that one yet.

Talking about yourself. Objective number two is to find out about you. Schools want nice parents who understand and support what they're about and whom they can work with if a bump turns up somewhere down the road. Conversely, they are looking to weed out parents who will become problems. Criticizing your current school? Not a good idea. Trying to impress the interviewer with your wealth, social pedigree, or high IQ? Likely to fall flat. Where most people misstep is in the general behavior domain: being polite, attentive, and enthusiastic about this school and your child's ability to fit in are all good; yawning, interrupting, not listening to the questions that are asked, or taking off your shoes (it has been done) are not.

Both spouses really, really should attend. If you're divorced and simply can't stand your formerly better half, we suggest you put aside your differences for the duration of the interview. If you ask to come separately, you're just admitting (what apparently is the truth) that you can't work together in the interests of your child—and that would not exactly be considered a factor in your child's favor. If you truly operate as a single parent, don't worry about dragging along a recalcitrant ex or soon-to-be ex. Schools today are pretty familiar with all different kinds of family units. It won't be held against you.

Expressing your intentions. Objective number three is to determine how serious you might be about the school. Often you'll get asked about the other schools to which you're applying. If you're looking at a bunch of schools—single sex and co-ed, a range of educational philosophies—you'd better be proactive in explaining why the list is so varied as well as why their school might be at the top of that list.

Quite naturally, you will be expected to have questions too, ideally ones that indicate you've at least spent some time trying to understand the school and given some thought to its benefits for your child.

Starring Your Child

The child's interview comes in as many shapes and sizes as they do. Sometimes it doesn't even factor into the admissions decision, especially for the younger kids. In the less-competitive preschools, you won't be doing much more than filling out an application and looking at the facility for yourself. But if there is competition for places at the school, you can lay a winning bet that the school's going to want to see your child. Most times, your child will participate in a group "interview" with a bunch of other kids also being evaluated, although there are schools that prefer to see kids individually or in pairs. Monitoring them in either format could be anyone from the head of the school (or lower school), the admissions director, or sometimes simply teachers from the school.

For preschool, it's play play play. Preschool interviews are almost always just playing. We're talking about 2-year-olds (sometimes younger) here, most of whom

What to Ask and How to Ask It

Julia's husband was completely annoyed by the fact that he wasn't supposed to ask penetrating questions on tours or interviews (a dictum he resolutely ignored). How was it, he queried, that one is supposed to buy something for thousands of dollars a year—an experience that will have a major impact on the development of his child—and not be permitted due diligence? Well, that's the way it is. Think prayer, not purchase, and you've got the right attitude.

Now, admissions people *do* like questions, but they differentiate between perceptive queries and obnoxious ones.

We'll give you one freebie. One question parents are dying to know the answer to is the number of available openings. It's okay to ask, but it helps to acknowledge the challenges of the admissions office when you're framing the question. "We know you have siblings and legacies [and congregation members, if it's a preschool] to worry about. Do you have any idea how many openings you might have for the incoming class?" And you can ask if they think they need more boys or girls or later birthdays or early birthdays as well, although the admissions people probably won't really know until pretty late in the admissions cycle.

are still parallel playing, and directors don't expect more even if it looks like the kids are being marched through a set of structured activities. They also understand that very young children have pretty variable behavior and the capability of letting loose with a tantrum, especially when confronted with new situations. Now, that's not a death knell. Kids who wail their way through their school playdates have been known to get in anyway. But, it's clearly not helpful, particularly if the meltdown occurs at a school that's seeing a surge in demand. These days, admissions directors are looking for ways to winnow the pool of applicants, and negative behavior, however normal it is, can be enough to eliminate you from consideration. There's no reason why you can't ask for a second chance on the grounds that little Emily was off her game that day; sometimes she'll be granted another shot. Separation issues are probably a lesser concern. They're so common you may well be able to arrange a second chance. On the other hand, if little Yoshi throws a block at the teacher or bites one of his co-interviewees, you might as well rip up the application right there.

In kindergarten, seeing is believing. Kindergarten interviews are generally much more involved, and admissions directors take them very seriously. With the jump in applications and the increase in test results tainted by illicit tutoring, schools have come to rely increasingly on what they see with their own eyes. Some schools are more concerned with a child's social skills, feeling that how a child plays with others is an excellent gauge of readiness. Other schools run kids through a gauntlet of tests that are intended to replicate and supplement any standardized tests already taken. The child's performance on these tasks can carry significant weight, particularly at more selective schools—because every admissions director's nightmare is being called up by a board of trustees wanting to know how all these underperforming fifth graders were ever let into the school.

Most times, the educators running these group sessions are really pros. They get what they're after without making it a drag for the kids. In fact, most kids have a pretty good time performing the activities. What types of things are they called upon to do? Drawing; listening to and discussing stories; responding to general questions about life, school, and hobbies; puzzle manipulation; and simple arithmetic activities. The specifics change all the time, "otherwise we'd get bored," said one admissions director. Some tasks we've heard children asked to perform: count backward from 30, cut out and glue three circles to make a snowman, write their name. Sometimes, however, the interview format will be one-on-one, child and teacher. The activities are quite similar, although they may have a slightly less playtime feel.

What's your role in all of this? Certainly, you will have to give your child an explanation of where you're going. You may want to tell your child that you're looking at a bunch of schools for him for the coming year and the "playgroups" are a chance for him to see the school. Just as you would with the admissions test, make sure he's fed and rested and that the interview is scheduled at a time of day when he's likely to be at his best (some schools reserve Saturday mornings for child interviews). Have him taken to the school by whomever he's likely to separate from best. Do not be late. To fill any dead time between the time you arrive and the start of the session, bring a coloring book, something to read to your child, or whatever he would enjoy playing with quietly.

How to Guarantee Your Child Flunks the Interview

1. Let him know how nervous you are. Tell him how important this is, that he's going to visit a school that Mommy and Daddy want him to go to next year *more than anything*, and that he'll be playing with some very nice children who might be in his class (he'll be sure to hate them). Be sure to give him lots of rules at the same time: Don't pick your nose, don't make those burping sounds, answer all the teacher's questions, shake hands when you leave.
2. Schedule the interview during his naptime or after a long day at preschool. (Are you nuts?)
3. Bring him way too early. That'll give him loads of time to get antsy.
4. Give him *lots* to think about besides the test. Some bad ideas: buying a Halloween costume right before the interview so it's all he can think about or promising him a whole lot of fun right after the test, like going out for sundaes and maybe even playing video games. He'll be focused, all right—just not on what his interviewer is asking him.

AND ALL THE REST (LITTLE THINGS THAT COUNT BIG)

Okay, you've done the applications, a zillion essays, your child's been interviewed, you've been grilled, you laid out a couple hundred dollars to get him tested—what else could schools possibly want from you? Plenty.

Recommendations

If your child's already in school, they'll want any existing school records plus a recommendation from his current school to be provided in a predetermined format (often area schools share a common format). Although those school recommendations tend to be written in the most favorable terms possible, they do nonetheless convey a lot of information. You will never see these reports, but you can probably assume the strengths and weaknesses that appeared on your child's nursery school evaluations will show up in some form. Some of *your* qualities may appear as well, since quite often the evaluation includes a section on the parents' involvement with the child and the school (this would be where a preschool director might indicate your predisposition to be "generous," for example). In fact, these school recommendations can go a long way to pushing your child into the yes pile—which is why you want to have been a good, involved parent at the school you're leaving.

Then there's the matter of personal recommendations: Some schools require them, some make them optional, and others make it clear they'd really prefer not to hear from anyone else. First rule of recommendations: Do not give a school more than it asks for. Second rule: Don't have a recommendation done unless it's by someone who really knows the child and family well. References written by a casual celebrity acquaintance are really a dime a dozen in cities chock-full of notables. They do not impress admissions officers, who get very jaded by parental attempts at influence. How about a recommendation from a family already at the school? "It's tricky," offered one preschool head. "We're all human beings, you know, so it depends if I like the person writing the recommendation." Ooohhh. That'll give you something to chew on: Not only do you need to find someone at the school who knows you well, you need to figure out if they're well liked. How about a letter from a trustee? It definitely gets more attention, but trustees get requests all the time, and some are very good at damning applicants with faint praise. On the other hand, if you do get a trustee to write a heartfelt letter on your behalf and your child is accepted, you darn well better make sure little Joe ends up attending.

Drop-By Visits

One other routine that kindergarten admissions directors employ—though less often when they're inundated with applications—is to visit a child at his preschool.

It's a great way to get a bead on what the child is really like in class. Generally, you'll get a heads-up from your preschool director. They want to make sure your kid shows, after all. But do not tell your child anything about the visit. Chances are, he won't really even notice anyone's watching him.

Thank-You Notes

We have heard diametrically opposed views about thank-you notes. Some professionals think they're de rigueur, but others have said they're just another unnecessary piece of paper. We could almost flip a coin on this, but even though neither of us ever did them (and our mothers are not happy about that), we recommend that you send them out. Just make sure you do them after the interview, rather than the tour, and certainly don't send two. Don't spend hours drafting the letter either. It's pretty much the same exercise as what you'd go through thanking a hostess for a nice dinner. Mention how much you enjoyed the meeting, describe some particular comments from the director (or whomever it was you actually spent time with) that resonated with you, and, ideally, make the school especially suitable for darling Jacqueline. Reiterate (because we assume you said this in the interview) how impressed you are with the school and then close politely. That's all there is to it.

First Choice Letters

The first choice letter is so named because it's the one you send to a school telling them that their institution is your "first choice" for little Sophie. It's not a designation to bestow lightly, because accompanying it is an implied promise that Sophie will indeed attend that school if she gets in. This letter is a tricky little proposition with a much greater chance of backfiring on you than a simple thank-you note can. Independent school associations have struggled over recent years with whether or not they should even be allowed because of the pressure it puts on parents. In really competitive cities, however, the cow is already out of the barn, and many parents send them because they think they have no choice. Do they? There's no question that admissions directors do consider them when weighing candidates. After all, the board will want to know their "yield"—how many of the children they accepted are actually coming. If the director sends out a bunch of acceptances only to find that half of those candidates are going elsewhere, that could really screw up a carefully constructed class. And if the openings are tight, having the first choice letters really makes life easier. Said one admissions officer, "If you have a class that's going to be full of siblings and have only 10 or 12 openings, you probably will make all your acceptances from the first choice pool."

But it's not an absolute rule. The admissions director quoted above was quite heartfelt in her insistence that she doesn't usually restrict herself to first choice letters to fill her slots. We've also heard of admissions directors who disregard the letters entirely because of the large number of parents who write first choice letters to every school on their short list. Yet another consideration for the child moving on from preschool is what the policy of the current school is. If it's known that the preschool director recommends first choice letters, an ongoing school that doesn't receive one from you may assume that you sent one elsewhere. Your takeaway:

Check out the competition. If you're in a competitive city and applying to competitive schools, you certainly should consider writing one, if you can. But try and get a sense of whether the letter is going to have any impact.

Send out a scout. Ideally, your preschool director will make a call to the relevant admissions director saying something like, "The Ricardos really love your school and would like to write a first choice letter to you. Is little Ricky in the ballpark?" A direct answer probably won't be forthcoming, so make sure your director writes down the exact words. If the answer is something like, "Well, it's a tough admissions year, and we have a lot of applicants (yada, yada, yada)," you're wasting a stamp. Sometimes, it may take a couple of attempts to get a favorable reception, so the whole process becomes one of determining what one preschool head calls a "negotiated first choice" (something to remember when all those other parents tell

And a Winning First Choice Letter Is . . .

The best advice we've heard is to "write from the heart." Sounds pat, but if you use some canned version that is purported to open all doors, you may just end up sounding like everyone else—and what good does that do?

- Admissions directors really are swayed by parents who genuinely like (and understand) their school and believe that it will provide a truly brilliant home-away-from-home for their child. If that's how you feel, write why you think that way, what really impressed you, and why it works for your child.
- A tome is neither necessary nor desired—no one's going to read it; just a thoughtful paragraph or two.
- If grammar and spelling are not your friends, get a more literate acquaintance to edit for you. Typos are just never a good idea (by the way, one admissions director told us how amazed she is at how often her name gets misspelled; and you thought they didn't notice).

How to Get Your Child Eliminated from Consideration in 10 Easy Steps

Step 1. Have your secretary (or consultant) call the school. Oh, schools hate that. It's rude. It makes you seem uninterested. It may even result in you never actually getting that application.

Step 2. Accept a cell phone call during a tour or interview. Every admissions person and consultant we talked to just about frothed at the mouth over this one. Turn the phone off before you go on the tour or to the interview—and lose the BlackBerry too; you don't want to be tempted.

Step 3. Ask a confrontational question like "Where's your diversity?" Or "Why should we send our son here?" Or simply be rude to anyone, anywhere, at some time in the process. You'll be nailed and probably appropriately. Schools don't want obnoxious people (even if you didn't intend to be obnoxious, that's the way you'll come off) because they tend to be the ones who are most difficult to deal with when little Jackson hits a bump at some point in his educational career.

Step 4. Dress inappropriately. You know, wear three-piece suits to that arty downtown school or jeans and tie-dye to that uptight uptown one. Schools want people who fit in with their gestalt (why shouldn't they?), and if you don't, you'll be pruned.

Step 5. Ask for special treatment, a personal interview if the school doesn't offer them, an extra tour. Schools have barely enough time to deal with the normal process, so they just looovvvve people who ask for more. Although they're prepared to be more than gracious after you get in (and before you accept), they have no patience with those who want extra attention before the fact.

Step 6. Give schools more (or less) than what they ask for. Stuffing your child's folder with CVs, art samples, and lukewarm personal references just irritates admissions directors.

Step 7. Renege on a first choice. This probably won't affect the child, but you'd better not have a second child coming along down the road.

Step 8. Apply later rather than earlier. Overburdened admissions offices, which have to discriminate among hundreds of pretty similar candidates, will just assume that you couldn't have been that interested if you applied a month after applications season opened.

Step 9. Reschedule an appointment. Schools just aren't terribly happy about moving stuff around, so if you don't have an excellent reason—major surgery comes to mind, business engagements don't—keep the appointment.

Step 10. Offer a cash bribe. We're not saying that money doesn't matter at all in this process, but, please, a bribe?

you that such-and-such school was their first choice; maybe it was, but only after three other "first choices" flashed a quick thumbs down).

When all else fails, test the waters yourself. If your child is not in school currently or your current school head is useless (it happens), you're on your own. You can try and get a sense from the admissions director yourself, but the conversation could easily become awkward if you ask directly about the first choice letter. A better route is to place a call (admissions directors really don't mind if you call once or twice with a question) to see how the applicant pool is shaping up and remind them how great you think the school is. You'll have to be perceptive, but the director's response might give you an idea of where you stand.

You have some time. You certainly don't want to write a first choice letter before you've completed all the steps at all the schools you're considering. Nor do you want to take a chance that the letter arrives too late. The best timing is probably right around the school's deadline for accepting applications. The letter can arrive after that date, but we wouldn't wait too long.

YES, NO, MAYBE SO: THE BEST STRATEGIES FOR THE WAITLISTED AND DENIED

You've been to more open houses than you care to admit, schmoozed endlessly with parents of kids attending the schools you aspire to, did the best you could to deliver a happy, well-rested child to the testing denizen. After a point, there is no more you can do—except wait to see if your prayers are answered. In many cities, acceptances are issued on a "common reply date." This is the date when members of the local independent schools all agree to send out their responses in order to eliminate confusion and timing issues for people caught between schools (these dates may be different for preschools and kindergartens). Generally there's also a common response date for acceptances, which means parents and schools muddle through a few anxious, confusing days waiting for all the dust to settle.

Of course, if your child is accepted at his top choice, no worries. Just make sure you *immediately* take your child's name out of contention at every other school to which he was either accepted or waitlisted, so that those places are freed for others still in the hunt. Some situations require a little more finesse.

You're Accepted at One School but Waitlisted at Your Favorite

Most likely, the school that gave you the nod also gave you a date to respond by; until then, you're free to play the field. Don't just sit around waiting for the phone to ring. Our advice:

Call the waitlist school. Tell them (1) you want to remain on the waitlist;

(2) you love the school; and (3) you will definitely attend if offered a place. You can certainly ask what your chances are. The admissions director may tell you to call back in a few days; otherwise, it's okay to check in every day.

Get appropriate third parties to place a call on your behalf. Round up whoever's predisposed to be helpful—your preschool director, an influential parent—and ask them to put in a good word for you.

Don't turn down another offer too soon. Your child needs a place so, no matter what, make sure you keep one acceptance on the hook. Bear in mind, wait-lists are funny things and each school uses them differently. Some keep very short ones; other schools have a reputation of putting almost everyone on a waitlist, sparing parents the sadness that comes from an outright rejection. Your chances of getting an actual acceptance can be great or terrible, but you won't know that from the sheer fact of being waitlisted.

You've Gotten All the Letters and Your Child Is Only on Waitlists

Immediately call every director of admissions and tell them your plight. Most are truly sympathetic to how difficult the process is for parents, and if you're on the cusp, your sad story may bump your child up on the list. If your child's in preschool, this is the moment when the preschool director should be burning up the phone lines on your behalf.

The Acceptance Period Is Over and Your Child Has Not Gotten in Anywhere

An admissions director described a phone call she had gotten at the end of her last admissions cycle. It was from a father ("it's usually from the father," she says) who was devastated to learn that his son had been rejected from every school to which he'd applied. "I feel like I failed," he said. "You didn't," she replied. "You just lost round one. Now you're on to round two." And she proceeded to give him a very sensible list of actions relevant for any parent with a child who seems like he's been left out in the cold.

Sit tight. If your child was waitlisted anywhere, let those schools know that you would like to remain on their waitlist (*if* they maintain it; some terminate it at the end of the current admissions cycle). Call periodically, particularly at the end of the summer, to see if there are any openings. Let them know that you're willing to hang out as long as you have to, to get your child in (and that you'll be back trying again the next year if that's what it takes). Persistence can pay off; just don't whine or become obnoxious.

Dig deeper. Find out if there are any openings that haven't been filled in schools to which your child didn't apply. Preschool directors often know of openings; local independent schools associations might be able to help (in New York City, the Educational Records Bureau and the Parent's League both track openings just for this reason). Call ongoing schools directly and ask if they have a place. See if you can submit an application for consideration should a spot free up.

Be safe. Find out what your public school options are (if you haven't already planned for this) and get Tiffany enrolled. Then do the work for first grade to move her to a better private or public situation if it's warranted.

Think out of the box. Consider having your child stay an extra year at his current preschool (if he was applying to kindergarten) and then reapply next year for either kindergarten or first grade. If the issue is preschool, think about bypassing a formal program entirely in favor of an ad hoc year that you construct out of a range of different classes you enroll your child in (art, movement, music, etc.). Alternatively, for either age, you can look at full-day day care centers that may not have been on your original list. Some do have kindergarten equivalent programs, and since many operate on a rolling admissions basis, slots often come open.

CHAPTER 13

YOU *CAN* WIN:
A PUBLIC SCHOOL PRIMER

▪ ▪

It hurts just thinking about it. The battles, the struggles, the emotional cuts and bruises you'll acquire over the next year as you set about to get your child the best city public education possible. Just trying to understand who's on first and what's on second can defeat even the hardiest of us.

We're not going to gloss over the grim stuff: Confusion reigns in just about every large public school system we've examined. And in too many places, Byzantine systems make what should be so straightforward, like applying to a neighborhood school, unbelievably complicated. In cities, where magnet schools and special programs abound, for instance, you'll need to apply to a bunch—10 to 15 schools is not unusual in Chicago these days—because the competition for the handful of great schools that exist in every city is so fierce.

We certainly can understand why some parents give up before even trying and haul off to the 'burbs. But don't let that be you. Because the rewards of winning this war are well worth a few minor scars: a great—no, in many cases, a spectacular—*free* education. Kathy is proud to have gone city public all the way through to her Ivy League college. And while she worried that public schools wouldn't cut it for Alice, now after having researched this chapter, she's more convinced than ever that Alice too will triumph in public school.

There are great schools, filled with great teachers, in every city. The trick is identifying them and then getting your child into them. *This is doable!* But it will entail an unusual degree of legwork, organization, and in some cases, a little urban assertiveness.

Every city works differently, but wherever you live, you must expect to do a major amount of research to validate the quality of your local school. You'll also need to get all your ducks in order for applying to that school and even find some backup or replacement schools, should this not work out. This will all take time—

and much more of it than you're probably anticipating. But before you can even get to the nitty gritty (did anyone say gritty?) of figuring out how to get Drea into perfect public school #1, you need a bird's-eye view of how things *really* work. We've outlined some underlying principles for you. The first four apply to identifying good schools, the rest to how you need to act, think, and even feel while dealing with them.

THE CITY PARENT RULES
A Public School Cheat Sheet

Rule #1: Money does talk. Ironically, unlike private school, where wealth may or may not be a factor, in the public domain just follow the money and you'll find the best schools. The public school options for Kathy's Alice are promising because Kathy and her husband decided that even the prospect of an Alice meant that schools should be a major factor in their apartment purchasing decision. Instead of buying a huge loft in a transitioning area (whose schools still reflected the area's more challenged times), they took the smaller space in a pricier area that had long-established great public schools. Parents of school-age children in cities across the country face the same sort of Hobson's choice: Go for less living space in a neighborhood with better schools or opt for the more attractive living conditions and lesser schools.

It's an ugly American truth—particularly to the many fervent public school advocates who believe wholeheartedly in equality of education—but the richer the 'hood, the better the schools. You'll find this to be the case whether you live in Chicago or Los Angeles or Phoenix or Houston. Others can argue the politics of it; we're just going to explore the facts. Here are some things to think about.

- Higher socioeconomic areas are usually associated with more parental involvement and louder, more vocal or politically astute parents—all crucial factors in public education.
- Research suggests that there is a relationship "between school system effectiveness, the socioeconomic status of families in the community, and the educational level of parents." William Bainbridge, CEO and president of SchoolMatch, a national educational research and consulting organization, points out that teachers tend to prefer higher socioeconomic districts. Working conditions are often perceived to be better, and posts in such areas are presumed to provide better potential for career advancement. Further, Bainbridge points out, teachers in such districts also tend to have: higher grade-point averages in their college work; higher achievement (according to

standardized tests scores); previous teaching experience; better, more influential references; more positive results on background-check.

- And here's something thoroughly depressing: In schools where 25 percent of the student population lives in poverty, *all* the students, including the rich and middle class ones, typically underperform compared to students from schools in wealthy communities.

Rule #2: The principal rules! In city schools, the principal is paramount. The most active and effective principals are those who have a strong sense of vision for their school and the know-how to implement it. They are open to parents and staff and reach out to the local community and businesses to expand the resources available to their schools. Look for the grants and outside programs, and you'll know a lot about the principal's effectiveness. "This indicates whether a principal is active and politically astute, whether the person can attract much needed outside funding. At the very least, it means someone is sitting down and writing out the proposals," says Lenore Michaels, whose son attends a New York City public school that has programs with the city's American Craft Museum, the Guggenheim, Midori violin, and the Museum of Natural History.

Of course, you have to establish that a school even has a principal. In the more tumultuous of city school systems, acting principals are often in place, and they don't have nearly the kind of clout or leadership needed for the best of schools. "When my son first went to his school," recalls one urban mom, "there was no principal for two years. We were starting to get very nervous, and if it had gone on one more year, it would have been disastrous."

Acting or not, you'll want to meet and greet the principals in place. You can get a sense of their style and the way they interact with passersby, teachers, and other staff, along with children and parents.

Rule #3: PTAs rule too! There's no question that parental involvement can make or break a school. In every city, the best schools have the most active parent-teacher associations. As the de facto watchdog over the school, good PTAs—run by and consisting entirely of parent volunteers—will make sure that the powers-that-be are doing their jobs. If a building is falling apart, for instance, an active PTA can make the difference between repairs and ruin. If parents don't like the quality of a certain teacher, rest assured a boisterous and powerful PTA will leave a principal with no choice but to rectify the situation. "In a school with high parental involvement," explains veteran PTA member Michaels, "the PTA will complain and complain and complain until something's done."

But perhaps even more important, local PTAs are now picking up the city's budgetary slack. Increasingly, PTAs have moved away from pure advocacy to fundraising, and their efforts are responsible for all those lovely "frills," which in today's era of economic frailty can mean paying for teachers' salaries, not just the extras. Art and music instruction, computers, drama classes, after-school programs, sports programs, whole-day kindergarten offerings, books, guidance counselors—you name it, the PTA is behind it. In the wealthiest city neighborhoods, PTAs have been known to bring in astronomical sums—$300,000 a year at New York City's posh PS 6, for example.

Active PTAs are prevalent, and highly effective, in less-posh neighborhoods too. In fact, parents we've spoken with take particular pride in the impact they can make in less well-to-do neighborhoods. Wherever you are, the best schools are helped by principals who work in tandem with, not against, the PTAs. So look for schools where there is a true spirit of cooperation. And please participate in PTA fund-raising efforts. Whatever you can afford will be appreciated; they're asking for necessities, not just frills.

Rule #4: Go where you're the minority. We know this sounds horribly racist to divide along these lines, but here's an unspoken truth: Applying to a predominantly ethnic school, where *your* child would be in the minority, ups her chances for gaining admission. Not that administrators always cop to this, but when they have admissions discretion, many schools make racial/ethnic balancing a priority. Some administrators do fess up. Clara Hemphill, author of *New York City's Best Public Elementary Schools*, reports on her site about NYC schools, Insideschools.org, that principal Janet Won, of top-rated Chinatown PS 124, would like the school "to be more ethnically diverse and particularly encourages applications from children who are not of Chinese ancestry." The "go where you're the minority" theory works for all races—if your child is African American applying to an all-white school, Asian applying to an all-Hispanic school, Native American applying to just about anywhere, etc.

By the way, you may want to get those Asian schools on your radar if they're not already. Asian children are among the highest-performing ethnic groups in school tests, and not unexpectedly quite a few Asian-dominated communities have schools that are among the best in their city. In San Francisco, for instance, four predominantly Chinese American Westside elementary schools recently topped the most competitive public school in that district, according to the city's Academic Performance Index (API). New York City's vibrant Chinatown schools, too, consistently turn out high test scores. In fact, of the neighborhood's seven schools, six boast top reading and math scores.

Rule #5: It pays to be pushy. Given our general inclination to be nice/be helpful, telling you to do otherwise may seem a bit hypocritical. But for the record, you can be pushy *and* polite. To get what you want out of public schools, absolutely everyone we spoke with expressed this sentiment in some form or another—from parents who learned the hard way to those who were successful from the start; from educators who deal with assertive parents all the time to administrators in mega positions of power.

What do we mean? Get out there, be vocal, and don't drop the ball. Chances are if you're willing to fight long and hard enough, you will ultimately prevail. Advocating for your child works not only in terms of getting, say, special education benefits or into the exact class you want, but also getting in altogether.

Take the case of Oakland public school mom Susan Bower. When she learned that her youngest, Emily, had not gotten into her older brother's elementary school (where the family was not zoned), did she give up? No, she went straight to the principal. "Being pushy and knowing that it's 'okay' to go and talk to the principal was key," she recalls. And apparently the tactic worked for quite a few other families that year. So many had expressed their dissatisfaction about not getting in that the school actually was able to add another kindergarten class to accommodate them! (Remember—power in numbers!)

Rule #6: Beware the bureaucrats. Never, never forget, many of the individuals involved in the process—from those answering phones at the district office to those reviewing applications for special needs or school choices—are civil service workers entrenched in a great deal of paperwork and bureaucracy. So don't make a mistake on applications and forms. You leave out a line, you forget to dot your i's, well, guess what? You don't pass Go!

CITY SAVVY

You Can Get the Teacher You Want

Assertiveness, apparently, works wonders in terms of teacher selection too. Pretty much everywhere, the official rule is you can't pick your children's teachers. But those in-the-know, know otherwise. Sharon Jones, who heads up the Gifted and Talented division of Atlanta's city schools and taught in gifted classes there for 20 years, believes that parents can advocate to "make sure their children get the good classes and the good teachers."

Our suggestion: Do your homework on next year's teachers to find the one who best suits your child's personality, learning style, and past school experience. Then write a note to the principal describing your child in those terms, suggesting that your choice would be a wonderful match. At the same time, lobby any of your contacts within the school for a little support.

3 Essential Reasons to Join the PTA

Here's why it behooves you to get active.

1. You'll learn about what's happening at the school on a political, citywide level.
2. You'll have valuable in-your-face presence with the movers and shakers of the school.
3. You can really impact the school for the benefit of your children and those who follow.

Rule #7: Watch for changes. In public schools, things change constantly all throughout and between school years. Districts, programs, principals—all can move with a rapidity that greatly surpasses the fluctuation in private schools. So, you have to stay on top of the dynamics in your child's school, district, and the city's public school system as a whole, because there can be meaningful change at each of these levels that will filter down to color your child's experience.

Rule #8: There are good public school parents. Now go become one. How? Get involved, make yourself helpful, and respect your children's teachers. The efforts of parents are critical to the success of good public schools and you need to do your part. You can get some ideas of how to participate from parent bulletin boards and the PTA. If group work at the PTA is not your thing, there's still a lot you can do on your own in Carly's classroom. Make sure the teacher knows you are "willing to do the grunt work that frees up their time to teach," writes one mother on the Salon.com message board, who now has a third child in her school's G&T program. Her strategy: Approach the teacher at the school's first scheduled informal visit to let her know her availability (once a week, twice a month, whatever); writing a note works well too. Offer to help in the classroom, make photocopies, set up bulletin boards—whatever the teacher wants. "Now," reports the savvy mom, the teachers "sometimes even contact me before the year starts if they know one of my kids will be in their class." And there's a fringe benefit to all this hard work. "You will be known in the school and known to the teachers, and they will respect that and so will your child. You can have influence over which teacher your child gets, what trips they go on, after-school activities, etc," writes one NYC public school elementary teacher on the Urban Baby message board.

Rule #9: There are bad public school parents. Hands down the worst public school parent in the city is the one who drops off Theo at school and thinks his education will take care of itself. Maybe you can get away with this in the private domain, but it's not the smartest behavior in the public one. Not only that, it's not fair to the other parents who will do the necessary pitching in and to your children who deserve more from you. So do your share. (Not sure how? Read rule #8 one more time.) A lesser, but still absolute no-no is being inconsiderate of teachers' time. Here's a profile of the drive-all-the-others-nuts parent: She goes up to Miss Clavel in the morning as all the other little imps are arriving and embarks on a lengthy discussion about her Madeleine, while Miss Clavel is trying to get her posse organized and settled. And just in case you think we're exaggerating, here's how one parent describes it: "I am all for finding out what Snotleigh is doing, but hey lady, I got a kid in this class too. Why the hell do you get to chat the teacher up for 20 mins. while we all wait?" If you have something to discuss with the teacher, leave a note, a phone message, or an e-mail if that's how she likes to correspond with parents.

No Child Left Behind: It May Affect You . . . If Only We Could Tell You How

Despite the fact it won't be fully implemented until 2005, President George W. Bush's No Child Left Behind legislation, conceived to enhance public education, is already having significant planned and unplanned impacts on city schools. The law, which has a variety of provisions aimed at improving poorly performing schools, requires that all states issue annual report cards for individual schools (FYI: many cities are already doing this). Parents of children in "failing" schools will be given top priority to transfer their children to a better-performing public school as well as be entitled to take advantage of free tutoring for their children.

Well-intentioned as it may be, it is completely unclear what impact the legislation will have on the size of classes in desirable schools and on the average parent's ability to get their child transferred into a good school—let alone on the overall quality of city schools. In New York City, parents whose children were at failing schools found their list of "choices" hardly an improvement: The local alternatives were often equally poor performers. The more acceptable schools were often located far away, even in other boroughs with commute times that were less than acceptable for elementary-age kids. And in high schools, where travel is much less of an issue, hugely overcrowded classes were reported at many of the more desirable schools. Clearly, the process has more than its share of kinks, and public school parents will be well-advised to stay abreast of developments.

PUBLIC SCHOOL OPTIONS AND M.O.S

In the city, when you make the decision to put your child in public school, you're barely at the starting line. You won't have just one school to consider: You potentially have dozens of possibilities to whittle down into a list of preferred candidates. And well before you even get to the point of looking at individual schools, you need to first understand the system. That means deciphering the types of schools that exist in a city and the application and admissions process for each. Sound complicated? You betcha.

Loosely defined, most urban public schools fall into one of three basic categories: (1) regular neighborhood school, often referred to as zoned schools; (2) specialty schools, which have some special form of educational programming and, depending on the city, may go by the names magnet, alternative, and focus (the latter not to be confused with poorly performing schools that are under special scrutiny); and (3) schools set up under special state mandate, referred to as charter schools. To these we add our own special group: (4) schools and programs for children deemed to be *gifted and talented*. Technically some of these would be considered to be alternative schools, but we're grouping them together because collectively they all have a shared admissions hurdle: *testing*.

The Neighborhood School: Regular or Zoned School

Statistically, this is the type of school that most kids attend. It's the school (or sometimes the small group of schools, as in San Francisco and Boston) that your child is zoned for and, by law, entitled to go to (except when you can't get in, read on). In a nutshell: Your local elementary school will either be good or bad. If yours happens to be the former (and we'll explain how to determine that later on), well hallelujah, you've found the holy grail of public education. Your school is: free; near your home (probably within walking distance); filled with lots of like-minded little tykes all primed and excited about learning; and the envy of all your friends. What's more, all you have to do to get Leo in is to register him. Period.

Yes, compared to some of the other public school options, this one's a fairy tale—but don't start celebrating quite yet. In some highly competitive and crowded cities, even though it's technically your right to send your child to the local school, it's eminently possible that your child could be left without a space if you're not on top of the situation. Most registrations are on a first-come, first-served basis. When the school fills up, your children will be redirected to another school; if your local school is a good one, the spaces will fill up fast.

If you're in a city that works this way, take nothing for granted. Make sure you understand the registration process. If the application is to be mailed, get it in by the earliest possible date. If you have to show up, get in line to register on the day you're supposed to, and fill out the forms correctly. And remember to bring all the documents that are required—usually your disease-free child's inoculation records, proof of address, and proof of birth. We recommend getting in line early in the morning the day of registration, if that's even early enough. The *Washington Post* reported parents at one school started lining up at 11—the night before! You gotta do it, but you gotta have a sense of humor too. As one NYC parent who was in line during the wee hours in a snowstorm quipped, "This is worse than a Bruce Springsteen concert!"

If you don't get in because there were just not enough places or you were a little late, do not give up. Go immediately to the school's principal, and tell him or her how disappointed you are and what a valuable asset you'll be to the school. Ask to be put on a waiting list. Enroll your child somewhere else, but then show up the day when school administrators are back at work (usually a week before the kids start; in many locales, this will be the day after Labor Day) to see if any spaces have opened up.

Specialty Schools (Magnet, Focus, Theme, Unzoned, Choice, and More)

Now, on the other hand, if your neighborhood school is underperforming or scary, your job is to do anything you can to get Destiny into a better one. It's time to exercise your right to choose. Sometimes that means trying to transfer to a better neighborhood school. Sometimes it means picking another type of school entirely.

In addition to regular schools, most cities offers a number of specially programmed schools (or sometimes programs within regular schools), open to kids from all over the city that, guess what, have their own unique application process.

Opting Out? How to Do It

Those parents who will be choosing not to have their children attend the local zoned school will have to follow whatever process is in place to move to a different school—and follow it carefully. This often entails filling out one form to register for the local zoned school and then another to apply for an intra- or inter-district transfer, depending on the location and type of the intended school. In some locales, this can be accomplished all in one spot; in others, you'll need to schlep just a little more.

Montessori for Free!

The Montessori method of educating children—where kids are encouraged to learn through hands-on experience and at their own pace (or in small groups) in mixed-age classes—is carving out a place in urban public school systems across the country. These Montessoris tend to be wildly popular, probably because interested parents believe that Montessori provides an excellent academic leg up for students. Formats differ. Some cities have full-fledged stand-alone Montessori schools; some run Montessori programs housed in a regular school (maybe even just one class). And admissions vary as much as the program type: Some are by lottery, some first-come, first-served, and some screened (children with some earlier Montessori experience do better in the latter case). And some will even ask parents to make donations; the average going rate is about $1,000 annually.

Here are three Web sites that will help your search for public Montessori programs in your city: www.montessoriconnections.com, www.amshq.org, and www.jolapub.com.

Many such schools were developed under magnet programs intended to foster desegregation, the theory being that focused or theme programming could draw all kinds of kids to a school, even one in a distressed neighborhood. Whatever the name, you can recognize these schools because they're typically organized around a special theme, say art/music, math/science, foreign languages, the humanities, etc., or a particular teaching method or philosophy.

Today, in fact, many specialty schools are praised as wonderful paradigms of diversity, with children of mixed socioeconomic and ethnic backgrounds (that's the point, after all) and academic abilities including English language skills. The mix notwithstanding, the school bodies are often surprisingly cohesive. Why? Possibly shared values. The very act of choice is a filter: Magnet parents are by nature proactive. As a result, these schools tend to have high levels of parent involvement, students who are often very motivated, and teachers who take pride in the school. The thinking goes: There's a built-in and desirable selectivity when parents go to all the effort to research a specialty school and then jump through whatever hoops are necessary to get their children into them.

In many cities, this "thinking" has borne out. A study of San Antonio, Texas, schools found that "relative to non-choosing parents, choosing parents are more educated, wealthier, more involved in their children's education at home and at school, and hold higher educational expectations for their children's education." Children applying to choice programs also were found to have higher standardized test scores. On magnets specifically, studies have shown that "virtually all magnets now have long waiting lists, despite that in many, students have to travel long distances to school, the class day is longer, and the work is harder than in nonmagnets." And in the magnet-heavy Chicago public school system, only two of its magnet schools didn't fall within the top third of the city's schools.

Of course, better may not be good enough, particularly if your baseline is the rather abysmal typical city school. So maybe not every specialty school is worth that second look—but many are, and you would be shortchanging your child to ignore the category completely.

And Keep in Mind . . .

If you do look, keep a couple of considerations top of mind. First, the good specialty schools generally have many more applicants than places. Most rely on a lottery to determine admissions, often first giving preference to siblings and children living within a specified geographic area. A few have other hurdles (and we're not talking about the academically advanced ones, which we've lumped into the next section)—mostly to determine that the parents and child are in sync with the theme of the schools. They sometimes require teacher recommendations and in-person meetings (of child or parents or both).

Second, free transportation is not guaranteed. Often it's limited to students living within a prescribed distance from the school. Fall outside that radius and you will have to provide your own wheels.

The very big plus: Some of these schools are really excellent. If the type of philosophy or subject meshes well with your child's own developing personality, it may be the best of all possible worlds (did we mention it's free?).

Charter Schools

Charters are public schools that operate independently of a city's board of education and are open to students throughout the city. Your tax dollars support them, but they are run by individuals or groups or private companies and are not bound by many of the state and city regulations, including those for curriculum, teacher hiring, pay, even number of school days, which sometimes hog-tie the typical public school.

Charters are certainly interesting from a historical and political perspective, but as an educational option for your child, you may be hard-pressed to find one to get really excited about. So far, charters' test results have not been great. In fact, in mid-2003, when RAND Education released a report on California charter schools that suggested their results were only on par with traditional public schools, that was heralded as good news. A slightly more favorable take comes from a study by the Manhattan Institute that compared charter schools with public schools having like demographic and geographic characteristics, rather than comparing them with public school averages. In that comparison, students at the charter schools showed slight percentage gains in math and reading tests over their public school equivalents.

Why have they not been more successful? Staffing is often comprised mostly of inexperienced teachers and administrators. On the positive side, the teaching staff tends to be young and gung-ho—but let's face it, all the enthusiasm in the world won't compensate for a lack of experience and expertise. Many of these schools are in extremely problematic financial condition, and they all risk having their charters removed at any given time. There are exceptions—a few shining stars that give hope to the prospects for the whole charter school movement—but they are few and far between.

And Keep in Mind . . .

As time goes on and more charters develop experience and track records, they may indeed become a more universally viable option. For now, you don't have a compelling reason to think charter unless your city is home to one of the really good ones or, conversely, your public school options are undesirable. If you are looking at a charter, think hard about the following:

- Charters differ tremendously in tone and philosophy, and the newer, more experimental, ones are generally so young that it's hard to judge whether they are good.
- Charters with a longer history and track record tend to perform better. Just the fact that they've lasted says something about their management and financial strength. A report by the California Charter Development Center showed that charters that had been open for 5-plus years outperformed traditional public schools on the state's Academic Performance Index.
- The better charters often require serious involvement, sometimes making parents sign a contract that commits them to a certain number of volunteer hours as a condition of their child's acceptance in the school.

Bottom line: Proceed with caution.

Gifted and Talented Schools and Programs

Every city has a special set of accelerated learning programs—sometimes even whole schools—geared to "gifted" children who qualify by surpassing some cutoff on a specified intelligence test. Surprise, surprise, these programs typically deliver high test scores and attract great teachers and involved parents. They become almost self-generating engines of success, and the best ones exceed anything you'll find outside a city. Admission to one of these babies is a coveted prize, as evidenced by the roughly 3,000 applicants who take a stab at one of the 48 kindergarten slots at New York City's nonpareil Hunter College Elementary School. Getting your child into a G&T program is absolutely a worthy goal for a city parent, but it isn't nirvana. There are side effects to the process, to getting a space, even to being part of that world should your child be brilliant enough, or fortunate enough, to get in. None of these should make you want to give up the hunt, but a little foreknowledge won't hurt either.

It Takes a Genius to Decipher the G&Ts

First and foremost, as those Hunter supplicants would testify, there just aren't enough gifted and talented spaces to go around. Many kids who meet the standards still get shut out, especially at the youngest ages and even in the largest cities, which service hundred of thousands of students. Chicago has 11 regional gifted elementary schools (of which four don't start until first grade) plus four gifted magnets that require testing. Dallas has only seven gifted and talented elementary schools (their Vanguard programs); Los Angeles reportedly only has 400 places for the 1,600 elementary school kids who meet its highly gifted standards. Smaller cities can be even worse: Your child's chances of getting into whatever G&Ts exist are only slightly better than winning the Nobel Peace Prize (making them possibly even harder to get into than the coveted private school "baby ivies").

The process of trying to secure one of those few places is more than a little wearing on everyone involved. It's not just the private school audience who has to deal with the emotional repercussions of kindergarten competition. The G&T race has the same sort of high stakes feel, which often precipitates somewhat unhealthy behavior on the part of the highly competitive city parents involved. Even for the most balanced parents, being part of that whole scene can definitely cast a little shade on the school experience. And sadly, many of the formerly proud parents of the kids who don't make the final cut walk away from the process feeling like they and/or their kids are complete losers. So if you're going to join this chase, we have one word for you: *grip* (as in get a).

Because it won't be all roses even if your child does get in. The first week won't be over before you hear the faint mumblings of "elitism" under someone's breath as you pass by them. And God help you if your star is in a gifted and talented program housed within a larger, regular school, you might as well prepare for out and out class warfare, as your G&T program probably operates independently, with its own PTA, teachers, and budget. Battles will erupt between the "haves" and "have nots," and the latter will almost certainly argue "classism." So along with that fabulous education for your child, you will be taking on a hot, political climate, and we've heard it can get pretty darned nasty. NYC's highly lauded Anderson program is a great example. When parents mobilized to extend the elite elementary school program to middle school—an ordinarily fabulous event, given the dearth of good middle schools in that city—opponents were vociferous that the first priority should be to bring ethnic balance to the existing program.

Another issue for G&T programs is that their "home" can be pretty rough; it may be in a school you'd ordinarily avoid at all costs. There are plenty of ramifications for bright kids housed in a bad school or a bad neighborhood. As one parent jibes, "You're not surrounded by lily white cherubs of the same socioeconomic level, so if that bothers you . . ." Other parents lament that things can get a little dicey in common spaces like playgrounds and cafeterias. In such schools, the aides will sometimes handle children a little more gruffly than the parents are comfortable with or look the other way when bad language is bandied about. Says Michaels, whose eldest son is in a G&T at a "so-so" NYC public school, "We're pretty lucky that Julian is not a wimp." If her local zoned school had been better, she says she would have opted for it over a G&T.

If the G&T format you're looking at is a "pull-out" program, the issues are a little different. In these arrangements, which usually go into effect after kindergarten, children matriculate to a regular school but have the opportunity to take accelerated classes several hours a week. Drawbacks? Probably the most important negative is that parents won't know if their child is in the pullout program until sometime after the child has been in the school. Then, there is the enormous variation in the programs. Some run only one hour a week, others are all-day programs—meaningful differences given the view of some experts that anything less than five hours a week is unlikely to have a real impact.

Cities that rely on the pull-out concept also tend to start gifted and talented differentiation later, with the separation done by the school, usually based on the results of the school's normal standardized testing. What's the implication for the parent of a pre-K'er? If you think you have a bright one on your hand, you'll probably want to check out the pull-out programs at the different elementary schools you're considering, notwithstanding the fact that the little tyke may not be taking advantage of pull-out for a few years *and* not to mention the possibility that all your fine research may be for naught if and when the time comes you've moved or your child doesn't qualify.

Admissions to G&Ts

For full-fledged G&T schools and programs, you can expect a separate admissions procedure *and* a screening process that will involve at least some kind of IQ test. Each state (and often each city; sometimes individual schools) establishes its own definition of giftedness and its own rules for governing gifted education services. Because it's so specialized and relevant for just a small percentage of the city's kids, just finding out about the specifics can be a laborious task. Rarely will it be highlighted on a city board of education site.

To figure out your options, it's helpful to contact the person in charge of gifted programs at your city's board of education, particularly since you may want to be considering programs that are outside of your geographic area. Unfortunately, there's no standard title for this function. The programs are known as G&T, GATE, TAG, and Accelerated. Their directors could also be called coordinators, curriculum coordinators, administrators, or facilitators. So you may have to make a few calls to locate the right person. If your city is set up with area or district administration, you may also, or alternatively, go to the office covering your region (and possibly other regions; hope the idea of a little travel doesn't frighten you) and ask for help (they might also be able to direct you to a higher level person at the board of ed if you've been unsuccessful in locating that individual yourself). Finally, once you find the school and programs you're interested in, contact each individual school's gifted education coordinator to get the local lowdown.

Taking the Tests

In most venues, your child will need to take a standardized IQ test. The Stanford-Binet is a common one; the WPPSI and the Metropolitan Readiness Test are others. Generally, your child will be required to exceed a certain minimum percentage level: The cutoff varies by school, but 90 percent is fairly common. It can be much higher. New York City's Hunter, for instance, hovers around 97 to 98 percent, depending on the year. Or IQ may make the difference: In Miami, they use 130 (although lower thresholds apply for children from lower income or non-English speaking backgrounds).

Because we're talking about little kids here, who mostly can't read or write or operate a computer, the test is administered by a licensed psychologist or practitioner. Schools go a lot of different ways

CITYWISE WARNING !

Never Assume That All the G&Ts Operate the Same Way in Your City

If you're applying to more than one G&T program—especially two different types (say a full-scale specialty school across town and a G&T program housed in your neighborhood school)—there is some likelihood that your child will face different applications, deadlines, and tests. This will add to the costs, time, and stress imposed on you and your child.

A Gift for the Gifted

If you suspect your child is gifted, you might want to check out some of the specialized sites that exist to help parents develop their children's intellectual capabilities and deal with some of the less-joyful characteristics or situations that can accompany giftedness.

- www.hoagiesgifted.org is a compendium of articles, advice, and links and provides a wonderful primer on giftedness.
- www.nagc.org, the site of the National Association for Gifted Children (NAGC), has links to state-affiliated gifted advocacy groups and associations.

on this. Some have the testing on their turf: They give you the date and time to show up. Others offer a small group of testers from which to choose. Almost always, you'll be footing the bill for the exam (the going rate is anywhere from $50 to $150), though the fee can be waived if sufficient financial need is established.

Anxious parents debate the wisdom of having their child tutored for these admissions tests. It's not worth it, for reasons you almost assuredly already know: inaccurate results that will set up your child for failure later on, risk of being found out, setting a bad example, cheating, etc. Just don't do it.

Occasionally, the standardized test is only phase one of the admissions process. In some schools, particularly the most competitive ones with huge applicant pools, all the little Jasons and Janelles who meet the percentile cutoffs are invited to go through a second round of tests, generally some sort of on-site evaluation. The formats can range from small group "play" interviews to another round of standardized testing.

A special note about the tester. Schools that have *you* arrange the tests will generally provide you a list of acceptable testers. Don't be cavalier about your ability to choose here. Testers come in a lot of shapes and sizes. For sure, they are all following quite detailed outlines pertaining to the tests they are giving, which may cover when they can rephrase a question, how they can prompt a hesitant child, when they should ask for clarification, even what's a correct response and what's not. But within those guidelines, there are matters of individual style that can become quite important, particularly as their style works or doesn't work with your little tyke. The reality is hard to plumb. You'll hear horror stories about testers who are unfriendly, even mean. Generally, that means the parent didn't like the score coming back. Was that the tester's fault? You'll never know. Without a doubt, testers do have reputations, and if you're a proactive parent, it's pretty hard to accept the luck of the draw when picking a tester off a list.

List in hand, narrow down the choices. If your child is in preschool, you might be able to get some recommendations from the preschool director. Talk to other parents who've been through the process (that's another good question to ask the preschool director) and maybe even your pediatrician, to see if they have names. When you get your short list, it's time to get personal. Roxana Reid, co-founder of SmartCityKids, one of the many local services that have sprung up to help parents navigate the maze of New York City schools, suggests calling the prospective tester to set up a time to talk on the phone or maybe even meet in person. Some testers will often write up the previsit as a kind of psychological consultation, which health insurance may even cover.

"You'll at least get a sense of who they are through a voice conversation," she offers. "How do they sound? Are they abrupt with you, or thoughtful? Do they slow down their speech to really hear you?" On your phone date, ask questions about the test setting. One important question, advises Reid: "Ask them what they do when a child is stuck on a question. Do they help them or move on?"

Your Test for the Tester

The goal is to determine whether this tester is responsible and kind, not just competent, and whether the person's style is likely to mesh well with your child's. Focus on the testing room setting and the tester's style and competence:

- What does the office look like?
- How will the tester manage your child's transition from mommy to stranger?

- Does the tester recommend bringing an item to break the ice?
- Are there any toys? Kid-sized furniture and books?
- How does the tester make a child feel when they first come?
- How does the tester help a child who is not understanding a question?

And of course, it's imperative to try to determine whether your child will do well with this person. Does your child cotton to men or women, younger peppy types or more reserved adults?

Two important caveats. First, good testers book up early. If your child is going to be taking these tests between September and December of the year before kindergarten (as is common), you can't wait until late November to start figuring this out. Start right after Labor Day; better yet, start the prior spring or summer when the testing cycle is dormant and testers are more likely to have the time to take your call or see you. The second point: Listen to other parents with a skeptical ear. In Reid's experience, "Parents tend to lie about how their children have done in this process." Best will in the world, parents find it hard to be objective about their own children, and there is that tendency to like testers if the child does well and not like them if the child does not. So when you're discussing a tester with another parent, keep the conversation on objective evidence (the tester wouldn't let Lila bring her teddy bear in, or the tester let Jonathan play with the cool pencil sharpener on the desk to help him focus).

Some parting thoughts:

1. The more relaxed you are, the more relaxed your kid will be and the better he'll do. This is a given.
2. Most testers won't discuss the results. If you want to understand your child better, you'll have to pay for another session—which may be worth your while if the scores are outstandingly good or bad; otherwise, move on.

FINDING YOUR WAY IN THE SCHOOL SYSTEM MAZE

Now that we've immersed you in the urban public school gestalt—the myriad, sometimes mysterious program options, the environmental tics of continually changing regimes, the duties of dutiful urban parents—you are either ready to pass out or are up to the challenge of navigating *your own city's* school system.

Gathering good top-to-bottom information starts with finding out what you need to know about how your city is governed, right on down to the workings of your little neighborhood school. Naturally, there are no hard and fast rules. Every city is governed differently, and in many big ones, districts and sometimes even schools operate independently.

Wherever you are, you'll need to get a handle on your system, figure out the pros and cons of your neighborhood school (if you have one), check out other options, and get your child set up to apply to the ones that catch your fancy. So much data to gather, so little time to do all you need to do.

The Official Route: Penetrating the Board of Ed— City and State

The first stop for any city parent should be the local board of education Web site. The good ones will clue you in on the terminology of the edu-speak that's used in your area, give you an overview of the school options and the application processes for each option, and help you figure out your zoned school (again, if any). You can also get "report card" information on the city's schools, the results of state exams and other statistics—typically percentage of kids being provided free lunch, percentage of suspensions, and percentage of kids for whom English is a second language. But we warn you, there is considerable variation in the quality of these Web sites. Even a good one—like LA's, where you plug in your address and immediately get the location of your "school of residence" along with a stunning amount of information on that school, including test results, demographics, and free lunches—is far from perfect. We defy you to find any organized information on magnets, G&T programs, or even the plain old kindergarten registration process. In this regard, however, Los Angeles is fairly typical. More and more cities are making it easy for you to get essential data on *individual* schools. Where they fall down is helping you understand the options for your child.

If you're not getting everything you want at the local level, check your state board of ed site as well. Since so much of education is controlled by the state, you may have better luck getting info on certain specifics, like gifted and talented education and charters, on the state Web site.

There's a hugely important offline source that should be on your agenda as well. Most big cities are probably subdivided geographically into districts (or zones, areas, regions, instructional divisions—terms vary, but we'll use *district* for our purposes). The district office in control of the area that you live in will invariably be an excellent source of information. Usually, you can get the contact info for your district office from the board of ed Web site. Be aware that in some cities, there may be separate offices within the district to deal with parent questions. In Boston, you'd probably be directed to the Family Resource Center covering your area; in the newly reorganized NYC bureaucracy, you'd want to go to the "Learning Support Center" for the "Region" in which your "Community School District" is housed. Confused? You can always just walk over to the elementary school nearest your home and go to the principal's office. Tell them you're looking for general information on the area's public schools and need to find the board of ed office covering the schools in your area (while you're at it, schmooze to get the name of a helpful person at that office).

Nomenclature notwithstanding, when you get to one of these offices, you will find they generally have loads of relevant info, from school brochures to school report cards (more on them later) to registration forms to variance request forms to the names of magnets, charters, and G&Ts. Where they also can really help out is on process questions—especially what you have to do to get to a school other than the one you're zoned for.

The Unofficial Route: Local Expertise

Sometimes even more valuable than the official sources are the many services that have sprung up to help wayward parents. Just about every major city community center or Y offers how-to lectures on school processes and programs at some point during the year. If you're lucky enough to live in a city with a local public school guidebook, definitely make the investment—although the rate of change in urban schools often renders these books outdated the day they hit the stores.

CITY SAVVY

Get the Inside Skinny from Teacher Trainees

Contact the coordinator of internships/externships at your local teachers college to get the insider's scoop. These schools often send their students into the local schools for course work as teacher's assistants and as a result may have an invaluable view of the school you are considering. Ask the coordinator to put you in touch with a student or graduate who is working in (or has recently worked in) the school you are considering. Additionally, someone from the office of the dean of academic affairs may be able to offer an overall take on your local schools.

The other usual suspects—your city's newspapers and parenting papers, as well as many of the city magazines—generally offer seasonal school stories and may have archival articles; these can be good sources of anecdotal information on particular schools or programs. Also, look for local advocacy groups. NYC's Advocates for Children of New York, for instance, has a miracle of a site, www.Insideschools.org—by far, the best we've seen in any city. It step-by-steps everything from how to get a bus pass to how to file a complaint—*and* has an invaluable, searchable database of schools, based on various criteria (i.e., locale, gifted, and special needs programs), a great time-saver. Even a site as good as this one, however, cannot be used on a stand-alone basis. Some information may not be the latest (test scores and student/teacher ratios), and parent comments are obviously subjective. You'll certainly want to recheck whatever you've come up with. But what a great way to start.

Supplemental Sources

If your own city's school data is inadequate or you're looking for another perspective, try some of these great national and regional sites.

http://eric.ed.gov. An online clearinghouse of literature and research focusing on early and elementary education. Sponsored by the U.S. Department of Education's Institute of Education Sciences and the U.S. Department of Education, ERIC has many valuable articles—some academic, some consumer-friendly. It's the perfect place to go if you're looking for theory- or research-related information on kindergarten readiness, dealing with exceptional children, or certain types of teaching, for example.

www.greatschools.net. Free all the way, GreatSchools.net's National School Guide provides some very basic information about virtually every K–12 school in the country. Its State School Guides are the real treasures, with in-depth school profiles, school search and sort tools, custom e-mail newsletters, and state-specific advice about navigating the public school system. California, Arizona, Texas, Florida, and Washington are the only states represented thus far, though the nonprofit does have expansion plans to others.

www.Just4Kids.org. Loads of reputable companies have contributed grants to this Texas-based foundation, established to help school communities achieve higher academic standards. Their rather expansive reports format existing school data into a parent-friendly report. You can get data by school or rank

Should Public School Parents Consider Consultants?

Contrary to our position on consultants servicing the private schools, the right consultant may be just the ticket if you're new to a system and under time pressure, or stymied by a truly Byzantine applications process, or desperate to get your child into any school but the one for which he is zoned. The best public school consultants know teachers and administrators at the school and district level and are constantly keeping track of all the changes in the system (hey, in some places that can be daily!). They also regularly visit the schools they cover. Oh, and here's something radical: They're cheap for the price. Maybe it's because their customer base doesn't have the deep pockets of the private school parents, so they just have to price accordingly. Or maybe it's because the bulk of their

schools based on similar income levels and levels of English proficiency. Material is free. The most comprehensive information is collected on Texas schools, but you can get comparative test info for 13 other states including Washington and Florida.

www.nces.ed.gov/ccd. This Web site for the National Center for Education Statistics provides basic data on all the public elementary and secondary schools (approximately 95,000) and school districts (approximately 17,000) in the country. Its search function allows users to obtain high-level information on specific schools but not much detail. Major drawback: Although the database purports to allow you to search in certain subcategories (special education, alternative, charter, or magnet schools), you will not be getting any information on gifted and talented programs or many specialty schools unless they were listed in those subcategories when entered into the database.

www.schoolmatch.com. This Ohio-based counseling and research service offers parents nationwide a free online directory of all U.S. public schools as well as special inexpensive individual school reports ($10 for the "SnapShot"). Schoolmatch offers other pay-as-you-go services, including a detailed report card on an individual school—which costs $34 and helps rank schools against a national, not local, standard—as well as counseling services via phone.

value is explaining the peculiarities of the process in their geographic region, which is cookie-cutter for them but gold for you. And if you're time crunched, a good consultant may be a lifesaver.

How do you know if a consultant is good? If you can find consultants who are retained by schools to work with their parents, that's certainly a good sign. A reference from a friend who successfully employed a consultant is obviously good too. Many give seminars or participate in panels on school topics; that's a good way to get a sense if someone's "real" or not. And, by the way, just as we advised with private school consultants, attend a seminar or two on public schools before hiring anyone. It may well turn out that all your questions are answered just by attending a group presentation.

SIZING UP A SCHOOL: PUTTING SOME COLOR ON YOUR DATA

It's not enough to get data: You have to know how to use it. And, of course, when we're talking about something as interactive and personal as school, you need to get some qualitative assessment into the mix. Your assignment: to analyze all the objective criteria—i.e., test scores, location, the state of the facility—and then balance your findings with your subjective reactions gained through school visits, personal references, the feeling you get from the school, its students, teachers, and its principal.

Looking at the Facts

"Measurables" are generally included in the school's annual report card. You'll see how a school is stacking up in terms of standardized test score results and, depending on the city, other measures such as student-teacher ratios, ethnic breakdown of student body, percentage of children receiving free lunches, and expenditures per pupil.

There are also practical considerations to take into account. And GreatSchools.net has a free downloadable form, "Imagining Your Ideal School: An Exercise for Setting Priorities," that we recommend to help get organized.

How far will your child have to travel? Remember, if you're going out of zone or district, you may no longer be eligible for free transportation.

What support services does the school have? Is there an on-site nurse? (In this age of asthma and lethal food allergies, a resident nurse can be pretty good to have.)

What are the school's "extras"? Art and music? After-school activities? Extended care programs? The type of special activities offered—fencing versus football, chess or congo drums—are also clues to what the parent body and school leadership value and how active the parents are in rounding out the school's resources.

What about outdoor space? And note: Just because a school has no playground, doesn't mean there will be no sports, athletics, or recreational space available to the children. Many schools lacking green space work with city parks departments and make use of nearby playgrounds and parks. Don't make assumptions; ask.

Subjective Criteria

Now comes the truly elusive part: getting a feel for a school's environment and how it will impact Misha's educational experience. You'll definitely want to step foot in the schools you are considering as often as you can. Many, particularly the in-demand schools, run several open houses for potential parents. Get the dates, and RSVP early if they're taking names. But don't stop there. You should attend a school tour—ideally, the season before you're planning on applying. Some schools run tours regularly, other schools may have parent guides with whom you'll set up a time directly. If it's a group tour, someone from the school's administration and often the principal will be available for a little bit, and you may have some opportunity to talk to other staff members and teachers. If you're on your own, it might be more difficult to get some face time with officials, but certainly ask if you can at least meet the principal.

CITYWISE WARNING

Scores Can Be Misleading

"If you're talking about predominantly white schools in upper- or middle-class neighborhoods, then yes, the tests probably tell a lot," says Kari Kling, an instructor of educators based in Phoenix. "But there are tons of other factors" to consider. A high quotient of ESL (English as a second language) students may bring down test scores and hide what might be an acceptable performance by native English speakers. Similarly, if the schools house a gifted and talented program, scores from the G&T kids may bring up scores for the school as a whole. In Chicago, local kibitzers pointed out that the fabulous increase in the performance of a local school, which resulted in many accolades for the principal, may *possibly* have had something to do with the installation of a gifted and talented program.

Also, experts advise caution with tests normed on a statewide rather than national basis. "Homegrown" state tests are subject to the vagaries of those in charge and not always with the most positive results. If you're wavering between public and private, a nationally normed scale may give you a better context from which to make your decision (it may be the best school in Arkansas, but if Arkansas schools rank pretty poorly against all others, that may not be good enough for you).

And here's some seriously bad news for public school parents who are still under the impression that they can behave any way they want. The more competitive schools, which usually have some degree of discretion over admissions, are starting to scrutinize parents' behaviors on school tours just the way the private schools do. On one tour Kathy attended, a parent answered her cell phone, and it was clear that the behavior was noted by the guide. It was oh-so-subtle but, we can bet you, oh-so-devastating for the admissions prospects of that parent's child. So, no answering cell phones, no being rude to volunteers, and no nasty questions.

Observing a classroom is mandatory for understanding how the school's philosophy works in action, what methods teachers are employing, and how the students are responding to it. What you *see* will undoubtedly be the most important part of your tour. Sure, sure everyone says to look for happy classrooms and lots of creative art and writing displayed on the walls (in fact, so many guides recommend this that you really have to wonder about a school that *doesn't* have kids' works on the walls). But you need to look beyond that. And,

Going on Tour: What to Ask the Principal

If you see the principal on a group tour or are lucky enough to get a personal interview, you don't want to bombard the principal with questions. We've selected a choice few:

1. Ask the principal to articulate what the philosophy of the school is and lest you're left with what is often a gobbledygoop response, ask the principal to explain, with specific examples, how this philosophy is implemented.

2. Don't forget to ask about any grants and externally funded programs the school has. You'll gain great insight into how active the principal really is.

3. Ask how long the principal has been there (FYI: stability is a good thing in public schools).

4. Ask about the teachers. They're the ones on the front lines with young Justin. Find out what the school offers teachers in the way of ongoing professional development. Such an investment in personnel indicates respect for the teachers' role and experience and is often central to a happy, respected staff.

5. Ask about the principal's goals for the school. You might find out something interesting.

Get Thee to a PTA Meeting

Going to a PTA meeting offers an instant window into the school world. Right away, you'll know whether there's an army of parents ready and able to raise money for the school, and you'll learn about what issues are in play. Contact the PTA head to find out when the next meeting is and ask to attend. Most will welcome you, but if not, keep trying. As a little experiment, Kathy asked a friend to go over to the school and find out if she could attend a meeting. The answer was "Absolutely not. These meetings are for people in the school only." Then Kathy called the PTA prez herself and pushed and cajoled and finally said: "I don't understand, isn't this meeting open to the public?" Something clicked, because she was suddenly allowed to go.

While you're at it, if the school has a Web site, see what other events are in the offing. No one's going to freeze you out of an auction or fund-raiser. Maybe there are sporting events or art fairs you can attend. The value: You have a chance to meet more parents who may be willing sources of inside info (and if you actually put a little money in their coffers, they'll love you for it).

if you're looking at private schools too, be prepared. Don't let your judgment be clouded completely by the fact that the public school's physical plant doesn't shine as brightly. Particularly if you're looking at an elementary school, bells and whistles should be less important than the quality of the teaching. So, what to focus on?

The quality of personal interaction—between kids and teachers, kids and kids, teachers and teachers (rudeness or harshness are not good signs). Really pay attention as you walk through the halls. According to Yvonne Jones, Ph.D., a Seattle-based educational consultant, with over 30 years experience in education, the "human climate" is quite telling. "Look to see what happens when class is not in session," recommends Jones. "How does the office staff deal with a child who comes into the office and says that he forgot his lunch? Or watch in the hall when children and adults are passing in the hallways. How do they interact?" Additionally, Jones recommends seeing how people act when they are relaxed. "Go to public events, like bake sales or sports days."

A parent bulletin board or corner. How much space is dedicated to it? This is a clue as to whether the principal is working with and respectful of parents.

The Loo Is for You

One experienced California educator says the bathroom is the tip-off. The condition of school restrooms speaks volumes about how the school is being run. It never would have occurred to us to check out the WC, but from now on . . .

The school newsletter. It's possibly available on the school Web site. (Actually a well-organized and exciting Web site is yet another indicator of a well-organized and exciting school.)

School security. If your child is starting at a K–8 or K–12 school, be prepared for some heavy-duty security. The intensity will either make you feel your child is in good hands or send you looking for less-dramatic environs.

Putting It All Together

Whether you plan on sticking with the school around the block, are trying to get Giselle into that fabulous school near your office, or lust over a spot in that impressive G&T program, your first obligation is to the process. If you've done the research, you'll know exactly the steps you have to take to apply or register (and presumably you've also done all the tours and open houses and checked data so you feel good about your choices). Now you just sit back and wait. Well, not exactly. There's that little thing called schmoozing.

Follow the lead of Chicago's excellent Northside Parents Network, which attests to the ability of clever parents to edge their kids into desirable magnet schools by taking advantage of the principal's ability to award a few spots at his or her discretion. Most good schools—probably any you'd want your child to attend—are not going to be able to take everybody. When it comes down to giving the final yeas or nays, being known to the powers-that-be (in a good way) can make all the difference. So by all means, become a person to the principal, not a faceless name. Do like they do in Chicago: Set up a meeting, write a letter, or have someone write a letter about you, and go to the open school meetings.

If luck is with you, your prayers will be answered. However, if Dahlia didn't get that place in the school of your dreams, all is not lost. Lots of movement occurs the day when the school term starts up again. Just like anywhere else, people move during the summer, or maybe a private school parent who was keeping a public school as a back-up finally got around to alerting the school, thus freeing up a spot in that gifted and talented program or hot neighborhood school.

Furthermore, there are things you can do to improve your chances, even if you think you have none. Often what you're told is an inflexible rule at the *board of ed* or *district* level may be bendable at the *school* level. If the official rule is that your third child will not be given preference for admittance into the school that your other kids currently attend, the unofficial rule is that school administrators do have some leeway in letting in children.

While most policies and processes work on a district-wide basis, if you need an exception, you'll probably need to work at the school level. (This is especially true if you're looking into post-kindergarten.)

Getting In on Round 2

If you haven't been successful getting into one of your top public school choices, here's what you can do.

First, just as with private schools, call the school you got shut out of immediately after having been rejected, to make sure you're on the waitlist.

Second, right away, start working it, baby: Visit the school, ask to speak to the principal or a program coordinator (if you're trying to get into a specialty program), find out who the PTA president is and work that angle too. Find out who the movers and shakers of the school are. And use whatever means you can, but not by whining or criticizing. Tell everyone along the way that it's your first choice. The key is to get your name known, but in a good way.

Third, repeat step two either right after Labor Day or the day that your local school system opens up for administrators. Call all your new contacts again and go back to the school; face time makes a difference. Oh, and smile: You attract more bees with honey.

NOTES

■ ■

Chapter 1: Apartment Living

p. 7   . . . kids "may view" . . .   KidsPlace study sponsored by Sacramento, California, as reported on www.Connectforkids.org.

Chapter 2: Keeping Sane in Small Spaces

p. 26   . . . open/semi-open . . . remote . . .   Glenna Morton, "Children's Room: Four Types of Storage," http://interiordec.about.com/library/weekly/aa060401a.htm.

p. 39   . . . All parents should consider . . .   *FamilyFun* Q & A on "Should Brother and Sister Share a Room," http://familyfun.go.com/raisingkids/child/dev/expert/dony127fasharebed/dony127fasharebed.html.

Chapter 3: The Rx for City Health Hazards

p. 42   . . . In 1946, . . .   Sharon Dowell, "Hospital on Cutting Edge of Children's Care," *The Sunday Oklahoman*, February 16, 2003.

p. 43   . . . There are more . . .   American Academy of Pediatrics, "Care of Children in the Emergency Department: Guidelines for Preparedness," *Pediatrics* 107, no. 4 (2001): 777–781.

p. 44   . . . Ninety percent . . .   Emergency Medical Services for Children, "Facility Recognition of Emergency Department Pediatric Capacity," EMSC Pediatric Care Resource Kit, 2000, www.ems-c.org/pie/media/e6.pdf.

p. 49   . . . Patients in Las Vegas . . .   Peter G. Gosselin, "Amid Nationwide Prosperity, ERs See a Growing Emergency," *Los Angeles Times*, August 6, 2001.

p. 53   . . . a survey by . . .   Jeffrey J. Stoddard, et al. "Providing Pediatric Subspecialty Care: A Workforce Analysis," for the AAP Committee on Pediatric Workforce Subcommittee on Subspecialty Workforce, *Pediatrics* 106 (December 2000):1325–1333.

p. 55   . . . One study examining . . .   James Gorman, "City Trees Outgrow Rural Cousins, and Study Credits Urban Chemistry," *New York Times*, July 10, 2003.

p. 55   . . . the impact of pollution . . .   The American Lung Association, "Children and Ozone Air Pollution," fact sheet no. 99, September 2000; Jane Woodward Elioseff, ed., "Danger in the Air: Toxic Air Pollution in the Houston-Galveston Corridor," Galveston-Houston Association for Smog Prevention, 1996; "Air Quality, Special Report," *Consumer Reports* 62, no. 8 (August 1997): 36.

p. 55   . . . their airways . . . cement and soil . . .   Jane Woodward Elioseff, ed., "Danger in the Air: Toxic Air Pollution in the Houston-Galveston Corridor."

p. 62   . . . children under 4 . . .   Pew Environmental Health Commission, "Attack Asthma: Why America Needs a Public Health Defense System to Battle Environmental Threats," report, May 2000.

p. 62   . . . all urban children . . .   American Thoracic Society, "Urban Living Biggest Risk for Asthma in Children," press release referring to a study by C. Andrew Aligne, of Strong

Children's Research Center, Rochester General Hospital, Rochester, New York, published in *American Journal of Respiratory and Critical Care Medicine,* September 2000.

p. 63 ... young lungs ... Mark Alpert, "The Invisible Epidemic," *Scientific American* (November 1999).

p. 63 ... stress is triggering ... "Understanding a Childhood Asthma Epidemic," *NPR,* February 13 2003, www.npr.org/display_pages/features/feature_984541.html.

p. 64 ... lead exposure may be ... Environmental Protection Agency, Emerging Issues section of "America's Children and the Environment," report, 2nd edition, February 2003.

p. 64 ... 88 percent ... Pamela A. Meyer, et al., "Surveillance for Elevated Blood Lead Levels Among Children—United States, 1997–2001," Centers for Disease Control and Prevention, *Morbidity and Mortality Weekly Report* 52, no. SS10;1 (September 12, 2003).

p. 65 ... one 5-year study ... "Very Low Lead Levels Linked with IQ Deficits, According to NJEM Study," adapted from news release issued by NIH/National Institute of Environmental Health Sciences, *Science Daily,* April 17, 2003.

p. 65 ... 5 IQ points ... Jane E. Brody, "Even Low Lead Levels Pose Perils for Children," *New York Times,* August 5, 2003.

p. 65 ... new guidelines ... Gardiner Harris, "Low Lead Levels Can Be Danger to Children," *Wall Street Journal Online,* September 11, 2002.

p. 66 ... according to the CDC ... American Public Health Association, "Protecting Children from Lead Poisoning and Building Healthy Communities," *American Journal of Public Health,* June 1999.

p. 67 ... in traffic-congested ... Howard W. Mielke, "Lead in the Inner Cities," *American Scientist,* January–February 1999.

p. 67 ... one study ... Helen J. Binns, "Lead Poisoning: Still a Common Problem in Chicago," *The Child's Doctor, Journal of Children's Memorial Hospital, Chicago,* Spring 2001.

p. 67 ... Washington D.C. residents ... David Nakamura, "Water in D.C. Exceeds EPA Lead Limits," *Washington Post,* January 31, 2004.

p. 67 ... San Francisco ... University of California at San Francisco, Office of Environmental Health and Safety, *OEH&S Safety Update* newsletter, May/June 1997, www.ehs.ucsf.edu/Program%20&%20Services/lead.htm#Lead%20Based%20Paint%20 Hazards.

p. 68 ... 21 percent ... Helen J. Binns, "Lead Poisoning: Still a Common Problem in Chicago," *The Child's Doctor, Journal of Children's Memorial Hospital,* Chicago, Spring 2001.

p. 71 ... real estate investor ... Paul Tharp, "Ritzy Apts. Turn into Solid Mold," *NY Post,* January 6, 2003.

p. 71 ... Airtight buildings ... Testimony of National Multi Housing Council/National Apartment Association, before the Subcommittee on Housing and Community Opportunity, Subcommittee on Oversight and Investigations, Committee on Financial Services, U.S. House of Representatives in their Joint Hearing, "Mold: A Growing Problem," July 18, 2002.

p. 72 ... see or smell ... California Department of Health Services, "Mold in My Home: What Do I Do?" Indoor Air Quality Information Sheet, revised July 2001.

p. 74   . . . A team at . . .   Vicki Monks, "Your Health," *National Wildlife*, April/May 1999; "Playing with Pesticides," *Environmental Health Perspectives*, 106, no. 1 (January 1998).

p. 76   . . . female German cockroach . . .   "Cockroaches," Pest Notes, University of California Division of Agriculture and Natural Resources, Publication 7467, November 1999.

Chapter 4: The Ins and Outs of City Safety

p. 77   . . . traffic-related pedestrian . . .   National Safe Kids Campaign, "Injury Facts, Pedestrian Injury," www.safekids.org/tier3_cd.cfm?content_item_it=1150& folder_id=540.

p. 81   . . . In pedestrian friendly . . .   "Large City Transportation Issues," Rudin Center for Transportation Policy and Management at the Robert F. Wagner Graduate School of Public Service, New York University, November 2000.

p. 82   . . . buses will take . . .   "Issues in Bus Rapid Transit," www.fta.dot.gov/7694_7695_ENG_HTML.htm.

p. 83   . . . leased taxis have . . .   Schaller Consulting, "Higher Pay, Safer Cabbies," a study prepared for *Transportation Alternatives*, January 2004, pp. 3–4.

p. 84   . . . passengers in . . .   Pete Donahue, "50 Cab Crashes Per Day," *New York Daily News*, March 1, 2001.

p. 84   . . . nearly 12 percent . . .   Schaller Consulting, "Taxi and Livery Crashes in New York City, 1990–1999," February 2001, p. 9.

p. 89   . . . fire safety experts . . .   Alisa Wolf, "What Went Wrong," *NFPA Journal*, May/June 1999.

p. 89   . . . In New York City . . .   Donna Klein, "First Deputy FDNY Commissioner Details Latest Fire Regulations," New York Association of Realty Managers, 2000.

p. 92   . . . studies suggest . . .   U.S. Consumer Product Safety Commission, "Test All Smoke Alarms (Detectors) and Annually Replace Batteries; Develop and Rehearse an Escape Plan," CPSC Document #5077.

Chapter 5: Taking Care of the Caregiving

p. 100   . . . 25 percent had . . .   Marcy Whitebook, et al. "Highlights—Then and Now: Changes in Child Care Staffing, 1994-2000," Center for Child Care Workforce, 2001, p. 5.

p. 102   . . . As researchers had noted . . .   Ibid.

p. 104   . . . the enormous crème de la crème . . .   Kay Hymowitz, "Fear and Loathing at the Daycare Center," *City Journal*, Summer 2001.

p. 104   . . . centers are often only . . .   Tom Frederickson, "Aiming to Be Manhattan Child Star," *Crain's New York Business*, October 21, 2002.

p. 108   . . . parents feel they . . .   Jill Hamburg Coplan, "Solving the Daycare Dilemma: Why good daycare is hard to find, and what you can do about it," *Baby Talk*, April 2002.

p. 109   . . . accounting for a quarter . . .   Ibid.

p. 111   . . . au pairs stumbling in . . .   Daniel Kadlec, "Au Pair Odyssey; Mine Weren't Dangerous, but They Drove Me Crazy," *Time*, November 24, 1997, 58.

p. 112   . . . as many as 40 percent . . .   Betty Reid Mandell, "The Future of Caretaking," *New Politics*, Winter 2003.

p. 114   . . . In one study . . .   Patricia Baquedano-Lopez, "A Stop at the End of the Bus Line: Nannies, Children and the Language of Care" (working paper no. 51, Center for Working Families, University of California, Berkeley, 2002).

p. 114   . . . In New York . . .   Shellee Colen, "'Like a Mother to Them,' Stratified Reproduction and West Indian Childcare Workers and Employers in New York," in *Conceiving the New World Order* (Berkeley and Los Angeles: University of California Press, 1995), 78–102.

p. 116   . . . In the West Indies . . .   Ibid.

p. 116   . . . a Guatamalen nanny . . .   Juanita Darling, "Latina Nannies Rear a Generation en Espanol," *Los Angeles Times,* September 19, 1999.

p. 116   . . . in St. Croix . . .   Denise Bennerson and Gia Richards, "Child Rearing: A Virgin Islands Model," Kraal Cultural Manual, Media Library Services, Department of Education, St. Croix District, US Virgin Islands, http://www.viaccess.net/~crucian/child.htm.

p. 117   Lyuba Konopasek . . .   Meegan Thompson and Kirsten Matthew, "Update: National Obesity Crisis Takes More Children Hostage," *Big Apple Parent,* July 2003, 13.

p. 117   . . . Dominican wonder drug . . .   "City Health Department Warns New Yorkers to Avoid Buying or Using "Litargirio," New York City Department of Health and Mental Hygiene Press Release, November 5, 2003.

p. 117   . . . this is, in many ways . . .   Lee Lusardi Connor and Susan Gilbert, "It's 10:00 A.M. Do You Know What Your Sitter's Doing?" *Redbook,* November 1997.

p. 118   . . . one study of children . . .   Baquedano-Lopez, "A Stop at the End of the Bus Line."

p. 121   . . . seminal study . . .   Institute of Medicine. *From Neurons to Neighborhoods: The Science of Early Childhood Development,* Institute of Medicine, 2000.

p. 121   . . . 40 percent . . .   Gilien Silsby, "Researcher Brings the Plight of Domestic Workers into the Open," *USC Chronicle,* April 9, 2001, www.usc.edu/dept/LAS/pase/FRAMES/NEWS/hondag2001.htm.

p. 122   . . . San Fran nannies . . .   "Nanny Shortage Spikes Salaries in Silicon Valley," CNN.com, July 10, 2002, www.cnn.com/2000/US/07/10/daddies.nannies.01.

p. 123   . . . According to one agency . . .   Charlotte Hildebrand Harjo, "A Nanny's Story," *The Jewish Journal of Greater Los Angeles,* September 1, 2000, online edition, www.jewishjournal.com/archive/09.01.00/coverstory1.09.01.00.html.

p. 123   . . . one agency's primer . . .   Aunt Ann's Nanny, Housekeeper and Estate Agency Web site, www.in-housestaffing.com.

p. 125   . . . Agencies are . . .   Pierrette Hondagneu-Sotelo, "Domestic Employment Agencies in Los Angeles," Department of Sociology, University of Southern California, Los Angeles, September 1996.

p. 127   . . . A survey . . .   "Berkeley Parents Network Nanny Survey Results," http://parents.berkeley.edu/survey/2002nanny_survey_results.html.

p. 129   . . . formed in 1995 . . .   Anita Hamilton, "Find It on Craig's List," *Time,* March 3, 2003, 76.

Chapter 6: Playground Nation and the Sporting Life

p. 148 ... Out of more ... Wendy Marquez, "How Safe is Your Child's Playground? Many City Playgrounds Fail Safety Test." November 2002, http://parentsknow.com/articles/article.php?id=1035834459.

p. 148 ... As many as 40 percent ... KidSource Online, "How Can We Provide Safe Playgrounds," www.kidsource.com/kidsource/content3/safe.playgrnd.t.p.k12.safe.html.

p. 148 ... A comprehensive study ... Deborah K. Tinsworth and Joyce E. McDonald, Directorate for Epidemiology, U.S. Consumer Product Safety Commission, "Special Study: Injuries and Deaths Associated with Children's Playground Equipment," Washington, D.C., April 2001.

p. 151 ... toddlers, who may ... "Playgrounds Test High for Arsenic: Study," CBC News, February 10, 2003, www.cbc.ca/stories/2003/01/15/Consumers/arsenic_030115.

p. 152 ... California, for example ... Tracy Davis, UC Davis Toxicology Intern, "Poisoned Playgrounds," *Enviro-Times Newsletter*, San Francisco Department of Public Health, Environmental Health Section, May 2002.

p. 152 ... a joint study ... M. Serratto, R. Chatrath, and D. Thoele, "Physical Fitness of Urban Children and Adolescents in the United States," *Pediatric Cardiology* 23, no. 6 (November–December 2002): 608-612.

p. 152 ... study after study ... Leonard H. Epstein, et al., "How Much Activity Do Youth Get? A Quantitative Review of Heart-Rate Measured Activity," *Pediatrics* 108, no. 3 (2001).

p. 154 ... Urban planners ... Katharine Q. Seelye, "Cities Made for Walking May Be Fat Burners," *New York Times*, June 21, 2003.

p. 158 ... During the latter ... American Academy of Pediatrics, "Organized Sports for Children and Preadolescents," *Pediatrics* 107, no. 6 (June 2001): 1459–1462.

Chapter 7: Finding Your Urban Backyard

p. 177 ... Day trip ideas ... Many of these suggestions from "Weekend Getaways with Kids" by Valerie Vaz, *Essence*, October 1995.

p. 185 ... castor bean and oleander ... "Common Poisonous Houseplants," Plant Information Fact Sheet No. 4, The New York Botanical Garden, Plant Information Service, the LuEsther T. Mertz Library; "Most Commonly Ingested Plants," www.kidsource.com.

Chapter 8: Getting Baby Up to Speed

p. 194 ... In 1898 ... Rebecca Webber, "Public Toilets," July 15, 2001, www.gothamgazette.com.

p. 194 ... In progressive San Francisco ... Ibid.

Chapter 9: That's Entertainment

p. 211 ... Boston's Le Meridien ... "Kids Love Boston," at Le Meridien, www.familytravelguides.com.

p. 221 ... Los Angeles' mariachi ... Frommer's Web site, "Attractions: Ethnic Neighborhoods," www.frommers.com.

p. 225   . . . Joachim Splichal . . .   Jessica Strand, "Baby Food Go Bye-Bye," *Los Angeles Times*, April 24, 2003.

p. 226   . . . when Boston-based . . .   June Naylor, "Restaurants gathering creative ways to revive a traditional favorite," *Fort Worth Star-Telegram*, April 2, 2003.

p. 227   . . . Korea . . .   "Food Menu," Lifeinkorea.com, www.lifeinkorea.com/cgi-bin/menu.cfm.

Chapter 10: From Sin City to Mayberry

p. 237   . . . William Damon . . .   William Damon, "Character Education the Right Way," Hoover Institution's Weekly Essays, February 5, 2001, www-hoover.stanford.edu/pubaffairs/we/current/damon_0201.html.

p. 237   . . . Damon reminds us . . .   William Damon, "Selections from: The Moral Development of Children," *Scientific American,* August 1999, www.teachon.com/zizi/articles/school/violence1.html.

p. 240   . . . Stephen L. Carter . . .   Stephen L. Carter, "The Etiquette of Democracy," www.religion-online.org/cgi-bin/relsearchd.dll/showarticle?item_id=213.

p. 243   . . . do it . . .   "Four Steps to a Moral Child," *Stanford Magazine,* www.stanfordalumni.org/news/magazine/2000/marapr/articles/damonside2.html.

p. 245   . . . Rebecca Bigler . . .   Brian Matmiller, "Exploring the Roots of Bias," *Wisconsin Week,* November 4, 1998, www.news.wisc.edu/wire/i110498/bias.html.

p. 245   . . . social judgments . . .   Hilary E. MacGregor,"Adopt, Then Adapt," *Los Angeles Times,* October 22, 2002.

p. 247   . . . teaching tolerance . . .   Lisa Lansman, "Color-Blindness: Teaching Children to Celebrate Diversity," www.preteenagerstoday.com; Dora Pulido-Tobiassen and Janet Gonzalez-Mena, "Teaching Diversity: A Place to Begin," http://teacher.scholastic.com/professional/teachdive/placetobegin.htm; Stephanie Irby Coard, Ph.D., "Preparing Children for a Multicultural World," www.aboutourkids.org.

p. 247   . . . Lindsay Friedman . . .   Matt Alderton, "How Not to Raise a Racist," *Chicago Parent*, July 2003.

p. 249   . . . *New York Times* book review . . .   Jose Padua, "Children's Books in Brief, Beegu," *New York Times Book Review,* November 16, 2003, 31.

p. 251   . . . in 2001 . . .   Aaron Friedman, et al., "Alarmingly Useless: The Case for Banning Car Alarms in New York City," Transportation Alternatives, www.transalt.org/info/caralarms/04cost.html.

p. 251   . . . the first study . . .   Gary W. Evans, Peter Lercher, et al., "Community Noise Exposure and Stress in Children," *Journal of the Acoustical Society of America* 109, no. 3 (March 2001): 1023–1102.

p. 251   . . . feelings of helplessness . . .   Science Daily, "Researchers Find Everyday Traffic Noise Harms the Health and Well-Being of Children," May 23, 2001.

p. 251   . . . One oft-quoted study . . .   Carol M. Ostrom, "Even Low-Level Noise Can Stress Your Body Out, Researchers Say," *Seattle Times,* July 17, 2003, www.freep.com/news/health/dnoise17_20030717.htm.

p. 251   . . . how passers-by . . .   U.S. Environmenal Protection Agency, Office of Noise Abatement and Control, "Noise: A Health Problem," August 1978.

p. 252   . . . psychologists point out . . .   Arline Bronzaft, "Beware: Noise Is Hazardous to Our Children's Development," *Hearing Rehabilitation Quarterly* 22, no. 1 (1997).

p. 252   . . . According to Frances Kuo . . .   Frances E. Kuo and William C. Sullivan, "Aggression and Violence in the Inner City," *Environment and Behavior* 33, no. 4 (July 2001): 543–571.

p. 254   . . . One recent study . . .   Michael Waldholz, "Taking a Garden Break," *Wall Street Journal,* August 26, 2003.

p. 255   . . . Researchers at . . .   Frances Kuo et al., "Coping With ADD," *Environment and Behavior* 33, no.1 (January 2001): 54–77.

p. 255   . . . having a few trees . . .   Kuo and Sullivan, "Aggression and Violence in the Inner City;" Kuo et al., "Coping With ADD."

p. 258   . . . a technique used . . .   Sheryl Gay Stolberg, "Stress Management for Kindergartners," *In Light Times,* March 2003.

p. 261   . . . Astonishing numbers . . .   "Hardwired to Connect: The New Scientific Case for Authoritative Communities," Institute for American Values press release, September 9, 2003.

p. 261   . . . the commission synthesized . . .   Ibid.

p. 262   . . . Dutch researchers . . .   "City Living Linked to Significantly Increased Risk of Psychotic Symptoms," *Reuters Health,* July 12, 2001.

p. 264   . . . When people know . . .   F.E. Kuo, et al, "Fertile Ground for Community: Inner-City Neighborhood Common Spaces," *American Journal of Community Psychology* 26 (6): 823–851.

p. 265   . . . Seattle is . . .   Janet I. Tu, "'Emerging Churches' Drawing Young Flock," *Seattle Times,* January 16, 2003.

p. 265   . . . Quest church operates . . .   Eugene Cho, "Why Quest?" and "New Interbay Area Church Embarks Upon an Authentic, Inclusive Quest," October 24, 2001, Quest Church Web site, www.seaq.org.

p. 267   . . . when there's a choice . . .   D'Vera Cohn, "Integrated People, Integrated Places: Multirace Residents Pick Neighborhoods of Diversity," *Washington Post,* July 29, 2002.

p. 268   . . . embrace the "birth culture" . . .   Amy Dickinson, "Bicultural Kids," *Time,* August 26, 2002.

p. 268   . . . "contributory activities" . . .   Robert Brooks, "Fostering Responsibility in Children: Chores or Contributions?" (part 1), November 1999, www.drrobertbrooks.com.

p. 269   . . . The Search Institute . . .   The Search Institute Web site, www.search-institute.org.

p. 269   . . . A conference on . . .   "Engaging Today's Youth," overview of Conference on Fostering Youth's Civic Engagement and Participation in Free and Democratic Societies, Stanford Center on Adolescence, Fall 2000, *CSHD Publications: Lifelines* 3.

p. 269   . . . teenagers will be . . .   The Search Institute, www.search-institute.org/assets/toddlers.html.

p. 269   . . . toddlers share toys . . .   Richard Gallagher, Ph.D.; Robin F. Goodman, Ph.D.; and Anita Gurian, Ph.D., "Raising Responsive and Responsible Children," aboutourkids.org.

p. 269   . . . (APA) reminds us . . .   American Psychological Association, "What Makes Kids Care? Teaching Gentleness in a Violent World," www.apa.org.

p. 270   . . . Dr. Brooks believes . . .   Brooks, "Fostering Responsibility in Children."

p. 272   . . . capture the action . . .   Idea from www.kidsforcommunity.org.

Chapter 11: Getting Off to a Great Start

p. 285   . . . Tom Wolfe . . .   George Neumayr, "Parochial Schools Are the Answer," Los Angeles Mission, June 2000, www.losangelesmission.com/ed/articles/2000/0600gn.htm, reprint of article appearing in *Investor's Business Daily,* January 21, 2000.

p. 285   . . . According to . . .   Martha Naomi Alt and Katharin Peter, "Private Schools, A Brief Portrait," National Center for Education Statistics, 2002.

p. 287   . . . when *U.S. News* . . .   Teresa Kennedy, "Private Schools," *Gotham Gazette,* December 9, 2002.

p. 289   . . . A broad study . . .   Final Report, San Antonio School Choice Research Project, Center for the Study of Education Reform, June 1997, www.coe.unt.edu/cser/finalreport.htm.

p. 289   . . . school is . . .   Internet poster "Lyndsey" on the "Life Is Like a Box of Chocolates: Volunteering at Your Kids' School," thread, May 6, 2003, Mothers Who Think message board, Table Talk section, Salon.com.

p. 289   . . . a U.S. Department of Education . . .   U.S. Department of Education, A Back to School Special Report on the Baby Boom Echo: Growing Pains, "Growing Pains: The Challenge of Overcrowded Schools Is Here to Stay," August 21, 2000.

p. 290   . . . the National Academy . . .   Stacey Colino, "A Big Fat F: When It Comes to Children's Health, Schools Are Getting Just That," *Women's Day,* March 2003.

p. 290   . . . 85 percent . . .   Statistics excerpted from the National Center for Education Statistics, "Private School Enrollment Continues to Climb," 2001 biennial private school survey as reported by the Council for American Private Education (CAPE), September 2002, www.capenet.org/facts.html.

p. 291   . . . dropout rates . . .   Mary Anne Raywid, "Focus Schools: A Genre to Consider," Urban Diversity Series No. 106, ERIC Clearinghouse on Urban Education, Institute for Urban and Minority Education, Hofstra University, November 1994.

p. 291   . . . 1990 RAND study . . .   Paul Hill et al., "High Schools with Character," RAND, August 1990.

p. 291   . . . in Washington D.C. . . .   Jason Boffetti, "Why Catholic Schools Deserve a Public Break," *Crisis,* September 2001.

p. 291   . . . Catholic schools have . . .   Raywid, "Focus Schools: A Genre to Consider."

p. 291   . . . schools appeal to . . .   Ibid.

p. 292   . . . such children can . . .   Paul T. Hill, "No Legal Barrier Prevents Private Funders from Helping Catholic Schools Teach Poor Children," June 4, 2000, Seattlepi.com.

p. 293   . . . of course . . .   The Economist, "Black v Teachers," May 8, 2001.

p. 295   . . . two-thirds of all . . .   Laurent Belsie, "Preschools Are Popping at the Seams," *The Christian Science Monitor,* July 9, 2002.

p. 297   . . . 45 percent . . .   "Prekindergarten in U.S. Public Schools: 2000–2001," U.S. Department of Education's National Center for Education Statistics, May 28, 2003.

p. 301   ... People have figured ...   Anonymous posting on New York Urban Baby message board, the School forum, http://newyork.urbanbaby.com/bbs/top.php3?category=14&city=New+York.

p. 302   ... one desperate LA parent ...   Kathleen Kelleher, "Education Panic in the Playground; Pressure on Parents to Place Children in Top Los Angeles Pre-Schools," *Los Angeles Magazine*, April 1998.

Chapter 12: The Agony and the Ecstasy: A Private School Primer

p. 303   ... Georgetown Day ...   Valerie Strauss, "Changes Are in the Works for Tyke Testing," *Washington Post*, June 20, 2000.

p. 304   ... the Latin School ...   Barbara Ballinger Buchholz, "A New Kind of Early Admission: Angst," *Chicago Tribune*, March 2, 2003.

p. 304   ... 2,221 kids ...   Jane Gross, "Right School for 4-Year Old? Find an Adviser," *New York Times*, May 28, 2003.

p. 307   ... 41,000 NYC families ...   Joanna Coles, "Parents Hire Help to Open Doors," *London Times*, December 4, 2000.

p. 307   ... quoted one consultant ...   Ibid.; Jane Gross, "Right School for 4-Year Old? Find an Adviser."

p. 316   ... what really makes ...   Jack P. Shonkoff and Deborah Phillips, editors, "From Neurons to Neighborhoods: The Science of Early Childhood Development," Board on Children, Youth and Families, National Research Council and Institute of Medicine, National Academy Press, 2000, p. 9.

Chapter 13: You *Can* Win: A Public School Primer

p. 331   ... there is a relationship ...   William Bainbridge and Thomas Lasley II, "Demographics, Diversity and K-12 Accountability," *Education and Urban Society* 34 (August 2002).

p. 332   ... teachers tend to prefer ...   William Bainbridge, "Ohio's Schools Need Equity in Quality of Teachers," *Columbus Dispatch*, December 17, 2002.

p. 332   ... In schools where ...   William Bainbridge, "Poverty, Not Race, Holds Back Urban Students," *Columbus Dispatch*, July 28, 2002.

p. 333   ... $300,000 a year ...   Clara Hemphill with Pamela Wheaton, *New York City's Best Public Elementary Schools*, Teachers College Press, 2002 edition.

p. 333   ... principal Janet Won ...   From profile of PS 124, District 2 school on Insideschools.org.

p. 333   ... In San Francisco ...   Nick Driver, "Westside Schools Are Tops," *San Francisco Examiner*, September 13, 2002.

p. 333   ... of the neighborhood's ...   Information derived from a review of District 2 schools on Insideschools.org.

p. 335   ... make sure the teacher ...   From "Snarky Bean" (screen name) poster April, 26, 2003 on the "Life Is Like a Box of Chocolates: Volunteering at Your Kids' School" thread, Mothers Who Think discussion area, Table Talk section, Salon.com.

p. 335   ... "You will be known ...   From anonymous poster on Urban Baby message board, October 20, 2002.

p. 336 ... "I am all for ... Posting by Lori Dee on "Parents Who Talk about Schools" message board, Salon.com, April 5, 2002.

p. 338 ... The *Washington Post* ... Rosalind S. Helderman, "Early Birds Get a Spot; Parents Wait for Hours at Kindergarten Registration," *Washington Post,* May 1, 2003.

p. 340 ... A study of San Antonio ... Final Report, Center for the Study of Education Reform, San Antonio School Choice Research Project, June 1997, www.coe.unt.edu/cser/finalreport.htm.

p. 340 ... virtually all magnets ... Morton Inger, "Improving Urban Education with Magnet Schools," ERIC clearinghouse on Urban Education, www.ericfacility.net/databases/eric.digestsled340813.html, August 1991.

p. 340 ... the magnet-heavy Chicago ... Elaine M. Allensworth and Todd Rosenkranz, "Access to Magnet Schools in Chicago," report, August 2000.

p. 340 ... RAND Education released ... "RAND Study Finds California Charter Schools Produce Achievement Gains Similar to Conventional Public Schools," news release, RAND Education, June 30, 2003.

p. 341 ... students of the charter schools ... Greg Winter, "Charter Schools Succeed in Improving Test Scores, Study Says," *New York Times,* July 20, 2003.

p. 341 ... A report by ... Michael Agostini, "Veteran Charter Schools Outperform Non-Charters on API," Charter Schools Development Center, 2003.

p. 342 ... roughly 3,000 ... Mackenzie Carpenter, "Squeaky Wheels: Parents Who Demand Gifted Classes Say They Only Want What's Best for Their Children," *Post-Gazette,* June 10, 2001.

p. 342 ... Los Angeles reportedly ... Amy Pyle, "Struggling to Teach the Very Brightest," *Los Angeles Times,* August 17, 1997.

p. 343 ... anything less than ... James Gallagher, "Questions Parents of Gifted Students Should Ask Schools," on the National Association for Gifted Children Web site, www.nagc.org/Publications/Parenting/question.html.

p. 356 ... Northside Parents Network ... Sandra Young, "Back to School," *Parent to Parent* (newsletter of the northside parents network), September 2000, 2.

INDEX

■ ■

<u>Underscored</u> page references indicate sidebars and tables.

Diversity
  age-specific concept of, <u>246</u>
  economic, lacking, in private schools,
    286
  ethnic, entertainment and, <u>206</u>
  game explaining, <u>248</u>
  in public schools, 289
  teaching children about, <u>247–49</u>
Documents kit, for emergencies, <u>96</u>
Dog(s)
  best breeds of, 183–85
  bites, preventing, <u>184</u>
  choosing, 182–83
Doormats, 29
Doormen, befriending, 264
Doors, storage on, <u>37</u>
Dry cleaning, pollutants from, <u>57</u>, <u>58</u>

E

E. coli, in swimming pools, <u>157</u>
Ear plugs, for noise reduction, <u>17</u>
Edamame, 232
Education. *See* Schools
Elderly persons, helping, 273
Electronic equipment, noise reduction
    from, 253
Elevator safety, 94, <u>94–95</u>
Emergency care, pediatric
  vs. adult care, <u>44</u>
  discussing
    with caregivers, <u>50</u>, <u>53</u>
    with pediatrician, 48–49, <u>49</u>
  outside your neighborhood, <u>47</u>, <u>49</u>
Emergency departments, pediatric
  advantages of, 43–45
  considerations for choosing, 45
  evaluating, 45–48, <u>46</u>
Emergency preparedness, <u>95–98</u>
Emergency supply kit, <u>98</u>
Entertainment, urban
  bookstore events, <u>207</u>
  early sign-up for, <u>206</u>
  ethnic, <u>206</u>, 220–22, 223–24, <u>223</u>
  evaluating access to, 5
  evening, <u>206</u>

finding information on, 203–4
free and low-cost, <u>204–6</u>
impromptu, <u>206–7</u>
at museums
  art, 216–18
  family activities, 211–12, <u>212</u>
  family membership to, 212–13
  games for, <u>218</u>
  guidelines for using, <u>213–16</u>
  specialty, <u>214</u>
performing arts, 219–20
street life, <u>207</u>
tourist attractions, 207, 210
  boating adventures, 210
  bridges, 210
  factory tours, 210–11
  horse and buggy rides, 210
  hotel stays, 211
  landmarks, 210
  outdoor art, 210
  star gazing, 211
EPA, for mold control information, <u>74</u>
Ethnic diversity, entertainment and, <u>206</u>
Ethnic festivals, 223–24, <u>223</u>, <u>248</u>
  Web sites on, <u>222</u>
Ethnic foods, 221
  Greek, 231–32
  Indian, 232
  Japanese, 232–33
  Korean, 233–34
  Mexican, 233
  Peruvian, 234
Ethnic museums, <u>216</u>
Ethnic neighborhoods, 220–22
Evacuation tips, <u>95</u>, <u>96</u>, <u>97</u>
Exercise. *See also* Physical activity
  for asthma prevention, <u>64</u>
  for new mothers, 198

F

Fabrics, for upholstered furniture,
    23–25
Factory tours, 210–11
Fajitas, 233
Falafel, 231

Giftedness, Web sites on, <u>345</u>
GoCityKids.com, <u>205</u>
Golden retrievers, 183
Gossip
 among nannies, <u>114</u>
 about school choices, <u>280</u>, <u>348</u>
Greek foods, 231–32
Guinea pigs, <u>180–81</u>
Gyoza, 232

H

Hair/Pelitos (Cisneros), 249
Hamsters, <u>180–81</u>
Hanging accidents, at playgrounds, 150
Harness, for walking with toddlers, <u>79</u>
Havanese dogs, 183
Health care, pediatric
 advantages of, 42–43
 emergency department, 43–49
 nanny and, 117, <u>120</u>
 from pediatric dentists, 50–52
 in plastic surgery, 52–53, <u>53</u>
 researching, 43
Helping others
 benefits of, 268–69
 books about, <u>272</u>
 in community, 272–74
 involving children in, <u>268</u>, 269–71,
  <u>271–72</u>
 modeling, for children, <u>269</u>
HEPA air filters, <u>59</u>
High chairs, alternative to, <u>22</u>
Hiking, 176–77, <u>176</u>
Holidays, ethnic celebrations of, <u>223</u>
Homeless
 helping, <u>242</u>
 panhandling from, 242
Horse and buggy rides, 210
Hotel stays, for touring cities, 211
Houston
 fire department response time in,
  89
 Museum of Fine Arts in, 211–12
 open space in, <u>170</u>

Humidifiers, cleaning, <u>62</u>
Hygiene, for lead protection, <u>70</u>

I

Ice skating, 154–55, <u>167</u>
 summer, <u>162</u>
Identification, for children, 81
Independence, encouraging, in children,
  <u>238</u>
Indianapolis, fire safety programs in,
  <u>92</u>
Indian foods, 232
Information processing, as urban stressor,
  252–53
Interest-based communities, for social
  connection, 267
Interviews
 approval, for apartment living, 11
 nanny, 129, <u>129–30</u>
 for private school admission
  child, 320–22, <u>321</u>, <u>322</u>
  parent, 317–20, <u>318</u>, <u>319</u>, <u>320</u>
It's Okay to Be Different (Parr), 249

J

Japanese foods, 232–33
Japchae, 233–34
Jogging strollers, <u>193</u>, 198
Journey around Boston from A to Z
  (Zschock), <u>209</u>

K

Kansas City, nanny salaries in, 123
Katsu, 232
Keeping Quilt, The (Polacco), 249
Kick ball, for indoor exercise,
  160–61
Kindergarten
 cutoff dates for, <u>284</u>
 interviews for, 321–22
Kitchen fires, <u>88</u>
Korean barbecue, 233

guidelines for using, <u>213–16</u>

natural history and science, <u>214</u>

transit, <u>214</u>

Music

classes, for children, <u>220</u>

family-friendly, 219–20

"Music for Aardvarks and Other
  Mammals," <u>220</u>

N

Nan, 232

Nannies

background checks on, 130–32

city mobility of, 112

finding

from agencies, 125–26, <u>126</u>

difficulties with, 112–13

through networking, <u>128–29</u>

by yourself, 126–28

gossip among, <u>114</u>

immigrant

child-rearing views of, 116–17, <u>138</u>

communications with, 118–19, <u>120</u>,
  <u>130</u>

effects of, 116–17, <u>138</u>

lack of training in, 120–21

language of, 117–18, <u>118</u>, <u>138</u>

interviewing, 129, <u>129–30</u>

male, <u>127</u>

networks of, pros and cons of, 113–15

paying taxes on, 123–25, <u>124</u>

respect for, 121–22

salaries of, 122–23

setting up, <u>133–38</u>

spying on, <u>132–33</u>, <u>137</u>, <u>138</u>

for summer programs, <u>166</u>

views of, on employers, <u>115</u>

Nanny Book, The (Carlton and Myers), 129

Nannycams, <u>132–33</u>, <u>137</u>

National Lead Information Center, <u>68</u>

Natural sanctuaries, healing from, <u>255</u>

Nature

activities, outdoor, <u>173–75</u>

centers, <u>174</u>

evaluating access to, 5

for stress reduction, 254–56

walks, <u>167</u>, 168

Neighborhood

beautifying, 272

researching, 3–5, <u>5–6</u>

social connections in, 263

Neighborhood schools, 336–38, <u>338</u>

Neighbor relations

cultivating, 11–13

noise affecting, 14–18

New Orleans, lead reduction in, 67

New York City

Asian schools in, <u>333</u>

Children's All Day School in,
  100–102

elevator inspection in, 94

ethnic walking tours in, 221

fire department response time in, 89

fire safety in, 89, <u>92</u>

lead reduction in, 67

mom/tot gatherings in, 199

open space in, <u>170</u>

outdoor art in, 210

ozone in, 55

park beautification in, 273

park events in, 171

public bathrooms in, 194

school admissions testing in, <u>315</u>

storybooks depicting, <u>209</u>

summer camps in, <u>164</u>, <u>165</u>

taxi accidents in, <u>83</u>

walking in, 154

No Child Left Behind legislation,
  <u>336</u>

Noise

effects of, on children, 251–52

evaluating, in apartment, 9, <u>9</u>, 11

legal action against, <u>18</u>, <u>19</u>

neighbor relations and, 14–18

ordinances on, 14, <u>15</u>

in preschools, <u>295</u>

reducing, <u>17–19</u>

Nuclear power plant accidents, <u>96</u>

Nursery schools. *See* Preschools